JESUS AND THE GOD OF ISRAEL

JESUS AND THE GOD OF ISRAEL

God Crucified and Other Studies
on the New Testament's Christology
of Divine Identity

Richard Bauckham

WILLIAM B. EERDMANS PUBLISHING COMPANY

GRAND RAPIDS, MICHIGAN / CAMBRIDGE, U.K.

Published 2008
in the United Kingdom by Paternoster,
an imprint of Authentic Media
www.authenticmedia.co.uk

Published 2009 in the United States of America by
Wm. B. Eerdmans Publishing Co.
2140 Oak Industrial Drive N.E., Grand Rapids, Michigan 49505 /
P.O. Box 163, Cambridge CB3 9PU U.K.
www.eerdmans.com

Printed in the United States of America

15 14 13 12 11 10 09   7 6 5 4 3 2 1

ISBN 978-0-8028-4559-7

To co-workers in early Christology

JIMMY DUNN

LARRY HURTADO

Contents

Introduction

In 1998 I published a small book entitled *God Crucified: Monotheism and Christology in the New Testament.*[1] For a small book it seems to have made a large impact. This is because it was a concise argument for a new proposal for understanding early Christology in its Jewish context. That book forms chapter 1 of the present collection, while the other chapters are further studies developing aspects of the proposal in more detail.

In *God Crucified,* I take current scholarly discussion about the nature of Jewish monotheism in the Second Temple period and attempts to find Jewish precedents for early Christology as my starting points, and argue that recently popular trends to find a model for Christology in semi-divine intermediary figures in early Judaism are largely mistaken. Working with the key category of the *identity* of the God of Israel – which appropriately focuses on *who* God is rather than what divinity is – I show that early Judaism had clear and consistent ways of characterizing the unique identity of the one God and, thus, distinguishing the one God absolutely from all other reality. When New Testament Christology is read with this Jewish theological context in mind, it becomes clear that, from the earliest post-Easter beginnings of Christology onwards, early Christians included Jesus, precisely and unambiguously, within the unique identity of the one God of Israel. They did so by including Jesus in the unique, defining characteristics by which Jewish monotheism identified God as unique. They did not have to break with Jewish monotheism in order to do this, since monotheism, as Second Temple Judaism understood it, was structurally

---

[1] Carlisle: Paternoster/Grand Rapids: Eerdmans. The book was a version of the Didsbury Lectures for 1996, given at the British Isles Nazarene College in Didsbury, Manchester, UK.

open to the development of the christological monotheism that we find in the New Testament texts.

The earliest Christology was already the highest Christology. I call it a Christology of divine identity, proposing this as a way beyond the standard distinction between 'functional' and 'ontic' Christology, a distinction which does not correspond to early Jewish thinking about God and has, therefore, seriously distorted our understanding of New Testament Christology. When we think in terms of divine identity, rather than divine essence or nature, which are not the primary categories for Jewish theology, we can see that the so-called divine functions which Jesus exercises are intrinsic to who God is. This Christology of divine identity is not a mere stage on the way to the patristic development of ontological Christology in the context of a Trinitarian theology. It is already a fully divine Christology, maintaining that Jesus Christ is intrinsic to the unique and eternal identity of God. The Fathers did not develop it so much as transpose it into a conceptual framework more concerned with the Greek philosophical categories of essence and nature.

The inclusion of Jesus in the unique, divine identity had implications not only for who Jesus is but also for who God is. This forms the second half of the argument of *God Crucified.* When it was taken seriously, as it was in the major forms of New Testament theology, that not only the pre-existent and the exalted Jesus, but also the earthly, suffering, humiliated and crucified Jesus belongs to the unique identity of God, then it had to be said that Jesus reveals the divine identity – who God truly is – in humiliation as well as exaltation, and in the connection of the two. God's own identity is revealed in Jesus, his life and his cross, just as truly as in his exaltation, in a way that is fully continuous and consistent with the Old Testament and Jewish understanding of God, but is also novel and surprising. While the Fathers successfully appropriated, in their own way, in Nicene theology, the New Testament's inclusion of Jesus in the identity of God, they were less successful in appropriating this corollary: the revelation of the divine identity in Jesus' human life and passion. To see justice done to this aspect of New Testament Christology we have to turn to the kind of theology of the cross which Martin Luther adumbrated and which has come into its own in the twentieth century.

God Crucified does not provide the detailed study of the texts and the thorough interaction with other interpretations of Jewish monotheism, New Testament Christology, and the key early Jewish and early Christian texts, which will be needed in order to establish my arguments adequately in the context of current scholarly discussion.

But, as a concise statement of my case, uncluttered by too much detail of exegesis and scholarly apparatus, many readers have found it useful. So it stands in first place in the present book as a statement of the broad proposal to which the other essays, as more detailed explorations of specific aspects of the proposal, are supplementary. These other essays were written originally for particular contexts and occasions (conferences and multi-authored volumes), though some have been revised and extended for the present volume. They are not yet the fully comprehensive study (provisionally entitled 'Jesus and the Identity of God: Early Jewish Monotheism and New Testament Christology') that I promised in the preface to *God Crucified*. They are more like working papers on the way to that book. Because of their origins as independent essays, each is a self-contained essay, intelligible in itself, and so they do not need to be read in the order in which they appear here, and readers can pick out those that initially interest them most. While not yet comprising the comprehensive study on which I continue to work, together they certainly provide much evidence and argument in support of the proposal made in *God Crucified*. Readers interested in the nature of monotheism in the Hebrew Bible and Second Temple Judaism will find much fresh material here, while readers interested in New Testament Christology will see how my proposal that a Christology of divine identity was the common form of all early Christology can be supported and developed in the cases of Paul, Hebrews and the Gospel of Mark. To a large extent these essays focus on the first half of the argument of *God Crucified*, but the last, which focuses on the understanding of Jesus' death in Mark's Gospel, makes a contribution to the further study of the line of thought adumbrated in the second half of that book (here the second half of chapter 1).

In the decade during which these essays were written and, in some cases, presented as conference papers or lectures, I have incurred many debts to those who have commented on them, alerted me to relevant material, asked questions – sometimes very penetrating ones – and offered criticism – sometimes quite radical – of my arguments and approach. I believe the essays are the better for having taken on board these helpful and challenging interactions. I have also been much encouraged by many readers of *God Crucified* who have e-mailed, written or spoken to me, conveying their appreciation of the book and the ways in which they have found it helpful. They have helped me retain the sense that this large research project, which must certainly continue for some time to come, is worth pursuing with as much thoroughness as I can achieve. People frequently ask when the full and detailed study is going to appear. I hope that, despite the delay of the latter, they will find some of their questions answered in this present collection.

1

God Crucified

1. Understanding Early Jewish Monotheism

1.1. Early Jewish monotheism and New Testament Christology in recent discussion

The key question this book addresses is the relationship between Jewish monotheism – the Jewish monotheism of the Second Temple period which was the context of Christian origins – and New Testament Christology. Recent discussion of New Testament Christology makes it abundantly clear that this relationship between Jewish monotheism and early Christology is central to the debate about the character and development of early Christology. How New Testament authors understand the relationship of Jesus to God, how far they attribute some kind of divinity to Jesus, what kind of divinity it is that they attribute to him – such questions are deeply involved with questions about the way Second Temple Judaism understood the uniqueness of God. Of course, assumptions about the character of Jewish monotheism have always informed modern scholarly interpretation of New Testament Christology. What is relatively new in recent discussion is that there is now a significant debate in progress about the nature of Jewish monotheism in this period.[1] Interestingly, most participants in this debate are concerned precisely with the way in which the view of Jewish monotheism they argue affects the interpretation of New Testament Christology. A range of different views as to the nature of Second Temple Jewish

---

[1] See the valuable survey in Larry W. Hurtado, 'What Do We Mean by "First-Century Jewish Monotheism"?' *SBLSP* (1993): 348–54.

monotheism (or, indeed, as to whether the term 'monotheism' is appropriate at all) correlate with a similar range of views as to the process by which Jesus came to be regarded as divine and the sense in which he was considered divine in the Christian churches of the New Testament period.

Simplifying somewhat the range of views for the sake of illustration, one can identify two main approaches. There is, first, the view that Second Temple Judaism was characterized by a 'strict' monotheism that made it impossible to attribute real divinity to any figure other than the one God. From this view of Jewish monotheism, some argue that Jesus cannot have been treated as really divine within a Jewish monotheistic context, so that only a radical break with Jewish monotheism could make the attribution of real divinity to Jesus possible.[2] In view of the obviously very Jewish character of earliest Christianity, this approach tends to interpret the evidence in such a way as to minimize the extent to which anything like really divine Christology can be found within the New Testament texts.

Secondly, there are revisionist views of Second Temple Judaism which in one way or another deny its strictly monotheistic character. Such views usually focus on various kinds of intermediary figures – principal angels, exalted humans, personified divine attributes or functions – who are understood to occupy a subordinate divine or semi-divine status, so that the distinction between the one God and all other reality was by no means absolute in the Judaism of this period, it is claimed. Such views are closely related to a search for Jewish precedents and parallels for early Christian Christology. Such scholars often recognize both that many New Testament texts really do treat Jesus as in some way divine and also that these texts are clearly working within a fundamentally Jewish conceptual context. The attempt to understand how such high Christology could develop within a Jewish movement focuses then on the intermediary figures of Second Temple Judaism who in some way participate in divinity. Such figures provide, as it were, an already existing Jewish category into which early Christian estimations of Jesus' exalted status fit. Because Jewish monotheism was not strict but flexible, and the boundary between the one God and all other reality relatively blurred by the interest in intermediary figures, the highest New

---

[2] A.E. Harvey, *Jesus and the Constraints of History* (London: Duckworth, 1982), chap. 7; P. Maurice Casey, *From Jewish Prophet to Gentile God* (Cambridge: J. Clarke/Louisville: WJK, 1991); idem, 'The Deification of Jesus,' *SBLSP* (1994): 697–714.

Testament Christology can be understood as an intelligibly Jewish development.[3]

The view I shall argue in the first two sections of this chapter differs from both these approaches. In common with the first view, I shall argue that the monotheism of Second Temple Judaism was indeed 'strict'. I shall argue that most Jews in this period were highly self-consciously monotheistic, and had certain very familiar and well-defined ideas as to how the uniqueness of the one God should be understood. In other words, they drew the line of distinction between the one God and all other reality clearly, and were in the habit of distinguishing God from all other reality by means of certain clearly articulated criteria. So-called intermediary figures were not ambiguous semi-divinities straddling the boundary between God and creation. Some were understood as aspects of the one God's own unique reality. Most were regarded as unambiguously creatures, exalted servants of God whom the literature often takes pains to distinguish clearly from the truly divine reality of the one and only God. Therefore, differing from the second view, I do not think such Jewish intermediary figures are of any decisive importance for the study of early Christology. While not denying that some of them have some relevance, I think the intensive interest in them as the key to understanding the Jewishness of early Christology has been misleading. The real continuity between Jewish monotheism and New Testament Christology is not to be found in intermediary figures.

The view I shall argue is that high Christology was possible within a Jewish monotheistic context, not by applying to Jesus a Jewish category of semi-divine intermediary status, but by identifying Jesus directly with the one God of Israel, including Jesus in the unique identity of this one God. Jewish monotheism clearly distinguished the one God and all other reality, but the ways in which it distinguished the

---

[3] Christopher Rowland, *The Open Heaven* (London: SPCK, 1982), 94–113; Andrew Chester, 'Jewish Messianic Expectations and Mediatorial Figures and Pauline Christology,' in *Paulus und antike Judentum*, ed. Martin Hengel and U. Heckel (WUNT 58; Tübingen: Mohr [Siebeck], 1991), 17–89; Margaret Barker, *The Great Angel: A Study of Israel's Second God* (London: SPCK, 1992); Charles A. Gieschen, *Angelomorphic Christology* (AGJU 42; Leiden: Brill, 1998). See also, for a variety of related views which stress the importance of Jewish intermediary figures for the development of Christology: Martin Hengel, *The Son of God*, trans. J. Bowden (London: SCM, 1976); James D.G. Dunn, *Christology in the Making* (London: SCM, 1980); idem, 'Was Christianity a Monotheistic Faith from the Beginning?' *SJT* 35 (1982): 303–36; idem, 'The Making of Christology – Evolution or Unfolding?' in *Jesus of Nazareth: Lord and Christ*, ed. J.B. Green and M. Turner (Grand Rapids: Eerdmans/Carlisle: Paternoster, 1994), 437–52; Larry W. Hurtado, *One God, One Lord: Early Christian Devotion and Ancient Jewish Monotheism* (Philadelphia: Fortress, 1988).

one God from all else did not prevent the early Christians including Jesus in this unique divine identity. While this was a radically novel development, largely unprecedented in Jewish theology, the character of Jewish monotheism was such that it did not require any repudiation of the ways in which Jewish monotheism understood the uniqueness of God. What has been lacking in the whole discussion of this issue has been an adequate understanding of the ways in which Second Temple Judaism understood the uniqueness of God. By acquiring such an understanding, we shall be able to see that what the New Testament texts in general do is take up the well-known Jewish monotheistic ways of distinguishing the one God from all other reality and use these precisely as ways of including Jesus in the unique identity of the one God as commonly understood in Second Temple Judaism.

Before proceeding to argue this view, I wish to make two brief general criticisms of the way the discussions of Jewish mono-theism and early Christology have tended to proceed. One is that the fundamentally important question – what, in the Jewish under-standing of God, really counts as 'divine' – is rarely faced with clarity. In the discussion of whether Jewish monotheism was more or less strict or flexible, and in the discussion of the status of so-called intermediary figures, scholars tend to apply a variety of unexamined criteria for drawing the boundary between God and what is not God or between the divine and the non-divine.[4] Consequently, it is also unclear what the attribution of divinity to Jesus in early Christology would really imply. Some (not all) scholars who seek Jewish precedent for early Christology in allegedly semi-divine or subordinately divine Jewish intermediary figures seem to think that this supports an interpretation of New Testament Christology favourable to later christological orthodoxy, the confession of the true divinity of Jesus Christ. In fact, such arguments often produce something much more like an Arian Christ, a demigod who is neither truly divine nor truly human. The whole discussion of Jewish monotheism and early Christology urgently requires clarification of the way Jewish monotheism understood the uniqueness of God and drew the distinction between God and what is not God.

Secondly, assessment of the evidence for the character of Second Temple Jewish monotheism has, in my view, been distorted by

---

[4] A good start towards clarity in discussion in this respect is the list of 'criteria of divinity' in Gieschen, *Angelomorphic Christology*, 31–3, though I would reduce and modify his list in some respects.

concentration on the so-called intermediary figures, in the belief that these constitute the parts of the evidence that will be most illuminating for understanding early Christology. Much of the clear evidence for the ways in which Second Temple Judaism understood the uniqueness of God has been neglected in favour of a small amount of highly debatable evidence. Intermediary figures who may or may not participate in divinity are by no means characteristic of the literature of Second Temple Judaism. They should not be the focus of a study of Second Temple Jewish monotheism. Rather we should proceed by studying the broader evidence of the way the uniqueness of God was understood, and then consider the intermediary figures in the context of this broader evidence.

1.2. *Second Temple Judaism as self-consciously monotheistic*

There is every reason to suppose that observant Jews of the late Second Temple period were highly self-conscious monotheists in this sense: they saw their worship of and obedience to the one and only God, the God of Israel, as defining their distinctive religious way in the pluralistic religious environment of their time. The best evidence is their use of two key monotheistic passages of Scripture. One was the Shema' (*Shema*), the passage in Deuteronomy (6:4–6) which begins, 'Hear, O Israel: YHWH our God, YHWH is one', and continues with the requirement of total devotion to this one God: 'You shall love YHWH your God with all your heart, and with all your soul, and with all your might.' The other was the Decalogue, whose first two command-ments forbid Israelites to have or to worship any gods but YHWH (Exod. 20:2–6; Deut. 5:6–10). Both passages were clearly understood in this period as asserting the absolute uniqueness of YHWH as the one and only God. The first, the Shema', was recited twice daily, morning and evening, by all Jews who were concerned to practise Torah faithfully, since it was believed that the Torah itself commanded such twice daily recitation of this passage. Moreover, there is evidence that, in this period, the passage recited included not only the Shema' itself but also the Decalogue. Observant Jews, therefore, were daily aware of their allegiance to the one God alone. Their self-conscious monotheism was not merely an intellectual belief about God, but a unity of belief and praxis, involving the exclusive worship of this one God and exclusive obedience to this one God. Monolatry (the worship of only the one God) as the corollary of monotheism (belief in only the one God) is an important aspect of Jewish monotheism to which we shall return.

1.3. *The unique identity of God in Jewish monotheism*

This kind of practical monotheism, requiring a whole pattern of daily life and cultic worship formed by exclusive allegiance to the one God, presupposes a god who is in some way significantly identifiable. The God who requires what the God of Israel requires cannot be merely the philosophical abstraction to which the intellectual currents of contemporary Greek thought aspired. Jews, in some sense, knew who their God was. The God of Israel had a unique identity. The concept which will be the central focus of the whole argument of this chapter is that of the identity[5] of God. Since the biblical God has a name and a character, since this God acts, speaks, relates, can be addressed and, in some sense, known, the analogy of human personal identity suggests itself as the category with which to synthesize the biblical and Jewish understanding of God. It is the analogy which is clearly at work in much of the literary portrayal of God in biblical and Jewish literature. In the narratives of Israel's history, for example, God acts as a character in the story, identifiable in ways similar to those in which human characters in the story are identifiable. He has a personal identity, as Abraham and David do. This is not to say that the human analogy is adequate. All biblical and Jewish literature, even those passages which on the surface seem naively anthropomorphic in their portrayal of God, are aware of the transcendence of God, such that language and concepts are stretched when applied to him. As we shall see, the identity of God, in the Jewish understanding, breaks out of the human analogy, but its starting-point is clearly the analogy of human personal identity.

The term identity is mine, not that of the ancient literature, but I use it as a label for what I do find in the literature, which is not, of course,

---

[5] For the notion of identity as I use it here, cf. H.W. Frei, *The Identity of Jesus Christ* (Philadelphia: Fortress, 1975); idem, 'Theological Reflections on the Accounts of Jesus' Death and Resurrection,' in *Theology and Narrative: Selected Essays*, ed. G. Hunsinger and W.C. Placher (New York/Oxford: OUP, 1993), 45–93; D. Patrick, *The Rendering of God in the Old Testament* (Philadelphia: Fortress, 1981); R.W. Jenson, *The Triune Identity* (Philadelphia: Fortress, 1982); R.F. Thiemann, *Revelation and Theology: The Gospel as Narrated Promise* (Notre Dame, Ind.: University of Notre Dame Press, 1985), chaps. 6–7; R.A. Krieg, *Story-Shaped Christology: Identifying Jesus Christ* (New York: Paulist, 1988), chap. 1; K.J. Vanhoozer, 'Does the Trinity Belong in a Theology of Religions? On Angling in the Rubicon and the "Identity" of God,' in *The Trinity in a Pluralistic Age*, ed. K.J. Vanhoozer (Grand Rapids: Eerdmans, 1997), 41–71. As Vanhoozer notes, '"Identity" is, of course, susceptible of several meanings: numeric oneness, ontological sameness or permanence in time, and the personal identity of self-continuity' (47). The last is the meaning employed here. Reference to God's identity is by analogy with human personal identity, understood not as a mere ontological subject without characteristics, but as including both character and personal story (the latter entailing relationships). These are the ways in which we commonly specify 'who someone is'.

necessarily a notion precisely the same as modern ideas of personal identity, but is nevertheless clearly a concern with *who God is*. The value of the concept of divine identity appears partly if we contrast it with a concept of divine essence or nature. Identity concerns *who* God is; nature concerns *what* God is or what divinity is. Greek philosophy, already in the period we are discussing and in a way that was to influence the Christian theological tradition significantly in the period after the New Testament, typically defined divine nature by means of a series of metaphysical attributes: ingenerateness, incorruptibility, immutability and so on. My point is not that the biblical and Jewish tradition had no use at all for statements about divine nature. Some Jewish writers in the later Second Temple period consciously adopted some of the Greek metaphysical language.[6] But even in these writers the dominant conceptual framework of their understanding of God is not a definition of divine nature – what divinity is – but a notion of the divine identity, characterized primarily in ways other than metaphysical attributes. That God is eternal, for example – a claim essential to all Jewish thinking about God – is not so much a statement about what divine nature is, more an element in the unique divine identity, along with claims that God alone created all things and rules all things, that God is gracious and merciful and just, that God brought Israel out of Egypt and made Israel his own people and gave Israel his law at Sinai and so on. If we wish to know in what Second Temple Judaism considered the uniqueness of the one God to consist, what distinguished God as unique from all other reality, including beings worshipped as gods by Gentiles, we must look not for a definition of divine nature but for ways of characterizing the unique divine identity.

1.4. *Characterizing the unique identity of God*

For convenience I will distinguish two categories of identifying features of the God of Israel. There are those which identify God in his relationship to Israel, and there are those which identify God in his relation to all reality. The categories are not, of course, unrelated, but the distinction will be helpful for my argument. To Israel God has revealed and is known by his name YHWH, which was of great importance to Second Temple Jews because it names the unique identity of God. In addition to his name, God's identity is known to Israel from the recital of his acts in history and from the revelation of

---

[6] E.g. Josephus, *A.J.* 1.15, 19; 8.107; *C. Ap.* 2.167–8.

his character to Israel. Through much of the Hebrew Bible, YHWH
is identified as the God who brought Israel out of Egypt and by the
remarkable events of the exodus period created a people for himself
(e.g. Exod. 20:2; Deut. 4:32–39; Isa. 43:15–17). In addition to identification
of him by his activities, there is also a character description, given by
God himself in his self-revelation to Moses, 'YHWH, YHWH, a God
merciful and gracious, slow to anger, and abounding in steadfast love
and faithfulness...' (Exod. 34:6 and constantly echoed elsewhere in the
biblical and later Jewish literature[7]). The acts of God and the character
description of God combine to indicate a consistent identity of the one
who acts graciously towards his people and can be expected to do so.
Through the consistency of his acts and character, the one called YHWH
shows himself to be one and the same.

Alongside such identifications of God in his covenant relationship
with Israel, there are also characterizations of his identity by reference
to his unique relationship to the whole of reality: most especially, that
he is Creator of all things and sovereign Ruler of all things. It is worth
noting at this point (since it will be important to us in a later section) that
the two categories of identifying features come together with special
combined significance in Israel's eschatological expectation. In the
future, when God will fulfil his promises to his own people, showing
himself to be finally and definitively the gracious God they have known
in their history from the exodus onwards, God will at the same time
demonstrate his deity to the nations, implementing his sovereignty as
Creator and Ruler of all things in establishing his universal kingdom,
making his name known universally, becoming known to all as the God
Israel has known. The new exodus of the future, especially as predicted
in the prophecies we call Deutero-Isaiah (Isa. 40 – 55), will be an event
of universal significance precisely because the God who brought Israel
out of Egypt is also the Creator and Ruler of all things.

For the moment, however, we leave aside the first category of identifying features of God. They did not cease to be of central importance
for the Jewish understanding of the identity of God, and we shall
return to them in the last section of this chapter. But we shall focus
now on those ways of characterizing the unique divine identity
which refer to God's relationship to the whole of reality. The reason
for doing so is that, in the literature of Second Temple Judaism, these
are the features of the divine identity on which Jews focused when

---

[7] Num. 14:18; Neh. 9:17; Ps. 103:8; Joel 2:13; Jonah 4:2; Sir. 2:11; Pr. Man. 7; 4 Ezra 7:132–40; Jos.
Asen. 11:10; 1QH[a] 11:29–30.

they wished to identify God as unique. To our question, 'In what did Second Temple Judaism consider the uniqueness of the one God to consist, what distinguished God as unique from all other reality, including beings worshipped as gods by Gentiles?', the answer given again and again, in a wide variety of Second Temple Jewish literature, is that the only true God, YHWH, the God of Israel, is sole Creator of all things[8] and sole Ruler of all things.[9] While these characteristics are by no means *sufficient* to identify God (since they say nothing, for example, about his goodness or his justice), they are the features which most readily distinguish God absolutely from all other reality. God alone created all things; all other things, including beings worshipped as gods by Gentiles, are created by him. God alone rules supreme over all things; all other things, including beings worshipped as gods by Gentiles, are subject to him. These ways of distinguishing God as unique formed a very easily intelligible way of defining the uniqueness of the God they worshipped which every Jew in every synagogue in the late Second Temple period would certainly have known. However diverse Judaism may have been in many other respects, this was common: only the God of Israel is worthy of worship because he is sole Creator of all things and sole Ruler of all things. Other beings who might otherwise be thought divine are by these criteria God's creatures and subjects.

The emphasis on God's uniqueness as Creator and sovereign Ruler of history occurs in the Hebrew Bible especially in the great divine assertions of God's unique deity in Deutero-Isaiah, where they are the basis of the expectation that God will demonstrate his unique deity to the ends of the earth in the future. We shall return frequently to Deutero-Isaiah in this chapter. Those chapters of Isaiah were, outside the Torah, the most important sources of Second Temple Jewish monotheism. Again and again Deutero-Isaiah's expressions of God's uniqueness are echoed in later Jewish literature. The Lord is God, and there is no god besides him,[10] who created all things and reigns supreme

---

[8] Isa. 40:26, 28; 42:5; 44:24; 45:12, 18; 48:13; 51:16; Neh. 9:6; Hos. 13:4 LXX; 2 Macc. 1:24; Sir. 43:33; Bel 5; *Jub.* 12:3–5; *Sib. Or.* 3:20–35; 8:375–76; *Sib. Or.* frg. 1:5–6; *Sib. Or.* frg. 3; *Sib. Or.* frg. 5; 2 *En.* 47:3–4; 66:4; *Apoc. Ab.* 7:10; Ps-Sophocles; *Jos. Asen.* 12:1–2; *T. Job* 2:4.

[9] Dan. 4:34–35; Bel 5; Add. Esth. 13:9–11; 16:18, 21; 3 Macc. 2:2–3; 6:2; Wis. 12:13; Sir. 18:1–3; *Sib. Or.* 3:10, 19; *Sib. Or.* frg. 1:7, 15, 17, 35; 1 *En.* 9:5; 84:3; 2 *En.* 33:7; 2 *Bar.* 54:13; Josephus, *A.J.* 1:155–6.

[10] This monotheistic formula appears very frequently in the Hebrew Bible and Second Temple Jewish literature: Deut. 4:35, 39; 32:39; 1 Sam. 2:2; 2 Sam. 7:22; Isa. 43:11; 44:6; 45:5, 6, 14, 18, 21, 22; 46:9; Hos. 13:4; Joel 2:27; Wis. 12:13; Jdt. 8:20; 9:14; Bel 41; Sir. 24:24; 36:5; 4Q504 [4QDibHam[a]] 5:9; 1Q35 1:6; Bar. 3:36; 2 *En.* 33:8; 36:1; 47:3; *Sib. Or.* 3:629, 760; 8:377; *T Ab.* A8:7; Orphica 16; Philo, *Leg.* 3.4, 82.

over all things: these themes run from Deutero-Isaiah right through the whole literature of Second Temple Judaism.

Both these aspects of God's unique identity are aspects of his absolute supremacy over all things, and are frequently connected very closely in the literature. There is one respect, however, which will be important for the argument of this chapter, in which they differ. In creation, God acted alone, 'I ... alone stretched out the heavens [and] ... by myself spread out the earth' (Isa. 44:24). As the only Eternal One (another frequent and related characterization of God in the Second Temple period[11]), God alone brought all other beings into existence. God had no helper, assistant or servant to assist or to implement his work of creation.[12] God alone created, and no one else had any part in this activity. This is axiomatic for Second Temple Judaism.

In his sovereignty over the universe and history, however, God, of course, employs servants, especially the myriads of angels. Here the dominant image is of God as the great emperor ruling the cosmos as his kingdom, and employing, like a human emperor, vast numbers of servants who do his will throughout his empire. In this sense, the activity of others who implement God's sovereignty is important, but the Jewish concern to emphasize the uniqueness of God's total sovereignty means that angels are invariably portrayed as servants whose role is simply to carry out the will of God in total obedience. They do not share in his rule; they serve. While God sits on his throne, the angels, even the greatest, stand, in the posture of servants, awaiting his command to serve.[13] The supremacy of God is frequently depicted in the evidently powerful imagery of height. God's great throne, from which he rules the whole cosmos, is situated in the heaven of heavens, exalted high over all the many heavenly realms[14] in which his glorious angelic servants sing his praise and do his will. Even the most exalted angels, God's ministers of state, cannot approach the high and lofty throne[15] which towers above them at the summit of the universe.

So the participation of other beings in God's unique supremacy over all things is ruled out, in the case of creation, by excluding them

---

[11] Tob. 13:1; Sir. 18:1; 2 Macc. 1:25; *T. Mos.* 10:7; *1 En.* 5:1.

[12] Isa. 44:24; *2 En.* 33:4; *4 Ezra* 3:4; Josephus, *C. Ap.* 2.192. Even Philo's exegesis of Gen. 1:26 in *Opif.* 72–75; *Conf.* 179 is only a minor qualification of this denial: he insists that God acted alone in the creation of all things *except* humanity, and holds that the plural in Gen. 1:26 involves subordinate co-workers of God so that, while good human actions may be attributed to God as their source, sins may not.

[13] Dan. 7:10; Tob. 12:15; 4Q530 2.18; *1 En.* 14:22; 39:12; 40:1; 47:3; 60:2; *2 En.* 21:1; *Ques. Ezra* A26, 30; *2 Bar.* 21:6; 48:10; *4 Ezra* 8:21; *T. Ab.* A7:11; 8:1–4; 9:7–8; *T. Adam* 2:9.

[14] Isa. 57:15; 3 Macc. 2:2; *4 Ezra* 8:20–1; *2 En.* 20:3J.

[15] E.g. *1 En.* 14:18–22.

from any role at all, and, in sovereignty over the cosmos, by placing them in strict subordination as servants, excluding any possibility of interpreting their role as that of co-rulers.

1.5. *Exclusive worship of YHWH as recognition of his unique identity*

Alongside these two principal ways of characterizing God's unique identity we must set an indication of the unique identity of God which plays a different, but essential role in Jewish monotheism. This is monolatry, the exclusive worship of the one God. There is no doubt that, in religious practice, this was the factor which most clearly signalled the distinction between God and all other reality.[16] God must be worshipped; no other being may be worshipped.[17] The pervasive concern of Jews in the Second Temple period for the uniqueness of their God can be seen in their scruples about any practice which could be construed as worship of humans or other beings regarded as gods by others.[18] From all non-Jews who believed in or worshipped a high god but never supposed this to be incompatible with the worship also of lesser divinities, Jews were sharply distinguished by their monolatrous practice.[19]

Some recent argument has tended to the position that the exclusive worship of the one God is really the factor that defines God as unique in Second Temple Judaism.[20] This, in my view, is a confusion, because

---

[16] Richard Bauckham, 'Jesus, Worship of,' in *ABD*, ed. David Noel Freedman, 6 vols. (New York: Doubleday, 1992), 3:816 ('Judaism was unique among the religions of the Roman world in demanding the *exclusive* worship of its God. It is not too much to say that Jewish monotheism was defined by its adherence to the first and second commandments'); idem, *The Climax of Prophecy: Studies on the Book of Revelation* (Edinburgh: T&T Clark, 1993), 118; idem, *The Theology of the Book of Revelation* (Cambridge: CUP, 1993), 58–9.

[17] For the slender evidence adduced for some kind of veneration of angels by Jews, see Loren T. Stuckenbruck, *Angel Veneration and Christology* (WUNT 2/70; Tübingen: Mohr [Siebeck], 1995), 45–203; C.E. Arnold, *The Colossian Syncretism* (Grand Rapids: Baker, 1996), 32–89. While there may be a few marginal instances of the worship of angels, as there is plentiful evidence of the invocation of angels in magical practice, it is very doubtful whether any substantial number of Jews treated angels in a way that they would themselves have regarded as comparable, even in degree, with the worship of God. Occasional prayer to angels should not be confused with worship.

[18] Add. Esth. 13:12–14; Philo, *Legat.* 116; cf. Acts 10:25–26.

[19] Cf. John M.G. Barclay, *Jews in the Mediterranean Diaspora from Alexander to Trajan (323 BCE–117 CE)* (Edinburgh: T&T Clark, 1996), 429–34.

[20] Hurtado, 'What Do We Mean,' 348–68. This takes his attempt to give worship the key role in the definition of Jewish monotheism further than his earlier *One God*. I tended to this view myself in Bauckham, 'Jesus, Worship of,' *ABD* 3:816, 'Judaism was unique among the religions of the Roman world in demanding the *exclusive* worship of its God. It is not too much to say that Jewish monotheism was defined by its adherence to the first and second commandments.'

the exclusive worship of the God of Israel is precisely *a recognition of and response to* his unique identity. It is God's unique identity which requires worship of him alone. Worship of other beings is inappropriate because they do not share in this unique identity. Worshipping God along with withholding worship from any other being is recognition of the absolute distinction between God and all other reality.

The distinction in cultic practice between Jews and others who acknowledged a high god is, in fact, correlative with a difference in monotheistic conception. The typical Hellenistic view was that worship is a matter of degree because divinity is a matter of degree. Lesser divinities are worthy of appropriate degrees of worship. Philosophical monotheists who held that all other divine being derives ultimately from the one, nevertheless held the derived divinity of lesser divine beings to be appropriately acknowledged in cultic worship. The notion of a hierarchy or spectrum of divinity stretching from the one God down through the gods of the heavenly bodies, the daemons of the atmosphere and the earth, to those humans who were regarded as divine or deified, was pervasive in all non-Jewish religion and religious thought, and inseparable from the plurality of cultic practices in honour of a wide variety of divinities. Jews understood their practice of monolatry to be justified, indeed required, because the unique identity of YHWH was so understood as to place him, not merely at the summit of a hierarchy of divinity, but in an absolutely unique category, beyond comparison with anything else. Worship was the recognition of this unique incomparability of the one God. It was the response to YHWH's self-revelation as the sole Creator and Ruler of all.

Hence, in Second Temple Judaism, monolatry was not a substitute for the lack of a clear concept of divine uniqueness. It was the corollary of a notion of God's unique identity which itself was carefully framed so as to indicate the absolute distinction between God and all other reality. The requirement of exclusive worship and the common ways of characterizing the unique identity of God correlated with and reinforced each other. On the one hand, that it is inappropriate to worship beings other than the one God could be justified by pointing out that they are created by him, benefit humans only in a way that derives ultimately from God, ministers of God's will, not independent sources of good.[21] In other words, they do not participate in the unique identity of God the Creator and Ruler of all things, and therefore do not deserve worship, which is acknowledgement of that unique identity.

---

[21] E.g. Josephus, *A.J.* 1.155–6; *2 En.* 66:4–5[J]; *Sib. Or.* 3:20–35.

On the other hand, when some Hellenistic philosophical accounts of the one supreme God as the sole source of all other being and providential overseer of all things correspond quite closely to Jewish monotheistic ideas,[22] the language of such accounts can be borrowed by some Jewish writers. In this case, the formal definition of the unique identity of the one God may be closely similar, but the Jewish claim that it requires exclusive worship heightens the significance of the distinction being made between the one God and all other reality. Whereas the tendency of non-Jewish thought is to assimilate such ideas of divine uniqueness to patterns of thought in which the supreme God is the summit of a hierarchy of divinity or the original source of a spectrum of divinity, the tendency of Jewish thought is to accentuate the absolute distinction between God and all else as the dominant feature of the whole Jewish worldview. The deeply rooted Jewish sense that the unique identity of God required exclusive worship played an important role in this difference.

1.6. *Jewish monotheism and 'intermediary' figures*

The evidence that Jews of this period could easily and were in the habit of drawing a firm line of clear distinction between the one God and all other reality is far more considerable than the small amount of evidence adduced by those who argue that so-called intermediary figures blur this distinction. Methodologically, it is imperative to proceed from the clear consensus of Second Temple monotheism to the more ambiguous evidence about so-called intermediary figures to which we now turn. The question that needs to be addressed in the case of such figures is: By the criteria which Second Temple Jewish texts themselves constantly use to distinguish the one God from all other reality, do these figures belong to the unique identity of God or do they fall outside it? Are they, so to speak, intrinsic to God's own unique identity as the one God, or are they creatures and servants of God, however exalted? The criteria which count are the criteria by which Jews of the period themselves distinguished the unique identity of God, not other possible criteria of divinity which were not the decisive ones for them. Once these criteria are applied, it seems to me that in almost every case the question I have just asked is readily answerable. In other words, some of these figures are unambiguously depicted as intrinsic to the unique identity of God, while others are

---

[22] See, for example, the doctrine of God in the Ps-Aristotelian treatise *De Mundo*, summarized by R.M. Grant, *Gods and the One God* (London: SPCK, 1986), 78–9.

unambiguously excluded from it. Unfortunately, there is no space here to argue the case in the way that it requires to be argued, by examining the texts in detail. All that is possible in the present context is to outline the argument very broadly.

1.7 Intermediary figures

Two categories of intermediary figures can be distinguished. One has been called principal angels and exalted patriarchs.[23] These are angelic or human figures who play a very important role in God's rule over the world. They are either very high-ranking angels, such as Michael in the Qumran literature or Yahoel in the *Apocalypse of Abraham*, or human figures such as Moses in the work of Ezekiel the Tragedian or the Son of Man in the *Parables of Enoch* (if it is correct to think that that work identifies the Son of Man with Enoch exalted to heaven). The second category of intermediary figures consists of personifications or hypostatizations of aspects of God himself, such as his Spirit, his Word and his Wisdom. (Because of their relevance to early Christology, I shall confine the present discussion to Word and Wisdom.) In my view, the Jewish literature in question for the most part unequivocally excludes the figures in the first category from the unique identity of God, while equally unequivocally includes the figures in the second category within the unique identity of God.

1.7.1. Principal angels and exalted patriarchs

Applying our criteria, there is no suggestion, anywhere in the literature, that principal angels or exalted patriarchs participate in the work of creation. They are clearly created beings.[24] With regard to God's sovereignty over the cosmos, Second Temple Jewish literature does certainly envisage a small group of very highly placed angels,[25] who form a kind of council of chief ministers of state, each in charge of some major aspect of the divine government of the cosmos.[26] This picture has been distorted by the assertion in much recent scholarship that the literature frequently envisages a single principal angel (though the identity of this angel varies in various texts), a sort of grand vizier or plenipotentiary, to whom God delegates the whole of his rule over the

---

[23] Hurtado, *One God*, 17.
[24] For angels as created, see, e.g. *Jub.* 2:2; *L.A.B.* 60:2; *2 Bar.* 21:6; *2 En.* 29:3; 33:7.
[25] Seven: *1 En.* 20:1–8; Tob. 12:15; Rev. 8:2; four: *1 En.* 9:1; 10:1–11; 40:3–10; 54:6; 71:8–9; 1QM 9:15–16; *Apoc. Mos.* 40:3.
[26] E.g. *1 En.* 20:2–8; 40:9.

cosmos.[27] In my view, such a figure appears in very few[28] of the texts. A less than careful reading of the texts has mistakenly manufactured such a figure. For example, in some works the archangel Michael, who is the heavenly patron of Israel, takes precedence as first in rank among the principal angels.[29] This corresponds to the pre-eminent position of Israel in God's rule over the world. But it does not mean that Michael is in charge of all the work of all the other angels. There is no suggestion, for example, that the angels who are in charge of the workings of nature, an extremely important part of the angelic activity in the world, come under the supervisory authority of Michael. Michael ranks higher than the other principal angels, but he is not set in authority over their spheres of government. So the notion of a heavenly viceroy, who, next to God, is in charge of the cosmos, as a standard idea in the Jewish conception of the cosmos is a fiction. This alleged precedent for Christology should be forgotten.

The most exalted angels serve God; they do not participate in his rule. Two features, among others, make this clear. In the first place, they never sit with God on his heavenly throne, the obvious symbol which Jewish writers could have used in their depictions of the heavens, to portray a viceroy or co-ruler. On the contrary, they stand, in the posture of servants.[30] Secondly, not only are they never worshipped, but they explicitly reject worship. They are portrayed as doing so in a series of texts which form a stereotyped literary tradition, clearly designed to distinguish exalted angels, who declare themselves mere servants of God, from God.[31] These texts clearly deploy the criteria of sovereignty

---

[27] E.g. Alan F. Segal, *Two Powers in Heaven* (SJLA 25; Leiden: Brill, 1977), 186–200; Hurtado, *One God*, 71–82; P. Hayman, 'Monotheism – A Misused Word in Jewish Studies?' *JJS* 42 (1991): 11; Barker, *Great Angel*.

[28] I find the idea of a single vicegerent of God in only the following cases, where special considerations can be seen to be at work: the archangel (probably Michael) in *Joseph and Aseneth*, where his role in heaven is modelled on Joseph's in Egypt (14:8–9; cf. Gen. 45:8); the Spirit of truth or Prince of light (also identified with Michael) in some Qumran texts (especially 1QS 3:15 – 4:1), where the role is due to the rather distinctive features of Qumran dualism; and the Logos in Philo who had his own philosophical-theological reasons for envisaging a single mediator of all divine relationship to the world. The other so-called intermediary figures have much more limited roles.

[29] *1 En.* 40:9; cf. *T. Mos.* 10:1; 1QM 17:7–8.

[30] Tob. 12:15; *T. Ab.* A7:11; 8:1–4; 9:7–8; cf. also Luke 1:19.

[31] The clearest examples in Jewish literature are Tob. 12:16–22; *Apoc. Zeph.* 6:11–15; *3 En.* 16:1–5; Cairo Genizah Hekhalot A/2, 13–18, and in Christian literature, Rev. 19:10; 22:8–9; *Ascen. Isa.* 7:18–23; 8:1–10; *Apoc. Paul* [Coptic ending]; *Apoc. Gos. Matt.* 3:3; cf. also *2 En.* 1:4–8; *3 En.* 1:7; *Lad. Jac,* 3:3–5; *Jos. Asen.* 14:9–12; 15:11–12. They are studied in Richard Bauckham, 'The Worship of Jesus in Apocalyptic Christianity,' *NTS* 27 (1980–81): 322–41; revised version in idem, *Climax of Prophecy,* chap. 4; see also Loren T. Stuckenbruck, 'An Angelic Refusal of Worship: The Tradition and Its Function in the Apocalypse of John,' *SBLSP* (1994): 679–96; idem, *Angel Veneration,* 75–103.

and worship to draw the line between, on the one hand, God who rules all things and should therefore be worshipped and, on the other hand, glorious heavenly beings who, being only servants of God, may not be worshipped.

There is one exception which proves the rule. In the *Parables of Enoch*, the Son of Man will in the future, at the eschatological day of judgement, be placed by God on God's own throne to exercise judgement on God's behalf.[32] He will also be worshipped.[33] Here we have a sole example of an angelic figure or exalted patriarch who has been included in the divine identity: he participates in the unique divine sovereignty and, therefore, in recognition of his exercise of the divine sovereignty he receives worship. His inclusion in the divine identity is partial, since he plays no part in the work of creation or indeed in the divine sovereignty until the future day of judgement, and therefore his inclusion in the divine identity remains equivocal. But he is the only such equivocal case, who shows, by contrast, the absence in other cases of any of the criteria by which Second Temple Jews would consider a heavenly figure to share the divine identity.[34]

1.7.2. *Personified or hypostatized divine aspects*
The second category of intermediary figures – personifications or hypostatizations of aspects of God – turns out, by the same criteria, to be quite different. Both the Word and the Wisdom of God take part in the work of creation, sometimes with distinguishable roles,[35] sometimes interchangeably.[36] The texts in question make it quite clear that they are not infringing the standard monotheistic insistence that

---

[32] *1 En.* 61:8; 62:2, 5; 69:27, 29; cf. 51:3.

[33] 48:5; 62:6, 9. This worship cannot be understood as merely an expression of submission to a political superior, since the Son of Man is seated on the throne of God. In such a context, it is recognition of the unique divine sovereignty over the world.

[34] A second case is frequently alleged: Moses in the *Exagoge* of Ezekiel the Tragedian (68–89) but, in my view, this passage has been widely misunderstood. Moses in a dream sees himself replacing God on the throne of the universe. Raguel's interpretation of the dream takes this to be a symbol of Moses' career as a king and prophet of Israel. What God is in relation to the cosmos, Moses will be in relation to Israel. Ezekiel is offering an interpretation of the statement in Exod. 7:1 that God will make Moses 'God'. The dream depicts this literally (God vacates his own cosmic throne and places Moses on it), but the *meaning* of the dream is its interpretation as a metaphor of Moses' earthly role. Cf. Gen. 37:9–10: in Joseph's dream, he receives the worship the heavenly bodies give to God, but the meaning of the dream is that his parents and brothers will serve him.

[35] Ps. 33:9; *4 Ezra* 6:38; *2 Bar.* 56:3–4; *2 En.* 33:4.

[36] Wisdom: Jer. 10:12; 51:15; Ps. 104:24; Prov. 3:19; 8:30; Sir. 24:3b, Wis. 7:22; 8:4–6; cf. 1QH^a 9:7, 14, 20; Wis. 9:2; Word: Ps. 33:6; Sir. 42:15; *Jub.* 12:4; *Sib. Or.* 3:20; *2 Bar.* 14:17; 21:4; 48:8; *4 Ezra* 6:38; *T. Ab.* A9:6; Wis. 9:1.

God created without assistance of any kind.[37] *2 Enoch* 33:4, in an echo of Deutero-Isaiah (Isa. 40:13),[38] says that God had no advisor in his work of creation, but that his Wisdom was his advisor. The meaning is clearly that God had *no one else* to advise him. His Wisdom, who is not someone else but intrinsic to his own identity, advised him. Similarly, Wisdom is depicted sitting on the great divine throne beside God, participating in the exercise of his sovereignty by playing the role of advisor or counsellor to the king (*1 En.* 84:2–3; Wis. 9:4, 10). Here the image which the literature refrains from applying to any angelic servant of God is applied to Wisdom, with no detriment to the clear distinction between God and all other reality, because precisely this symbol serves to include Wisdom in the unique identity of the one God who rules the cosmos from his uniquely exalted throne. In general, the personifications of God's Word and God's Wisdom in the literature are not parallel to the depictions of exalted angels as God's servants. The personifications have been developed precisely out of the ideas of God's own Wisdom and God's own Word, that is, aspects of God's own identity. In a variety of ways, they *express* God, his mind and his will in relation to the world. They are not created beings, but nor are they semi-divine entities occupying some ambiguous status between the one God and the rest of reality. They belong to the unique divine identity.

My conclusion that the Word and the Wisdom of God are intrinsic to the unique divine identity, as understood in Jewish monotheism, does not decide the question (which, in my view, must be secondary) whether the personification of these figures in the literature is merely a literary device or whether they are envisaged as having some form of distinct existence in reality. I think there is a good argument for the latter at least in some of the texts about Wisdom (e.g. Wis. 7:22 – 8:1). But this does not mean that Wisdom is there envisaged as a subordinate divine being extrinsic to the identity of the one God. It means that these Jewish writers envisage some form of real distinction within the unique identity of the one God. If so, they are not abandoning or in any way compromising their Jewish monotheism. The Second Temple Jewish understanding of the divine uniqueness does not define it as unitariness and does not make distinctions within the divine identity inconceivable. Its perfectly clear distinction between God and all other reality is made in other terms, which in this case place God's Wisdom unequivocally within the unique divine identity.

---

[37] Isa. 44:24; *2 En.* 33:4; *4 Ezra* 3:4; Josephus, *C. Ap.* 2.192.
[38] Cf. Sir. 42:21; *1 En.* 14:22; Wis. 9:13, 17; 1QS 11:18–19.

2. Christological monotheism in the New Testament

2.1. *Introduction: divine identity Christology*

In the previous section, I outlined an analysis of the nature of Second
Temple Jewish monotheism, arguing that the unique identity of the God
of Israel is the category by means of which we can best grasp the way
Jews of the period understood God. I argued that the Judaism of the
period was pervasively, self-consciously and strictly monotheistic, in
the sense of having a clear concept of the absolute distinction between
God and all other reality, with extensive implications for religious
practice. The uniqueness of the divine identity was characterized
especially by two features: that the one God is sole Creator of all
things and that the one God is sole Ruler of all things. To this unique
identity corresponds monolatry, the exclusive worship of the one and
only God who is so characterized. Worship, in the Jewish tradition, is
recognition of the unique divine identity, and so must be accorded to
the one who created and rules all things, but may not be accorded to
any other beings, all of whom are created by and subject to the one true
God. Finally, I argued (without being able to present the evidence in
detail) that the so-called intermediary figures which feature in some
Jewish texts of the period do not, as is often alleged, blur or bridge
the line of absolute distinction which Jewish monotheism maintained
between God and all other reality. On the contrary, if we allow the texts
to operate, as they do, Judaism's own criteria of distinction between
God and all other reality, we find that, almost without exception, these
figures belong unambiguously either outside the unique identity of
God, so that there is no proper Jewish sense in which they count as
divine, or else within the unique identity of God, such that they are
intrinsic to God's own identity as the one God. Principal angels and
exalted patriarchs do not participate in the unique creative work of
God, nor do they participate in the exercise of God's rule by sharing
the divine throne, but only carry out God's will as servants, and so,
finally, they are not worshipped. The Word and the Wisdom of God,
on the other hand, do participate in the creative work of God and in
his sovereignty, and so belong intrinsically to God's unique identity.
In neither case, once we understand the way Jewish monotheism drew
the distinction between God and all other reality, is there any blurring
of the line.

The present section will build on this understanding of Jewish
monotheism an argument about New Testament Christology. Once
again, there is no possibility of providing more than a small sampling

of the evidence for this case, which ought properly to encompass all the important christological texts of the New Testament. I shall concentrate on illustrating a way of reading the texts which puts the whole question of the character of New Testament Christology in a new light. In this argument, the understanding of Jewish monotheism which I have proposed will function as the hermeneutical key to understanding the way in which the New Testament texts relate Jesus Christ to the one God of Jewish monotheism. It will enable us to see that the intention of New Testament Christology, throughout the texts, is to include Jesus in the unique divine identity as Jewish monotheism understood it. They do this deliberately and comprehensively by using precisely those characteristics of the divine identity on which Jewish monotheism focused in characterizing God as unique. They include Jesus in the unique divine sovereignty over all things, they include him in the unique divine creation of all things, they identify him by the divine name which names the unique divine identity, and they portray him as accorded the worship which, for Jewish monotheists, is recognition of the unique divine identity. In this way, they develop a kind of christological monotheism which is fully continuous with early Jewish monotheism, but distinctive in the way it sees Jesus Christ himself as intrinsic to the identity of the unique God.

I shall be arguing what will seem to anyone familiar with the study of New Testament Christology a surprising thesis: that the highest possible Christology – the inclusion of Jesus in the unique divine identity – was central to the faith of the early church even before any of the New Testament writings were written, since it occurs in all of them. Although there was development in understanding this inclusion of Jesus in the identity of God, the decisive step of so including him was made at the beginning of Christology. Essential to this argument is the recognition that this high Christology was entirely possible within the understanding of Jewish monotheism we have outlined. Novel as it was, it did not require any repudiation of the monotheistic faith which the first Christians axiomatically shared with all Jews. That Jewish monotheism and high Christology were in some way in tension is one of the prevalent illusions in this field that we must allow the texts to dispel. The New Testament writers did not see their Jewish monotheistic heritage as in any way an obstacle to the inclusion of Jesus in the divine identity; they used its resources extensively in order precisely to include Jesus in the divine identity; and they saw in this inclusion of Jesus in the divine identity the fulfilment of the eschatological expectation of Jewish monotheism that the one God will be universally acknowledged as such in his universal rule over all things.

As I observed at the beginning of section 1, recent attempts to make high Christology intelligible as a development within a thoroughly Jewish context have focused on the so-called intermediary figures as providing precedents or parallels for high Christology. The conviction has been that a direct identification of Jesus with the one God would have been impossible for Jewish monotheism, whereas the various figures alleged to occupy ambiguous or semi-divine status, participating in divinity in some subordinate way, make room within Jewish monotheism for the attribution of divine attributes and functions to Jesus. This conviction is, in my view, almost the exact opposite of the truth. What Jewish monotheism could not accommodate were precisely semi-divine figures, subordinate deities, divinity by delegation or participation. The key to the way in which Jewish monotheism and high Christology were compatible in the early Christian movement is not the claim that Jewish monotheism left room for ambiguous semi-divinities, but the recognition that its understanding of the unique identity of the one God left room for the inclusion of Jesus in that identity. Though such a step was unprecedented, the character of Jewish monotheism did not make it impossible. Moreover, it was not a step which could be, as it were, approached gradually by means of ascending christological beliefs. To put Jesus in the position, for example, of a very high ranking angelic servant of God would not be to come close to a further step of assimilating him to God, because the absolute distinction between God and all other reality would still have to be crossed. The decisive step of including Jesus in the unique identity of God was not a step that could be facilitated by prior, less radical steps. It was a step which, whenever it was taken, had to be taken simply for its own sake and *de novo*. It does not become any more intelligible by being placed at the end of a long process of christological development. In my view, the New Testament evidence is best explained if this step was taken very early, as the fundamental step on which all further christological development then rested.

2.2. *The exalted Jesus participates in God's unique sovereignty over all things*

At a very early stage, which is presupposed and reflected in all the New Testament writings, early Christians understood Jesus to have been exalted after his death to the throne of God in the highest heaven. There, seated with God on God's throne, Jesus exercises or participates in God's unique sovereignty over the whole cosmos. This decisive step of understanding a human being to be participating now in the unique divine sovereignty over the cosmos was unprecedented. The principal angels and exalted patriarchs of Second Temple Jewish literature provide no precedent. It is this radical novelty which leads to all the other exalted christological claims of the New Testament texts. But, although a novelty, its meaning depends upon the Jewish monotheistic conceptual context in which the early Christians believed it. Because the unique sovereignty of God over all things was precisely one of the two major features which characterized the unique identity of God, in distinction from all other reality, this confession of Jesus reigning on the divine throne was precisely a recognition of his inclusion in the unique divine identity, himself decisively distinguished, as God himself is, from any exalted heavenly servant of God. We shall see further evidence of this as we proceed.

2.3. *Psalm 110:1 in early Christology*

Early Christian theology, like other Jewish theology of the period, proceeded primarily by exegesis of the Hebrew Scriptures. Creative exegesis of the Scriptures was the principal medium in which early Christians developed even the most novel aspects of their thought, a point of which we shall have to take much notice especially in later parts of this chapter. But the point is important now, because the participation of Jesus in the unique divine sovereignty was understood primarily by reference to one key Old Testament text (Ps. 110:1) and other texts brought into exegetical relationship with it. Psalm 110:1 (LXX 109:1) is the Old Testament text to which the New Testament most often alludes (twenty-one quotations or allusions, scattered across most of the New Testament writings,[39] with the Johannine literature the one notable exception). It reads:

> The LORD said to my Lord,
> 'Sit at my right hand
> until I make your enemies your footstool.'[40]

The verse certainly does not have to be read as meaning that the person referred to as 'my Lord' (the Messiah) is seated on the divine

---

[39] Matt. 22:44; 26:64; Mark 12:36; 14:62; 16:19; Luke 20:42–43; 22:69; Acts 2:33–35; 5:31; 7:55–56; Rom. 8:34; 1 Cor. 15:25; Eph. 1:20; 2:6; Col. 3:1; Heb. 1:3, 13; 8:1; 10:12–13; 12:2; 1 Pet. 3:22; Rev. 3:21. All these allusions are certain except Rev. 3:21, which is probable.

[40] On the early Christian use of this text, see D.H. Hay, *Glory at the Right Hand: Psalm 110 in Early Christianity* (SBLMS 18; Nashville: Abingdon, 1973); Martin Hengel, 'Sit at My Right Hand!' in *Studies in Early Christology* (Edinburgh: T&T Clark, 1995), 119–225.

throne itself and exercises the divine sovereignty over the cosmos. It could, for example, be read to mean simply that the Messiah is given a position of honour as a favoured subject beside the divine throne, where he sits inactively awaiting the inauguration of his rule on earth. This is how some of the rabbis later read it.[41] It is quite clear, however, that early Christians read it differently: as placing Jesus on the divine throne itself, exercising God's own rule over all things. The point is sometimes made by combining the verse with Psalm 8:6:

> You made him ruler over the works of your hands
> and placed all things under his feet.[42]

The discontinuity between early Christology at this decisive point and the beliefs and expectations of Second Temple Jewish literature can be illustrated from the fact that, whereas this text Psalm 110:1 is the most quoted Old Testament text in the New Testament, in the whole of the literature of Second Temple Judaism there is only one probable allusion to the verse, in the *Testament of Job* (33:3),[43] where its use bears little resemblance to its significance for early Christians. Nowhere in early Judaism is it applied to one of the exalted heavenly figures – angels or patriarchs – who occupy important places in heaven now or in the future. Nowhere is it applied to the Messiah, who is never, of course, supposed in early Jewish expectation to rule the cosmos from heaven, but only to be a ruler on earth. The messianic interpretation of the royal psalms in general would lead us to expect that, when Jews in the Second Temple period did interpret Psalm 110, they would apply it to the Messiah. But its absence from the literature shows that it had no importance for them, whereas for early Christians it was of key importance. The difference simply reflects the fact that early Christians used the text to say something about Jesus which Second Temple Jewish literature is not interested in saying about anyone: that he participates in the unique divine sovereignty over all things.

---

[41] Hay, *Glory*, 28–31.

[42] Ps. 110:1 and Ps. 8:6 conflated or associated: Matt. 22:44; Mark 12:36; 1 Cor. 15:25–28; Eph. 1:20–22; 1 Pet. 3:22; cf. Heb. 1:13 – 2:9.

[43] The point is that, in place of his throne and splendour in this world, which is passing away, Job has an eternal splendour reserved for him in heaven. The point is not to give him a position of authority in God's rule over the world, but to depict his heavenly reward as the eternal reality of which his kingdom in this world has been only a worthless shadow. This provides no precedent for early Christian use of the text, in which Christ's enthronement at God's right hand is not merely his individual heavenly reward but his unique cosmic status and role.

My argument is that the exaltation of Jesus to the heavenly throne of God could only mean, for the early Christians who were Jewish monotheists, his inclusion in the unique identity of God, and that, furthermore, the texts show their full awareness of that and quite deliberately use the rhetoric and conceptuality of Jewish monotheism to make this inclusion unequivocal. As evidence for this I will refer to four further aspects of the way the texts envisage the exaltation of Jesus.

2.4. Jesus' sovereignty over 'all things'

First, the texts frequently refer to Jesus' exaltation or sovereignty as over 'all things'. Though New Testament scholars commonly fail to recognize this and in individual texts debate the extent of the 'all things' to which the text refers, the phrase belongs to the standard rhetoric of Jewish monotheism, in which it constantly refers, quite naturally, to the whole of the created reality from which God is absolutely distinguished as its Creator and Ruler.[44] God's servants may be said, by his permission, to rule some things, as earthly rulers do, but only God rules over all things from a throne exalted above all things. The frequent New Testament christological uses of this phrase[45] should not be studied atomistically, but their cumulative weight appreciated as testimony to the way the texts habitually define Christ's exaltation or rule in the terms Jewish monotheism reserved for God's unique sovereignty.

2.5. Jesus shares God's exaltation above all the angelic powers

Secondly, many of the texts emphasize Jesus' exaltation and sovereignty over all the angelic powers, sometimes with emphatic use of the potent Jewish imagery of height. For example, Ephesians 1:21–22:

> [God] raised [Jesus] from the dead and seated him at his right hand in the heavenly places, far above all rule and authority and power and dominion, and above every name that is named, not only in this age but also in the age to come. And he has put all things under his feet.

---

[44] E.g. Isa. 44:24; Jer. 10:16; 51:19; Sir. 43:33; Wis. 9:6; 12:13; Add. Esth. 13:9; 2 Macc. 1:24; 3 Macc. 2:3; *1 En.* 9:5; 84:3; *2 En.* 66:4; *Jub.* 12:19; *Apoc. Ab.* 7:10; *Jos. Asen.* 12:1; *Sib. Or.* 3:20; 8:376; *Sib. Or.* frg. 1:17; Josephus, *B.J.* 5.218; 1Qap Gen^ar 20:13; 4QD^b 18:5:9.
[45] Christ's lordship over 'all things': Matt. 11:27; Luke 10:22; John 3:35; 13:3; 16:15; Acts 10:36; 1 Cor. 15:27–28; Eph. 1:22; Phil. 3:21; Heb. 1:2; 2:8; cf. Eph. 1:10, 23; 4:10; Col. 1:20. Christ's participation in the creation and sustaining of 'all things': John 1:3; 1 Cor. 8:6; Col. 1:16–17; Heb. 1:3.

That 'far above' evokes the image of the high and lofty divine throne at the summit of the heavens (cf. also Eph. 4:10), exalted far above the various angelic powers which rule as God's servants in the lower heavens.[46] Jesus is not here being placed in the position of any angelic figure, nor are the angelic powers being demoted. The spatial relationship between Jesus on the divine throne and the angelic powers is precisely how Jewish pictures of the heavenly realms portrayed the relationship between the divine throne and the angelic powers subject to God. The point is that Jesus now shares precisely God's exaltation and sovereignty over every angelic power. Similarly, in the great christological passage in Hebrews 1, where a catena of seven scriptural quotations is deployed to explicate the full meaning of Psalm 110:1 with which the catena concludes, the significance of Jesus' exaltation to the right hand of God is expounded by proving his superiority over all the angels. This superiority is both imaged as spatial height (1:3–4) and expounded as qualitative difference. The angels, argues the passage, are no more than servants of God, whereas Christ, who occupies the divine throne itself, participates in God's own sovereignty and is, therefore, served by the angels (1:7–9, 13–14). The purpose is not a polemic against angels or angel Christology. Nothing that is said about the angels would have been controversial to any Jewish reader. The function of the angels in the passage is to assist theological definition of the one God, to portray the line of distinction which Jewish monotheism always insisted on drawing between God, the only sovereign Ruler, and all other reality. When this line is drawn, even the highest angels are only servants of God. But if Jesus is superior to the angels, participating in the divine sovereignty, this means precisely, for Jewish monotheistic conceptuality, that he is included in the unique identity of the one God. Careful study of Hebrews 1, for which we lack space here, would reveal with what care and sophistication the passage employs all the key features by which Jewish monotheism standardly characterized the uniqueness of God in order to include Jesus within the unique divine identity.

2.6. *Jesus given the divine name*

Thirdly, the exalted Jesus is given the divine name, the Tetragrammaton (YHWH), the name which names the unique identity of the one God, the name which is exclusive to the one God in a way that the sometimes

---

[46] Cf. especially *T. Levi* 3:4, 'In the highest of all [the heavens] dwells the Great Glory in the holy of holies far above every holiness.'

ambiguous word 'god' is not. Hebrews 1:4 states that Jesus, exalted to the right hand of God, became 'as much superior to the angels as the name he has inherited is more excellent than theirs'. Though most of the commentators do not think so, this can only refer to the divine name, as must 'the name that is above every name', which according to Philippians 2:9 was bestowed on Jesus when God exalted him to the highest position. Connected with this naming of the exalted Jesus by the divine name is the early Christian use of the phrase 'to call on the name of the Lord',[47] as a reference to Christian confession and to baptism. The Old Testament phrase[48] means to invoke God by his name YHWH,[49] but the early Christian use of it applies it to Jesus. It means invoking Jesus as the divine Lord who exercises the divine sovereignty and bears the divine name.

2.7. *Worship of Jesus as recognition of his exercise of the unique divine sovereignty*

Fourthly, the exalted Christ's participation in the unique divine sovereignty is recognized by worship. As we observed in section 1, worship in the Jewish tradition is precisely recognition of the unique divine identity. It is accorded to God, especially as sole Creator of all things and as sole Ruler of all things. It most obviously puts into religious practice the distinction Jewish monotheism drew between the one God and all other reality. So the significant christological evidence is not only that which shows, as has been increasingly recognized in recent scholarship, that the practice of worshipping Jesus goes far back into early Jewish Christianity, but also the evidence that worship was thought to be due to Christ precisely as response to his inclusion in the unique divine identity through exaltation to the throne of God. Therefore, very significant are the depictions of universal worship in Philippians 2:9–11 and Revelation 5, two passages we shall consider in more detail in the next section, in both of which it is precisely the exaltation of Christ to the divine throne which evokes the worship of all creation. Also noteworthy is Matthew 28:17, where, in the closing scene of this Gospel, the disciples worship Jesus as he declares that all authority in heaven and on earth has been given to him.[50]

---

[47] Acts 2:17–21, 38; 9:14; 22:16; Rom. 10:9–13; 1 Cor. 1:2; 2 Tim. 2:22.
[48] Note especially Ps. 80:18; Isa. 12:4; Joel 2:32; Zeph. 3:9; Zech. 13:9.
[49] Cf. Gen. 4:26; 1 Kgs. 18:24–39.
[50] Note also Heb. 1:6; John 5:21–23.

2.8. *The pre-existent Christ participates in God's unique activity of creation*

The evidence we have considered so far amounts to what could be called christological and eschatological monotheism. Jesus is seen as the one who exercises God's eschatological sovereignty over all things, with a view to the coming of God's kingdom and the universal acknowledgement of God's unique deity. Jesus is included, we might say, in the *eschatological* identity of God. Clearly the dominant early Christian concern was with Jesus' present and future participation in the divine sovereignty. It is, therefore, all the more remarkable that early Christians included Jesus in the unique divine sovereignty, not only eschatologically but also *protologically*, not only in the present and future but also from the beginning. This must be mainly because, for Jewish monotheism, the eternal divine sovereignty, including God's unique creative activity in the beginning as well as his providential ordering of all things and his future completion of his purpose for his reign over all things, is properly indivisible. God alone rules all things and will rule all things because he alone created all things. If Jesus is no mere servant of God but participates in the unique divine sovereignty and is, therefore, intrinsic to the unique divine identity, he must be so eternally. The participation of Christ in the creative work of God is necessary, in Jewish monotheistic terms, to complete the otherwise incomplete inclusion of him in the divine identity. It also makes even clearer that the intention of this early Christology is precisely to include him in the unique divine identity, since, in the creative work of God, there was, for Jewish monotheists, no room even for servants of God to carry out his work at his command. Creation, axiomatically, was the sole work of God alone.

Whereas the inclusion of Jesus in the eschatological sovereignty of God is found in all the New Testament literature, his inclusion in the work of creation is less widespread, but is found in 1 Corinthians, Colossians, Hebrews, Revelation and the Gospel of John.[51] Since it is of less direct relevance to most of the concerns of the New Testament writers, this is not surprising. What is noteworthy is that in three of these cases (1 Corinthians, Hebrews and John) the purpose, in my view, is precisely to express Jewish monotheism in christological terms. It is not that these writers wish to say anything about the work of creation for its own sake or even that they wish to say anything about the relationship of Christ to creation for its

---

[51] John 1:1–5; 1 Cor. 8:6; Col. 1:15–16; Heb. 1:2–3, 10–12; Rev. 3:14.

own sake, but that they wish precisely to include Jesus Christ in the unique divine identity. Including him precisely in the divine activity of creation is the most unequivocal way of excluding any threat to monotheism – as though Jesus were a subordinate demigod – while redefining the unique identity of God in a way that includes Jesus. To illustrate the point, we shall examine the earliest of these texts: 1 Corinthians 8:6. This passage in its context reads:

> [4]Hence, as to the eating of food offered to idols, we know that 'there is no idol in the world' and that 'there is no God except one.' [5]Indeed, even though there may be so-called gods in heaven or on earth – as in fact there are many gods and many lords – [6]but for us there is one God, the Father, from whom are all things and we for him, and one Lord, Jesus Christ, through whom are all things and we through him.

Paul's concern in this context is explicitly monotheistic. The issue of eating meat offered to idols and participation in temple banquets is an instance of the highly traditional Jewish monotheistic concern for loyalty to the only true God in a context of pagan polytheistic worship. What Paul does is to maintain this Jewish monotheistic concern in a Christian interpretation for which loyalty to the only true God entails loyalty to the Lord Jesus Christ. He takes up from the Corinthians' letter (at the end of verse 4) the typical Jewish monotheistic formula 'there is no God except one' in order to agree with it and to give, in verse 6, his own fuller monotheistic formulation, which contrasts the 'many gods and many lords' of the Corinthians' pagan environment (verse 5) with the one God and one Lord to whom Christians owe exclusive allegiance.

Verse 6 is a carefully formulated statement,

a but for us [there is] one God, the Father,
b from whom [are] all things and we for him,
c and one Lord, Jesus Christ,
d through whom [are] all things and we through him.

The statement has been composed from two sources, both clearly recognizable. One is the Shemaᶜ, the classic Jewish statement of the uniqueness of God, taken from the Torah itself, recited twice daily by all observant Jews, as we noticed in section 1. It is now commonly recognized that Paul has here adapted the Shemaᶜ and produced, as it were, a Christian version of it.[52] Not so widely recognized is the full significance of this. In the first and third lines of Paul's formula (labelled a and c above), Paul has, in fact, reproduced all the words of the statement about YHWH in the Shemaʿ (Deut. 6:4: 'The LORD our God, the LORD, is one'),[53] but Paul has rearranged the words in such a way as to produce an affirmation of both one God, the Father, and one Lord, Jesus Christ. It should be quite clear that Paul is including the Lord Jesus Christ in the unique divine identity. He is redefining monotheism as christological monotheism. If he were understood as *adding* the one Lord to the one God of whom the Shemaʿ speaks, then, from the perspective of Jewish monotheism, he would certainly be producing, not christological monotheism, but outright ditheism. The *addition* of a unique Lord to the unique God of the Shemaʿ would flatly *contradict* the uniqueness of the latter. The only possible way to understand Paul as maintaining monotheism is to understand him to be including Jesus in the unique identity of the one God affirmed in the Shemaʿ. But this is, in any case, clear from the fact that the term 'Lord', applied here to Jesus as the 'one Lord', is taken from the Shemaʿ itself. Paul is not adding to the one God of the Shemaʿ a 'Lord' the Shemaʿ does not mention. He is identifying Jesus as the 'Lord' whom the Shemaʿ affirms to be one. Thus, in Paul's quite unprecedented reformulation of the Shemaʿ, the unique identity of the one God *consists of* the one God, the Father, *and* the one Lord, his Messiah. Contrary to what many exegetes who have not sufficiently understood the way in which the unique identity of God was understood in Second Temple Judaism seem to suppose, by including Jesus in this unique identity Paul is certainly *not* repudiating Jewish monotheism, whereas were he merely associating Jesus with the unique God he certainly *would* be repudiating monotheism.

Whereas the first and third lines of the formulation divide the wording of the Shemaʿ between God and Jesus, the second and fourth lines (labelled b and d above) similarly divide between God and Jesus another Jewish monotheistic formula, one which relates the one God as Creator to all things. The description in its undivided,

---

[52] F.F. Bruce, *1 and 2 Corinthians* (NCB; London: Oliphants, 1971), 80; D.R. de Lacey, '"One Lord" in Pauline Christology,' in *Christ the Lord*, ed. Harold H. Rowdon (D. Guthrie FS; Leicester: IVP, 1982), 191–203; Dunn, *Christology*, 180; Hurtado, *One God*, 97; N. Thomas Wright, *The Climax of the Covenant* (Edinburgh: T&T Clark, 1991), 128–9; D.A. Hagner, 'Paul's Christology and Jewish Monotheism,' in *Perspectives on Christology*, ed. M. Shuster and R. Muller (P.K. Jewett; Grand Rapids: Zondervan, 1991), 28–9; Neil Richardson, *Paul's Language about God* (JSNTSup 99; Sheffield: JSOT Press, 1994), 300; B. Witherington III, *Jesus the Sage* (Edinburgh: T&T Clark, 1994), 316.

[53] The 'our' of the Shemaʿ appears as the 'for us' at the beginning of Paul's reformulation.

unmodified form is used elsewhere by Paul – in Romans 11:36a: 'from him and through him and to him [are] all things'. Here the statement simply refers to God, whereas, in 1 Corinthians 8:6, Paul has divided it between God and Christ, applying to God two of the prepositions that describe God's relationship as Creator to all things ('from' and 'for' or 'to') and the third of these prepositions ('through') to Christ. Although Paul's formula in Romans 11:36 does not appear precisely in this form elsewhere, there are enough Jewish parallels[54] to make it certain that Paul there simply quotes a Jewish formulation. That God is not only the agent or efficient cause of creation ('from him are all things') and the final cause or goal of all things ('to him are all things'), but also the instrumental cause ('through him are all things') well expresses the typical Jewish monotheistic concern that God used no one else to carry out his work of creation, but accomplished it alone, solely by means of his own Word and/or his own Wisdom. Paul's reformulation in 1 Corinthians 8:6 includes Christ in this exclusively divine work of creation by giving to him the role of instrumental cause.

Implicit in the reformulation is an identification of Christ with either the Word or the Wisdom of God or both. It hardly matters which, since the Jewish habit of explaining God's sole creative work by saying that he created through his Word or through his Wisdom merely gives Paul the opportunity for apportioning the work of creation in such a way as to include Christ in it. We can now see that, in this and other New Testament passages where the pre-existent Christ is described in terms corresponding to Jewish language about the Word or the Wisdom of God, it is not the Jewish concepts of Word and Wisdom themselves which are driving the christological development. The purpose is to include Jesus completely in the unique identity of God, protologically as well as eschatologically. The role of the Word and/or Wisdom was appropriate for this purpose, since, as we saw in section 1, they represent Jewish ways of making some form of distinction within the unique divine identity, especially with reference to the work of creation. Their activity in creation by no means compromises the monotheistic uniqueness of the divine creative activity since they are intrinsic to the unique divine identity. This is exactly what Paul means to say of Jesus. In this passage, Paul exhibits the typically strong Jewish monotheistic self-consciousness; he distinguishes the one God to whom alone allegiance is due from all pagan gods who are no gods;

---

[54] Josephus, *B.J.* 5.218; Philo, *Cher.* 127; cf. Heb. 2:10.

he draws on classic Jewish ways of formulating monotheistic faith; and he reformulates them to express a christological monotheism which by no means abandons but maintains precisely the ways Judaism distinguished God from all other reality and uses these to include Jesus in the unique divine identity. He maintains monotheism not by adding Jesus to but by including Jesus in his Jewish understanding of the divine uniqueness.

2.9. Conclusion: New Testament Christology as Christology of divine identity – beyond 'functional' and 'ontic' Christology

A higher Christology than Paul already expresses in 1 Corinthians 8:6 is scarcely possible, and the way I have just summed it up may stand as a summary of what a much more extensive review of the christological material throughout the New Testament would show to be the common character of all New Testament Christology. In conclusion to this section, I shall point out the general significance of the category of divine identity, as I have used it, as the key to understanding New Testament Christology, by contrast with the categories which have dominated discussion of New Testament Christology in recent decades, which are so-called 'functional' Christology and so-called 'ontic' (or 'ontological') Christology. A Christology of divine identity will take us, I suggest, beyond the fundamentally misleading contrast between 'functional' and 'ontic' Christology as categories for reading the New Testament texts. In my view, these categories have proved inadequate to the task of illuminating the texts, not least because they do not reflect an adequate understanding of the way Jewish monotheism understood God.

Thus, for example, while much of what we have observed in this chapter about the New Testament's portrayal of Jesus' participation in the unique sovereignty of God has been observed before, its full significance has been largely missed through reliance on misleading presuppositions and use of inappropriate categories. The dominance of the distinction between 'functional' and 'ontic' Christology has made it seem unproblematic to say that, for early Christology, Jesus exercises the 'functions' of divine lordship without being regarded as 'ontically' divine. In fact, such a distinction is highly problematic from the point of view of early Jewish monotheism. For this understanding of the unique divine identity, the unique sovereignty of God was not a mere 'function' which God could delegate to someone else. It was one of the key identifying characteristics of the unique divine identity, which distinguished the one God from all other reality. The unique divine sovereignty is a matter of *who God is*. Jesus' participation in the unique divine sovereignty is, therefore, also not just a matter of what Jesus does, but of *who Jesus is* in relation to God. Though not primarily a matter of divine nature or being, it emphatically *is* a matter of divine identity. It includes Jesus in the identity of the one God. When extended to include Jesus in the creative activity of God, and therefore also in the eternal transcendence of God, it becomes unequivocally a matter of regarding Jesus as *intrinsic to* the unique identity of God.

The distinction commonly made between 'functional' and 'ontic' Christology has been, broadly, between early Christology in a Jewish context and patristic Christology which applied Greek philosophical categories of divine nature to Christ. Even when ontic Christology is seen to begin well within the confines of the New Testament, it is seen as the beginnings of the patristic attribution of divine nature to Christ. The assumption usually is that, whereas first-century Jewish monotheists could attribute divine 'functions' to Jesus without difficulty since this would not infringe Jewish monotheism, they could not easily attribute divine 'nature' to him without raising difficult issues for monotheism with which only later Trinitarian developments could cope (successfully or not). However, this is to misconstrue Jewish monotheism in Hellenistic terms as though it were primarily concerned with *what divinity is* – divine nature – rather than with *who YHWH, the unique God, is* – divine identity. The whole category of divine identity and Jesus' inclusion in it has been fundamentally obscured by the alternative of 'functional' and 'ontic', understood to mean that either Christology speaks simply of what Jesus does or else it speaks of his divine nature. Once the category of divine identity replaces those of function and nature as the primary and comprehensive category for understanding both Jewish monotheism and early Christology, we can see that the New Testament's lack of concern with the divine nature of Christ is by no means an indication of a merely functional Christology. We can see that, throughout the New Testament texts, there is a clear and deliberate use of the characteristics of the unique divine identity to include Jesus in that identity. Once we have rid ourselves of the prejudice that high Christology must speak of Christ's divine nature, we can see the obvious fact that the Christology of divine identity common to the whole New Testament is the highest Christology of all. It identifies Jesus as intrinsic to who God is.

3. God crucified: the divine identity revealed in Jesus

3.1. Introduction: from the exalted and pre-existent Christ to the earthly Jesus

In the first two sections, I have argued that, if we attend carefully and accurately, on the one hand, to the ways in which Second Temple Judaism characterized the unique identity of the one and only God and, on the other hand, to what New Testament writers say about Jesus, it becomes abundantly clear that New Testament writers include Jesus in the unique identity of the one God. They do so carefully, deliberately, consistently and comprehensively, by including Jesus in precisely those divine characteristics which for Second Temple Judaism distinguished the one God as unique. All New Testament Christology is, in this sense, very high Christology, stated in the highest terms available in first-century Jewish theology. It is certainly not a merely functional Christology, but is, I have suggested, best characterized as a Christology of divine identity. Jesus, the New Testament writers are saying, belongs inherently to *who God is*.

My argument so far has been designedly selective in two ways. First, I have focused on those features of the identity of the God of Israel which Second Temple Judaism regularly highlighted as characterizing the uniqueness of God by distinguishing God absolutely from all other reality: notably, that God is the Creator of all things and sovereign Ruler of all things. Other features of the identity of the God of Israel, which I pointed out in the first section were essential to Jewish understanding of God, were nevertheless left aside in my argument so far because they were not the aspects to which Jews were accustomed to appeal in defining the uniqueness of the one God. Secondly, in illustrating the way in which New Testament writers employ these key features of the unique identity of God in order to include Jesus in it, I have focused on the pre-existent Christ, who participated in the creative activity of God, and on the exalted Christ, who at the right hand of God participates in God's eschatological sovereignty over all things. To the earthly Jesus, his life and death, I have not referred, because it is the pre-existent and exalted Christ who most obviously shares in the unique creative and sovereign relationship of God to all other reality. It was in Jesus' exaltation to share the divine throne in heaven that the early Christians recognized his inclusion in the divine identity.

However, we now reach the stage of my argument in which it is appropriate to consider the earthly Jesus, and this will also, in due course, bring into play those other essential features of the identity of the God of Israel which have not so far figured in my christological argument. Initially, however, focusing on the earthly Jesus turns the issue of the divine identity around. For the early Christians, the inclusion of the exalted Jesus in the divine identity meant that the Jesus who lived a truly and fully human life from conception to death, the man who suffered rejection and shameful death, also belonged to the unique divine identity. What did this say about the divine identity? Whereas hitherto we have considered what the New Testament writers' understanding of the relation of Jesus to God says about Jesus, we must now ask what it says about God. In other words, we must consider Jesus as revelation of God. The profoundest points of New Testament Christology occur when the inclusion of the exalted Christ in the divine identity entails the inclusion of the crucified Christ in the divine identity, and the christological pattern of humiliation and exaltation is recognized as revelatory of God, indeed as the definitive revelation of who God is. Such a revelation could not leave the early Christian understanding of God unaffected, but, at the same time, the God whose identity the New Testament writers understood to be now defined by the history of Jesus was undoubtedly the God of Israel. His identity in Jesus must be consistent with his identity in the Hebrew Scriptures. So, with the New Testament writers, we shall have to identify the continuity within the novelty, the already known identity of the God of Israel in the newly revelatory history of Jesus.

3.2. Christological monotheism: The early Christian reading of Isaiah 40 – 55

Within the limited space available, I shall pursue just one approach to the way New Testament writers understood the inclusion of the earthly life and death of Jesus within the identity of God. As we have noticed in section 2, much of the creative theological thinking in earliest Christianity was done by way of Old Testament exegesis. Early Christians did theologically creative exegesis in the Jewish tradition. They did not, of course, read the Jewish Scriptures in the historicizing manner of modern Old Testament scholarship, but nor did they, as some accounts of New Testament interpretation of the Old seem to suggest, simply read into the Old Testament ideas they held in any case independently of the Old Testament. They brought the Old Testament text into relationship with the history of Jesus in a process of mutual interpretation from which some of their profoundest theological insights sprang.

No part of the Old Testament was more important to them than the chapters we know as Deutero-Isaiah (Isaiah 40 – 55). (Of course, for early

Christians, these chapters were simply part of the book of the prophet Isaiah, but the term Deutero-Isaiah can serve as a convenient label for this section of the book, which they would certainly have seen as a distinguishable section of Isaiah's prophecy.) For the early Christians, these chapters of Isaiah, above all, were the God-given account of the significance of the events of eschatological salvation which they had witnessed and in which they were involved: Isaiah's vision of the new exodus, the divine act of redemption of Israel in the sight of all the nations and for the sake of the nations themselves also, leading to, in the following chapters we call Trito-Isaiah, the new Jerusalem and the new creation of all things. The New Testament writers' extensive indebtedness to Deutero-Isaiah has been widely acknowledged, even if its precise extent has been debated. The fact that the very word 'gospel' was taken by the earliest Christians from Deutero-Isaiah (Isa. 40:9) is an indication of the key importance of these chapters for them, as is the fact that all four evangelists highlight the way the beginning of the gospel story, the ministry of John the Baptist, fulfilled the beginning of Deutero-Isaiah's prophecy of the new exodus (Isa. 40:3–4).[55] What has not been recognized sufficiently is that, behind many of the New Testament texts, lies an integrated early Christian reading of these chapters as a connected whole. Allusions to the narrative of the Suffering Servant in chapter 53, for example, should not be read as though early Christian use of this one chapter alone can explain them, nor only in connection with the other servant passages in Deutero-Isaiah, but as integral to a reading of Isaiah 40 – 55 as a prophecy of the new exodus which leads to the salvation of the nations.

For our purposes, it is important to notice the way in which the monotheistic theme in Deutero-Isaiah coheres with the themes of these chapters as a whole. Outside the great monotheistic texts of the Torah, the divine speeches in Deutero-Isaiah constitute the classic monotheistic sources of Second Temple Judaism. The speeches in which God declares his uniqueness ('I am the LORD and there is no other'), asserting it polemically against the idols who are no gods, defining his uniqueness as Creator of all things and sovereign Ruler of history, contain all the characteristics of divine uniqueness which we considered in section 1. It was in the unique identity of this God of Deutero-Isaiah, in his cosmic and historical lordship, that early Christians so clearly and deliberately included the pre-existent and exalted Christ. But the monotheism of Deutero-Isaiah is also eschatological. It looks to the day when the God of Israel will demonstrate himself to be the one and only

---

[55] Matt. 3:3; Mark 1:2–3; Luke 3:4–6; John 1:23.

God in the sight of all the nations, revealing his glory and his salvation in the deliverance of his people, so that all the ends of the earth will acknowledge him as God and turn to him for salvation. It is in his great act of eschatological salvation, the new exodus, that the one and only God will demonstrate his unique deity universally. This is also the coming of his kingdom, announced by the messenger who brings good news (the gospel) of salvation, saying to Zion, 'Your God reigns' (Isa. 52:7; cf. 40:9). The one God implements his universal sovereignty in the new exodus which demonstrates his deity to the nations. It was in this context of the necessary link between the uniqueness of God and his eschatological acts for the salvation of Israel and the world that the early Christians read of the enigmatic figure of the Servant of the Lord, who witnesses to God's unique deity and who, in chapters 52–53, both suffers humiliation and death and also is exalted and lifted up.

What I hope to show is that, in the early Christian reading of Deutero-Isaiah, the witness, the humiliation, the death and the exaltation of the Servant of the Lord is the way in which God reveals his glory and demonstrates his deity to the world. The witness, the humiliation and the exaltation of the Servant are the eschatological salvation event, the new exodus, by which the unique deity of God is now identified, such that the ends of the earth acknowledge that God is God and turn to him for salvation when they see the exaltation of his Servant. One important key to this early Christian reading of Deutero-Isaiah, in my view, lies in the connections between Isaiah 52:13, which introduces the crucial passage about the Suffering Servant, and other passages of Isaiah. The three relevant texts in translations of both their Hebrew original and their Greek version are:

Isaiah 52:13 Heb.: Behold, my Servant shall prosper; he shall be *exalted* (*yārûm*) and *lifted up* (*niśśā'*) and shall be very high (*gāvah*).

LXX Gk.: Behold, my Servant shall understand, and shall be *exalted* (*hupsōthēsetai*) and shall be *glorified* (*doxasthēsetai*) greatly.

Isaiah 6:1 Heb.: I saw the Lord (*'ădōnāi*) sitting on a throne, *exalted* (*rām*) and *lofty* (*niśśā'*); and his train filled the temple.

LXX Gk.: I saw the Lord sitting on a throne, *exalted* (*hupsēlou*) and *lifted up* (*epērmenou*); and the house was full of his glory.

Isaiah 57:15 Heb.: For thus says the *exalted* (*rām*) and *lofty* (*niśśā'*) One who inhabits eternity, whose name is Holy: 'I dwell in the high (*mārôm*) and holy place, and also with those who are crushed (*dakkā'*; cf. Isa. 53:5, 10) and lowly in spirit, to revive the spirit of the lowly and to revive the heart of the crushed.'

LXX Gk.: Thus says the Lord Most High (*hupsistos*) who dwells in *the heights* (*en hupsēlois*) forever, Holy among the holy ones (*en hagiois*) is his name, the Lord Most High (*hupsistos*) resting among the holy ones (*en hagiois*), and giving patience to the faint-hearted, and giving life to the broken-hearted.

Isaiah 52:13 states, with emphasis, the exaltation of the Servant, presumably following the humiliation and death described in the following passage. There are two points to notice about it: (1) The words 'exalted' and 'lifted up' ('my Servant shall be exalted and lifted up') occur also in Isaiah 6:1, introducing Isaiah's vision of God on his throne (where the throne is described as 'exalted and lifted up'), and in Isaiah 57:15, which describes God, dwelling in the heights of heaven, as himself 'exalted and lifted up'. The combination of the two Hebrew roots *rûm* ('to be high', 'to be exalted') and *nāśā'* ('to lift up') is rare in the Hebrew Bible, and the verbal coincidence between these three verses is striking. Modern Old Testament scholars think the two later passages, Isaiah 52:13 and 57:15, must be dependent on Isaiah 6:1. Early Christians would have observed the coincidence and applied the Jewish exegetical principle of *gezērâ šāvâ*, according to which passages in which the same words occur should be interpreted with reference to each other. (In my view, most early Christian exegesis of the Old Testament was done with reference to the Hebrew text, even when the Greek text was also employed. In this case, the texts can be connected on the basis of the Septuagint Greek translation, but are more strikingly connected in the Hebrew.) So, in the light of the connections with Isaiah 6:1 and 57:15, the meaning of Isaiah 52:13 is that the Servant is exalted to the heavenly throne of God. This is why, in John 12:38–41, Isaiah 53 and Isaiah 6 are brought together, and Isaiah is said to have seen Jesus' glory, that is, when he saw the glory of the Lord in his vision in chapter 6 of his prophecy. (2) If Isaiah 52:13 means that the Servant was exalted to share the heavenly throne from which God rules the universe, then it is readily connected with Psalm 110:1, which was, as we have seen in section 2, the central Old Testament text for the early Christian inclusion of Jesus in the identity of God. Therefore two New Testament references to the exaltation of Jesus to the right hand of God combine allusion to Psalm 110:1 with allusion to Isaiah 52:13 (Acts 2:33; 5:31) and one combines allusion to Psalm 110:1 with allusion to Isaiah 57:15 (Heb. 1:3).

The Servant, in both his humiliation and his exaltation, is therefore not merely a human figure distinguished from God, but, in both his humiliation and his exaltation, belongs to the identity of the unique

God. This God is not only the high and lofty one who reigns from his throne in the high and holy place; he also abases himself to the condition of the crushed and the lowly (Isa. 57:15). And when the nations acknowledge his unique deity and turn to him for salvation, it is the Servant, humiliated and now exalted to sovereignty on the divine throne, whom they acknowledge.

3.3. *Christological monotheism in three examples of the Christian reading of Isaiah 40 – 55*

We now turn to three parts of the New Testament in which we can see this reading of Deutero-Isaiah reflected and developed in particular ways: Philippians 2:6–11, the book of Revelation and the Gospel of John.

First, we shall see how in each of these three parts of the New Testament monotheistic motifs from Deutero-Isaiah are applied to Jesus. These are some of the most remarkable instances of the inclusion of Jesus in the unique identity of the one God who declares his uniqueness in the divine speeches of Deutero-Isaiah. Each has been noticed before, but separately. What has gone unnoticed is the convergence of Paul, Revelation and the Fourth Gospel in this inclusion of Jesus in Deutero-Isaianic monotheism.

3.3.1. *Philippians 2:6–11*

Philippians 2:6–11 is one of the central christological passages of the Pauline literature, and therefore also one of the earliest passages of christological reflection that we have in the New Testament. The climax of the passage is reached when Jesus is exalted to the position of divine sovereignty over all things and given the divine name itself, which names the unique divine identity,

> so that at the name of Jesus
> > *every knee should bend,*
> > > in heaven and on earth and under the earth,
> > [11] *and every tongue should acknowledge*
> > > that Jesus Christ is Lord,
> > > to the glory of God the Father (vv. 10–11).

The allusion (indicated by the italics above) is to Isaiah 45:22–23:

> Turn to me and be saved,
> > all the ends of the earth!
> > For I am God, and there is no other.

> By myself I have sworn,
>> from my mouth has gone forth in righteousness
>> a word that shall not return:
>> 'To me every knee shall bow,
>>> every tongue shall swear'

We should note the characteristic Old Testament, and especially Deutero-Isaianic, assertion of the absolute uniqueness of YHWH: 'I am God and there is no other.' This passage in Deutero-Isaiah depicts – indeed it is *the* passage in Deutero-Isaiah which depicts – the eschatological demonstration of YHWH's unique deity to the whole world. This is the point at which the one Creator of all things and Sovereign over all things proves himself to be so, acknowledged as both only God and only Saviour by all the ends of the earth which turn to him in worship and for salvation. The Philippians passage is, therefore, no unconsidered echo of an Old Testament text, but a claim that it is in the exaltation of Jesus, his identification as YHWH in YHWH's universal sovereignty, that the unique deity of the God of Israel comes to be acknowledged as such by all creation. Precisely Deutero-Isaianic *monotheism* is fulfilled in the revelation of Jesus' participation in the divine identity. Eschatological monotheism proves to be christological monotheism.[56]

3.3.2. *The book of Revelation*
Secondly, we turn to a set of titles which the book of Revelation applies both to God and to Jesus Christ:[57]

[God says]	I am the Alpha and the Omega (1:8).
[Christ says]	I am the first and the last (1:17; cf. 2:8).
[God says]	I am the Alpha and the Omega, the beginning and the end (21:6).
[Christ says]	I am the Alpha and the Omega, the first and the last, the beginning and the end (22:13).

The three phrases – the Alpha and the Omega, the first and the last, the beginning and the end – are clearly treated as equivalent phrases (since Alpha and Omega are the first and last letters of the

---

[56] I have argued this view of Philippians 2:9–11 more fully in Richard Bauckham, 'The Worship of Jesus in Philippians 2:9–11,' in *Where Christology Began: Essays on Philippians 2*, ed. Ralph P. Martin and Brian J. Dodd (Louisville: WJK, 1998), 128–39.

[57] For a more detailed treatment, see Bauckham, *Theology*, 25–8, 54–8.

Greek alphabet), and are claimed both by God (1:8; 21:6) and by Christ (1:17; 22:13), in declarations of unique divine identity strategically located in the opening and closing sections of the book. These declarations are modelled on those of YHWH in Deutero-Isaiah (44:6; 48:12; cf. 41:4):

> Isaiah 44:6   I am the first and I am the last; besides me there is no God.
> Isaiah 48:12 I am he; I am the first, and I am the last.

The four declarations in Revelation form a deliberately cumulative pattern, in which the first three declarations attribute different, though equivalent, phrases to God and Christ respectively, but in which the fourth declaration claims for Christ all three forms of the title. One form of the title ('the first and the last') is attributed only to Christ, but the other two ('the Alpha and the Omega, the beginning and the end') are attributed to both God and Christ. Indeed, they are the only title shared by both God and Christ in the book of Revelation. They say something significant about this work's inclusion of Jesus in the unique divine identity.

In the form, 'the first and the last', the title comes from Deutero-Isaiah, where it is one of the terms that encapsulates Deutero-Isaianic monotheism. It expresses the unique eternal sovereignty of the one God, who precedes all things as their Creator, and as the Lord of history brings all things to their eschatological fulfilment. He is the source and the goal of all things. Revelation thus includes Christ both protologically and eschatologically in the identity of the one God of Deutero-Isaianic monotheism. Indeed, it is to Christ rather than to God that it attributes the specifically Deutero-Isaianic form of the title, 'the first and the last', on which the other two forms are variations. Once again, Deutero-Isaianic monotheism is interpreted as christological monotheism. God proves to be not only the first but also the last, the end, the Omega of all things, when his kingdom comes in that coming of Christ towards which the whole book of Revelation is orientated.

3.3.3. *The Gospel of John*
It is the eschatological orientation of the book of Revelation, directed to the future achievement of the unique sovereignty of the one God, which makes the title 'the first and the last' particularly appropriate, among the monotheistic motifs of Deutero-Isaiah, for christological use in that book. The Gospel of John understandably makes a different choice when it places on the lips of Jesus during his ministry another

of the characteristically Deutero-Isaianic declarations of unique divine identity. The Johannine choice is the concise statement 'I am he', in Hebrew *'ᵃnî hû'*, usually translated in the Septuagint Greek as *egō eimi* ('I am'), the form in which it appears in John's Gospel.[58] This sentence occurs as a divine declaration of unique identity seven times in the Hebrew Bible: once in Deuteronomy, in one of the most important monotheistic passages of the Torah, and six times in Deutero-Isaiah.[59] It serves to declare, in the most concise of forms, the uniqueness of God, equivalent to the more common 'I am YHWH'. On the lips of Jesus in the Fourth Gospel, its ambiguity, in contexts where it need not be recognized as the uniquely divine self-declaration, enables it to identify Jesus with God, not in a blatantly explicit way which, even in the Fourth Gospel, would be inappropriate before Jesus' exaltation, but in a way which becomes increasingly unambiguous through the series of seven absolute 'I am' sayings (John 4:26; 6:20; 8:24, 26, 58; 13:19; 18:5, 6, 8). It is certainly not accidental that, whereas in the Hebrew Bible there are seven occurrences of *'ᵃnî hû'* and two of the emphatic variation *'ānokî 'ānokî hû'* (Isa. 43:25; 51:12), in John there are seven absolute 'I am' sayings, with the seventh repeated twice (18:5, 6, 8) for the sake of an emphatic climax (thus seven or nine in both cases). The series of sayings thus comprehensively identifies Jesus with the God of Israel who sums up his identity in the declaration 'I am he'. More than that, they identify Jesus as the eschatological revelation of the unique identity of God, predicted by Deutero-Isaiah.

So, in these three major representatives of New Testament Christology – Philippians 2:6–11, Revelation, John – we see, in different forms, the early Christian interpretation of Deutero-Isaiah's eschatological monotheism as christological monotheism. The use of monotheistic motifs from Deutero-Isaiah in these passages of high christological reflection shows that monotheism is not an incidental concern, but a central concern in the Christology of these texts. Moreover, the application of monotheistic motifs from Deutero-Isaiah to Jesus means more than his inclusion in the unique identity of God. It means that he is the revelation of that unique identity of God to the world. So far from the inclusion of Jesus in divinity constituting a problem for monotheism, these New Testament writers present it as the way in which the unique God demonstrates his unique divinity to the world.

---

[58] P.B. Harner, *The 'I Am' of the Fourth Gospel* (Facet Books; Philadelphia: Fortress, 1970); D.M. Ball, *'I Am' in John's Gospel* (JSNTSup 124; Sheffield: Sheffield Academic Press, 1996).

[59] Deut. 32:39; Isa. 41:4; 43:10, 13; 46:4; 48:12; 52:6.

3.4. *The humiliation and exaltation of Jesus revealing the divine identity in three examples of the Christian reading of Isaiah 40 – 55*

What we must now investigate, as the second stage of our argument in relation to all three of these New Testament texts, is the way they present the suffering, humiliation and death of Jesus in Deutero-Isaianic terms closely related to the monotheistic motifs from Deutero-Isaiah. Jesus fulfils the eschatological monotheism of the prophecies because he is the Servant of the Lord of Deutero-Isaiah, whose humiliation and exaltation together reveal the identity of the one God.

3.4.1. *Philippians 2:6–11*

Philippians 2:6–11 is the subject of one of the most complex exegetical debates in New Testament scholarship.[60] I cannot here argue all the disputed issues, but will merely indicate the positions I take on some of the key exegetical points as preliminary to the theme I want to draw out for our present purposes. (1) Against the majority view that the passage is a pre-Pauline hymn, I am inclined to think Paul himself composed it. So I shall speak of the author as Paul, but the issue makes no difference to my exegesis. (2) Against those recent interpreters who think that from the outset the passage concerns the human Jesus, I maintain the traditional view, still that of the majority of exegetes and vindicated in most recent discussions,[61] that the passage begins by speaking of the pre-existent Christ in eternity and proceeds to speak of his incarnation. (3) I do not think the passage embodies an Adam Christology. If Adam is in view at all, he is in view only very indirectly. In my view, Adam has proved a red herring in study of this passage. (4) On the difficult translation issue of the meaning of verse 6b, I think the best linguistic argument now suggests the translation: 'he did not think equality with God something to be used for his own advantage'. In other words, the issue is not whether Christ gains equality or whether he retains it, as in some translations. He has equality with God and there is no question of losing it; the issue is his attitude to it.[62] (5) The 'form of God' (v. 6)

---

[60] An invaluable survey of scholarship is in Ralph P. Martin, *Carmen Christi: Philippians 2:5–11 in Recent Interpretation and in the Setting of Early Christian Worship*, rev. ed. (Grand Rapids Eerdmans, 1983); and see now most recently *Where Christology Began*, ed. Martin and Dodd.

[61] L.D. Hurst, 'Re-Enter the Pre-Existent Christ in Philippians 2:5–11?' *NTS* 32 (1986): 449–57; C.A. Wanamaker, 'Philippians 2.6–11: Son of God or Adam Christology,' *NTS* 33 (1987): 179–93; N.T. Wright, *Climax of the Covenant*, 56–98 (but, in my view, Wright is trying to have his cake and eat it in combining a divine incarnational and an Adam christological approach).

[62] N.T. Wright, *Climax of the Covenant*, 62–90.

and the 'form of a servant (slave)' (v. 7), which are clearly intended to be contrasted, refer to forms of appearance: the splendour of the divine glory in heaven contrasted with the human form on earth.[63]

These preliminary points about the exegetical decisions I make result in the following exegesis of verses 6–11. The pre-existent Christ, being equal with God, shared the divine glory in heaven. But he did not consider his equality with God something he should use for his own advantage. He did not understand his equality with God as a matter of being served by others, but as something he could express in service, obedience, self-renunciation and self-humiliation for others. Therefore, he renounced the outward splendour of the heavenly court for the life of a human being on earth, one who lived his obedience to God in self-humiliation even to the point of the peculiarly shameful death by crucifixion, the death of a slave. This radical self-renunciation was his way of expressing and enacting his equality with God, and *therefore* (v. 9) it qualified him to exercise the unique divine sovereignty over all things. His exaltation to the highest position, the heavenly throne of God, is not a matter of gaining or regaining equality with God, which he has always had and never lost, but of acquiring the function of implementing the eschatological sovereignty of God. Exercising the unique divine sovereignty, he bears the unique divine name, the Tetragrammaton, and receives the worship of the whole creation. Since he had expressed his equality with God in a human life of obedient service to God, his exercise of the divine sovereignty also does not compete with his Father's deity, but redounds to the glory of his Father (v. 11). This is the way in which the one and only God reveals his identity to his whole creation and is acknowledged as God by his whole creation.

To fill out this basic exegesis, I will make three further points. First, what is going on in this passage is a profound interpretation of Deutero-Isaiah. The allusion to Isaiah 45 in verses 10–11 we have already discussed: it is universally agreed, though its full significance is by no means always appreciated. More debatable is allusion to Isaiah 52 – 53 in verses 7–9, but I think the verbal connections are easily strong enough to establish such allusion.[64] The most important are as follows:

---

[63] Wanamaker, 'Philippians 2.6–11,' 183–7.

[64] Cf. L. Cerfaux, 'Hymne au Christ-Serviteur de Dieu (Phil., II, 6–11 = Is., LII, 13–LIII, 12),' in *Receuil Lucien Cerfaux: Études d'Exégèse et d'Histoire Religieuse* (BETL 6–7; Gembloux: Duculot, 1954), 2:425–37.

Philippians 2:6–11	**Isaiah 52 – 53; 45**
[Christ Jesus], though he was in the form of God,	
did not regard equality with God as something to be used for his own advantage,	
⁷but *poured himself out*,	53:12: because he poured himself out …
taking the *form* of a slave,	
being born in human *likeness;*	(52:14; 53:2: form… appearance)
and being found in human *form,*	
⁸he *humiliated* himself,	(53:7: he was brought low)
becoming obedient *to the point of accepting death*	53:12: … to death.
– even death on a cross.	
⁹*Therefore* also God *exalted him to the highest place*	53:12: Therefore … 52:13: he shall be exalted and lifted up and shall be very high.
and conferred on him the Name that is above every name,	
¹⁰so that at the name of Jesus	45:22–23: Turn to me and be saved,
every knee should bend,	all the ends of the earth!
in heaven and on earth and under the earth,	For I am God, and there is no other.
¹¹*and every tongue should acknowledge*	²³By myself I have sworn,
that Jesus Christ is Lord,	from my mouth has gone forth in righteousness
to the glory of God the Father.	a word that shall not return: 'To me every knee shall bow, every tongue shall swear.'

What has not been noticed, even by those who see that Paul has the Suffering Servant of Isaiah 53 in view here, is the way the allusions to Isaiah 52 – 53 and to Isaiah 45 cohere. Paul is reading Deutero-Isaiah to mean that the career of the Servant of the Lord, his suffering, humiliation, death and exaltation, is the way in which the sovereignty of the one true God comes to be acknowledged by all the nations.

The key verse in Isaiah 53 is verse 12, the concluding verse of the passage: '*Therefore* I will allot him a portion with the great … *because* he poured out himself to death …' The prophet says that *because* the Servant humiliated himself, *therefore* God exalted him. This is precisely the message and the structure of the Philippians passage. Verses 7–8 of the passage are Paul's exegesis of the second of those two clauses in Isaiah 53:12 ('because he poured himself out to death'). Paul understands this clause to summarize the whole movement of the Servant's self-renunciation and self-humiliation, ending in death, and so he expands it by inserting further explanation between 'he poured himself out' (which in Paul's Greek is a literal translation of Isaiah's Hebrew[65]) and 'to death'. The pouring out or emptying is the self-renunciation in service and obedience, which begins with incarnation and leads inexorably to death. Paul then glosses the word 'death' (from Isaiah) with the phrase 'even death on a cross' – to indicate that the form of death was this appropriately shameful end to the self-humiliation already described in Isaiah 53. But Isaiah says that because the Servant poured himself out, therefore God will exalt him ('allot him a portion with the great'), a theme already announced at the beginning of the Isaianic passage (52:12): 'my servant shall be exalted and lifted up, and shall be very high'. Paul echoes this verse in his verse 9 ('Therefore God exalted him to the highest place') and, understanding it in the way we have already explored – to mean that the Servant was exalted to the divine throne – he adds that he receives the divine name. The Servant thus exalted to the divine throne is the one to whom the ends of the earth turn in acknowledgement of his unique divine identity, according to Isaiah 45.

Secondly, the central themes of the passage are the relation between high and low status, and between service and lordship. Certainly, one who belongs to the unique divine identity ('equal with God') becomes also human, but the issue is not seen in terms of a contrast between divine and human natures. The question is not: how can the infinite God become a finite creature, how can the omnipotent, omniscient and omnipresent God take on human limitations, how can the immortal God die? These questions arise when the contrast of divine and human natures comes to the fore, as it did in the patristic period. Here in Philippians 2 the question is rather one of status. Can the one who inhabits the heights of heaven, high on his throne above all creation, come down not merely to the human level, but even to the ultimate degradation: death on a cross? Can he renounce the form of God, the honour and glory of divine status in the heavenly palace, where the myriads of angels serve him, for the form of a servant, the dishonour, the loss of all status, that a human life that ends on a cross entails? The self-humiliation and obedience to which verse 8 refers are no mere ethical attitudes, but the repudiation of status, the acceptance of the slave's lack of status, the voluntary descent to the place furthest removed from the heavenly throne to which he is then – and Paul says 'therefore' – exalted. This is not the contrast of two natures, divine and human, but a contrast more powerful for first-century Jewish theology

---

[65] J. Jeremias, 'Zu Phil. 2,7: EAYTON EKENΩΣEN,' *NovT* 6 (1963): 182–8.

with its controlling image of the God as the universal emperor, high on his heavenly throne, inconceivably exalted above all he has created and rules. Can the cross of Jesus Christ actually be included in the identity of this God?

Can the Lord also be the Servant? The passage, inspired both by Deutero-Isaiah and by the Christ-event, answers: only the Servant can also be the Lord.

Thirdly, the passage amounts to a christological statement of the identity of God. The exaltation of Christ to participation in the unique divine sovereignty shows him to be included in the unique divine identity. But, since the exalted Christ is first the humiliated Christ, since indeed it is *because* of his self-abnegation that he is exalted, his humiliation belongs to the identity of God as truly as his exaltation does. The identity of God – who God is – is revealed as much in self-abasement and service as it is in exaltation and rule. The God who is high can also be low, because God is God not in seeking his own advantage but in self-giving. His self-giving in abasement and service ensures that his sovereignty over all things is also a form of his self-giving. Only the Servant can also be the Lord. Only the Servant who is also the Lord receives the recognition of his lordship – the acknowledgement of his unique deity – from the whole creation.

3.4.2. *The book of Revelation*

We turn now more briefly to the second of our three New Testament examples of reading Isaiah 40 – 55 in relation to the humiliation and exaltation of Jesus: the book of Revelation. Chapter 4 of the book depicts, like many another apocalyptic disclosure, the great divine throne in heaven on which the one who created all things sits. The rest of the book reveals his purpose for achieving his eschatological sovereignty over the creation in which his rule is presently contested. Chapter 5, the continuation of the vision of the divine throne in heaven, reveals in a preliminary way how this will occur and anticipates its result: the worship of God by every creature in the whole creation. The scene is a close parallel to Philippians 2. John sees the exalted Christ on the divine throne, represented in his vision as a lamb standing as though it were slaughtered. The lamb receives the worship of the heavenly attendants just as God had in chapter 4, but now the circle of worship expands, so that every creature in heaven and on earth and under the earth and in the sea worships 'the One who is seated on the throne and the Lamb' (v. 13). Thus it is the enthronement of the slaughtered lamb, his exercise of the divine sovereignty, which leads to the universal acknowledgement of God to whose identity he belongs. The lamb is undoubtedly the Passover lamb and belongs to the image of eschatological salvation as the new exodus, which is one of the overarching images of the book. But the picture of the lamb standing as though it were slaughtered is also an allusion to Isaiah 53:7. In the context of Deutero-Isaiah's own dominant image of the new exodus, the picture of the Servant as a lamb led to the slaughter casts the Servant himself in the role of Passover lamb for the new exodus. Thus, although Revelation is primarily concerned to look forward from the exaltation of Christ to his achievement of the divine lordship at his future coming, still it makes, with its image of the slaughtered lamb on the throne of the universe, essentially the same point as Philippians 2 about the divine identity and rule. The sacrificial death of Christ belongs to the divine identity as truly as his enthronement and his Parousia do, and the divine sovereignty is not fully understood until it is seen to be exercised by the one who witnessed to the truth of God even to the point of death. Only as the slaughtered lamb is the Christ of Revelation also the first and the last, the Alpha and the Omega.[66] Once again, the inclusion of the earthly Jesus and his death in the identity of God means that the cross reveals who God is.

3.4.3. *The Gospel of John*

To complete our account of the early Christian reading of Isaiah 40 – 55 in our three New Testament examples, we must turn again to the Gospel of John. We observed earlier how John places Deutero-Isaiah's great monotheistic self-declaration of God – 'I am he' – on the lips of Jesus in the series of seven absolute 'I am' sayings. We must now see how John relates this making known of God's unique identity in Jesus to the humiliation and passion of Jesus. Approaching this topic via John's interpretation of Deutero-Isaiah will give us a fresh angle on the much debated subject of the Johannine understanding of the cross.

The opening verse of the great Suffering Servant passage in Isaiah (Isa. 52:13) reads:

> Behold, my Servant shall prosper;
> he shall be *exalted* and *lifted up* and shall be very high.

Or in the Septuagint Greek version:

> Behold, my Servant shall understand,
> and shall be *exalted* (*hupsōthēsetai*) and shall be glorified
> (*doxasthēsetai*) greatly.

---

[66] Cf. Bauckham, *Theology*, 64, 70–1.

Most readers of the Suffering Servant passage, including Paul in Philippians 2 and other New Testament authors, take this first verse to be an anticipatory statement of the exaltation of the Servant which will follow the humiliation, suffering and death that the passage goes on to describe. Isaiah 52:13 announces in advance the exaltation of the Servant which is otherwise only reached at the end of the whole passage (53:12). John, I believe, has interpreted this verse differently. He has taken it as a summary statement of the theme of the whole of the passage it introduces. In other words, the exaltation of the Servant of which this verse speaks is the whole sequence of humiliation, suffering, death and vindication beyond death which chapter 53 describes. The Servant is exalted and glorified in and through his humiliation and suffering. This is the exegetical source for John's theologically profound interpretation of the cross as Jesus' exaltation and glorification.

In the Fourth Gospel there are two principal ways in which Jesus refers to the cross as his coming destiny. Both within the narrative context are enigmatic; both, for the perceptive reader, are theologically potent. Each of them features one of the two verbs with which the Septuagint of Isaiah 52:13 describes the exaltation of the Servant: *hupsoō* ('to lift up', 'to raise high', 'to exalt') and *doxazō* ('to honour', 'to glorify'). We shall consider each in turn.

In place of the passion predictions of the Synoptic Gospels, which state that the Son of Man must suffer, with concrete details of his rejection and death and with probable reference to Isaiah 53 as the prophetic destiny he must fulfil,[67] John has three passion predictions which state that the Son of Man must be 'lifted up' (*hupsoō*):

3:14–15: 'And just as Moses lifted up (*hupsōsen*) the serpent in the wilderness, so must the Son of Man be lifted up (*hupsōthēnai*), [15]that whoever believes in him may have eternal life.'

8:28: So Jesus said, 'When you have lifted up (*hupsōsēte*) the Son of Man, then you will realize that I am he, and that I do nothing on my own, but I speak these things as the Father instructed me.'

12:32–34: 'And I, when I am lifted up (*hupsōthō*) from the earth, will draw all people to myself.' [33]He said this to indicate the kind of death he was to die. [34]The crowd answered him, 'We have heard from the law that the Messiah remains forever. How can you say that the Son of Man must be lifted up (*hupsōthēnai*)? Who is this Son of Man?'

---

[67] Matt. 16:21; 17:23; 20:19; Mark 8:31; 9:31; 10:33–34; Luke 9:22; 18:33.

Compared with the passion predications in the Synoptics, in these Johannine sayings the allusion to the Suffering Servant is both more direct and, in its peculiar conciseness (the one word 'lifted up'), deliberately riddling. Such Johannine enigmas tease the reader into theological enlightenment. In this case, the key is the double meaning of the word. It refers both literally to the crucifixion as a lifting up of Jesus above the earth (as 12:33 makes clear) and figuratively to the same event as Jesus' elevation to the status of divine sovereignty over the cosmos. The cross is already his exaltation. Its physical character, as a literal elevation from the earth, symbolizes its theological character as the decisive movement upwards to heaven as the place of divine sovereignty. The literal elevation, which Jesus' executioners intended as humiliation, an exhibition of his disgrace for all to see, John's readers see, through Deutero-Isaianic eyes, as the event in which Jesus' divine identity is manifested for all to see, thereby drawing all people to himself (12:32). But the full significance in terms of Deutero-Isaianic monotheism we can appreciate only when we observe, as hardly anyone has done, the conjunction in 8:28 of the allusion to Isaiah 52:13 (the lifting up of the Son of Man) with the divine self-declaration, 'I am he', also from Deutero-Isaiah. This saying is the central one of the three sayings about the lifting up of the Son of Man (3:14–15; 8:28; 12:32–34), and it is also the central saying of the series of seven absolute 'I am' sayings.[68] It deliberately brings the two sets of sayings into theological relationship. *When* Jesus is lifted up, exalted in his humiliation on the cross, *then* the unique divine identity ('I am he') will be revealed for all who can to see. The hope of Deutero-Isaiah, that the one true God will demonstrate his deity to the world, such that all the ends of the earth will turn to him and be saved, is fulfilled when the divine identity is revealed in Jesus' death. These three Son of Man sayings together, not simply repeating but complementing each other, make this comprehensive point: the cross reveals the divine identity in Jesus (8:28), such that all people are drawn to him (12:32) for salvation (3:14–15).

The sayings which refer to Jesus' death as his glorification (two more Son of Man sayings, as well as some others) take up the second key verb from Isaiah 52:13 (*doxazō*), and make in a different way the same point as those which refer to the lifting up of the Son of Man:

12:23: 'The hour has come for the Son of Man to be glorified (*doxasthē*).'

---

[68] John 4:26; 6:20; 8:24, 26, 58; 13:19; 18:5–8.

13:31–32: 'Now the Son of Man has been glorified (*edoxasthē*), and God has been glorified (*edoxasthē*) in him. If God has been glorified in him, God will also glorify (*doxasei*) him in himself and will glorify him at once.'

The verb (*doxazō*) can mean 'to honour' and, in that sense, points to the same Johannine paradox of the cross. Just as Jesus' humiliation is at the same time his exaltation, so his rejection, his shaming and disgrace in this peculiarly shameful form of death is paradoxically his honouring by God, in which he also honours God and God also is honoured in him. But John's use of the verb means more than 'honour': it relates to that heavenly splendour (glory) with which other New Testament texts associate the exalted Christ exercising the divine sovereignty. The Fourth Gospel itself gives programmatic prominence to that glory (the heavenly splendour) which is the appearance of God, the manifestation of God's being, when the Prologue claims that 'we have seen his glory, the glory as of a father's only son' (1:14). This glory is the visible manifestation of who God is, reflected in the earthly life of Jesus, a son who is (as it were) the spitting image of his father. It appears in the miracles of Jesus, which reveal his glory, but supremely in the hour of his glorification when finally the divine identity is manifested on earth as it is in heaven. It is not, of course, that the words 'the Son of man is glorified' can have the literal meaning: 'he manifests the divine glory'. We are dealing rather with a play on words, which links the glorification of the Servant of the Lord (Isa. 52:13) with the revelation of the glory of the Lord, also a Deutero-Isaianic theme:

> Then the glory of the LORD shall be revealed,
> and all flesh shall see it together (Isa. 40:3).

This eschatological manifestation of God's glory – the revelation of who God is – to the world takes place in Jesus' death.

In both sets of sayings – those which refer to the cross as Jesus' lifting up and those which refer to the cross as his glorification – the divine identity is revealed in the paradox of Jesus' death: his humiliation which is in divine reality his exaltation, his shame which is in divine reality his honour. This is a kind of intensification of the theme of Philippians 2:6–11. There the divine identity is revealed in the humiliation and the exaltation as a sequence, in the one who first pours himself out to the ultimate degradation of the cross and is then exalted to the highest position of all. In Philippians the paradox which transforms the meaning of exaltation is that the one who humiliated himself to the utmost is *therefore* exalted to the utmost. But in John the paradox intensifies: Jesus' self-humiliation actually is his exaltation by God. Precisely the same happens with the contrast of lord and servant, which in Philippians 2 is a sequence: the one who is obedient even to the point of dying the death of a slave is therefore exalted to cosmic sovereignty as Lord. Jesus is servant and lord in succession. But in John the whole passion narrative fuses the two themes of lordship and servanthood in simultaneity. Jesus is the king in humility (at the entry into Jerusalem), the king in humiliation (before Pilate and on the cross) and the king in death (his royal burial). Jesus is the lord who serves, who enacts the meaning of his death when he washes the disciples' feet, the menial task exclusive to slaves. His kingship consists in his humiliating service to the point of death. Just as he is exalted in his humiliation and glorified in his disgrace, so also he reigns in being the servant. In this way he reveals who God is. What it means to be God in God's sovereignty and glory appears in the self-humiliation of the one who serves. Once again the Prologue provides the programmatic key, this time in its use of the word 'grace' (1:14, 17). Because God is who God is in his gracious self-giving, God's identity appears in the loving service and self-abnegation to death of his Son. Because God is who God is in his gracious self-giving, God's identity, we can say, is not simply revealed but enacted in the event of salvation for the world which the service and self-humiliation of his Son accomplishes.

3.5. *The humiliation and exaltation of Jesus revealing the divine identity in three examples of the Christian reading of Isaiah 40 – 55: Summary*

Briefly to recapitulate the testimony of the three New Testament witnesses we have studied to the effect of recognizing the crucified Jesus as belonging to the identity of God: Here God is seen to be God in his radical self-giving, descending to the most abject human condition and, in that human obedience, humiliation, suffering and death, being no less truly God than he is in his cosmic rule and glory on the heavenly throne. It is not that God is manifest in heavenly glory and hidden in the human degradation of the cross. The latter makes known who God is no less than the former does. The divine identity is known in the radical contrast and conjunction of exaltation and humiliation – as the God who is Creator of all things, and no less truly God in the human life of Jesus; as the God who is Sovereign over all things, and no less truly God in Jesus' human obedience and service; as the God of transcendent majesty who is no less truly God in the abject humiliation of the cross. These are not contradictions because God is self-giving love, as much in his creation and rule of all things as in his human incarnation and death. The radical contrast of humiliation and exaltation is precisely the revelation of who God is in his radically self-giving love. He rules only as the one who also serves. He is exalted above all only as the one who is also with the lowest of the low. This is the meaning of the *therefore* of Philippians 2 (*because* Jesus degraded himself to the lowest position, *therefore* he was exalted to the highest position). This is the meaning of the slaughtered Lamb's standing as slaughtered on the heavenly throne of God in Revelation 5. This is the meaning of the Johannine paradox that Jesus is exalted and glorified on the cross.

Finally, before we move into the next stage of the argument, it is important to stress that this revelation of the divine identity in the cross does not, for the New Testament writers, mean that the life and death of Jesus are merely an illustration of a general truth about God: that Jesus reveals that God is always like this. In some sense, as we shall shortly see, that was known already to Israel. The story of Jesus is not a mere illustration of the divine identity; Jesus himself and his story are intrinsic to the divine identity. The history of Jesus, his humiliation and his exaltation, is the unique act of God's self-giving, in which he demonstrates his deity to the world by accomplishing salvation for the world. In the words of the Johannine Prologue, through Jesus Christ, grace and truth *happened* – the divine self-giving occurred in full reality – and in this way the glory of the God whom no one has ever seen was revealed (John 1:14–18). In this act of self-giving God is most truly himself and defines himself for the world.

3.6. *God crucified and the God of Israel: novelty and consistency*

Now we turn to the stage of our argument in which we must relate this result to our starting-point, in other words, to the identity of the God of Israel revealed in the Hebrew Scriptures. If Jesus reveals who God is, if God's identity is as God crucified, how does this revelation relate to the identity of the God of Israel? Is this the same God? Is his identity in Jesus consistent with his identity in the Old Testament revelation? Is the revelation of his identity in Jesus only the universal revelation, to the world, of the divine identity already fully known to Israel? Or is his identity more fully known in Jesus?

To answer such questions, we must revert to my initial account, in section 1, of the way biblical and post-biblical Israel understood the identity of Israel's God. From that account, I isolated two of the key features of the divine identity, and pursued the rest of my argument in the first two sections in terms of these two features, which were the creative and sovereign activity of God. The point of isolating these two features was that it was on God as the Creator of all things and God as the sovereign Ruler of all things that Jewish understanding of the uniqueness of the one God focused. These are the two features of the divine identity which serve most clearly to distinguish God from all other reality and to identify God as the unique One, who alone relates to all other things as their Creator and Sovereign. These features, therefore, also served to make unequivocally clear the New Testament writers' inclusion of Jesus in the unique divine identity. However, while these two features serve most clearly to distinguish God from all other reality, they by no means sufficiently characterize God's relationship to his creation and by no means sufficiently identify God as he was known in his self-revelation to Israel. Israel had much else to say about the divine identity. In this connection, in section 1, I made two main points, both of which concern God's relationship to his covenant people. First, God is identified by his acts in Israel's history, especially in the exodus. Secondly, God is known from his character description given to Moses: 'merciful and gracious, slow to anger, and abounding in steadfast love and faithfulness' (Exod. 34:6). The acts of God in Israel's history and the character description of God together identify God as the one who acts graciously towards his people. Together they serve for Israel to define who God is.

However, the God so identified was expected, on the basis of this very identity, to act again in the future, in a way consistent with his already known identity. Thus Deutero-Isaiah, in a way especially important for the early Christians, expects a new exodus event, on the model of the first exodus but far transcending it. God will demonstrate his deity to Israel and to the ends of the earth, and will act for the salvation not only of Israel but of all peoples. It is no accident that Deutero-Isaiah's God is both the covenant God of the exodus and also the Creator and Ruler of all things. In the eschatological exodus, he will prove to be the God of all peoples, Sovereign and Saviour of all, in a way consistent with his identity as the gracious God of his people Israel. His uniqueness as Creator and Ruler of all will be universally acknowledged when he acts graciously for the salvation of Israel and the world.

It follows that, for those – the early Christians – who have experienced this new exodus, a new narrative of God's acts becomes definitive of his identity. Just as Israel identified God as the God who brought Israel out of Egypt and by telling the story of God's history with Israel, so the New Testament identifies God as the God of Jesus Christ and by telling the story of Jesus as the story of the salvation of the world. The new story is consistent with the already known identity of the God of Israel, but new as the way he now identifies himself finally and universally, the Creator and Ruler of all who in Jesus Christ has become the gracious Saviour of all. So far the novelty is what could be expected of the God known to Israel. But is there not something more radically novel because it is unexpected and surprising? When early Christians included Jesus himself, a human being, humiliated and exalted, in the identity of God; when they told the story of Jesus, whether in summary form in Philippians 2:6–11 or in extended detail in the Fourth Gospel, as the story of God's own human obedience, humility, degradation and death, were they not saying something radically new about the identity of God? If so we must press the question of its consistency with the known identity of the God of Israel. An important point to make in this connection is that the identity of the God of Israel does not exclude the unexpected and surprising. Quite the contrary, this is God's freedom as God requires his freedom from all human expectations, even those based on his revealed identity. He may act in new and surprising ways, in which he proves to be the same God, consistent with his known identity, but in unexpected ways. He is both free and faithful. He is not capricious, but nor is he predictable. He may be trusted to be consistent with himself, but he may surprise in the ways he proves consistent with himself. The consistency can only be appreciated with hindsight.

The question then is how the early Christians found the consistency in the novelty. If God crucified introduces radical novelty into the identity of God, wherein lies the consistency of identity? The first point to make is simply to reiterate what we established earlier in this chapter, that Jewish monotheism did not characterize the uniqueness of God in such a way as to make the early Christian inclusion of Jesus in the unique identity of God inconceivable. Those scholars, including many New Testament scholars, who assume that no Jewish monotheist could have accepted divine Christology, including Jesus in the divine identity, without abandoning Jewish monotheism have not understood Jewish monotheism. However, this – so to speak – negative consistency was clearly not sufficient for the early Christians. What is so impressive in the material we have studied is the way they developed their fresh understanding of the christological identity of God *through* creative exegesis of the Hebrew Scriptures. To illustrate this (which could certainly also have been illustrated in other ways) I have focused on their exegesis of Deutero-Isaiah. Precisely at the points where they appreciate most fully the new identity of God in Jesus, they are engaged in exegesis, in the process of bringing the texts of the Hebrew Scriptures and the history of Jesus into mutually interpretative interplay. We misunderstand this process if we see it as an attempt, by reading

Christology back into the texts, to pretend that actually nothing at all was unexpected. The first Christians knew better than we do that some of the key insights they found in Deutero-Isaiah had not been seen in Deutero-Isaiah before. But the work of creative exegesis enabled them to find consistency in the novelty. They appreciate the most radically new precisely in the process of understanding its continuity with the already revealed. With deliberate hindsight they understand the identity of the God of Israel afresh in the light of his new identity as the God of Jesus Christ. They find him to be one and the same God, not in ways which could have been predicted, but in ways which in this light now come to light.

So I will make three further main points about this question of consistency and novelty in the identity of God. First, we return to the contrast in Philippians 2 between high and low status, exaltation and humiliation, honour and shame. This contrast seems to me the point at which the inclusion of the human life and shameful death of Jesus in the identity of God must have seemed, for Second Temple Judaism's understanding of God, most remarkable. The image of God the sovereign Ruler on his majestic throne high above all the heavens was so dominant in Second Temple Judaism that the notion of divine self-degradation to the lowest human status could easily have seemed quite inconceivable. This issue of divine and human status would be the stumbling-block, rather than the problems which the Christian doctrine of incarnation was to encounter subsequently: the unitary nature of a God who cannot be internally differentiated, or definitions of divine and human nature which present them as incompatible. Such problems are barely visible in the New Testament, but the contrast of divine height and human lowliness, sovereign exaltation and servile degradation is a preoccupation. Yet, whatever the impression some post-biblical Jewish literature may give, the identity of the God of Israel already includes, in some sense, his lowliness as well as his exaltation. Isaiah 57:15, a text we have already encountered in relation to Philippians 2:6–11, reads:

> ... thus says the exalted and lofty One
> who inhabits eternity, whose name is Holy:
> 'I dwell in the high and holy place,
> *and also* with those who are crushed and lowly in spirit ...

The God of Israel, indeed, is characteristically the God of the lowly and the humiliated, the God who hears the cry of the oppressed, the God who raises the poor from the dust, the God who from his throne on high identifies with those in the depths, the God who exercises his sovereignty on high in solidarity with those of lowest status here below. In drawing on the narrative of the Servant of the Lord, humiliated and exalted, from Isaiah 53, Paul in Philippians 2:6–11 thereby evokes this characteristic of the identity of the God of Israel. The radical novelty in Philippians 2 lies in the way in which God in Jesus Christ dwells in the depths, not only with but *as* the lowest of the low. God's characteristic exaltation of the lowest becomes a pattern in which he participates himself. This could not have been expected, but nor is it uncharacteristic. It is novel but appropriate to the identity of the God of Israel.

Secondly, the way the Prologue to John relates the revelation of God in the incarnation to the identity of the God of Israel is instructive. The last verses of the Prologue (John 1:14–18) claim that God, who has never been seen by human eyes, has been revealed in the human life of Jesus Christ, who reflects his Father's glory and is full of grace and truth. All these terms allude to the story of God's revelation of himself to Moses in Exodus 33 – 34, in which the central Old Testament character description of God occurs. There Moses asks to see God's glory (33:18), is told that he cannot see God's face, but as God covers Moses' eyes and passes by, he hears God proclaim his name and his character: 'YHWH, YHWH, a God merciful and gracious, slow to anger, and abounding in steadfast love and faithfulness' (Exod. 34:6) – or in John's translation 'full of grace and truth' (John 1:14).[69] Moses could only hear God's word proclaiming *that* God is full of grace and truth. He could not see God's glory. But in the Word made flesh, God's glory was seen in human form, and grace and truth (according to John 1:17) happened or came about (*egeneto*). Thus, God's gracious love, central to the identity of the God of Israel, now takes the radically new form of a *human life* in which the divine self-giving happens. This could not have been expected, but nor is it uncharacteristic. It is novel but appropriate to the identity of the God of Israel.

Thirdly, the point which may well seem to us most startlingly novel about the new identity of God in Jesus is one which I have deliberately not made explicit until now: that the inclusion of Jesus in the identity of God means the inclusion in God of the interpersonal relationship between Jesus and his Father. No longer can the divine identity be purely and simply portrayed by analogy with a single human subject. And since the portrayal of God in the Hebrew Bible does, to a large

---

[69] Cf. A.T. Hanson, *Grace and Truth* (London: SPCK, 1975), chap. 1.

extent, employ the analogy of a human agent, this might seem such a radical innovation as to throw doubt on the consistency of the divine identity. But, if we think so, we may be attributing to the biblical writers too unsubtly anthropomorphic ways of thinking. While human identity may be the common analogy for thinking about the divine identity, the God of Israel clearly transcends the categories of human identity. The categories are used in awareness that God transcends them. In God's unique relationship to the rest of reality as Creator of all things and sovereign Ruler of all things, the human analogies, indispensable as they are, clearly point to a divine identity transcendently other than human personhood. Nothing in the Second Temple Jewish understanding of divine identity contradicts the possibility of interpersonal relationship within the divine identity but, on the other hand, there is little, if anything, that anticipates it.

The novelty of divine identity revealed as intra-divine relationship is, in my view, strikingly acknowledged in one New Testament text in the way most appropriate to the biblical tradition of understanding the divine identity. In this text, God acquires a new name which identifies him in this newly revealed form of his identity. In order to appreciate this text, it may help first to go back to the occasion in the Old Testament narrative on which God discloses his name, YHWH, by which he had not previously been known. To Moses at the burning bush in Exodus 3, God identifies himself as the God of the patriarchs, the God of Abraham, Isaac and Jacob (3:6), but this identity is not sufficient for the events in which he is to bring Israel out of Egypt and make them his people. The disclosure of the name by which his people are now to know him is required for his new identity, in which his old identity as the God of the patriarchs is by no means repudiated but is certainly surpassed. Since the patriarchal stories have appropriately been called 'the Old Testament of the Old Testament',[70] the transition from the God of the patriarchs to YHWH the God of Israel is a kind of precedent for the transition from the latter to the God of Jesus Christ. Once again a new name identifies the newly disclosed identity, although this clearly occurs only in one New Testament text: Matthew 28:19.

Though unique, this text is a significant one and deserves attention to its context. To a Gospel in which God has, of course, repeatedly been identified as the God of Israel, but in which the inclusion of Jesus in this divine identity has also repeatedly been indicated,[71] the last five

---

[70] R.W. Moberly, *The Old Testament of the Old Testament* (OBT; Minneapolis: Fortress, 1992).

[71] Cf. D.D. Kupp, *Matthew's Emmanuel: Divine Presence and God's People in the First Gospel* (SNTSMS 90; Cambridge: CUP, 1996).

verses form a climax. The risen Jesus receives worship and declares his exaltation to exercise of the divine sovereignty over all things (Matt. 28:18: 'all authority in heaven and on earth'). His inclusion in the divine identity is now unequivocal. The scene is a Gospel equivalent to the last part of the christological passage in Philippians 2:6–11. But, whereas in that passage it is the Old Testament divine name, YHWH, that the exalted Christ receives, here the disciples are to baptize 'in the name of the Father and of the Son and of the Holy Spirit' (v. 19). The formula, as in the phrase 'calling on the name of the Lord' which New Testament usage takes up from the Old with reference to baptism and profession of Christian faith, requires precisely a divine name. 'The Father, the Son and the Holy Spirit' names the newly disclosed identity of God, revealed in the story of Jesus the Gospel has told.

In conclusion, therefore, to this discussion of consistency and novelty in the New Testament revelation of the identity of God, we can say that in Christ God both demonstrates his deity to the world as the same unique God his people Israel had always known, and also, in doing so, identifies himself afresh. As the God who includes the humiliated and the exalted Jesus in his identity, he is the Father, the Son and the Holy Spirit, that is, the Father of Jesus Christ, Jesus Christ the Son, and the Spirit of the Father given to the Son.

3.7. *Evaluating later christological-theological developments*

This all-too-brief concluding section will indicate what the implications of my argument about New Testament Christology would be for evaluating later theological developments, in the patristic period and later. It may be helpful here to reiterate for the last time the two key points I have argued about the relationship between monotheism and Christology in the New Testament: (1) New Testament writers clearly and deliberately include Jesus in the unique identity of the God of Israel; (2) The inclusion of the human life and shameful death, as well as the exaltation of Jesus, in the divine identity reveals the divine identity – who God is – in a new way.

If we look beyond the New Testament, this interpretation of New Testament Christology makes possible a fresh evaluation of the continuity between the New Testament and the patristic development of dogma, in particular the achievement of Nicene orthodoxy in the fourth century. Broadly speaking, there seem to be two dominant ways of interpreting the development from New Testament Christology to the Council of Nicaea and beyond. The first sees the New Testament as containing, in embryonic form, the source of the development which culminated in the Nicene theology of the fourth century. In other words, New Testament Christology is moving in the direction of recognizing Jesus Christ as truly and fully God, but it was left to the theologians of the fourth century to bring such fully divine Christology to full expression and to find adequate ways of stating it within the context of a Trinitarian doctrine of God. Against this first interpretation, my argument has been that, once we understand Jewish monotheism properly, we can see that the New Testament writers are already, in a deliberate and sophisticated way, expressing a fully divine Christology by including Jesus in the unique identity of God as defined by Second Temple Judaism. Once we recognize the theological categories with which they are working, it is clear that there is nothing embryonic or tentative about this. In its own terms, it is an adequate expression of a fully divine Christology. It is, as I have called it, a Christology of divine identity. The developmental model, according to which the New Testament sets a christological direction only completed in the fourth century, is therefore seriously flawed.

The second way of interpreting the evidence supposes that a Christology which attributed true divinity to Jesus could not have originated within a context of Jewish monotheism. On this view, divine Christology is the result of a transition from Jewish to Hellenistic religious and, subsequently, Hellenistic philosophical, categories. Nicaea represents the triumph of Greek philosophy in Christian doctrine. This way of reading the history seems to me to be virtually the opposite of the truth. In other words, it was actually not Jewish but Greek philosophical categories which made it difficult to attribute true and full divinity to Jesus. A Jewish understanding of divine identity was open to the inclusion of Jesus in the divine identity. But Greek philosophical – Platonic – definitions of divine substance or nature and Platonic understanding of the relationship of God to the world made it extremely difficult to see Jesus as more than a semi-divine being, neither truly God nor truly human. In the context of the Arian controversies, Nicene theology was essentially an attempt to resist the implications of Greek philosophical understandings of divinity and to re-appropriate, in a new conceptual context, the New Testament's inclusion of Jesus in the unique divine identity.

The conceptual shift from Jewish to Greek categories was from categories focused on divine identity – who God is – to categories focused on divine being or nature – what God is. The creedal slogan of Nicene theology – the *homoousion* (that Christ is of the same substance as the Father) – may look initially like a complete capitulation to Greek categories. But the impression is different when we understand its function within the Trinitarian and narrative context it has in, for example, the Nicene and Niceno-Constantinopolitan Creeds. This context identifies God as Father, Son and Holy Spirit, and identifies God from the narrative of the history of Jesus. The *homoousion* in this context functions to ensure that this divine identity is truly the identity of the one and only God. In its own way it expresses the christological monotheism of the New Testament.

However, if the patristic development of dogma secured for a new conceptual context the New Testament's inclusion of Jesus in the unique divine identity, the Fathers were much less successful in appropriating the second key feature of New Testament Christology to which I have drawn attention: the revelation of the divine identity in the human life of Jesus and his cross. Here the shift to categories of divine nature and the Platonic definition of divine nature which the Fathers took for granted proved serious impediments to anything more than a formal inclusion of human humiliation, suffering and death in the identity of God. That God was crucified is indeed a patristic formulation, but its implications for the doctrine of God the Fathers largely resisted. Adequate theological appropriation of the deepest insights of New Testament Christology, such as we have observed in Philippians 2:6–11 and the Fourth Gospel, was not to occur until Martin Luther, Karl Barth and more recent theologies of the cross.[72]

---

[72] See Richard Bauckham, *Moltmann: Messianic Theology in the Making* (Basingstoke: Marshall Pickering, 1987), 65–72; idem, 'Cross, Theology of the,' in *New Dictionary of Theology*, ed. S.B. Ferguson and D.F. Wright (Leicester: IVP, 1988), 181–3; idem, 'Jesus the Revelation of God,' in *Divine Revelation*, ed. P. Avis (London: Darton, Longman & Todd/Grand Rapids: Eerdmans, 1997), 182–7; W. von Loewenich, *Luther's Theology of the Cross*, trans. H.J.A. Bouman (Belfast: Christian Journals, 1976); A.E. McGrath, *Luther's Theology of the Cross* (Oxford: Blackwell, 1985); D.K.P. Ngien, *The Suffering of God According to Martin Luther's 'Theologia Crucis'* (Bern/New York: Peter Lang, 1995); Jürgen Moltmann, *The Crucified God*, trans. R.A. Wilson & J. Bowden (London: SCM, 1974); E. Jüngel, *God as the Mystery of the World*, trans. D.L. Guder (Edinburgh: T&T Clark, 1983).

2

Biblical Theology
and the Problems of Monotheism[1]

1. Introduction

That the issue of 'monotheism' is a central issue for biblical theology hardly needs arguing. But there are a number of specific ways in which 'monotheism' has been problematized in recent biblical studies (hence the plural 'Problems of Monotheism' in my title). Major studies of the historical origins and development of 'monotheism' in ancient Israel, contextualized in the ancient Near Eastern context, have repeatedly challenged any traditional reading of the Old Testament's own telling of Israel's story. How far ancient Israel was 'monotheistic' at all before the latest strata of the Old Testament literature is very debatable, as is also, therefore, the extent to which Old Testament texts should be read in a 'monotheistic' way. For biblical theology, the methodological question of the role that a reconstructed history of ancient Israel should play in a biblical theology becomes unavoidable, if these historical debates are taken seriously by biblical theologians.

However, the problems of 'monotheism' are not confined to the Old Testament. Some recent studies have questioned how far it is really correct to describe early Judaism (in the period up to and including the period in which the New Testament was written) as 'monotheistic', and this question about early Jewish 'monotheism' is closely related to much recent debate about the origins and character of early Christology. Do the New Testament writers presuppose 'monotheism' as the Old Testament and Jewish form of religious faith, not repudiating it but somehow incorporating their innovatory understanding of Jesus

[1] This essay was first published in *Out of Egypt: Biblical Theology and Biblical Interpretation*, ed. Craig Bartholomew et al. (Scripture and Hermeneutics Series 5; Milton Keynes: Paternoster/ Grand Rapids: Zondervan, 2004), 187–232.

into it? Or does their high Christology arise from Jewish traditions that were not 'monotheistic'? The old question of how heirs of Jewish 'monotheism' could have come to include Jesus in the deity of the one God has been posed and answered in a variety of fresh ways in the light of debates about 'monotheism' in the Old Testament and early Judaism. We have a fresh opportunity for considering 'monotheism' as a truly pan-biblical issue, not one confined to the specialisms of either testament.

I have put 'monotheism' and 'monotheistic' in inverted commas throughout the previous paragraphs in order to alert us at once to the fact that the term 'monotheism' itself has become problematic and potentially misleading, if we do not take the trouble to be clear precisely how we are using it. An important recent contribution to this whole area of debate has argued forcefully that not only is the term a peculiarly modern one, but that the set of ideas it evokes are characteristically Enlightenment ones, seducing us into reading the biblical writings in terms of a view of religion that belongs to the Enlightenment and is inappropriate to the texts. This claim provides a fruitful point of entry for us into the complex of 'problems of monotheism' with which we shall be concerned in this paper.

There is one large and important area of discussion in which it is unfortunately not possible to engage within the scope of this chapter. This can be broadly characterized by the question, 'Is monotheism bad for people?' In recent years, critiques of monotheism as leading to absolute monarchical forms of government (in church as well as state), hierarchical structures in society, a dualistic exaltation of the male over the female, exclusion of the other and violence against the other, have been multiplying.[2] Such critiques pose searching questions for biblical theology, and they are not unrelated to the rather narrower historical and exegetical issues with which this chapter is concerned. But they also require serious engagement with the post-biblical history of ideas. The fact that they cannot be addressed in the present context should not be mistaken for failure to appreciate their importance.

---

[2] E.g. P. Ciholas, 'Monothéisme et violence,' *RSR* 69 (1981): 325–54; J. Ochshorn, *The Female Experience and the Nature of the Divine* (Bloomington: Indiana University Press, 1981); G. Ruggieri, 'God and Power: A Political Function of Monotheism?' in *Monotheism*, ed. C. Geffré and J.-P. Jossua (*Concilium* 177 [1/1985]; Edinburgh: T&T Clark, 1985), 16–27; Christian Duquoc, 'Monotheism and Unitary Ideology,' in *Monotheism*, ed. Geffré and Jossua, 59–66; Jürgen Moltmann, *The Trinity and the Kingdom of God*, trans. M. Kohl (London: SCM, 1981), 191–202; Daphne Hampson, 'Monotheism,' in *Dictionary of Ethics, Theology and Society*, ed. P.B. Clarke and A. Linzey (London/New York: Routledge, 1996), 582–5; R.M. Schwartz, *The Curse of Cain: The Violent Legacy of Monotheism* (Chicago: University of Chicago Press, 1997).

2. Monotheism as a misleading category

A major contribution to our topic has been made by Nathan MacDonald in his recent book, *Deuteronomy and the Meaning of 'Monotheism.'*[3] MacDonald argues that the idea of 'monotheism' (like 'polytheism') is an invention of the Enlightenment that is inappropriate for understanding the Old Testament and that the use of this category has seriously distorted Old Testament scholarship's account of Israel's faith in YHWH. Tracing the invention of the word 'monotheism' and its early use by the seventeenth-century Cambridge Platonists, he associates it with the intellectualization of religion in seventeenth-century English thought, which tended to identify religion with a body of theoretical knowledge and to judge the truth or falsity of a religion by the truth or falsity, rationally assessed, of the propositions that constituted it. 'Monotheism' was an organizing principle in the categorization of religions according to their intellectual claims and, as such a principle, made the question of the number of gods a priority in the classification and evaluation of religions. The term 'monotheism', especially as subsequently taken over by the Deists, became associated with the Enlightenment's philosophical construction of a rational, ethical and universally evident religion. The identification of emergent 'monotheism' in ancient Israel was thus in danger of being a mere projection of Enlightenment beliefs and values and of being understood within a developmental understanding of the necessary progress of humanity through various stages towards ethical monotheism, which, being rationally compelling, is bound to prevail everywhere.

MacDonald shows how this Enlightenment idea of monotheism has influenced major accounts of Israelite religion from Wellhausen onwards. He acknowledges that von Rad is an exception in that he deliberately distinguished Israelite 'monotheism' from the modern conception that, he observes, derives from the Enlightenment. In my view, Yehezkel Kaufmann is also more of an exception than MacDonald allows. Whatever other criticisms may be made of Kaufmann's claim that the 'basic idea of Israelite religion is that God is supreme over all',[4] there is nothing peculiarly modern about it (whereas Enlightenment Deism was by no means happy with an *actively* sovereign God like Kaufmann's

---

[3] FAT 2/1; Tübingen: Mohr Siebeck, 2003. This is a revised version of his Durham doctoral thesis, *One God or One Lord?: Deuteronomy and the Meaning of 'Monotheism'* (2001).

[4] Quoted by MacDonald, *Deuteronomy*, 36, 37. MacDonald refers to the criticism of Kaufmann's claim by Jon D. Levenson, *Creation and the Persistence of Evil*, new ed. (Princeton: Princeton University Press, 1994).

YHWH): it is the teaching of traditional Judaism, Christianity and Islam.[5] Allowing that Kaufmann's understanding of universalism is not the Enlightenment concept,[6] MacDonald nevertheless takes the fact that Kaufmann understands Israelite monotheism as in *any* sense universalistic to align him with the Enlightenment notion. The same seems to be true of transcendence.[7] MacDonald's discussion of Kaufmann shows that he needs the specifically Enlightenment idea of monotheism to do more work than it can. From his perspective he evidently needs to critique not only the influence of Enlightenment monotheism on Old Testament scholarship, but also the influence of the entirely traditional, pre-modern belief of the 'monotheistic' religions (Judaism, Christianity and Islam) in the transcendence, unrivalled sovereignty and universal deity of the one God. However, he is on firmer ground, in my view, in seeing the persistence of the influence of the Enlightenment concept in the developmental models applied to Israelite religion, in light of the impact of the new archaeological evidence for Israelite polytheism, by two representatives of recent scholarship, Robert Gnuse and Walter Dietrich.

These matters are preliminary to MacDonald's study of Deuteronomy, which argues that 'Deuteronomy does not, at any point, present a doctrine of God that may be described as "monotheism"', while 'the description of Deuteronomy's message as "monotheistic" obfuscates at least as much as it enlightens'.[8] The following seem to me the most important ways in which he distinguishes Deuteronomy's 'doctrine of God' from Enlightenment monotheism:

(1) Deuteronomy does not deny the existence of other gods. MacDonald observes, with many others, that the Shemaʿ and the first commandment of the Decalogue require monolatry, the exclusive devotion of Israel to YHWH, but do not deny the existence of other gods. They may even be said to presuppose it in treating them as real competitors for Israel's devotion.[9] Less usual, though not unprecedented,[10] is MacDonald's denial that Deuteronomy itself teaches that YHWH is the only god.

---

[5] MacDonald himself writes that 'YHWH's universal control provides the background of election' (*Deuteronomy*, 167).

[6] MacDonald, *Deuteronomy*, 39.

[7] MacDonald, *Deuteronomy*, 40.

[8] MacDonald, *Deuteronomy*, 209–10.

[9] MacDonald, *Deuteronomy*, 77, 210.

[10] Cf. Robert K. Gnuse, *No Other Gods: Emergent Monotheism in Israel* (JSOTSup 241; Sheffield: Sheffield Academic Press, 1997), 206, with references to other scholars in n. 47.

(MacDonald, in line with his thesis, translates *ʾelōhîm* as 'god', except on the few occasions when it has the article, for which he uses 'God'.) The two key statements in chapter 4 – 'so that you would acknowledge that YHWH is God (*hāʾelōhîm*); there is no other besides him' (4:35) and 'acknowledge ... that YHWH is God (*hāʾelōhîm*) in heaven above and on the earth beneath; there is no other' (4:39) – he takes to mean that YHWH is unique (the only god who is God) and is the only god *for Israel*.[11]

(2) The 'intellectualization' of religion implicit in 'monotheism' is lacking in Deuteronomy. 'Monotheism' 'represents a call to recognize the objective state of metaphysical affairs'. That there is only one God is presented as 'a fact that one must assimilate', part of a body of objective knowledge about the world that is rationally accessible. 'In Deuteronomy, however, the recognition of YHWH's oneness is a call to love YHWH, a love expressed in obedience and worship.'[12] This does not mean that MacDonald denies that Deuteronomy makes cognitive truth-claims about YHWH, but that he sees these as inseparable from the relational requirement of devotion to YHWH.

(3) By contrast with the facile, intellectual recognition of monotheism as a fact, Deuteronomy – here exemplified in the Shemaʿ – requires of Israel (not others) a love of or devotion to YHWH that is 'all consuming and incomparably demanding'.[13] The emphasis is on a demand that is supremely difficult to fulfil. Moreover, it is not self-evident, as it is for the 'ethical monotheism' of the Enlightenment, what the obligation entails, since it is not a matter of general ethical values but of specific concrete acts of obedience laid down by YHWH for his own people Israel.

(4) Deuteronomy presumes that, devotion to YHWH being as difficult and demanding as it teaches, Israel will easily forget YHWH and needs careful disciplines of remembrance. This distinguishes it from the Enlightenment view of monotheism as an intellectual step in human history that, once made, could not conceivably be reversed, so obvious is its intellectual superiority to polytheism. MacDonald quotes Schleiermacher: 'as soon as piety has anywhere developed to the point of belief in one God over all, it may be predicted that man will not in any region of the earth remain stationary on one of the lower planes.... There

---

[11] MacDonald, *Deuteronomy*, 79–85.
[12] MacDonald, *Deuteronomy*, 210.
[13] MacDonald, *Deuteronomy*, 210.

is nowhere any trace, so far as history reaches, of a relapse from Monotheism, in the strict sense.'[14] The modern conception of a historical progress, in which monotheism is a necessary stage, has strongly influenced Old Testament scholars' ideas about a monotheistic development or monotheistic breakthrough in Israel.

(5) Finally, there is a strong contrast between the universalism of Enlightenment monotheism (the meaning of which is especially clear when it is seen as the opposite pole from particularism) and the centrality of Israel's election in Deuteronomy. For the Enlightenment approach, true monotheism required the one God to be freed from any special attachment to Israel (this approach has strongly influenced New Testament as well as Old Testament scholarship). By contrast, for Deuteronomy, YHWH's 'uniqueness cannot be recognized apart from his election of Israel. For Deuteronomy, there is no access to YHWH apart from this relationship ... This is true not only for Israel, but also for the nations ... How the nations respond to Israel determines their response to YHWH.'[15]

These arguments are very important and, in my view, largely convincing. My serious reservations concern point (1) and will be explained below. Of course, MacDonald's study is confined to Deuteronomy, but points (2) – (5) seem to me to be broadly valid for much of the Old Testament (though some different things might also need to be said about the Wisdom literature and about Genesis), and certainly they expose very sharply and usefully the ways that Enlightenment ideas of monotheism have distorted study of the Old Testament.

What I find disappointing in MacDonald's work is his failure to deal systematically with the issue of YHWH's uniqueness vis-à-vis the other gods. Given that Deuteronomy affirms the uniqueness of YHWH (as alone God [4:35, 39; 7:9] and as alone 'god of gods' [10:17]) without denying the existence of other gods, in what does that uniqueness consist? In his conclusion he writes that 'monotheism'

does not capture what it means in Deuteronomy to say that 'YHWH is God' (*hā'elōhîm*). 'Monotheism' has been generally understood, with exceptions such as Albright, as the denial of the existence of other gods, but one. In Deuteronomy the existence of other gods is not denied.

---

[14] MacDonald, *Deuteronomy*, 124.
[15] MacDonald, *Deuteronomy*, 180.

Nevertheless it is still claimed that 'YHWH is God', or 'god of gods'. This claim to be a unique divinity is based not on creation, or YHWH's role in parcelling out the nations to other gods, but on YHWH's faithfulness, mercy and jealousy demonstrated by his election of Israel. In his particular actions for his people, YHWH shows that he is God. We might say, to use the language of theological discourse, that YHWH's claim to be God is not primarily an ontological claim, but more a soteriological one (though such a claim carries with it ontological implications).[16]

There are several questions to ask about this passage:

(1) What is the sense of 'primarily' in the last sentence?[17] One could say that the claim is *primarily* soteriological *in the order of knowledge,* but not in the order of being. In other words, YHWH is unique (even apart from his election of Israel), but Israel recognizes this uniqueness only through what he does for Israel. This would be parallel to the 'Nicene' argument in the Trinitarian debates of the fourth century, which proposed (against Arius) that Christ could only save, in the sense claimed by Christian soteriology, if he were fully divine. On the other hand, MacDonald's statement could mean that YHWH's claim to be God is *primarily* a soteriological one *in the order of being.* In other words, he is unique as a result of what he has done for Israel. In this case, his election of Israel constitutes his uniqueness. The penultimate sentence of the passage ('In his particular actions for his people, YHWH shows that he is God')[18] seems to me to make best sense if MacDonald intends the first of these two possible senses of 'primarily', but the lack of clarity is disturbing if one is looking to his work for an answer to the question how Deuteronomy understands the uniqueness of YHWH.

---

[16] MacDonald, *Deuteronomy*, 215.

[17] Bernhard Lang, *Monotheism and the Prophetic Minority* (Sheffield: Almond Press, 1983), 55, makes a superficially similar point in relation to his view that monotheism was a response to the political circumstances of exile: 'There is a dimension of doctrine in monotheistic thought, it is true; but, unlike later scholastic speculation, Yahweh-aloneists and Jewish monotheists are not primarily concerned with dogma and doctrine. Theirs is a theology of hope ... In theological jargon one could say that soteriological monotheism is older than monotheistic dogma, or that hope precedes belief.' Lang seems to make two points: one about the main concern of Jewish monotheists ('not primarily concerned with dogma'), the second a chronological one ('soteriological monotheism is older than monotheistic dogma').

[18] Cf. also, for example, MacDonald, *Deuteronomy*, 195: 'YHWH's uniqueness was *revealed* in his electing actions on Israel's behalf' (my italics).

(2) How does what is said here about YHWH's unique claim to be God differ from the claim that he is the national god of Israel (and Israel should worship him exclusively because he has so extravagantly committed himself to Israel as his people), whereas other gods are similarly the national gods of their peoples (even though they cannot claim to have benefited their peoples in the outstanding way that YHWH has benefitted Israel)? Is YHWH unique only in, so to speak, taking his commitment to his people more seriously than other national gods do and, therefore, requiring more exclusive allegiance than other national gods do?[19] I do not think MacDonald intends to say this (and I am sure Deuteronomy does not), but he says nothing else in his conclusion that enables us to give more content than this to the assertion of YHWH's uniqueness.

(3) An understanding of YHWH's uniqueness vis-à-vis the other gods also requires that we know more about the other gods than simply that Deuteronomy does not deny their existence. If all that matters is that Israel is not to worship them, we seem to be back with the idea that YHWH's uniqueness really is nothing more than his election of Israel. His difference from other gods would be only that he is more committed to his people than they are. MacDonald is well aware that Deuteronomy has more than this to say about the contrast between YHWH and other gods,[20] but he does not draw these insights into a systematic presentation of the nature of YHWH's uniqueness.

MacDonald's failure to conclude more about YHWH's uniqueness than he does in the passage quoted above from his conclusion probably results from his concern to distinguish Deuteronomy from Enlightenment monotheism's assumption that the uniqueness of the one and only God is simply a fact to be recognized. He wants to stress that YHWH's uniqueness is knowable to Israel (and to anyone else) only in the context of Israel's relationship with YHWH. The problem is that this concern seems to lead him to reduce YHWH's uniqueness to that relationship. But this is not necessary. Given that Israel can *recognize* YHWH's uniqueness only from what YHWH does for Israel, it does not

---

[19] Cf. Morton Smith's opinion that, while the theology of the Old Testament is in general 'the common theology of the ancient near East', what does require explanation is 'Yahweh's abnormal jealousy': 'The Common Theology of the Ancient Near East,' in *Studies in the Cult of Yahweh*, ed. S.J.D. Cohen (Religions in the Graeco-Roman World 130/1; Leiden: Brill, 1996), 1:15–27, here 26.

[20] MacDonald, *Deuteronomy*, 92, 195–7.

follow that this uniqueness cannot include what YHWH objectively is, even independently of Israel.

Deuteronomy seems to me to require an account of YHWH's uniqueness that takes full account of such passages as these: 'YHWH is God (*hāʾᵉlōhîm*) in heaven above and on the earth below' (4:39); 'heaven and the heaven of heavens belong to YHWH your god, the earth with all that is in it' (10:14); 'YHWH your god is god of gods and lord of lords, the great god' (10:17); and the divine self-declaration of 32:39 in relation to what is said about the gods in the Song of Moses. But, in order to establish my point, I want particularly to engage with MacDonald's exegesis of the crucially important passage Deuteronomy 4:32–40.

The two key statements of YHWH's uniqueness (vv. 35, 39) come as the climaxes to the two sections, verses 32–35 and verses 36–39:

> ³²For ask now about former ages, long before your own, ever since the day that god created human beings on the earth; ask from one end of heaven to the other: has anything so great as this ever happened or has its like ever been heard of? ³³Has any people ever heard the voice of a god speaking out of a fire, as you have heard, and lived? ³⁴Or has any god ever attempted to go and take a nation for himself from the midst of another nation, by trials, by signs and wonders, by war, by a mighty hand and an outstretched arm, and by terrifying displays of power, as YHWH your god did for you in Egypt before your very eyes? ³⁵To you it was shown so that you would acknowledge that YHWH is God (*hāʾᵉlōhîm*); there is no other besides him (*ʾên ʿôd milᵉbadô*).

> ³⁶From heaven he made you hear his voice to discipline you. On earth he showed you his great fire, while you heard his words coming out of the fire. ³⁷And because he loved your ancestors, he chose their descendants after them. He brought you out of Egypt with his own presence, by his great power, ³⁸driving out before you nations greater and mightier than yourselves, to bring you in, giving you their land for a possession, as it is still today. ³⁹So acknowledge today and take to heart that YHWH is God (*hāʾᵉlōhîm*) in heaven above and on the earth beneath; there is no other (*ʾên ʿôd*).

> ⁴⁰Keep his statutes and his commandments, which I am commanding you today for your own wellbeing and that of your descendants after you, so that you may long remain in the land that YHWH your God is giving you for all time.

> (NRSV altered)

MacDonald takes Israel's recognition of YHWH as *hāʾᵉlōhîm* in verse 35 to be the consequence of his election of Israel, while in verse 39 it is the consequence of his revelation at Horeb.[21] I do not think this is adequate. The passages seem to me to stress in both cases YHWH's supreme power, and it is because of YHWH's exercise of power on their behalf that Israel is to recognize him as *hā'ᵉlōhîm*. In the second case (while MacDonald must be right to see a connection between heaven and earth in v. 36 and heaven and earth in v. 39), the recognition that YHWH is 'God in heaven above and on the earth beneath' implies not just his presence in heaven and earth (as MacDonald argues), but also his power throughout heaven and earth. The parallel in Joshua 2:11 surely strongly supports this interpretation.[22] What makes YHWH, by comparison with the gods of the nations, 'the God' (or 'god of gods and lord of lords, the great god' as 10:17 puts it) is his unrivalled power. Thus, although it is only in what he does for Israel that Israel recognizes YHWH to be 'the God', this status is not only what he is in relation to Israel, but what he is in any case and, particularly, in relation to the other gods. Of course, it is essential to Israel's relationship with YHWH that he exercises his power in love for Israel, in electing and favouring Israel, but he would not be 'the God' were he not powerful enough to make his election and favour effective in ways that are beyond the power of other gods.

The phrase with which verses 35 and 39 conclude – 'there is no other (besides him)' (*'ên 'ôd mil°badô*) – is found, in this and other forms, quite frequently elsewhere and is generally considered a 'monotheistic formula'. MacDonald argues that here the meaning is that YHWH is the only god for Israel – not absolutely. I find his linguistic argument about the use of *'ên 'ôd*[23] unconvincing, since it cannot apply in several other instances of this formula where YHWH is the subject (1 Kgs. 8:60; Isa. 45:5, 6, 14, 18, 22). He has shown only that, when *'ên 'ôd* is used, there can be a limitation supplied by the context, but not that the phrase itself entails a limitation. First Kings 8:60 is the closest parallel[24] to Deuteronomy 4:35, 39. Solomon (at the dedication of the temple) prays that YHWH will 'maintain the cause of his servant and the cause of his people Israel' (v. 59)

> so that all the peoples of the earth may know that YHWH is God (*hā'ᵉlōhîm*); there is no other (*'ên 'ôd*) (1 Kgs. 8:60).[25]

---

[21] MacDonald, *Deuteronomy*, 191–6.

[22] Eccl. 5:1 (English 5:2), to which MacDonald especially appeals, is a considerably more remote parallel.

[23] MacDonald, *Deuteronomy*, 81–4.

[24] Note also 2 Sam. 7:22, 28.

[25] Other instances of the formula 'YHWH is God (*hā'ᵉlōhîm*)' or 'you are God (*hā'ᵉlōhîm*)' are Josh. 22:34; 2 Sam. 7:28; 1 Kgs. 18:21, 37, 39 (*bis*); 2 Kgs. 19:15 = Isa. 37:16; 2 Chr. 33:13; Isa. 45:18.

This is presumably a direct echo of Deuteronomy 4, and it is worth noting that, at the outset of his dedication prayer, Solomon says that 'there is no God like you in heaven above or on earth beneath' (8:23). The conclusion of verse 60 can surely not mean that all the peoples of the earth will know that YHWH is the only god *for Israel*. What they will recognize is that YHWH alone is 'the God'. They need not deny that there are other *gods*, but will recognize the uniqueness of YHWH as the only one who can be called 'the God'. It is in this category that 'there is no other'. This seems to me a good meaning also in Deuteronomy 4:35, 39. This interpretation agrees with MacDonald that the claim that 'YHWH is God (*hā'elōhîm*)' is a claim for uniqueness that does not deny the existence of other gods, but allows *'ên 'ôd mil'badô* to reinforce this uniqueness as such, rather than reducing it again to its significance only for Israel.

What Israel is able to recognize about YHWH, from his acts for Israel, that distinguishes YHWH from the gods of the nations is that he is 'the God' or 'the god of gods'. This means primarily that he has unrivalled power throughout the cosmos. The earth, the heavens and the heaven of heavens belong to him (10:14). By contrast, the gods of the nations are impotent nonentities, who cannot protect and deliver even their own peoples. This is the message of the Song of Moses (see especially 32:37–39). The need to distinguish among 'the gods' between the one who is supreme (YHWH) and the others, who are not just subordinate but powerless, creates, on the one hand, the usages 'the God' and 'the god of gods' and, on the other hand, the contemptuous 'non-god' (32:17: *lō' 'elōâh*; 32:21: *lō' 'ēl*) and 'their mere puffs of air' (32:21: *hab'lēhem*). Though called gods, the other gods do not really deserve the term, because they are not *effective* divinities, acting with power in the world.[26] YHWH alone is the God with supreme power:

> See now that I, even I, am he;
> there is no god besides (or: with) me.
> I kill and I make alive;
> I wound and I heal;
> and no one can deliver from my hand (32:39).

This is not Enlightenment monotheism, and nothing of what MacDonald writes about the existential and relational import of

---

[26] Cf. Werner H. Schmidt, *The Faith of the Old Testament*, trans. John Sturdy (Oxford: Blackwell, 1983), 279: The Old Testament 'regarded the gods not as nothing, but as good for nothing; it does not deny their existence but their power and effectiveness'.

YHWH's uniqueness should be surrendered. But we do seem here to be at least approaching the 'monotheism' of the 'Abrahamic' religions in their traditional forms, as well as 'monotheism' as Kaufmann understood it. It is not enough to observe that Deuteronomy does not deny the *existence* of other gods. We should also recognize that, once we do attend to the ontological implications that MacDonald admits Deuteronomy's 'doctrine of God' must have, this theology is driving an ontological division through the midst of the old category 'gods', such that YHWH appears in a class of his own.

3. The quest of the historical monotheism

MacDonald's work, apart from his introductory survey of scholarship, is, of course, limited to Deuteronomy and to the final form of the text. He attempts neither to place this in a historical context in relation to the historical place of other Old Testament texts, nor to place it in a canonical context of the rest of the texts read synchronically. The larger task of biblical theology clearly requires that one attempt at least one of these tasks, but whether the first is necessary or desirable for biblical theology immediately raises questions about the method and nature of biblical theology. In some ways, the issue of monotheism is similar, in Old Testament theology, to the issue of the historical Jesus in the New. Has New Testament theology any need to take an interest in the historical reconstruction of Jesus attempted in the quest of the historical Jesus, or are the canonical renderings of Jesus in the four Gospels the only proper and sufficient concern of New Testament theology? Similarly, is a history-of-religions account of the origins and development of ancient Israel's exclusive Yahwism relevant to the understanding of faith in Yahweh that must be central to an Old Testament theology, not to mention a pan-biblical theology? James Barr, for one, thinks that this is one of the key areas in which an absolute demarcation between the history of religion and biblical theology should not be maintained and where the results of history-of-religions scholarship are important for biblical theology.[27] Some of those who have contributed recently to the study of the origins and development

---

[27] J. Barr, *The Concept of Biblical Theology: An Old Testament Perspective* (London: SCM, 1999), 137–8. The other two of the three examples he gives are, in fact, closely connected with the issue of monotheism: the 'convergence' of deities (YHWH and El), and 'sexuality in the deity' (including the evidence for a female consort of YHWH).

of exclusive Yahwism in Israel are also convinced of the relevance of their results to biblical theology.[28]

The question arises particularly acutely because, as MacDonald points out, 'from its conception "monotheism" has been tied to questions of origin',[29] and this is also true of the discussion of monotheism in Israel and the Old Testament. To put a blunt question: Did YHWH reveal his exclusive deity to Israel at the time of the origins of the nation before the settlement in the land, as Deuteronomy claims, making this claim the basis for Israel's exclusive devotion to YHWH? Of course, historical study could never answer the theological question about the action of YHWH as such, and even a scholar like Robert Gnuse, who is deeply concerned with the theological implications of the historical work in this field, does not ask this theological question as such. But he would have to answer it negatively because, like many recent scholars,[30] he thinks that Israelite religion was originally indistinguishable from Canaanite religion, and that exclusive Yahwism was a late development of the monarchical period. (Others would not date it earlier than the exile.) Can we affirm the theological teaching of the Old Testament while allowing that the historical 'facts' could have been as different from the Old Testament's own narrative as this? Could YHWH really be as the Old Testament portrays him if, historically, even the claim of exclusive Yahwism has merely been projected back through fictionalized history from the exile all the way to Moses? The status of 'history' in Old Testament theology is, of course, a familiar issue,[31] but this instance of it seems to me to pose the problem most acutely.

As in the case of the historical Jesus, I would be reluctant simply to let history and theology go their separate ways, and so, though I can speak only as a novice in the field, it may be worth observing that I seriously doubt that the emerging consensus that Israelite religion was in origin simply Canaanite religion really has a historically persuasive basis in

---

[28] E.g. Walter Dietrich, 'Über Werden und Wesen des biblischen Monotheismus: Religionsgeschichtliche und theologische Perspektiven,' in *Ein Gott allein?* ed. Walter Dietrich and Martin A. Klopferstein (Freiburg: Swiss Academy of Humanities and Social Sciences, 1994), 13–30; Gnuse, *No Other Gods*; B. Becking, 'Only One God: On Possible Implications for Biblical Theology,' in B. Becking et al., *Only One God? Monotheism in Ancient Israel and the Veneration of the Goddess Asherah* (London: Sheffield Academic Press, 2001), 189–201.

[29] MacDonald, *Deuteronomy*, 53.

[30] E.g. Herbert Niehr, 'The Rise of YHWH in Judahite and Israelite Religion: Methodological and Historical Aspects,' in *The Triumph of Elohim: From Yahwisms to Judaisms*, ed. D.V. Edelman (Contributions to Biblical Exegesis and Theology 13; Kampen: Kok Pharos, 1995), 48–50.

[31] Cf., e.g. Barr, *Concept*, chap. 21.

the evidence. Archaeology has indeed shown that the worship of gods besides Yahweh, especially the goddess Asherah, was widespread in Israel and Judah in the monarchical period.[32] This is hardly inconsistent with the biblical narratives, which require only the supposition that, in addition to widespread polytheistic practice, there was a tradition of exclusive Yahwism – the tradition from which the biblical writings derive – which, whatever its varying degrees of influence and strength over centuries, went back to a much earlier period. It is important not to confuse such a tradition, which can be regarded as normative only as a theological judgement or in historical retrospect from its achievement of normative status in practice in the post-exilic period, with the religion of Israel in the pre-exilic period understood as the practice of most Israelites and evidenced by the archaeology as well as the texts, insofar as they can be considered reliable evidence for the practices they criticize. While archaeology provides no evidence of the existence of exclusive Yahwism before the end of the monarchical period (for which period the amulets from Ketef Hinnom and the tomb graffiti from Khirbet beit Lei are plausibly evidence of such),[33] the evidence it offers for the nature of Israelite religion is, in total, very small and can hardly be said to make it even probable that exclusive Yahwism did not exist.

The conclusion that exclusive Yahwism did not exist until the late monarchical period results mainly from treating the biblical texts not just with historical scepticism but with historical scepticism based on very considerable ideological suspicion of the texts, along with the use of religio-historical models for interpreting the non-biblical evidence and making a plausible story out of it. Such models are inescapable in any history of religions, and the smaller the amount of evidence and the more ambiguous it is, the more it is the models that control the conclusions drawn from the evidence. Once the biblical texts have been discounted as reliable evidence, not only because of very late datings given them but also because they are so ideologically shaped, the remaining evidence is, it must surely be admitted, rather easily malleable according to the models and analogies employed. While the historical reconstruction may indeed fully respect the integrity of

---

[32] The evidence is especially well presented and discussed in the essays in Becking et al., *Only One God?*

[33] K.J.H. Vriezen, 'Archaeological Traces of Cult in Ancient Israel,' in Becking et al., *Only One God?* 45–80; and R. S. Hess, 'Yahweh and his Asherah? Epigraphic Evidence for Religious Pluralism in Old Testament Times,' in *One God, One Lord in a World of Religious Pluralism*, ed. Andrew D. Clarke and Bruce W. Winter (Cambridge: Tyndale House, 1991), 5–33, offer balanced and sensible assessments of what the archaeological evidence shows.

this evidence, it is not so easy to tell whether an alternative historical reconstruction might not do so just as well. Ironically, there is a clear danger of historiography that is no less ideologically shaped than it considers that of the Deuteronomists to have been. In particular, most such reconstructions seem controlled by a developmental model, however nuanced, that envisages a series of steps that advance by stages towards full monotheism and cannot reckon with serious departure from monotheism once this has been attained.

I find two instances of the way Robert Gnuse deals with proposals that are not in line with the emerging consensus rather revealing. One of the valuable aspects of his book is the careful presentation of the work of most recent scholars in this field and the development of his own critical synthesis out of his assessment of these. The major recent study that is probably most out of line with what Gnuse identifies as the mainstream within which he situates himself is *The Rise of Yahwism* (1st edition, 1990) by Johannes C. de Moor.[34] This very learned work, which handles a wide range of ancient Near Eastern sources with expertise, proposes 'a new paradigm for the early history of Yahwism'.[35] As far as origins go, he proposes that exclusive worship of El, in the form of YHWH-El, originated, in the context of a wider tendency to put one god above others, among 'proto-Israelites' in late thirteenth-century Canaan, and that a form of this cult that can be more precisely identified as exclusive Yahwism originated with Moses (whom de Moor argues in detail to have been the Egyptian chancellor Beya of Egyptian texts) at the end of the twelfth century.[36]

This is how Gnuse evaluates de Moor's work:

> It is brilliantly argued, but it is incredibly hypothetical. He has reconstructed detailed history on the basis of apparently archaic sounding poetry in the Bible, a dangerously subjective procedure. His theory is possible, but not probable. Such a theory is difficult to refute, but also impossible to prove. Any hypothesis which increasingly turns literary allusions into specific historical reconstructions becomes less likely to have been the true historical scenario. De Moor's theory runs counter to the direction in which scholars are moving in their understanding of monotheistic evolution, so he will convert few readers to his hypothesis.[37]

---

[34] Writing in 1997, Gnuse refers to the 1990 edition. I have used the revised and enlarged edition: Johannes C. de Moor, *The Rise of Yahwism: The Roots of Israelite Monotheism* (BETL 91; Leuven: Leuven University Press/Peeters, 1997).

[35] De Moor, *Rise of Yahwism*, 9.

[36] The dating of Beya at 'the end of the 13th century' in de Moor's concluding summary (*Rise of Yahwism*, 372) seems to be a mistake.

[37] Gnuse, *No Other Gods*, 109.

The judgement that de Moor's work is very speculative is fair, but I wonder whether it is really *more* 'hypothetical' or its use of evidence *more* 'subjective' than the reconstructions Gnuse favours. The really decisive point against de Moor seems to be Gnuse's final sentence, which puts remarkable faith in a scholarly trend just because it is a scholarly trend, even given that Gnuse identifies this trend as 'a paradigm shift'.[38] (Gnuse himself is aware that many factors – not just the evidence – go into the making of scholarly trends.) What I find valuable is Gnuse's admission that de Moor's theory is 'possible'. He does not claim that there is evidence against it, only that the evidence for it is weak. This is a revealing indication of the status of all historical claims in this area. I have adduced this example, not because I wish to defend de Moor's theory (I lack the competence to assess it in detail), but because Gnuse's treatment of it seems to me to illustrate how far a controlling model can be the decisive factor in both making and judging historical reconstructions in this area.

My second instance of Gnuse's evaluation is not of a particular reconstruction but of a proposed model for interpreting the evidence. This is from Werner Schmidt's fine work, *The Faith of the Old Testament* (first published in 1968), which Schmidt himself characterized as standing midway between a history of Israelite religion and a theology of the Old Testament,[39] not in principle unlike the way Gnuse seems to position his own work. To characterize the way in which exclusive Yahwism related to other cults, Schmidt spoke of a 'double process of recognition and rejection'.[40] Yahweh took over some characteristics of other gods, while being sharply distinguished from other characteristics of the other gods. This was a process of recognizing what was compatible and rejecting what was incompatible with Israel's core faith in Yahweh. But such a process presupposes some criterion for such distinctions. Schmidt writes,

> It remains unsatisfactory however simply to state this polarity of contact and rejection. After the religio-historical comparison has been made, the question (for which there is historical justification too) is bound to arise: what made possible for Israel this history in which it deprived Yahweh's opponents of their power? What was the criterion which allowed rejection on the one hand, borrowing and change on the other? This is a difficult problem, and one to which the same answer cannot be given in every

---

[38] Gnuse, *No Other Gods*, 12.
[39] J.R. Porter, foreword to *The Faith*, by Schmidt, ix.
[40] Schmidt, *The Faith*, 180.

case. But Yahweh's demand for exclusivity and the prohibition of images are bound to be cited as the decisive criterion.[41]

Gnuse, who praises these categories of 'recognition', 'rejection' and 'core' (i.e. the criteria that guided the double process of recognition and rejection), correctly notices that the first two come close to the two categories which Mark Smith, in his much more recent major work, identifies as 'convergence' and 'differentiation' of deities.[42] What he does not note is the way that Schmidt's model supplies a clear deficiency in Smith's, in that the latter lacks an equivalent to Schmidt's category of 'core'. Smith's model provides an enlightening *description* of the relationship between Yahweh and the other gods, but lacks any clear explanation of the process.[43] But this advantage in Schmidt's model is lost in Gnuse's evaluation:

> Schmidt's categories are excellent for future discussion, except for his propensity to date the process too early [Schmidt considers the 'core' of Yahwism, as he identifies it, to date from the pre-settlement period] and to articulate the 'core' too concretely. The exclusivity of Yahweh and the aniconic portrayal were probably not important factors in the pre-exilic religion of Israel, as archaeology and the newer critical understanding of the biblical texts indicate ... The so-called 'core' of Yahwistic faith was probably more nebulous and would be difficult to define.[44]

But the historically explanatory value of the 'core' is entirely lost when thus reduced to the nebulous and indefinable! It seems to me that Schmidt quite correctly saw that it is a necessary *historical* question (as well as one important for Old Testament theology) to ask about the criteria that guided the double process of recognition and rejection or the already early core of faith in YHWH that accounts for its distinctive later development. His answer is, of course, as a historical explanation, a hypothesis, but has a lot of plausibility to it.[45] Gnuse rejects it, not

---

[41] Schmidt, *The Faith*, 180.

[42] Mark S. Smith, *The Early History of God: Yahweh and the Other Deities in Ancient Israel* (San Francisco: Harper & Row, 1990).

[43] This is explicit: Smith, *Early History*, 155–6, where Smith shows, from one point of view, laudable historical caution.

[44] Gnuse, *No Other Gods*, 239.

[45] For a similar historical argument, see R. Albertz, *A History of Israelite Religion in the Old Testament Period*, trans. John Bowden, (London: SCM, 1994), 1:61–2: 'there must have been a potential for difference within Yahweh religion which distinguished it from the usual polytheistic religions, a potential to which opposition groups which saw the exclusive worship of Yahweh as the only possibility of overcoming crises could appeal' (62).

really on grounds of hard evidence (the archaeology actually favours the early origin of Yahwistic aniconism rather than disproving it[46]) but because he is committed to a different model, so much so that, in my judgement, he has failed to recognize the superiority of Schmidt's model in accounting for the evidence.

These two examples of Gnuse's reasons for rejecting alternatives to the emerging consensus suggest that one should not have too much confidence in the historical basis for this consensus (i.e. for the view that Israelite religion was originally indistinguishable from Canaanite religion and that exclusive Yahwism was a late development). But Gnuse's work must retain our attention for the next stage of our argument also, because he is not only an enthusiastic champion of the emerging consensus. He is also its theologian, convinced that it has important implications for biblical theology.

The thread that runs through the whole of Gnuse's book is his evolutionary understanding of the emergence of monotheism from Israelite religion. This is for him not only a heuristic model for historical understanding of what happened, but also a crucially important theological category. He draws from much of the recent scholarship the impression that monotheism did not develop simply in a gradual process over a long period, as the evolutionary model has in the past tended to suggest, but through a combination of evolution and revolution, i.e. 'an evolutionary process which occurs in revolutionary fashion'. He envisages 'a series of intellectual revolutions over a period of years which culminated in the exile', when 'true' monotheism emerged out of the politico-religious crisis of the period.[47] (Gnuse uses a variety of terms to describe the culmination of the development, Deutero-Isaiah's monotheism with its denial of the existence of other gods: true monotheism, absolute monotheism, theoretical monotheism, pure monotheism, radical monotheism.)

The development through intellectual 'leaps' precipitated by specific circumstances has been a fairly common picture, while Mark

---

[46] See especially T.N.D. Mettinger, *No Graven Image? Israelite Aniconism in Its Ancient Near Eastern Context* (CB [NT] 42; Stockholm: Almqvist & Wiksell, 1995). He distinguishes *de facto* aniconism, which is as old as Israel itself (194), from 'the programmatic prohibition of images of the deity', which he attributes probably to the influence of Deuteronomistic theology (135, but cf. 196 for a possibly earlier date). Considering Israelite aniconism as such a form of a more general phenomenon of West Semitic aniconism, he does not see it as one of Israel's *differentia specifica*, though it may well be that 'the express veto on images' is (195–6). He perhaps does not allow sufficiently for the way that, in a given historical context, Yahwistic aniconism could be seen as distinctive and differentiating.

[47] Gnuse, *No Other Gods*, 69.

Smith already spoke of a combination of evolution and revolution.[48] Gnuse's contribution is to show that this combination need not involve abandoning a biological model of evolution, since contemporary understanding of the latter itself incorporates the idea of periodic 'leaps' forward, rather than a purely gradual process. He calls this model 'Punctuated Equilibria'. It is quite unclear to me how this explicitly biological model is supposed to function. Is it no more than an illustration (with 'pedagogic' usefulness, as Gnuse sometimes says) or is it supposed to have some explanatory value? Does the fact that the historical developments can be plotted in a way that resembles biological evolution somehow make that way of plotting them more convincing? Even for someone who believes as strongly as Gnuse does in the overall progressive nature of human intellectual and religious history, as well as in biological evolution, I cannot see any reason at all why the former should be supposed to advance in the same way as the latter.[49]

Old Testament scholars have often attached to their accounts of the development of monotheism in ancient Israel remarks to the effect that monotheism was the great Jewish contribution to the world or that what happened in Israel laid the foundations for the modern world.[50] But Gnuse claims for the emergence of Israelite monotheism its status as 'a great evolutionary advance for humanity'[51] by placing it within a world-historical scheme of evolutionary intellectual advance. Along with comparable intellectual breakthroughs in the 'Axial Age' in Greece, Persia, India and China, it belongs to the third great stage of intellectual evolution, succeeded either at the Renaissance or the Enlightenment by the modern intellectual world to which we belong.[52] Of course, this is a prime instance of the influence of the Enlightenment model of which Nathan MacDonald complains, but Gnuse not only envisages

---

[48] Gnuse, *No Other Gods*, 102.

[49] Even James Barr's moderate defence of evolutionary models of Israelite religion (*Concept*, chap. 7), while in my judgement associating the ideas of biological evolution and historical development too closely, does not seem to presume that there can be a useful comparison between the *ways* in which the two processes operate.

[50] B. Halpern, '"Brisker Pipes than Poetry": The Development of Israelite Monotheism,' in *Judaic Perspectives on Ancient Israel*, ed. J. Neusner, B. Halpern and E.S. Frerichs (Philadelphia: Fortress, 1987), 107, ends his quite sober interpretation of the historical development in this extraordinary way: 'The resultant communal religion remains at the heart of Western culture; the successful socialization of the radical monotheistic insight illustrates the interaction between the theory and the reality. In that sense, synthetic monotheism, as it may be called, was a movement towards theoretical empiricism, toward the "scientific method." It is in that sense that it has contributed most to the progress and progressiveness of Western thought.'

[51] Gnuse, *No Other Gods*, 125.

[52] Gnuse, *No Other Gods*, 233–6.

monotheism in highly intellectualizing terms (he often speaks of the Israelite intelligentsia achieving intellectual breakthroughs, and he more often speaks of intellectual history than of intellectual and religious history, as though the intellectual were the important aspect). He also sees the whole value of the developments he describes as consisting in the way they lead humanity on from one stage of intellectual development to the next, with the modern age as the culmination of the process. Thus, however much or little Enlightenment ideas of monotheism have influenced his understanding of the content of Israelite faith in YHWH, it is especially important to notice that the significance he sees in the development of this faith is quite different from the way any Old Testament writer could conceivably have seen it.

Gnuse has accomplished something theologically interesting. In effect, he has adopted a reconstruction of the historical evolution of monotheism in Israel which replaces the biblical narrative of Israel's history with YHWH and, at the same time, he has supplied a new theological understanding – a modernist salvation history – that corresponds to the new historical reconstruction, replacing the Old Testament's own theological account of Israel's history with YHWH. The procedure is parallel to that of radical reconstructions of the historical Jesus, which, since nineteenth-century liberalism, have frequently been inextricably linked with theologies alternative to those of the Gospels. It is merely rather surprising that Gnuse sees his work, in its theological aspect, as biblical theology.

Although Gnuse accords the emergence of monotheism in Israel world-historical significance, precisely this evaluation distances us modern people from it: 'We may be built upon biblical thought, but we have moved beyond it, too.'[53] The revolutionary breakthrough achieved by Israel's monotheistic intellectuals in the exile is, like all such evolutionary breakthroughs but the beginning of a further process of evolution – 'the Judaeo-Christian tradition' – in which 'the implications of radical monotheism are [still] being worked out in terms of their social and religious imperatives'.[54] (One wonders why the Muslim world is not also part of the evolutionary process deriving from Israelite monotheism.) In other words, 'the implications of monotheistic religion are unfolding still in our own age. Perhaps, this is *the cardinal conclusion* to be drawn from contemporary critical studies *for the theological task before us*' (my italics).[55] Gnuse is oblivious to such obvious questions

---

[53] Gnuse, *No Other Gods*, 235.
[54] Gnuse, *No Other Gods*, 273.
[55] Gnuse, *No Other Gods*, 275.

as: If western intellectual development is the leading edge of human evolution, does it not look rather as if a new evolutionary breakthrough to some kind of post-modern atheism is already in process?

Gnuse's more detailed thoughts on the implications for biblical theology revolve around the difference between the old biblical theology's penchant for a contrastive picture of Israel's distinctiveness vis-à-vis its Canaanite environment and his evolutionary picture of difference emerging from major continuity. About this difference he makes two interesting points. One is that, whereas the old biblical theology fostered a dialectical model of the church's opposition to the world with a corresponding attitude to social and political change, the new understanding will stress continuity and look for gradual processes of greater justice and equality, sensing the presence and activity of God in the human cultural processes of the whole contemporary world.[56] To this, one might respond that drawing any such conclusions from biblical theology to the actual possibilities for change in specific social and political situations is hardly the way to do applied theology.

The second implication of his evolutionary picture is that we should abandon the 'quest to find something unique in biblical thought that was so much in fashion ... We should not search for the unique, but rather for how old ideas were transformed'.[57] This seems to me a more insightful comment. It is surely true that the old fashion in Old Testament theology for outlining the Old Testament's theological ideas as in contrast at every point to the Near Eastern context 'produced forced generalizations'.[58] It would be refreshing to look for the Old Testament's own critiques of its religious environment rather than at historically reconstructed contrasting worldviews. We might discover that, in the last resort, it is not so much an issue of unique ideas as of YHWH's own uniqueness. As Peter Machinist shows, while Old Testament scholars find it increasingly difficult to locate anything truly unique in Israel's religion, a strong sense of the uniqueness of YHWH and of Israel (and the two as closely connected) pervades the writings of the Hebrew canon.[59] Gnuse reduces this to Israel's position as a kind of evolutionary bridgehead to the intellectual future of humanity; Machinist himself to Israel's sociological need for a 'counter-identity' in the face of the older and dominant cultures of Egypt and Mesopotamia.

---

[56] Gnuse, *No Other Gods*, 277–8.
[57] Gnuse, *No Other Gods*, 271.
[58] Gnuse, *No Other Gods*, 271.
[59] Peter Machinist, 'The Question of Distinctiveness in Ancient Israel,' in *Essential Papers on Israel and the Ancient Near East*, ed. F.E. Greenspan (New York: New York University Press, 1991), 420–42.

In a quest for the unique identity of YHWH in Old Testament theology, we should surely be looking not only to the 'monotheistic' claims, which may or may not have convincing parallels in other ancient cultures, but to the fact that these claims (that YHWH is the unique Creator and sovereign Lord of all reality) are made with no diminution of the particularity of YHWH the God of Israel. Particularity of this kind *cannot* be reduced to a general religious idea and so absorbed either into the general religious climate of the ancient world or into an ongoing process of intellectual evolution. What gets lost in the massive intellectualization of the subject by Gnuse is not simply the sense that Israelite religion was more than a set of ideas about reality, but also the particularity of YHWH. Gnuse's God does not, of course, really do any of the particular things the Old Testament's YHWH does, while his election of Israel becomes Israel's remarkable intellectual achievement as a signal contribution to the intellectual evolution of humanity. The most important warning we can take from a critique of Gnuse's work is that biblical 'monotheism', whether or not we choose to use the word and however we find it necessary to define it, is a claim about the God who defines himself by his covenant with Israel and the particular name YHWH that cannot be abstracted from his particular identity in his history with Israel.

Gnuse's is not the only attempt to draw theological conclusions from the emerging consensus about the emergence of monotheism in Israel. There are also those for whom the triumph of monotheism in the post-exilic period was not at all a good thing but a victory for oppressive patriarchal religion over the generous diversity of pre-exilic polytheism, in which Yahweh had a consort, and female spirituality found expression both in the household religion evidenced by the commonly found figurines of Asherah and also in cult centres not reserved for the exclusive worship of a single male god. Again, in its happy recovery of what it was really like from behind the ideological suppression and distortions of the canonical accounts, this resembles nothing so much as some forms of the quest of the historical Jesus, in which the real Jesus is rescued from the dogmatic Christology imposed on him by the Gospels. Of course, there is no real future for Old Testament theology, even of a suspicious and reconstructive kind, in this direction. If the attractive religious paradigm is that of Israel when Israelite religion was very much like most other ancient Near Eastern religious cultures, then there can be no good reason for continuing to be religiously interested in Israel in particular. Ancient polytheistic religion is, after all, much better documented outside Israel, and has left much more impressive religious literature elsewhere than the few polytheistic fragments that might be recoverable from the monotheistic censuring to which Israel's religion was subject in the literature that survives in the Old Testament.

4. The Old Testament – a monotheistic book?

Nathan MacDonald's book makes an indispensable contribution in demonstrating the inappropriateness of the categories of Enlightenment monotheism for understanding Old Testament faith in YHWH. However, not everyone who speaks of 'monotheism' has the Enlightenment model mainly in view. There are those whose thinking is much more influenced by the ways in which the Jewish and Christian traditions have read the Bible and understood the uniqueness of the God of Israel and the Christian God. There are also those who are well aware of at least some of the differences between Old Testament and modern 'monotheism', but continue to find it appropriate to speak of 'monotheism' in the former case, while seeking to avoid misunderstanding. My sense is that those New Testament scholars and scholars of early Judaism who speak of 'Jewish monotheism' in the Hellenistic and Roman periods are less influenced by the Enlightenment model than Old Testament scholarship has been. What term other than 'Jewish monotheism' could one use to characterize the very strong awareness that Jews of the post-biblical periods certainly had of the uniqueness of their God by contrast with the many and various gods worshipped by all other people they knew? (Perhaps one might propose 'mono-Yahwism', were that not reminiscent of the 'YHWH-alone' movement of the late monarchical period hypothesized by Morton Smith and Bernhard Lang. I use 'exclusive Yahwism' as a general term to cover what may be no more than monolatry as well as what I call 'Jewish monotheism'.) I shall continue to speak of 'late Second Temple period Jewish monotheism' ('Jewish monotheism' for convenience) for the kind of religion that I find in the Jewish literature of that period and that seems to me presupposed by the New Testament. The most important task is not that of finding a fully satisfactory label, but that of characterizing accurately just how the uniqueness of YHWH was understood.

This is itself a controversial subject, to which other chapters of this book make contributions. But it seems to me relevant to our understanding of the Old Testament, as biblical theologians, in the sense that what I am calling 'Jewish monotheism' is what Jews in the period of the formation of the Hebrew canon found in these Jewish Scriptures. This category is not alien to the texts in the way that Enlightenment monotheism is. Arguably, what I call 'Jewish monotheism' is the theology of the canon, in the sense that it was the theological context for the formation and editing of the canonical collection and the way in which this collection was intended to be read by those who made it the Scriptures of that very scriptural religion, early Judaism. It would seem quite appropriate at least to consider whether it can be read in that way without violence to a historically informed understanding of the texts. I am not suggesting that all the ways in which early post-biblical Judaism read the biblical texts are valid for us, only whether and how the basic understanding of the uniqueness of YHWH that the Hebrew canon's early readers found in it can also be found in it by us. If I am right that this is also the understanding of the God of the Old Testament that is presupposed by the New Testament in the course of its also very innovatory christological reading of the Old, then the issue is also vital for the task of 'pan-biblical' theology.

For Jewish monotheism, the one God has a unique name, YHWH, and a unique relationship with his chosen people Israel, to whom he has revealed not only the supreme power he exercises in mighty acts of salvation and judgement in relation to Israel, but also the moral dispositions (in the classic characterization of Exod. 34:6–7) that characterize his dealings with Israel. All these elements of YHWH's particular identity as the God of Israel are essential to Jewish monotheism, as are the requirements on Israel summed up in the first commandment of the Decalogue and in the Shema', which make Israel's monotheism no mere matter of intellectual belief but a matter of distinctive cultic practice and loving obedience that encompasses the whole of life.[60] (This is inadequately called monolatry, but it is true that Jews of the late Second Temple period were peculiarly conscious of the obligation to worship only YHWH and that this, with its negative corollary of non-participation in anything implicated in the cult of other gods, marked out Jewish monotheism most obviously in religious practice.)

This God of Israel is the one and only Creator of all things and sovereign Lord over all things. Among the many other things that late Second Temple period Jews said about the uniqueness of their God, these two aspects of his unique relationship to all other reality were the most commonly cited, repeatedly used to put YHWH in an

---

[60] Barclay, *Jews in the Mediterranean Diaspora*, 429, is right to find the term 'monotheism' inadequate if it is taken to place 'the emphasis on a concept – the belief that there is one, and only one, being rightly called "God" – and obscures the significance of *cultic practice* in defining acceptable or unacceptable religion.'

absolutely unique category. Most Jewish writers had no hesitation in making clear that, in this sense, YHWH is the only true God there is and ought to be acknowledged as such by all people. All pagan worship of other gods was giving to others what only the one Creator and Lord of all things ought to receive. Much Jewish literature of the period can be said to hold to an eschatological monotheism that expected that, since YHWH is the one and only Lord of all reality, he must come to be acknowledged as such universally in the end. But this universalism was not in tension with the particularity of YHWH's election of Israel, for other nations would come to recognize precisely YHWH, the God of Israel, as the only true God. It would be his salvific acts on Israel's behalf that would create this universal recognition, and recognition of the one God, Creator and Lord of all, would be inseparable from recognition of his special relationship to his covenant people. While, in the diverse literature of early Judaism, there are certainly more universalistic perspectives and more particularistic perspectives, often related to specific contextual factors such as Diaspora Jewish apologetic or Palestinian Jewish resistance to Roman rule, on the whole it is fair to say that universalism and particularism are not contradictory aspects. Jewish monotheism is characterized by its way of relating YHWH's particularity as Israel's God to his universality as Creator and sovereign Lord of all.

This is the kind of Jewish reading of the Jewish Scriptures that the New Testament seems everywhere to presuppose. Most scholars would allow that parts of these Scriptures give strong support to this kind of 'monotheism', but is it a plausible or valid canonical reading of the whole? Several writers have proposed that the Hebrew canon as a whole can be described as 'monotheizing', if not 'monotheistic', literature. This distinction is made by James Sanders, in a brief treatment that claims that 'every bit of [the Bible] monotheizes – more or less well'. He explains that each era from which biblical writings come 'left a residue of idioms derived from the polytheisms of its culture, precisely because of the struggle to monotheize'.[61] After a few examples, he concludes:

> The Bible is a monotheizing literature displaying the struggles of genera-
> tions over some fifteen to eighteen centuries to pursue the Integrity of
> Reality. In this sense the Bible is a paradigm; it conjugates the nouns and
> verbs of the divine integrity in a plethora of different kinds of situations
> and conditions. To monotheize, in this sense, is not to progress or evolve

[61] James A. Sanders, *Canon and Community: A Guide to Canonical Criticism* (Philadelphia: Fortress, 1984), 51.

toward monotheism, but rather to struggle within and against polytheistic contexts to affirm God's oneness, both in antiquity and today.[62]

These are very suggestive remarks, especially noteworthy for the way in which they allow polytheistic materials to be seen as subject to a monotheizing dynamic without proposing a developmental or evolutionary model. Unfortunately, Sanders does not seem to have pursued his suggestions any more fully, and nor, so far as I am aware, has anyone else. Sanders appears to be speaking about the individual biblical writings, rather than about a 'monotheizing' editing of them to form the canon, but his model seems at least to require a process of 'monotheizing' selection of material as part of the process of canon formation. Similarly, any plausible proposal that the process of canonization was in part a 'monotheizing' process cannot attribute the 'monotheizing' purely to canonical editors, but must presuppose the prior existence of some 'monotheizing' literature. It could, however, also be open to the presence in the canon of material that is not itself obviously 'monotheizing' at all, but that 'monotheizing' editors did not consider resistant to a 'monotheizing' reading encouraged by other parts of the canon.

Bernhard Lang who, unlike Sanders, appears unsympathetic to the canonical suppression of polytheistic aspects of Israelite religion, emphasizes the role of the editors of the canon, who were 'committed monotheists',[63] and explains that the exclusion of unequivocal polytheism from the canon results not only from the exclusion of explicitly polytheistic writings, but also from the more subtle methods of 'assimilating, adopting and re-interpreting traditions which may conserve polytheistic elements within a monotheistic context'.[64] One of his examples is the Israelite goddess Wisdom in Proverbs 1 – 9, where the polytheistic material has survived only because it could be read monotheistically in a way that reduced Wisdom to 'a mere figure of poetic speech'.[65] Again, this promising proposal has not been followed up by further argument that 'polytheistic' texts in the Old Testament are limited to ones that could be read in a monotheistic way, consistent with the explicit monotheism of other parts of the canon.

John Sawyer's article, 'Biblical Alternatives to Monotheism', implicitly counters Lang's argument, by arguing that there are three categories of

---

[62] James A. Sanders, *Canon*, 52.
[63] Lang, *Monotheism*, 53.
[64] Lang, *Monotheism*, 50.
[65] Lang, *Monotheism*, 53; see further Bernhard Lang, *Wisdom and the Book of Proverbs: A Hebrew Goddess Redefined* (New York: Pilgrim, 1986).

text in the Old Testament. There is (1) a small group of 'texts in which monotheism is explicit: that is to say, statements in which the existence of other gods apart from Israel's God, Yahweh, is denied';[66] and (2) 'a second group of texts which, although not originally monotheistic, have, under the influence of the [monotheistic] Deuteronomic texts, been so interpreted'.[67] But there is also (3) a third category of texts 'which are explicitly and embarrassingly polytheistic texts'.[68] With reference to the second category, he asks, 'Can a few explicitly monotheistic passages be used to change the meaning of other texts whose meaning is less explicit?'[69] After discussing the third category, he claims to 'have demonstrated that the plain meaning of the biblical text as a whole is far from monotheistic'.[70] In a response, Ronald Clements argued that

> Read diachronically, in the light of a critical awareness of the varying stages through which the Israelite religious tradition passed, monotheism does not seem to have been all that prominent a feature.... Nevertheless when read synchronically, as a connected body of religious texts which are believed to offer a coherent and unified revelation, the idea of monotheism would appear to be very important.[71]

The disagreement between Sawyer and Clements seems to be over two points: whether it is proper to read some texts in conformity with others in the canon if this means 'changing' their original meaning, and whether there are texts that cannot even be plausibly subjected to such a reading.

I shall return to these issues after making a further, crucially important point about Jewish monotheism. The essential element in what I have called Jewish monotheism, the element that makes it a kind of monotheism, is not the denial of the existence of other 'gods', but an understanding of the uniqueness of YHWH that puts him in a class of his own, a wholly different class from any other heavenly or supernatural beings, even if these are called 'gods'. I call this YHWH's transcendent uniqueness. (Mere 'uniqueness' can be what distinguishes one member of a class from other members of it. By 'transcendent uniqueness' I mean a form of uniqueness that puts YHWH in a class

---

[66] John F.A. Sawyer, 'Biblical Alternatives to Monotheism,' *Theol.* 87 (1984): 172–80, here 173.
[67] Sawyer, 'Biblical Alternatives,' 174.
[68] Sawyer, 'Biblical Alternatives,' 176.
[69] Sawyer, 'Biblical Alternatives,' 175.
[70] Sawyer, 'Biblical Alternatives,' 179.
[71] Ronald E. Clements, 'Monotheism and the Canonical Process,' *Theol.* 87 (1984): 336–44, here 338.

of his own.) Especially important for identifying this transcendent uniqueness are statements that distinguish YHWH by means of a unique relationship to the whole of reality: YHWH alone is Creator of all things, whereas all other things are created by him; YHWH alone is the sovereign Lord of all things, whereas all other things serve or are subject to his universal lordship. I think that a dynamic of distinguishing YHWH's uniqueness as, in this sense, transcendent is how the 'monotheizing' that Sanders rightly identifies throughout the biblical texts largely occurs (though I would not insist that there are not individual texts and perhaps whole biblical books where this dynamic cannot be identified). It is in this manner that the biblical texts, in Sawyer's words, 'struggle within and against polytheistic contexts to affirm God's oneness'.

From this perspective, it is clear that explicitly monotheistic texts are far from confined to those in Sawyer's first category, which he defines as 'statements in which the existence of other gods apart from Israel's God, Yahweh, is denied'.[72] For example, a text like Nehemiah 9:6, which Sawyer does not count as monotheistic, can now be seen to be a very strong expression of the monotheistic dynamic:

> You are YHWH, you alone; you have made heaven, the heaven of heavens, with all their host, the earth and all that is on it, the seas and all that is in them. To all of them you give life, and the host of heaven worships you (NRSV altered).

By attributing to YHWH the creation of all other reality, by emphasizing that all creatures without exception have been created by YHWH, this text is making an absolute distinction between the unique identity of YHWH and all other reality. The fact that other heavenly beings, YHWH's retinue, 'the host of heaven', are included does not qualify the uniqueness of YHWH but, on the contrary, serves to underline YHWH's uniqueness by making it unequivocally clear that YHWH does not belong to a class of heavenly beings that includes him along with the host of heaven, but is absolutely distinguished from the host of heaven in that he created them. This text makes the transcendent uniqueness of YHWH as clear as could be.

This example illustrates how it is not the existence of heavenly beings besides YHWH that is at stake in the 'monotheizing' dynamic of the texts and the canon, but the nature and status of such beings.

---

[72] Sawyer, 'Biblical Alternatives,' 173. He reckons only twenty-five such texts, mostly in the Deuteronomic writings and Deutero-Isaiah.

Within the Hebrew canon, most 'gods' besides YHWH fall into one of two categories. They are either members of YHWH's retinue, serving his rule, or they are impotent nonentities. In the former case, they are called by a variety of terms (gods, sons of gods, sons of the Most High, holy ones, watchers, the host of YHWH, the host of heaven). They accompany YHWH as warriors or attendants, and they assemble in YHWH's presence in heaven. We should avoid the 'etymological fallacy' of determining the significance of this heavenly retinue of YHWH by reference to its origins in a properly polytheistic context rather than its functions in the biblical text. Despite the rather misleading sense suggested by the commonly used English term 'divine council', the assembly around YHWH are not counsellors. He does not consult them in an open decision-making process in which they contribute advice on which he acts. Unless we count Satan's unsolicited suggestions in Job 1:9–12; 2:4–7, which YHWH allows him to implement, the only instance of advice given by one of the assembly to YHWH is in 1 Kings 22:19–22, where YHWH asks for a volunteer to lead Ahab to his death and, when 'a spirit' offers to do it, asks him 'how?' and approves of his suggestion. Not even this degree of participation in planning or decision-making occurs anywhere else. In Isaiah 6, there is only YHWH's request for a volunteer (v. 8). When Jeremiah speaks of prophets standing in 'YHWH's council' (*sôd*, a word that implies intimacy, a circle that is privy to YHWH's plans, but not necessarily debate or advice), he expects them to hear YHWH's decrees announced in the assembly, not to be involved in or present at some kind of discussion (Jer. 23:18, 22). The general point is that these 'gods' are not independent powers but servants of YHWH who no more qualify his unique status than do human beings who worship and obey YHWH. YHWH's retinue are the attendants of an absolute monarch, whose sheer numbers evidence his greatness and whose constant praises serve precisely to define and to proclaim his transcendent uniqueness.

The other category of 'gods' is the gods of the nations reduced to the status of powerless nonentities by the biblical texts' insistence on YHWH's uniquely supreme power and ridiculed as 'non-gods' and 'nothings', as we observed in section 2 in the case of Deuteronomy 32. Again, the monotheizing dynamic is apparent, not in absolutely denying their existence, but in denying them a status that could conceivably detract from YHWH's transcendent uniqueness.

The mere use of *ᵉlōhîm*, or other terms for divine beings, is not decisive for Jewish monotheism; everything depends on how such beings are defined in relation to YHWH. However, it is interesting –

and deserves much more attention than it has received – to observe some steps toward linguistic distinctions, such as the use of *'ᵉlōhîm* with the article in some cases to distinguish 'God' from 'the gods' (see section 2 on Deuteronomy's usage); the use of *'ᵉlōhîm* with a meaning something like 'the deity' (e.g. in Gen. 1); and the contemptuous descriptions of the foreign gods or idols by such terms as 'non-gods' (*lō' 'ēl*) or *'ᵉlîlîm*, a deliberate malformation of *'ᵉlōhîm* (as in Ps. 96:5, 'For all the gods [*'ᵉlōhê*] of the peoples are *'ᵉlîlîm*, but YHWH made the heavens').[73] In the literature of later Second Temple Judaism, the words for 'god' (in Hebrew, Aramaic and Greek) almost entirely cease to be used for the heavenly beings who serve YHWH, except in the Qumran community's own compositions, and in the special case of Philo (whose use of *theos* is strongly affected by Hellenistic use), and even the use of 'holy ones' strongly declines.[74] There is clearly a concern to reduce the use of terms that could designate both YHWH and other heavenly beings. The Qumran community continued to use almost all the biblical terms for heavenly beings to describe the angels (as they were now most often called), perhaps as a deliberate continuation of scriptural usage, but it would be a mistake to think the community less monotheistic than other Jews of the period. Terminology was affected by monotheizing, but not always decisively.

Sawyer distinguished a group of explicitly monotheistic texts (which I have argued should be much larger than he allows) from a category of texts which were not originally monotheistic but have been interpreted as such under the influence of the explicitly monotheistic texts. He doubts that such interpretation – 'changing' the original meaning of texts – is legitimate. I think this is too stark a contrast and propose that my concept of a monotheizing dynamic can help us identify more continuity between these two types of text. Let us take Sawyer's examples: in the first category, he focuses on the texts that use the formula 'and there is no other [besides YHWH]', while, in the second category, he focuses on the passages which emphasize the incomparability of YHWH. Not all of the texts in the former category say exactly that there is no other 'god' besides YHWH, as 2 Samuel 7:22 and Isaiah 45:5, 14, 21 do. More typically, they put YHWH in a class of his own, for example:

---

[73] See H.D. Preuss in TDOT 1:285–7.
[74] Similarly, statements of YHWH's incomparability, common in the Old Testament, are in the post-biblical literature almost entirely confined to the Qumran community's writings. This is doubtless because they state YHWH's incomparability *among the gods*.

'YHWH is the God (*hā'elōhîm*); there is no other besides him' (Deut. 4:35);
'there is no Holy One like YHWH, no one besides you' (1 Sam, 2:2);
'that all the people of the earth may know that YHWH is the God
    (*hā'elōhîm*); there is no other' (1 Kgs. 8:6);
'I am YHWH, and there is no other' (Isa. 45:5, 6, 18);
'I, YHWH, am your God, and there is no other' (Joel 2:27).

Compare some of the 'incomparability' texts:

'Who is like you, YHWH, among the gods?' (Exod. 15:11);
'For who is like me? Who can summon me?
Who is the shepherd who can stand before me?' (Jer. 49:19; 50:4);
'For who in the skies can be compared to YHWH?
Who among the sons of gods is like YHWH? ...
YHWH God of hosts, who is as mighty as you, YHWH?' (Ps. 89:6, 8).

The 'incomparability' texts usually say that YHWH is incomparable
among 'the gods' (though sometimes the comparison is more generally
with any creature at all) and so seem superficially polytheistic, in the
sense of admitting the existence of other heavenly beings. In fact,
however, they are expressions of the 'monotheizing' dynamic that is
constantly driving a line of absolute distinction between YHWH and
other 'gods'. The effect of 'there is none like YHWH' is precisely to put
YHWH in a class of his own, exactly as the first category of texts do in
denying that there is any 'other' besides YHWH. Whether the existence
of other gods is denied or whether YHWH is simply said to be in a
class of his own by comparison with them is of small importance to
the general sense of all these texts. This is confirmed by the fact that
examples of the two kinds of text sometimes occur in close association
with each other, for example:

'there is no one like you, and there is no god besides you' (2 Sam. 7:22);
'I am God, and there is no other; I am God, and there is no one like me'
    (Isa. 46:9).

There remains Sawyer's third category of texts, the 'explicitly and
embarrassingly polytheistic' ones. The most important texts here are
those which depict the battle between YHWH and the chaos monsters
(Rahab, Leviathan, the Sea), whether these represent the forces over
which YHWH triumphed when he created the world (Ps. 74:13–14) or the
persistent threat of chaos or evil that threatens creation and will require
a further victory of YHWH in the future (Isa. 27:1). This topic deserves a
full discussion for which this is not the place. But the idea that there are
powers opposed to God which God must defeat is part and parcel of the

traditional monotheistic religions, along with, of course, the conviction that God is unquestionably able to defeat such powers of evil, and can be expected to do so in the end. Jon Levenson is right to argue that there is real theological loss when this theme in the Hebrew Bible is dismissed in favour of an impression of YHWH's power as serene supremacy that is never challenged.[75] But the recognition of YHWH as the sole Creator of all things and the sole sovereign Lord of all things need not require that. What matters is that, as Herbert Niehr puts it,

> No other divinity is the subject of the processes of creation or the taming of chaos in the [Hebrew Bible]. YHWH alone is the creator and he alone fights chaos. The [Hebrew Bible] texts show that he is a universal god having power over everything in heaven and earth and that he is the supreme god fulfilling deeds other gods cannot fulfil.[76]

In other words, YHWH's defeat, restraint or taming of chaos (in a variety of texts) does not, in the perspective of Jewish monotheism, put his sole deity in doubt but precisely demonstrates his sole deity.

Recognition of the 'monotheizing' dynamic in the form I have proposed does not prevent us recognizing in the Hebrew Bible material that in a wide variety of ways resembles the language and myths of Canaanite and other Near Eastern religions. Rather, it shows us the way such material is constantly being re-functioned to serve the purpose of asserting and characterizing the transcendent uniqueness of YHWH. The texts were composed in cultures in which polytheism was always near to hand and had to be engaged. As Sanders put it, there is, in the texts, a 'struggle within and against polytheistic contexts to affirm God's oneness'.[77] They are texts in which (with some possible exceptions, such as Ecclesiastes[78]) we do not see monotheism securely achieved and taken for granted, but rather the many creative ways in which it is constantly being recovered and rethought. Moreover, as Nathan MacDonald's work

---

[75] Levenson, *Creation.*

[76] Niehr, 'The Rise of YHWH,' 67.

[77] Sanders, *Canon*, 52.

[78] Cf. T. Frydrych, *Living under the Sun* (VTSup 90; Leiden: Brill, 2002), 107–8: 'Qoheleth's perspective is thoroughly monotheistic, in the most rigid sense of that word. There is not a single hint in the book that Qoheleth is prepared to consider more than one deity, or a force of any kind, in operation alongside God, nor is there any apologetic against polytheistic views. This latter fact is of some interest, for Hellenistic influence on the society of Qoheleth's day was significant, and the documented tension between traditional Judaism and the penetrating Hellenism would have been impossible to escape. Yet, this tension is not at all reflected in the book. We have to conclude from this that Qoheleth has in mind an audience that needs no convincing with respect to the monotheistic perspective he puts before them.'

makes very clear, in distinguishing Deuteronomy from Enlightenment monotheism, exclusive Yahwism in the biblical tradition is not an easily made intellectual proposition, but a demand for radical and complete devotion to YHWH. So the 'monotheizing' dynamic always works in favour of a recognition of YHWH's transcendent uniqueness that is inseparable from his uniquely demanding requirement of loyalty and devotion from his covenant people.

So my proposal does not suppress the diversity of the texts, but does show how the whole of the Hebrew Bible can be read in accordance with early Jewish monotheism. It rejects a developmental reading of the texts. Not only is an evolutionary account of the emergence and development of monotheism simply not the story the canonical narratives of Israel tell. Recent scholarship also seems to me to have made the idea that we can stratify all the texts chronologically (with minute dissection of the texts into earlier and later layers and interpolations), and thereby construct a developmental reconfiguration of the biblical material, hugely problematic. All attempts to do this are hopelessly speculative, because the texts have not been preserved in such a way as to make it possible. Undoubtedly, the texts emerge out of a complex history, but they do not contain sufficient, or sufficiently clear, traces of their own pre-history to make tradition history a viable vehicle for biblical theology.[79] What they do contain is a dialectic of 'convergence' and 'differentiation' (Mark Smith's terms), or 'recognition' and 'rejection' (Werner Schmidt), driven by the core apprehension of YHWH's uniqueness. I use these terms not to describe a developmental history, as Smith and Schmidt do to some extent, but to characterize what is happening throughout the texts in many different ways. There is no evolution visible in the texts, but there is a dynamic.

Finally in this section, I must comment on the significance of the parallels in ancient Near Eastern religious texts to much of the kind of language I have identified as 'monotheizing' or monotheistic in the Old Testament. Here, for example, is part of a Sumerian prayer to the moon god Nanna-Suen (Sin):

> O lord, who decides destinies in heaven and on earth, whose saying no
>   one can alter,
> who holds water and fire in his hands, who guides living creatures – who
>   among the gods is as you are?

---

[79] Therefore I disagree with Barr, *Concept*, 61, when he suggests that 'the idea of monotheism' is one of those topics in biblical theology for which 'a historical framework with dating of different sources would very likely prove necessary'.

Who is exalted in heaven? You alone are exalted!
When you have spoken your word in heaven, the Igigi [gods of heaven]
　　pray to you,
when you have spoken your word on earth, the Anunnaki [gods of the
　　earth or underworld] kiss the ground....
O lord, your rule has no counterpart in heaven nor your heroic power
　　among your divine brothers on earth,
mighty one, exalted king, whose 'divine powers' no one dares to wrest
　　from you,
none of the gods can be compared with your deity.[80]

Such prayers, addressed to many different gods, are not uncommon
in the religious literature of Mesopotamia. There seem to be various
explanations, which Gnuse reports thus,

> Mesopotamia produced several deities who received apparently exclusive
> veneration, most notably Marduk and Sin in Babylon and Ninurta and
> Ashur in Assyria. However ... the existence of other gods is not denied,
> thus suggesting that each deity, when worshipped exclusively, merely
> absorbed the other gods temporarily and with respect for their continued
> existence. In some texts the elevation of one god was connected to the
> rhetoric of imperial aspiration of a conquering empire, in others the
> deity was symbolically representative of all the gods, and in prayers and
> laments the petitioner addressed the deity with exaggerated language of
> exclusivity in order to motivate the god to act.[81]

Quite similar material appears also in Egypt (quite apart from the
atypical episode of Akhnaton's cult of Aton), where, for example, it was
possible to praise Amon-Re as the sole creator of all things including
even the gods.[82] But different gods were variously praised as creator
of the world, on different occasions or by different worshippers
each praising their own personally favoured god. There was also an

---

[80] W. Beyerlin, ed., *Near Eastern Religious Texts relating to the Old Testament*, trans. J. Bowden
　　(London: SCM, 1978), 105–6. This text is no later than the seventeenth century BCE.
[81] Gnuse, *No Other Gods*, 268; cf. his fuller survey on pp. 154–61. Cf. Norbert Lohfink, 'The
　　Polytheistic and the Monotheistic Way of Speaking about God in the Old Testament,' in
　　Great Themes from the Old Testament, trans. R. Walls (Edinburgh; T&T Clark, 1982), 142:
　　'Theoretical polytheism among Israel's neighbours, in practice, always left open the
　　possibility of monolatry – the tendency, indeed, toward monolatry. Divine figures could
　　split themselves up, then join together again. New gods could step in.... But it always
　　happened that the man who worshipped one of these gods more or less consciously
　　summed up in that divinity all that godhead meant to him.'
[82] See the hymn in Beyerlin ed., *Near Eastern Religious Texts*, 13–16.

Egyptian tendency to merge deities.[83] In Greco-Roman religion, there was a rhetorical practice of praising a god as uniquely superior to all others.[84]

It is quite true that many such statements are, considered in themselves, semantically indistinguishable from similar ones about YHWH in the Old Testament.[85] The tendency to exalt one god to a *sui generis* position as compared with the others really is a 'monotheizing' move, whatever the reasons for it, as is the tendency to absorb features of various gods into one. However, these tendencies never, apparently, relate consistently and permanently to only one god. It seems not to have been thought inconsistent to apply the same kinds of language to more than one god on different occasions or by different individuals. Perhaps this also happened in pre-exilic Israel. But what characterizes the Old Testament as a canonical collection of literature is that this kind of language is invariably reserved for YHWH with whom all other gods are consistently contrasted. There is nothing occasional or optional about its application to YHWH. Thus the Old Testament language that can be paralleled elsewhere nevertheless needs, within the Old Testament, to be understood in its context as part of the Old Testament's overall delineation of the unique identity of YHWH.

5. The Shema῾ in the New Testament

Some scholars have proposed connections between non-monotheistic material in the Old Testament and Christology in the New Testament. John Sawyer, for example, thinks his view that the Old Testament is not predominately monotheistic helps to explain how belief in the divinity of Christ and the doctrine of the Trinity developed.[86] Bernhard Lang argues that an old tradition of two gods in Israel persisted in early Judaism and fed into New Testament Christology,[87] while

---

[83] Gnuse, *No Other Gods*, 161–74.

[84] Jerome H. Neyrey, '"First", "Only", "One of a Few", and "No One Else": The Rhetoric of Uniqueness and the Doxologies in 1 Timothy,' *Bib.* 86 (2005): 59–87.

[85] Machinist, 'The Question,' 423.

[86] Sawyer, 'Biblical Alternatives,' 179.

[87] Bernhard Lang, 'Die monarchische Monotheismus und die Konstellation zweier Götter im Frühjudentum: Ein neuer Versuch über Menschensohn, Sophia und Christologie,' in *Ein Gott allein?: JHWH-Verehrung und biblischer Monotheismus im Kontext der israelitischen und altorientalischen Religiongeschichte*, ed. W. Dietrich and M.A. Klopfenstein (Freiburg, Switzerland: Universitätsverlag, 1994), 559–64; idem, *The Hebrew God* (New Haven/London: Yale University Press, 2002), 197.

Margaret Barker has pursued this approach in much more detail, arguing that, in the older Israelite tradition that survived alongside monotheism, El and YHWH were distinct gods, father and son, and that the early Christians identified Jesus with YHWH.[88] In my view, there is no good evidence for the idea that non-monotheistic forms of Israelite religion survived through the Second Temple period to be available to the early Christians. The literature of early Judaism is uniformly monotheistic. But there is, in any case, another reason not to make this kind of connection between non-monotheistic Israelite religion and the New Testament: it is clear that the New Testament writers presuppose the kind of Jewish monotheism that I have described in the last section and that is found throughout early Jewish literature. Their christological innovations proceed on the basis of this presupposed monotheism, and they do not intend to depart from it.

In the present chapter, we shall confine ourselves to three important instances of the New Testament's appropriation of the Shema',[89] which, as a considerable amount of evidence shows, was central to the Jewish faith of the period, recited twice daily by observant Jews and echoed frequently in the literature. The first example does not involve Christology, the second and third do.

5.1. *Romans 3:28–30*

> For we hold that a person is justified by faith apart from works prescribed by the law. Or is God the God of Jews only? Is he not the God of Gentiles also? Yes, of Gentiles also, since God is one; and he will justify the circumcised on the ground of faith and the uncircumcised through that same faith (NRSV).

In this passage, with its obvious allusion to the Shema' ('God is one'), Paul draws a relatively novel[90] conclusion from the understanding of the Shema' that was normal in the late Second Temple period. Indeed, the form of the allusion (*heis ho theos*) is itself more or less standard. The usual form is *heis theos (esti)* (*Sib. Or.* 3:11; *Sib. Or.* frg. 1:7, 32; Josephus, *A.J.* 4.201; Ps-Sophocles; Philo, *Opif.* 171; *Spec.* 1.30), though James 2:19 has *heis estin ho theos*. It follows from reading the Shema' as 'YHWH

---

[88] Barker, *Great Angel*.
[89] Other allusions to the Shema' are Matt. 22:37; Mark 12:29–30, 32; Luke 10:27; Gal. 3:20; 1 Tim. 2:5; Jas. 2:19.
[90] Probably Philo comes closest in what he says about proselytes in *Spec.* 1.52.

our God, YHWH is one',[91] which is probably also how the Septuagint (*kurios ho theos hēmōn kurios heis estin*) should be understood. The words were understood to mean that YHWH, the God of Israel ('our God') is the one and only God of all reality, the one Creator and Lord of all. In this way, they express exactly that combination of particularity and universalism that is characteristic of early Jewish monotheism.

Paul takes up precisely that combination. He does not deny that God is, in a distinctive sense, the God of his people Israel, but insists that, since he is the one and only God there is, he must also be the God of Gentiles. In itself even this might not be controversial. But he interprets it to mean that Gentiles do not have to become Jews in order to be 'justified'. Mark Nanos puts it well:

> Gentiles are forbidden to become Jews . . . because to do so would be to deny the universalistic oneness of God (he is the One God of all the nations), which would implicitly deny his election of Israel and the privilege of Torah, because if he is not the One God of all outside Israel who believe in him then he is not the One God of Israel; he is not the One God at all. His oneness has been compromised if he is *only* the God of Israel, *only* the God of the circumcised, *only* the God of Torah, and not *also* the God of the nations, not *also* the God of the uncircumcised, and not *also* the God of those outside the Torah.[92]

Although there is no indication that Paul had it in mind, there is a kind of Old Testament precedent for insisting that YHWH is not the one God unless he is the God of the nations as well as the God of Israel. In the only echo of this part of the Shemaʿ within the Hebrew Bible, Zechariah 14:9 predicts that 'YHWH will become king over all the earth; on that day YHWH will be one and his name one.' The thought is evidently that YHWH cannot be truly one until he is in fact universally acknowledged as the one true God. The passage goes on to envisage an annual pilgrimage of the nations to worship YHWH by celebrating the Feast of Tabernacles in Jerusalem. The festival was associated with God's gift of the rains, and so it is appropriate that the punishment of any nation that does not make this pilgrimage to Jerusalem will be drought (Zech. 14:16–19). But the gift of the rains was also associated with the Shemaʿ (Deut. 10:13–14 – this passage was probably part of the

---

[91] For convincing arguments that this is also the meaning within Deuteronomy, see R. Walter L. Moberly, '"YHWH is One": The Translation of the Shemaʿ,' in *From Eden to Golgotha: Studies in Biblical Theology* (South Florida Studies in the History of Judaism 52; Atlanta: Scholars, 1992), 75–81; MacDonald, *Deuteronomy*, 62–70.

[92] Mark D. Nanos, *The Mystery of Romans* (Minneapolis: Fortress, 1996), 184.

twice daily recitation of the Shema'), and so it seems that Zechariah 14 envisages a universalizing of the Shema'. All peoples will be YHWH's peoples, all will love YHWH as the Shema' requires, all will therefore worship him at Tabernacles, and all will receive the paradigmatic divine blessing on those who love him. Thus, even Paul's characteristically radical conclusion from the Shema' is in line with the way the Shema' was understood even within the Old Testament. Israel's election, as God's people, becomes paradigmatic (and so never simply dissolved in an undifferentiated universalism) rather than exclusive.

5.2. First Corinthians 8:1–6

> Now concerning food sacrificed to idols: we know that 'all of us possess knowledge.' Knowledge puffs up, but love builds up. Anyone who claims to know something does not yet have the necessary knowledge; but anyone who loves God is known by him.
> Hence, as to the eating of food offered to idols, we know that 'no idol has real existence in the world,' and that 'there is no God but one.' Indeed, even though there may be so-called gods in heaven or on earth – as in fact there are many gods and many lords – yet
>> for us there is one God, the Father,
>>> from whom are all things and for whom we exist,
>> and one Lord, Jesus Christ,
>>> through whom are all things and through whom we exist
>
> (NRSV altered).

It is widely recognized that, in verse 6, Paul offers a Christian formulation of the Shema'. But we should first notice how, throughout his discussion of the issue of food offered to idols, Paul draws on the tradition of Jewish monotheistic rhetoric and especially on Deuteronomy. The issue, of course, is a very traditional issue of Jewish monolatry in a pagan religious context. Thus, the two statements that Paul takes up in verse 4 in order to explain them in the following verses are typically Jewish monotheistic formulae: 'we know that "no idol has real existence in the world," and that "there is no God but one"' (*oidamen hoti ouden eidōlon en kosmō kai hoti oudeis theos ei mē heis*). No doubt, these statements come from the Corinthians' letter, but the Corinthians may have been citing back to Paul what he himself had taught them and, in any case, the assertions are typically Jewish monotheistic ones. The designation of other gods as 'idols' can, of course, only be Jewish. The two statements together are reminiscent of the common Jewish monotheistic formula which claims that there is no other God besides YHWH, especially those versions of this formula which give it an explicitly cosmic context, like the *en kosmō* ('in the world')[93] of 1 Corinthians 8:4, which Paul echoes in the *eite en ouranō eite epi gēs* ('in heaven or on earth') of the following verse, and especially also those versions of the formula which link it with an allusion to the Shema''s assertion of the uniqueness of God. For example:

> YHWH is God; there is no other besides him.... YHWH is God in heaven above and on the earth beneath; there is no other (Deut. 4:35, 39).

> For there is no other besides the Lord, neither in heaven, nor on the earth, nor in the deepest places, nor in the one foundation (2 *En.* 47:3J).

> He is one, and besides him there is no other (Mark 12:32).

The first of the two statements is probably best translated: 'no idol has real existence in the world'. The alternative translation, 'an idol is a nothing in the world', is tempting, because it could echo the biblical use of *hebel* ('a vapour, a mere puff of air', i.e. nothing of any consequence) for the pagan gods, as in Deuteronomy 32:21 and elsewhere.[94] But the linguistic parallel between the two statements favours the former translation, which also makes better sense of 'in the world'. This last phrase also makes it obvious that 'idol' here does not mean the physical object as such (which, of course, undeniably exists) but the pagan god supposedly pictured by it, which, in Jewish usage, could also be called *eidōlon*. When Paul returns to the topic in chapter 10, now in order to urge the Corinthians to 'flee from the worship of idols' (10:14), he is aware that his argument might seem to contradict his agreement with the Corinthians that 'no idol has real existence in the world':

> What do I imply then? That food sacrificed to idols is anything, or that an idol is anything (*eidōlon ti estin*)? No, I imply that what pagans sacrifice, they sacrifice to demons and not to a god. I do not want you to be partners with demons (10:19–20: NRSV altered).

Paul's point may be that what the idol-worshippers think the idol represents, a god, does not exist but, as Jewish tradition believed on the basis of Deuteronomy 32:21 and Psalm 106:37, evil spirits exploit

---

[93] The biblical prohibition of idolatry is associated with specific rejection of the worship of anything in the cosmos: Deut. 4:15–19; 5:8.

[94] Cf. also Jub 20:8 ('all those who trust in them trust in nothing'); 2 *Bar.* 41:2; 2 *En.* 34:1. LXX translates *hebel* as *ouden* on one occasion, in Isa. 49:4, though the reference there is not to gods or idols.

their fantasy, so that, though they do not know it, they are actually worshipping 'demons'.[95] (The alternative view is that, both in 8:4 and 10:19, Paul means that pagan gods do not exist *as gods*, i.e. there is nothing godlike about them, but they do exist as minor supernatural forces – *daimonia*.)

In any case, what matters most here is Paul's resort to the Song of Moses, a classic resource for the Jewish insistence on the exclusive worship of YHWH. He cites Deuteronomy 32:17, 'They sacrificed to demons and not to a god' (LXX: *daimoniois kai ou theō*). The Hebrew of this verse probably means 'to demons, to what is not divine' (*lō' 'elōâh*).[96] As a translation of this, the Septuagint Greek should mean 'to demons and not to a god' or 'to demons, that is no-god', though a reader who did not know the Hebrew *Vorlage* could read it as 'to demons and not to God'. This meaning is possible in Paul's use of the allusion, but 'to demons and not to a god' is more appropriate to the Pauline context.[97] The same words Paul cites from Deuteronomy 32:17 are also echoed in Baruch 4:7 (*daimoniois kai ou theō*); *Jubilees* 11:17; *1 Enoch* 19:1; and *Sibylline Oracles* fragment 1:22.[98] They are a Jewish monotheistic commonplace. But Paul is well aware of their context in the Song of Moses, understood as recounting the history of Israel's idolatrous behaviour to which Paul had appealed in the earlier part of chapter 10.

He goes on to allude to the same passage of the Song of Moses again in 10:22: 'Or are we provoking the Lord to jealousy? Are we stronger than he?' The first question alludes to Deuteronomy 32:21, 'They have provoked me to jealousy with what is not a god' (LXX: *ep' ou theō*).[99] This is the only occasion on which Paul speaks of the divine jealousy (unless 2 Cor. 11:2 counts). His choice of the allusion shows that he takes very seriously the Jewish understanding of monolatry as required by God's jealous desire for the sole devotion of his covenant people (Exod. 20:5; Deut. 4:23–34; 5:9; 6:15; 32:16, 19, 21). In this sense, God's jealousy is closely connected with the Shema°. This makes it the more noteworthy

---

[95] Bar. 4:7; *Jub.* 11:4–5, 17; *1 En.* 19:1; 99:7; *Sib. Or.* frg. 1:22; 8:47, 386, 394.

[96] *1 En.* 19:1 paraphrases this as 'sacrifice to demons as to gods'; cf., similarly, *Sib. Or.* 8:394: 'dead demons, as if they were heavenly beings'.

[97] Gordon D. Fee, *The First Epistle to the Corinthians* (NICNT; Grand Rapids: Eerdmans, 1987), 472; Richard H. Bell, *Provoked to Jealousy: The Origin and Purpose of the Jealousy Motif in Romans 9–11* (WUNT 2/63; Tübingen: Mohr [Siebeck], 1994), 253–4.

[98] Note also Ps-Philo, *L.A.B.* 25:9 ('the demons of the idols'). Several of these passages understand the demons to be spirits of the dead (connecting Deut. 32:17 and Ps. 106:37 with Ps. 106:28; Deut. 26:14): *Jub.* 11:27; *Sib. Or.* frg. 1:22 ('sacrifices to the demons in Hades').

[99] The second question is probably an ironic reference to 'the strong' in the Corinthian church, but it may also allude to Deut. 32:39, which declares YHWH's unrivalled and unchallengeable power.

that Paul here attributes the divine jealousy of Deuteronomy to Jesus Christ. In Deuteronomy 22:21, YHWH speaks in the first person, but in turning the passage into a third person statement Paul could supply 'the Lord' (*kurios*) from verse 19. But since 'the cup of the Lord' and 'the table of the Lord' in the preceding verse must refer to Christ, this must be one of those quite frequent occasions on which Paul interprets the *kurios* of an Old Testament YHWH text as Jesus.[100] The implication for Jewish monotheism and Christology is remarkable: the exclusive devotion that YHWH's jealously requires of his people is required of Christians by Jesus Christ. Effectively he assumes the unique identity of YHWH.

This is coherent with the suggestion that Paul already has the Song of Moses in mind in 10:4 ('the rock was Christ'), alluding to the description of YHWH as Israel's Rock that is characteristic of the Song (Deut. 32:4, 15, 18, 31; note the close association with the theme of Israel's idolatry in v. 18).[101] But more certainly and more importantly, Paul has already prepared for his christological appropriation of the themes of monolatry and jealousy by means of his reformulation of the Shemaˁ in 8:6.

Paul has the Shemaˁ in mind from the beginning of chapter 8, for 'loves God' in verse 3 is already an allusion to it.[102] He is well aware that the faith of the Shemaˁ is not just a matter of objective knowledge that God is unique, but of wholehearted devotion to the one God. Thus, in verse 5, he is already shifting the emphasis from the mere existence or otherwise of gods (which v. 4 stressed) to the question of allegiance, devotion and worship. The sense in which there are 'many gods and many lords' (v. 5) is that pagans give allegiance and worship to them, whereas 'for us' (v. 6) there is one God and one Lord. While the phrase 'many gods and many lords' is accurate – the term *kurios* was used in many Greek cults – it also makes a neat contrast with the one God and one Lord of Paul's remarkable rewriting of the Shemaˁ. The carefully structured formulation reads:

> *all' hēmin heis theos ho patēr*
> *ex hou ta panta kai hēmeis eis auton*

---

[100] A.C. Thiselton, *The First Epistle to the Corinthians* (NIGTC; Carlisle: Paternoster/Grand Rapids: Eerdmans, 2000), 778. See also chapter 6 below.

[101] Fee, *Corinthians*, 449; Bell, *Provoked*, 254.

[102] If 'being known' by God (8:3) should be understood in terms of divine election (cf. Amos 3:2), then the association in that verse between loving God and being known by God could be further explored as a Deuteronomic theme related to the Shemaˁ (cf. Deut. 7:7–9) which Paul also reflects in Rom. 8:28–29.

kai heis kurios Iēsous Christos
di' hou ta panta kai hēmeis di' autou.

but for us [there is] one God, the Father,
from whom [are] all things and we for him,
and one Lord, Jesus Christ,
through whom [are] all things and we through him.

In stating that there is one God and one Lord, Paul is unmistakably echoing the monotheistic statement of the Shemaʿ ('YHWH our God, YHWH, is one'), whose Greek version in the Septuagint reads: 'The Lord our God, the Lord, is one' (*kurios ho theos hēmōn kurios heis estin*). Paul has taken over all of the words of this Greek version of the Shemaʿ,[103] but rearranged them in such a way as to produce an affirmation of both one God, the Father, and one Lord, Jesus Christ.

If Paul were understood as *adding* the one Lord to the one God of whom the Shemaʿ speaks, then, from the perspective of Jewish monotheism, he would certainly be producing, not christological monotheism, but outright ditheism. Over against the many gods and many lords (v. 5) whom pagans worshipped, the Shemaʿ demands exclusive allegiance to the unique God alone. Even if 'Lord' in verse 6 means no more than 'lords' in verse 5 – and it must certainly mean at least this – there can be no doubt that the *addition* of a unique Lord to the unique God of the Shemaʿ would flatly *contradict* the uniqueness of the latter. Paul would be not reasserting Jewish monotheism in a Christian way nor modifying or expanding the Shemaʿ, but repudiating Judaism and radically subverting the Shemaʿ. The only possible way to understand Paul as maintaining monotheism is to understand him to be including Jesus in the unique identity of the one God affirmed in the Shemaʿ. But this is, in any case, clear from the fact that the term 'Lord', applied here to Jesus as the 'one Lord', is taken from the Shemaʿ itself. Paul is not adding to the one God of the Shemaʿ a 'Lord' the Shemaʿ does not mention. He is identifying Jesus as the 'Lord' whom the Shemaʿ affirms to be one. In this unprecedented reformulation of the Shemaʿ, the unique identity of the one God *consists of* the one God, the Father, *and* the one Lord, his Messiah (who is implicitly regarded as the Son of the Father).

Paul rewrites the Shemaʿ to include both God and Jesus in the unique divine identity. But the point might not have been sufficiently clear had he not combined with the Shemaʿ itself another way of characterizing

---

[103] The *hēmōn* appears as the *hēmin* and repeated *hēmeis* of Paul's formulation.

the unique identity of YHWH. Of the Jewish ways of characterizing the divine uniqueness, the most unequivocal was by reference to creation. In the uniquely divine role of creating all things, it was, for Jewish monotheism, unthinkable that any being other than God could even assist God (Isa. 44:24; *4 Ezra* 3:4; Josephus, *C. Ap.* 2.192). But, to Paul's unparalleled inclusion of Jesus in the Shema', he adds the equally unparalleled inclusion of Jesus in the creative activity of God. No more unequivocal way of including Jesus in the unique divine identity is conceivable, within the framework of Second Temple Jewish monotheism.

As well as dividing the wording of the Shema' between God and Jesus, Paul also divides a description of God as the Creator of all things between God and Jesus. The description in its undivided, unmodified form is used elsewhere by Paul – in Romans 11:36a: 'from him and through him and to him [are] all things' (*ex autou kai di' autou kai eis auton ta panta*), where the context is one of Jewish monotheistic praise of the uniqueness of God.

It is true that there are some non-Jewish Hellenistic parallels to the formulation which relates 'all things' (*ta panta*) to God by a variety of prepositions. The best examples are in Pseudo-Aristotle, *Mund.* 6 (*ek theou panta kai dia theou sunestēke*); Marcus Aurelius, *Medit.* 4.3 (*ek sou panta, en soi panta eis se panta*); and Asclepius 34 (*omnia enim ab eo et in ipso et per ipsum*). The point of such formulae is that they describe God as the cause of all things, indicating the various types of causation (as standardly recognized in ancient philosophy) which are appropriate to God's relation to the world by means of the various prepositions: i.e. efficient causation (*ek*), instrumental causation (*dia* or *en*) and final causation (*eis*).[104] But such formulae would clearly be very congenial to Jewish usage, since Jews were, in any case, much in the habit of describing God as the Creator of 'all things' (e.g. Isa. 44:24; Jer. 10:16; 51:19; Sir. 43:33; Wis. 9:6; 2 Macc. 1:24; 3 Macc. 2:3; *1 En.* 9:5; 84:3; *2 En.* 66:4; *Jub.* 12:19; *Apoc. Ab.* 7:10; *Jos. Asen.* 12:1; *Sib. Or.* 3:20). Josephus (*B.J.* 5.218), without the use of the prepositions, says much the same as the non-Jewish Hellenistic formulations: 'all things are from God and for God' (*tou theou panta kai tō theō*). Philo explicitly takes up the standard philosophical set of types of causation and applies to God's relation to the world the three which can be so applied: God himself is the efficient

---

[104] Material and formal causation could not appropriately describe the relationship between God and the universe. Eph. 4:6 uses a different kind of formula, which also relates God to all things by means of three different prepositions, but has the prepositions governing *panta*, 'one God and Father of all, who is above (*epi*) all and through (*dia*) all and in (*en*) all.'

cause ('by whom [*huph' hou*] it was made'), his Word is the instrumental cause ('by means of which [*di' hou*] it was made') and the final cause ('on account of which [*di' ho*]') is 'the display of the goodness of the Creator' (*Cher.* 127). In Hebrews 2:10, God is the final and instrumental cause of his creation: the one 'on account of whom (*di' hou*) are all things and through whom (*di' hou*) are all things'.

We can, therefore, be confident that Paul's formulation – 'from him and through him and to him [are] all things' (Rom. 11:36) – is neither original to Paul nor borrowed directly from non-Jewish sources, but was known to him as a Jewish description precisely of God's unique relationship to all other reality. When he uses it in Romans 11:36, there is no christological reference, but when he incorporates it into his Christianized version of the Shema‛ in 1 Corinthians 8:6, he divides it between God and Christ, just as he divides the wording of the Shema‛ between God and Christ. The relationship to God expressed by the first and the last of the three prepositions (*ek* and *eis*) is attributed to the one God, the Father ('from whom [are] all things and we for him'), while the relationship expressed by the second of the three prepositions (*dia*) is attributed to the one Lord, Jesus Christ ('through whom [are] all things and we through him'). The fact that, in Romans 11:36, all three prepositions apply to God whereas, in 1 Corinthians 8:6, one of them applies to Christ, does not mean that they no longer all describe the Creator's relationship to the whole of creation. On the contrary, it means precisely that Christ is included in this relationship as the instrumental cause of creation.

The variation between 'all things' and 'we' in 1 Corinthians 8:6 results from Paul's desire to situate himself and his readers within the 'all things' who are thus related to their Creator. In this way, Paul is continuing the emphasis of the *hēmin* ('for us') with which he began his adaptation of the Shema‛, and reflecting the Shema‛'s own reference to 'the Lord *our* God'. He wishes it to be clear that the God whose unique identity is characterized by being the Creator of all things has that identity not only for all things in general, but specifically *for us*, who therefore owe exclusive allegiance to this God. The fact that Paul associates 'all things' with one preposition ('from whom all things'), 'we' with another ('we for him'), and both 'all things' and 'we' with the last preposition ('through whom all things and we through him'), is a rhetorical variation adapted to the needs of verbal symmetry. Paul does not mean that 'we' are not also 'from God' or that 'all things' are not also 'for God'. The whole is a condensed form of what would otherwise have been the more cumbersome and less symmetrical formulation:

one God, the Father,
  from whom [are] all things and we from him,
  for whom [are] all things and we for him,
and one Lord, Jesus Christ,
  through whom [are] all things and we through him.

By formulating his version of the Shemaᶜ in terms both of God's relationship to 'all things' and of his relationship to 'us', Paul reflects the two aspects of the divine identity according to the Shemaᶜ, as Jews of this period understood it: the one God is both the God of his covenant people and the universal God.

In conclusion, therefore, we can say that Paul is carefully and profoundly faithful to Jewish monotheism's understanding of the Shemaᶜ in both its affirmation that YHWH, the God of Israel, is the one and only God, and in its requirement that this one God's people be exclusively devoted to him. The only (!) novel element in Paul's reformulation is the inclusion of Jesus Christ within the unique divine identity so understood.

5.3. *John 10:30*

I and the Father are one.

It is surprising that this does not seem to have been previously recognized as an allusion to the Shemaᶜ, but we have already noticed (in the discussion of Rom. 3:28–30) that the formula 'God is one' was a common abbreviation of the Shemaᶜ. It is true that, in all Greek echoes of the Shemaᶜ, the word for one is masculine (*heis*), as we should expect, whereas in John 10:30 it is neuter (*hen*). But this is a necessary adaptation of language. Jesus is not saying that he and the Father are a single person, but that together they are one God. The statement should perhaps be understood as Jesus' understanding of the Shemaᶜ, corresponding to the allusion to the Shemaᶜ by 'the Jews' in 8:41: 'we have one Father, God' (cf. Mal. 2:10).

Jesus' assertion of oneness with the Father occurs twice more in the Gospel, both in the prayer of chapter 17, where Jesus prays that his disciples 'may be one, as we are one' (17:11: *ōsin hen kathōs hēmeis*; 17:22: *ōsin hen kathōs hēmeis hen*). This analogy between the oneness of Jesus and his Father, on the one hand, and the oneness of the disciples, on the other, has been used to argue that the former indicates no more than closeness of association or concurrence of will. But again the background in Jewish monotheistic reflection will clarify the issue considerably. Jewish writers sometimes say that to the one God there corresponds 'one' of something else in what belongs especially to him in the world: one holy city, one temple, one altar, one law, and especially one chosen people (*2 Bar.* 48:23–4; Josephus, *A.J.* 4.201; 5.111; *C. Ap.* 2.193; Philo, *Spec.* 1.52, 67; cf. also *2 Bar.* 85:14). Such formulations presumably lie behind the creedal list of seven 'ones' (also related to the Shema') in Ephesians 4:4–5: 'one body and one Spirit ... one hope of your calling, one Lord, one faith, one baptism, one God and Father of all' (cf. 1 Cor. 12:13).

For the particular case of one people corresponding to the one God, there may be an Old Testament source. In the Old Testament, this correspondence is found only in 2 Samuel 7:22–23,[105] but the context in David's prayer makes this an important passage, which would have been well known and could easily have been connected with Ezekiel 37:15–28, where the repeated use of 'one' does not apply to God but does to Israel, who are to be 'one nation' under 'one king' (37:22) or 'one shepherd' (37:24). In Ezekiel 34:23, the 'one shepherd' is 'my servant David'. This last passage evidently influenced John 10:16 ('one flock, one shepherd'), showing that John's interest in oneness language has Old Testament roots.

The Jewish *topos* that correlates one God with one people, of course, in no way implies that God is a unity in the same sense as his people are. Josephus and Philo understand the correspondence in the sense that service and worship of the one God unites the people of God into one (Josephus, *A.J.* 5.111; Philo, *Spec.* 1.52; 4.159; *Virt.* 7.35). The divine singularity draws the singular people of God together into a relational unity. It is this kind of unity that the Johannine Jesus desires for his people. He prays that his disciples be a single community corresponding to the uniqueness of the one God in which he and his Father are united (17:11, 22).

The Johannine Jesus' claim to oneness with the Father amounts to including himself with his Father in the unique identity of the one God as understood in Jewish monotheism. Within this divine identity, there is the uniquely intimate relationship of the Father and the Son. The oneness statements are clearly related to the statements of reciprocity: 'I am in the Father and the Father is in me' (10:38; 14:10, 11; cf. also 14:20; 17:21, 23). The first of these, in 10:38, is the climax of Jesus' defence of

---

[105] Only the people are explicitly called 'one', but the parallel between v. 22 (about YHWH) and v. 23 (about Israel) is so clear that it is natural to think that a correspondence between the 'one' people and the 'one' God is implicit. Against correcting 'one' (*'eḥad*) to 'another' (*'aḥer*) in v. 23, in accordance with the LXX, see N. Lohfink and J. Bergman in TDOT 1:198.

his earlier claim that 'I and the Father are one' (10:30). Both are taken to be blasphemous, and clearly they are, in some sense, equivalent claims. Evidently, this reciprocal indwelling – the closest conceivable intimacy of relationship – is the inner reality of the oneness of Father and Son. Their unity does not erase their difference, but differentiates them in an inseparable relationship.[106] We should also notice that the terms 'Father' and 'Son' entail each other. The Father is called Father only because Jesus is his Son, and Jesus is called Son only because he is the Son of his divine Father. Each is essential to the identity of the other. So to say that Jesus and the Father are one is to say that the unique divine identity comprises the relationship in which the Father is who he is only in relation to the Son and vice versa. It is in the portrayal of this intra-divine relationship that John's Christology steps outside the categories of Jewish monotheistic definition of the unique identity of the one God. It does not at all deny or contradict any of these (especially since the Shema᾿ asserts the uniqueness of God, not his lack of internal self-differentiation) but, from Jesus' relationship of sonship to God, it redefines the divine identity as one in which Father and Son are inseparably united in differentiation from each other.

There is much else in New Testament Christology to show that early Christians presupposed the Jewish monotheism of the late Second Temple period and its monotheistic reading of the Hebrew Bible. But these three case studies of New Testament interpretation of the Shema᾿ are examples that make the point with reference to early Judaism's central affirmation of the uniqueness of YHWH. The christological innovations – remarkable as they are – cannot be properly understood unless they are seen to work with – not at all to abandon – precisely the contours of early Jewish monotheism. With the inclusion of Jesus in the unique identity of YHWH, the faith of the Shema᾿ is affirmed and maintained, but everything the Shema᾿ requires of God's people is now focused on Jesus. Exclusive devotion is now given to Jesus, but Jesus does not thereby replace or compete with God the Father, since he himself belongs to the unique divine identity. Devotion to him is also devotion to his Father.

---

[106] M.L. Appold, *The Oneness Motif in the Fourth Gospel* (WUNT 2/1; Tübingen: Mohr [Siebeck], 1976), 281–2.

3

The 'Most High' God and the Nature of Early Jewish Monotheism[1]

1. Introduction

The nature of Jewish monotheism in the late Second Temple period has been much discussed and debated in recent decades.[2] Such discussion can now make significant progress mainly, in my view, through careful study of the ways Jewish writers of the period talk about God. There is a huge amount of evidence, but little study of it. It would be extremely useful, for example, to have complete listings of the use of various divine names and titles in early Jewish literature, because only then can we observe which were popular, which were not, in which types or categories of literature. Then we shall be able to write the kind of close studies of such terms in early Jewish literature that TWOT/TDOT provides for the Hebrew Bible. The present chapter is a step in that direction. The table at the end of the chapter lists all the occurrences, so far as I have tracked them, of the title 'the Most High' in early Jewish literature. The chapter attempts to account for this title's relatively high frequency, asks about its significance and seeks thereby to shed some light on the nature of early Jewish monotheism.

In order to situate the discussion, it will be helpful to begin with some comments on the distinction between 'exclusive' and 'inclusive' monotheism. The terms are used by William Horbury in a recent study

---

[1] This essay was first published in David B. Capes, April D. DeConick, Helen K. Bond and Troy A. Miller ed., *Israel's God and Rebecca's Children: Christology and Community in Early Judaism and Christianity: Essays in Honor of Larry W. Hurtado and Alan F. Segal* (Waco: Baylor University Press, 2007), 39–53.
[2] Among recent contributions, see especially Loren T. Stuckenbruck and Wendy E.S. North, ed., *Early Jewish and Christian Monotheism* (JSNTSup 263; London: T&T Clark [Continuum], 2004).

of 'Jewish and Christian Monotheism in the Herodian Age'.[3] He states
the argument of his paper thus:

> It is argued overall that the interpretation of Judaism as a rigorous
> monotheism, 'exclusive' in the sense that the existence of other divine
> beings is denied, does less than justice to the importance of mystical and
> messianic tendencies in the Herodian age – for these were often bound
> up with an 'inclusive' monotheism, whereby the supreme deity was
> envisaged above but in association with other spirits and powers.[4]

The problem here is the meaning of 'other divine beings', a term
that Horbury apparently equates with 'other spirits and powers'. If
it supposed that 'rigorous' or 'exclusive' monotheism must deny the
existence of any supernatural or heavenly beings besides God, then it
is clear that such monotheism never existed until the modern period.
Traditional monotheism in the Jewish, Christian and Islamic traditions
has always accepted the existence of vast numbers of supernatural
beings: angels who serve and worship God, demons who oppose God
within an overall sovereignty of God over all. But such beings have
been considered creatures, created by and subject to God, no more a
qualification of monotheism than the existence of earthly creatures is.
With this view of their nature, we can properly and, in my view, still
usefully speak of 'rigorous' or 'exclusive' monotheism.

Misunderstanding of this point has recurrently muddied the waters
of recent discussion of early Jewish monotheism.[5] The key question
is how the uniqueness of the one God is understood. In 'inclusive'
monotheism, the one God is the highest member of a class of beings
to which he[6] belongs. He is unique only in the sense of superlative: he
is the most powerful of the gods (and can therefore subject them to his
will), the wisest, has his residence higher in the cosmos than all others,
and so forth. He is unique in the sense of supreme. Something like
this view of God and the gods developed in antiquity out of an older
polytheism in which the gods acted independently and competitively.

---

[3] William Horbury, 'Jewish and Christian Monotheism in the Herodian Age,' in *Early Jewish,*
ed. Stuckenbruck and North, 16–44; cf. also idem, *Messianism among Jews and Christians*
(London/New York: T&T Clark, 2003), 12–19, where he takes issue with my arguments in
God Crucified.

[4] Horbury, 'Jewish,' 17.

[5] E.g. Hayman, 'Monotheism,' 1–15; Michael Mach, 'Concepts of Jewish Monotheism during
the Hellenistic Period,' in *The Jewish Roots of Christological Monotheism: Papers from the St.
Andrews Conference on the Historical Origins of the Worship of Jesus,* ed. Carey C. Newman,
James R. Davila and Gladys S. Lewis (JSJSup 63; Leiden: Brill, 1999), 21–42.

[6] In the ancient world, such a god is always grammatically 'he'.

It developed over much of the Near Eastern and, later, the Hellenistic and Roman worlds in antiquity.[7] It takes a 'gradient' view of reality that does not draw sharp ontological distinctions between the supreme God and other gods, or between gods and humans.[8]

By contrast, 'exclusive' monotheism understands the uniqueness of the one God in terms of an absolute difference in kind from all other reality. We could call it transcendent uniqueness. It means that there is no class of beings to which God belongs and of which he can be the supreme instance. It takes a 'binary' view of reality.[9] In my view, early Jewish literature (with few, if any, exceptions) is strongly committed to such a view by the way it constantly understands the uniqueness of the God of Israel as that of the one Creator of all things and the one sovereign Ruler of all things.[10] Because these definitions of God's uniqueness drive an absolute difference of kind between God and 'all things', they override any older gradient features of the Israelite-Jewish worldview (such as survive in some of the vocabulary used) and create an essentially binary view of reality. This does not and need not deny the existence of many heavenly beings, but simply insists that they are created by God and subject to the sovereign will of God. In early Judaism, the binary distinction between God and all other reality was observed and inculcated – in daily religious observance – by monolatry. In a gradient worldview (such as the pagan, inclusive monotheism of antiquity), many beings are accorded honour, each to a degree appropriate to its rank in the cosmic scale. Early Judaism turned monolatry (which had originally been a concomitant of henotheism) into a powerful symbol of exclusive monotheism. While appropriate honour might be accorded high-ranking creatures (but not in contexts where it might be mistaken for divine worship, and so usually not to angels or to rulers who claimed divinity), worship was different because it *was* acknowledgement of the transcendent uniqueness of the God of Israel. Study of Jewish God-talk in the Second Temple period must be alert to these distinctions if it is to achieve more than superficial understanding.

---

[7] See Martin L. West, 'Towards Monotheism,' in *Pagan Monotheism in Late Antiquity*, ed. Polymnia Athanassiadi and Michael Frede (Oxford: Clarendon, 1999), 21–40, here 21–9.

[8] This is not to deny that steps towards a stronger definition of the uniqueness of God can be found in pagan monotheism, especially that of the philosophers; cf. Michael Frede, 'Monotheism and Pagan Philosophy in Later Antiquity,' in Athanassiadi and Frede, *Pagan Monotheism*, 41–67.

[9] I borrow the terminology 'gradient' and 'binary' from David H. Aaron, *Biblical Ambiguities: Metaphors, Semantics, and Divine Imagery* (Leiden: Brill, 2001) without meaning to agree with all the uses to which he puts these terms.

[10] Richard Bauckham, 'The Throne of God and the Worship of Jesus,' in *Jewish Roots*, ed. Newman, Davila and Lewis, 43–69, here 45–8.

There are several reasons why investigation of the divine title or name 'the Most High' should be important for the nature of early Jewish monotheism. In the first place, it was remarkably common. In the Hebrew Bible, excluding Daniel,[11] it occurs thirty-one times.[12] According to my calculations, set out in the table, there are no fewer than 284 occurrences in literature we can, with certainty or reasonable probability, date to the period 250 BCE to 150 CE.[13] This figure is the more impressive when we notice that the voluminous works of Philo and Josephus – much the largest corpora of Jewish literature from this period – account for only fourteen of these 284 occurrences. But, secondly, another comparison with the usage of the Hebrew Bible is illuminating. There, with the only partial exception of Genesis 14:18–22,[14] the title is found exclusively in poetic passages, mostly psalms (which account for twenty-one of the thirty-four instances). In the literature of early Judaism, on the other hand, this title occurs across all the main genres of literature that were used. Clearly the title came into much more general use in the later Second Temple period than had been the case previously. But, thirdly, this conclusion appears correct only with regard to Palestinian Jewish literature. Of the 284 occurrences, 250 are in Palestinian Jewish literature,[15] only thirty-four in literature from the western Diaspora.[16] This difference cries out for some explanation.

---

[11] I exclude Daniel from this count and include it in early Jewish literature simply because it so clearly belongs chronologically with the latter.

[12] Gen. 14:18, 19, 20, 21; Num. 24:10; Deut. 32:8; 2 Sam. 22:14; Ps. 7:18(17); 9:3(2); 21:8(7); 46:5(4); 47:3(2); 50:14; 57:3(2); 73:11; 77:11(10); 78:17, 35, 56; 82:6; 83:19(18); 87:5; 91:1, 9; 92:2(1); 97:9; 107:11; Isa. 14:14; Lam. 3:35, 38. For conjectural emendations that, if accepted, would supply a few other instances, see Hans-Jürgen Zobel, 'עֶלְיוֹן, 'elyôn,' TDOT 11:121–39, here 122–3; Baruch A. Levine, *Numbers 21–36* (AB 4A; New York: Doubleday, 2000), 188, 193–4 (Num. 24:3).

[13] The Enoch literature collected in *1 Enoch* accounts for only seventeen of these occurrences. There is therefore no substance at all to Margaret Barker's claim that the use in *1 Enoch* is evidence of continuity between the Enoch literature and the Elyon cult of the First Temple (Margaret Barker, *The Older Testament: The Survival of Themes from the Ancient Royal Cult in Sectarian Judaism and Early Christianity* [London: SPCK, 1987], 246). The occurrences in *1 Enoch* are part of a much broader phenomenon.

[14] Even here the other uses are ancillary to the two occurrences in the liturgical blessing of 14:19–20.

[15] Major works of Palestinian Judaism that do not use it include 1 Maccabees and the Psalms of Solomon.

[16] Martin Hengel, *Judaism and Hellenism*, trans. J. Bowden (London: SCM, 1974), 298, misleadingly states that 'the designation "Hypsistos" … appears particularly often in the early evidence from the diaspora'. The evidence he cites from R. Marcus (200–1, n. 265) consists of only twelve passages in Diaspora literature (the references to *Sib. Or.* 1, *Sib. Or.* frg. 1, Ezek. Trag., Ph. E. Poet, Wis., 2 Macc., 3 Macc., given in my list), besides some inscriptional evidence.

In addition to the pattern of usage, there are also reasons why the use of this title in particular may throw light on the question of the nature of the Jewish monotheism of the period. In the first place, it is usually thought that the Hebrew term עליון (sometimes אל עליון), meaning 'the Most High', designates this god 'the highest god', supreme over other gods.[17] It is also common to associate this title with the idea of a council of the gods at which Elyon presides. We might therefore expect it, in early Judaism, to be associated with an inclusive monotheism that envisages many divine beings among whom the 'one' God is supreme. But then, secondly, we should notice how easily this inclusive monotheistic sense could attach to the usual Greek translation of the term. In the Septuagint, the divine title עליון is always translated as ὁ ὕψιστος (אל עליון as ὁ θεος ὁ ὕψιστος). This word was in widespread non-Jewish use to designate the supreme God. For example, Celsus, the second-century pagan critic of Christianity, says that 'it makes no difference whether we call Zeus the Most High (Ὕψιστον), or Zen, or Adonai, or Sabaoth, or Amon like the Egyptians, or Papaeus like the Scythians' (*apud* Origen, *Cels.* 5.41).[18] Celsus accepted a supreme God, the Most High God, known by various names to various peoples, including the Jews, but thought the Jews quite mistaken in abandoning the worship of other gods (1.23).

2. Interpretation of Deuteronomy 32:8–9

An important biblical text about the Most High that has played a prominent part in discussion of Jewish monotheism is Deuteronomy 32:8–9. There are important differences between the Masoretic Hebrew, the Septuagint Greek and Hebrew texts from Qumran (4QDeut[j]).[19] The MT reads

When the Most High (עליון) apportioned the nations,
when he divided humankind (בני אדם),
he fixed the boundaries of the peoples
according to the number of the sons of Israel (בני ישראל);
for YHWH's portion is his people,
Jacob his allotted share.

---

[17] Zobel, 'עֶלְיוֹן,' 126.
[18] Translation from Henry Chadwick, *Origen: Contra Celsum* (Cambridge; CUP, 1965), 297; cf. Also *Cels.* 1.24; 8.69.
[19] For the textual issues see P. Sanders, *The Provenance of Deuteronomy 32* (Oudtestamentliche Studiën 37; Leiden: Brill, 1996), 154–60.

In place of 'the sons of Israel', the Qumran text has 'the sons of God'
(בני אל[20]) and the LXX 'the angels of God' (ἀγγέλων θεοῦ). 'The angels of
God' in the Greek is doubtless a translation of the Hebrew as attested
by the Qumran manuscript. The MT looks like a modification of the
text motivated by concern for monotheism, but both forms of the text
were evidently extant in the Second Temple period.

As far as the relationship of the two divine names (Most High,
YHWH) goes, there are two possible ways of reading the text. On one
reading, the Most High apportions the nations to his sons ('the sons
of God' in 4QDeut[j]), of whom YHWH is one. According to the other
reading, the Most High and YHWH are the same. In his exercise of
universal sovereignty over the nations (as the Most High), he allocates
them to the heavenly beings of his entourage ('the sons of God' in
4QDeut[j]), but reserves Israel for his own direct rule (as YHWH the
covenant God of Israel).

The former reading has been claimed as the original meaning of the
text,[21] but it is hard to believe that, in its present context in Deuteronomy
32, it could ever have been read in this way (cf. YHWH's words in
32:39, which hardly leave room for his subordination to another god).[22]
Margaret Barker is obliged to admit: 'how such a "polytheistic" piece
came to be included in Deuteronomy, with its emphasis on monotheism,
is a question we cannot answer.'[23] But this reading of the text is the
foundation stone for her argument that, in the pre-exilic temple cult,
YHWH was worshipped as the son of the high God and that this belief
survived to become the source of early Christology, in which Jesus
was identified with YHWH and God his Father with the Most High.
Deuteronomy 32:8–9 seems indispensable to this case, since scarcely
any other text in the Hebrew Bible can be read as designating YHWH
a son of God.[24]

Moreover, Barker's argument that this 'ditheistic' reading of
Deuteronomy 32:8–9 survived to become available to the first Christians
in the Judaism they knew ignores the good evidence we have for the
interpretation of this text in early Judaism:

---

[20] The text is fragmentary: אל, אלים and אלהים are all possible.

[21] E.g. Mark S. Smith, *Early History*, 7–8; Gnuse, *No Other Gods*, 182.

[22] Note also that 'created' (קנך) in 32:6 is typically El/Elyon language (cf. Gen. 14:19, 22), but has
YHWH as its subject: see John Day, *Yahweh and the Gods and Goddesses of Canaan* (JSOTSup
265; Sheffield: Sheffield Academic Press, 2000), 20. For other features of El attributed to
YHWH in Deut. 32:6–7, see Mark S. Smith, *Early History*, 11.

[23] Barker, *Great Angel*, 6.

[24] Barker, *Great Angel*, 6–7, can only read Job 1–2 and Ps. 29:1 in this way because she reads
them in the light of her interpretation of Deut. 32:8–9. Contrast, for example, Day, *Yahweh*,
22.

He appointed a ruler (ἡγούμενον) for every nation,
But Israel is the Lord's own portion (Sir. 17:17).[25]

And he sanctified them [Israel] and gathered them from all the sons of man because (there are) many nations and many people, and they all belong to him, but over all of them he caused spirits to rule so that they might lead them astray from following him. But over Israel he did not cause any angel or spirit to rule because he alone is their ruler and he will protect them and he will seek for them at the hand of his angels and at the hand of his spirits and at the hand of all his authorities so that he might guard them and bless them and they might be his and he might be theirs henceforth and forever (*Jub.* 15:31–32).[26]

But from the sons of Isaac one would become a holy seed and he would not be counted among the nations because he would become the portion of the Most High and all his seed would fall (by lot) to the Lord, a (special) possession from all people, and so that he might become a kingdom of priests and a holy people (*Jub.* 16:17–18).[27]

When God divided and partitioned off the nations of the soul, separating those of one common speech from those of another tongue, and causing them to dwell apart; when he dispersed and put away from himself the children of earth, then did he fix the boundaries of the offspring of virtue corresponding to the number of the angels … But what are the portions of his angels, and what is the allotted share of the All-sovereign Ruler (τοῦ παντάρχου καὶ ἡγεμόνος)? The particular virtues belong to the servants, to the Ruler the chosen race of Israel (Philo, *Post.* 91–92).[28]

Marvel not at all, then, if the title of special portion of God the universal Ruler, to whom sovereignty over all pertains (τοῦ πανηγεμόνος θεοῦ τὸ ἐφ᾽ ἅπασι κράτος), is bestowed upon the company of wise souls, whose vision is supremely keen … Is not this the explanation of that utterance in the Greater Song [Deut. 32:7–9]? (Philo, *Plant.* 58–59).[29]

It is clear that all these interpretations of Deuteronomy 32:8–9, including Philo's allegorical interpretations (which presuppose a literal reading), take the Most High and YHWH in the text to be one and the same. They derive from three very different forms of early Judaism. The passages from Philo are of particular interest in revealing Philo's understanding of the title 'the Most High'. He took it to refer to God's sovereign rule

---

[25] NRSV. This verse is not extant in Hebrew.
[26] Translation from O.S. Wintermute, 'Jubilees,' in *The Old Testament Pseudepigrapha*, ed. James H. Charlesworth (London: Darton, Longman & Todd, 1985), 2:34–142, here 87.
[27] Translation from Wintermute, 'Jubilees,' 88.
[28] This is part of an allegorical exegesis of Deut 32:7–9, quoted in *Post.* 89. Translation by F.H. Colson and G.H. Whitaker in LCL.
[29] Translation by F.H. Colson and G.H. Whitaker in LCL.

over all things – one of the essential elements in the early Jewish understanding of God.

Early Jews and early Christians were, of course, capable of innovative exegesis. Given an appropriate theology, it was possible for any such exegete to adopt a ditheistic interpretation of this text, but we have no evidence that anyone did so before Eusebius of Caesarea in the early fourth century.[30] This is not a text that features in the rabbinic discussion of the 'two powers in heaven' heresy.[31]

William Horbury does not accept Barker's idea of a Jewish ditheism based on Deuteronomy 32:8–9, but he does call that biblical text, along with the interpretations of it in Sirach 17:17 and Jubilees 15:31, 'clear expressions of an inclusive monotheism'.[32] But this begs the question of the nature of those beings to whom the Most High allotted the Gentile nations. We should note that all these post-biblical texts, like the LXX, avoid calling them 'sons of God' (as in 4QDeut[j]). Philo, following the LXX, calls them 'angels', while Ben Sira calls them 'rulers', and Jubilees 'his angels', 'his spirits' and 'his authorities'. There is nothing to suggest their 'divinity'. In all cases, they are entirely subject to God, while in Jubilees, at least, they are unequivocally beings created by God (2:2). Jubilees, and perhaps Ben Sira, understand them to be beings worshipped as 'gods' by the Gentile nations, but this acceptance that the 'gods' of the nations exist does not entail that they exist *as* gods, as in any way comparable with YHWH the Most High God, who created and rules over them. Deuteronomy, in fact, calls the gods of the nations 'non-gods' (32:17: לא אלה, οὐ θεῷ; 32:21: לא אל, οὐ θεῷ): they exist, no doubt, but are not fit to be called gods,[33] any more than human rulers are. The mere existence of supernatural beings does not make 'inclusive monotheism'.

3. The 'Most High' in early Jewish literature

It is not possible to explain why specifically this divine title is used in every one of its occurrences. Sometimes, no doubt, it is used for the sake of variation, especially in poetic parallelism, and some writers

---

[30] Eusebius, *Dem. ev.* 4.9, quoted in Barker, *Great Angel*, 192. It should be noted that Eusebius' theology was rather closer to Arius than to Nicene Trinitarians, and could appropriately be called ditheistic.

[31] Segal, *Two Powers*.

[32] Horbury, 'Jewish,' 19.

[33] On the uniqueness of YHWH in Deuteronomy, see chapter 2 above, where I take issue to some extent with MacDonald, *Deuteronomy*.

use it more habitually than others. Nevertheless, a large percentage of the occurrences belong to three identifiable fields of associations.[34] These are:

3.1. *Temple, cult and prayer*

Often the Most High is the God to whom one has access in the temple rituals. The repeated use of this title in Ben Sira's description of temple worship (Sir. 50:1–21: significantly seven times) corresponds to usage in many other texts. The temple itself can be called the house or temple of the Most High.[35] This title is commonly associated with sacrifice,[36] with worship, praise and thanksgiving,[37] and with blessing (i.e. pronouncing God's blessing on people).[38] Prayer, whether or not offered in the temple, is often to the Most High and it is the Most High who answers prayer.[39] A select few (Melchizedek, Levi and the Hasmoneans) are called 'priests of the Most High (God)'.[40]

3.2. *God's sovereign rule over all things*

The holy of holies in the temple on earth corresponds to the throne-room of God in the heights of heaven. This is why the God who is accessible to his people in the temple is called 'the Most High'. It is as the one who is supreme over all things that praise and prayer are addressed to him. In many cases, use of the title 'the Most High' is accompanied by other

---

[34] For these usages in the Hebrew Bible, see Zobel, 'עֶלְיוֹן, 126–7. Robert C.T. Hayward, 'El Elyon and the Divine Names in Ben Sira,' in *Ben Sira's God*, ed. Renate Egger-Wenzel (BZAW 321; Berlin: de Gruyter, 2002), 180–8, provides a detailed study of Ben Sira's usage. A particular usage that does not fit obviously within these three fields is 'the law of the Most High': Sir. 9:15; 19:17; 23:23; 41:8; 42:2; 44:20; 49:4; 4Q525 [2QBeat] 2 24; 11Q5 [11QPs^a] 18:14; cf. (using terms equivalent to 'law') Ps. 78:56; 107:11; 2 *Bar.* 77:4; 82:6; *Jub.* 21:23; 1 *En.* 99:10; *Sib. Or.* 3:580, 719. On this usage in Ben Sira, see Hayward, 'El Elyon,' 185–7.

[35] Ps. 46:4(5); Sir. 50:7; Tob. 1:4; 2 *Bar.* 80:3; Philo, *Flacc.* 46; *Legat.* 278. Cf. Ps-Eupolemus 1:5.

[36] Sir. 7:9; 34:23; 35:8, 12; 50:14, 15; 1Qap Gen^{ar} 10:17–18; 21:2, 20; Tob. 4:11; Cairo Genizah *T.Levi* (Bodl. d 16); 1 Esd. 6:30(31); Philo, *Legat.* 157, 317.

[37] Ps. 7:18(17); 9:3(2); 50:14; 92:2(1); Dan. 4:31(34); Sir. 17:27; 47:8; 50:17; *Jub.* 16:27; 20:9; 4Q242 [4QPrNab ar] 1–3 5; Ps. 154:3, 10; 11Q5 [11QPs^a] 22:15; 4Q291 1 3; 1 Esd. 9:46. Cf. vows: Ps. 50:14.

[38] Sir. 50:21; *Jub.* 22:11, 13, 19; 25:11; 36:16; 1Qap Gen^{ar} 22:16; 11Q14 1 2:4, 7; Jdt. 13:18.

[39] Ps. 57:3(2); Sir. 35:21; 39:5; 46:5; 47:5; 50:19; 2 *Bar.* 64:8; 71:2; *Jub.* 12:19; 13:16, 29; 22:6; 25:11; 1 *En.* 9:3; 4Q242 [4QPrNab ar] 1–3 3; 3 Macc. 6:2. Prayers made away from the temple might well be associated with the temple because offered to the God who makes himself accessible to his people in the temple, and as assisted by the sacrifices and incense offerings in the temple.

[40] Gen. 14:18; *Jub.* 32:1; 1Qap Gen^{ar} 22:15; *T. Mos.* 6:1; Cairo Genizah *T. Levi* (Bodl. b 5–6); Philo, *Leg.* 3:82; Josephus, *A.J.* 16:163.

indications that this God is the universal Ruler.[41] Closely related is the use of this title in connection with God's judgement.[42]

3.3. Use by or to Gentiles

Evidently this title was thought appropriate for Gentiles to use when referring to the God of Israel as the supreme God (thirty-two occurrences)[43] or for Jews (and heavenly beings) to use when addressing Gentiles (nineteen occurrences).[44] Some of the uses by Gentiles are undoubtedly authentic (notably those by the Emperor Augustus in Josephus, *A.J.* 16.163; Philo, *Legat.* 157, 317),[45] but probably the usage also became a Jewish literary convention. Some of these instances overlap with others: e.g. Philo, addressing Gentiles, calls the Jerusalem temple 'the temple of the Most High God' (Philo, *Flacc.* 46; *Legat.* 278), while Pseudo-Solomon tells Gentile kings: 'your dominion was given you from the Lord, and your sovereignty from the Most High' (Wis. 6:3). Indeed, it was this connotation of universal sovereignty that made this title for the Jewish God appropriate for Gentiles. Over the course of the Second Temple period, it took the place of the title 'God of heaven' that had played this role in early post-exilic Jewish literature.[46]

---

[41] Pss. 47:3(2); 83:19(18); 97:9 ('over all the earth'); Sir. 50:15 ('king of all'); Dan. 4:14(17), 21(24), 22(25), 29(32), 31(34); 5:18, 21 ('sovereign over all human kingdoms'); *Jub.* 22:27 ('God of all,' 'Creator of all'); 1Qap Gen^ar 20:12–13 ('Lord and Master of everything and rule all the kings of the earth'); 22:21 ('Lord of heaven and earth'); 4Q491 15 6–7 ('over all the nations'); 4Q550c 3:1 ('governs the whole earth'); Philo, *Plant.* 58–59 ('the universal Ruler, to whom sovereignty over all pertains'); Philo, *Post.* 89–92 ('the All-sovereign Ruler'); 3 Macc. 6:2 ('governing all creation'); Ph. E. Poet 3 ('Lord of all'); Ps-Aeschylus ('power over all'). For other uses of 'Most High' that clearly connote universal lordship, see Sir. 41:4; 1 Esd. 2:2(3); *Sib. Or.* 3:718 ('he alone is sovereign').

[42] Ps. 82:8; *2 Bar.* 13:8; *Jub.* 39:6; *1 En.* 9:3; 10:1; 97:2; 100:4; 1Qap Gen^ar 20:12–13, 16; *T. Mos.* 10:7; *Sib. Or.* 1:179; 3:519, 718.

[43] Gen. 14:19–20; Dan. 3:26, 32(4:2); 4:14(17), 21(24), 22(25), 29(32), 31(34); 5:18, 21; *2 Bar.* 80:3; 4Q242 [4QPrNab ar] 1–3 3, 5, 6; Philo, *Legat.* 157, 317; 1 Esd. 2:2(3); 6:30(31); 8:19, 21; *Sib. Or.* 3:519, 574, 580, 719; *Sib. Or.* 1:179, 200; Ezek. Trag. 239; 3 Macc. 7:9; 2 Macc. 3:31; Josephus, *A.J.* 16:163; Ps-Aeschylus. Acts 16:17 is a New Testament instance of this usage.

[44] Gen. 14:22; Dan. 4:14(17), 21(24), 22(25), 29(32); 5:18, 21; 4Q550c 3:1; Philo, *Flacc.* 46; *Legat.* 278; *Sib. Or.* 3:519, 574, 580, 719; *Sib. Or.* 1:179, 200; Wis. 5:15; 6:3; Ps-Aeschylus. The *Sibylline Oracles* are ascribed to the pagan prophetess, the Sybil, and addressed (ostensibly at least) to Gentiles. Wisdom is ostensibly addressed by Solomon to Gentile rulers.

[45] Note also that the Emperor Julian gave the Jews permission to rebuild the temple of the Most High God (τοῦ ὑψίστου θεοῦ): Stephen Mitchell, 'The Cult of Theos Hypsistos between Pagans, Jews and Christians,' in *Pagan Monotheism*, ed. Athanassiadi and Frede, 81–148, here 111 n.82.

[46] Hebrew Bible: 'God of heaven' used by Gentiles: 2 Chr. 26:23; Ezra 1:2; 6:9, 10; 7:12, 21, 23; (Rev. 11:13; 16:11 also conform to this usage); used by Jews addressing Gentiles: Ezra 5:11, 12; Neh. 2:20; Dan. 2:44; Jonah 1:9; also used in Neh. 1:4, 5; 2:4; Ps. 136:26; Dan. 2:18, 19. Post-biblical Jewish literature: Tob. 7:12; 8:15; Jdt. 11:17 (Jew addressing Gentile); 3 Macc. 6:28

One feature of the evidence that these fields of association do not entirely explain is the frequent use of the title 'the Most High' in the two apocalypses, *2 Baruch* and *4 Ezra*, both being from the end of the Second Temple period and closely related to each other. In *4 Ezra*, this title is overwhelmingly dominant (sixty-eight occurrences), except in the seer's direct address to God, where he uses 'Lord' (*domine:* eleven occurrences)[47] or 'Sovereign Lord' (*dominator domine:* nine occurrences).[48] God is never called 'the Lord' in third-person usage. The term 'the Mighty One' (*fortis*) occurs five times, four of these in parallelism with 'the Most High' (6:32; 10:24; 11:43; 12:47) where another divine title was needed for literary reasons.[49] God is called 'God' only four times (7:19, 21, 79; 9:45), two of these in parallel with 'the Most High' (7:19, 79). This overwhelming dominance of the title 'the Most High' in *4 Ezra* has been remarked, but apparently never discussed.[50] In *2 Baruch*, the pattern is different in that this writer uses 'the Mighty One' much more often than 'the Most High' (forty-three occurrences of 'the Mighty One';[51] four of 'the Mighty God';[52] twenty-four of 'the Most High'). But here also 'Lord' occurs only in the seer's direct address to God (twenty-two times, sometimes 'my Lord', sometimes 'Lord, my Lord'), while the word 'God' is hardly used at all (10:1; 54:12).

In general, it could be said that the titles 'the Most High' and 'the Mighty One' are both appropriate in these works, where God is presented overwhelmingly as the one who is sovereign over history and the nations. But it may also be that these titles fill the gap left in Jewish God-talk by, on the one hand, the avoidance of the Tetragrammaton, as normally in this period (and, with it, avoidance of divine titles including YHWH, such as YHWH Sabaoth), and, on the other hand, a tendency to avoid also the word אלהים, because of its ambiguity as a term referring

---

(Gentile speaking); *Jub.* 12:4 (Abraham to his pagan father); 20:7; 22:19 (in parallel with 'God Most High'); cf. also 'Lord of heaven' in Tob. 6:18; 7:11, 16; 10:13; 1Qap Gen^ar 12:17; Cairo Genizah *T.Levi* (Bodl. b 6); *1 En.* 106:11; 'Lord God of heaven' in Jdt. 6:19.

[47] 5:41, 56; 6:38, 55, 57; 8:20, 24, 36, 63; 9:29; 14:2. This presumably represents אדני (not as substitute for YHWH). Ezra also uses it in addressing the angel.

[48] 3:4; 5:23, 38; 6:11; 7:17, 45, 58; 12:7; 13:51. Perhaps this represents יהוה אדני in the original Hebrew.

[49] The fifth instance is 9:45. On this title in *4 Ezra*, see Michael E. Stone, *4 Ezra* (Hermeneia; Minneapolis: Fortress, 1990), 175. The original Hebrew may have been גבור (as in 1Q19 2:5) or אדיר (as in 1QM 19:1).

[50] Cf. Stone, *4 Ezra*, 57; Jacob M. Myers, *I and II Esdras* (AB 42; New York: Doubleday. 1974), 121 ('No particular significance can be attached to these terms'!).

[51] This title is also frequent in the *Apocalypse of Abraham*, along with 'the Eternal One'. Probably in this work these two titles represent אל and יהוה respectively (cf. the combined name Yahoel in 17:13).

[52] 6:8; 7:1; 13:2, 4. It is used by Gentiles in 7:1. The Oxyrhynchus fragment preserves the Greek in 13:2 (ἰσχυροῦ θεοῦ).

very generally to all the gods of all the nations. The major writings of the Qumran sect also avoid using אלהים of God, while using אל.[53] This avoidance of the ordinary word for 'god' is very significant for our understanding of early Jewish monotheism. It indicates a recognition of the transcendent uniqueness of the one God, who cannot belong with others to a class of 'gods'. 'The Most High', on the other hand, is appropriate to the uniqueness of the God of Israel as the one who alone is Sovereign over all things.

3.4. The 'Most High' and the gods

For scholars of the Hebrew Bible, the divine title 'the Most High' (עליון) suggests the divine council in which Elyon presides over other gods, variously called 'gods', 'sons of God/gods' and 'holy ones'. But it is important to note that few biblical texts explicitly bring the title 'the Most High' into connection with lesser gods, however described. This is really only the case in Deuteronomy 32:8–9 (discussed above), Psalm 97:9 ('For you, YHWH, are the Most High over all the earth; you are exalted far above all gods') and Psalm 82:6 ('You are gods, sons of the Most High')[54] where the context is explicitly the divine council.[55] For an early Jewish reader of Scripture, these would be unusual cases that would not necessarily influence his or her own understanding or use of the title 'the Most High'. He or she would be much more likely to be influenced by many passages in which the title is associated with YHWH's transcendent supremacy over all other reality and, especially, the nations. Moreover, we should note that the word עליון itself by no means necessarily conveys the meaning 'highest of the gods'. As Randall Garr puts it, 'the superlative degree of the epithet עליון is not morphologically marked but semantically inferred'.[56] It merely situates God 'on high'.

---

[53] For the possibility that at Qumran אל was sometimes a substitute for יהוה, see Sean M. McDonough, *YHWH at Patmos: Rev. 1:4 in its Hellenistic and Early Jewish Setting* (WUNT 2/107; Tübingen: Mohr Siebeck, 1999), 69–70; Martin Rösel, 'The Reading and Translation of the Divine Name in the Masoretic Tradition and the Greek Pentateuch,' *JSOT* 31 (2007): 411–28, here 414. According to Arthur Marmorstein, *The Old Rabbinic Doctrine of God* (Oxford: OUP, 1927; 2nd edn, Farnborough: Gregg, 1969), 67–8, early rabbinic literature avoids both אל and אלהים.

[54] This is the only instance of בני עליון in the Hebrew Bible. In post-biblical Jewish literature, see Sir. 4:10; 4Q246 [4QapocrDan ar] 2:1.

[55] That Psalm 47 calls on the gods to worship their Ruler, the Most High (Tryggve N.D. Mettinger, *In Search of God: The Meaning and Message of the Divine Names*, trans. Frederick H. Cryer (Philadelphia: Fortress, 1988], 122), is not at all apparent in the text of the psalm itself.

[56] W. Randall Garr, *In His Own Image and Likeness: Humanity, Divinity, and Monotheism* (Culture and History of the Ancient Near East 15; Leiden: Brill, 2003), 211 n. 49.

Finally, we should note that even in Psalm 82:8, the most 'polytheistic' of passages in the Hebrew Bible, the idea of a real kinship of nature between 'the Most High' and his 'sons', the gods, is already contradicted by the former's judgement that the latter 'will die like humans' (Ps. 82:7). The strong impulse to draw an absolute distinction of kind between YHWH and all other reality, characteristic of Second Temple Judaism, is here already at work, despite the use of the very old terminology that was not designed to express that.

It is important to avoid 'reading forward' from the way passages in the Hebrew Bible are understood by modern scholars in search of their original meaning to assumptions about the way such passages would have been read by Jews in the late Second Temple period or the way they would have used the terminology of such passages. This mistake is commonly made in arguments that early Judaism – or parts of it – was not monotheistic, or did not espouse exclusive monotheism. Early Jewish readers of Scripture read it in the context of a monotheizing dynamic that was already at work in the formation of the Hebrew canon.[57] They were not in search of diversity but of uniformity and consistency. They read the 'non-monotheistic' or 'less monotheistic' passages in the light of the strongly monotheistic ones. Language that may originally have had polytheistic significance was refunctioned in early Jewish use in the service of monotheism. The divine title 'the Most High' is a significant case in point.

If there are few passages in the Hebrew Bible that bring this title into relationship with explicit reference to lesser gods, it is even harder to find such passages in the post-biblical literature of early Judaism. One might, for example, cite the Genesis Apocryphon (1Qap Gen[ar] 2:4–5), where Lamech, suspecting his son Noah may be a child of the Watchers, adjures his wife 'by the Most High, by the Great Lord, by the King of all ages' to tell him the truth, and refers to the Watchers as 'the sons of heaven'. But this periphrasis is surely meant to avoid the term 'sons of God', used in Genesis 6:2, 4 and thus to dissociate them from kinship with 'the Most High'. This title, in the literature of early Judaism, does not function to evoke YHWH's presidency of a council of other gods.

Imagery of height is pervasive in early Jewish picturing of God. It pictures God's transcendent supremacy over all things, in heaven or on earth. The very 'lofty' throne of God[58] is situated in the highest of

---

[57] See chapter 2 above.
[58] Isa. 6:1; *1 En.* 14:18; *2 En* 20:3J; Ps-Philo, *L.A.B.* 12:8.

the heavens,[59] or even 'above the heavens',[60] far above all the many ranks of angels that worship and serve him. It represents the absolute sovereignty of God over the whole cosmos. It coheres with one of the essential aspects of the uniqueness of the one God that are repeated everywhere in early Jewish literature:[61] that God is the only sovereign Ruler over all things, while all beings other than God are his creatures, subject to his will.[62] Sometimes this idea of God's unlimited sovereignty is explicitly expressed in the context of use of the title 'the Most High' (e.g. Dan. 4:34–35; 1Qap Gen[ar] 20:12–13; *Jub.* 22:27; 3 Macc. 6:2; Ps-Aeschylus). But, in the context of Second Temple Judaism, the title itself must have evoked this pervasive idea of God. This is surely what explains its widespread popularity.

However, we must notice again that this popularity, as far as the extant literature goes, is largely confined to the writings of Palestinian Judaism. We can now further specify the evidence that almost all the uses in literature from the western Diaspora fall within the third of the three fields of association we identified above: use by or to Gentiles. The only exceptions[63] are 1 Esdras 9:46 ('Ezra blessed the Lord God Most High, the God of hosts, the Almighty'), 3 Maccabees 6:2 (Eleazar the priest prays: 'King of great power, Almighty God Most High, governing all creation with mercy'), Philo the Epic Poet fragment ('the Most High, great Lord of all') and the few occasions on which Philo quotes and discusses those texts in the Greek Pentateuch that use the title.[64] It may not be accidental that, in the three exceptions other than Philo and in several of the exceptions in the works of Philo (*Post.* 91–2; *Plant.* 58–60; *Leg.* 3:82), 'the Most High' is accompanied by other divine titles or descriptions that reinforce the significance of the title 'the Most High' as indicating the unique divine sovereignty over all things. Perhaps, in the Diaspora context, this unpacking of the title was necessary as it does not seem to have been in Palestine.

The difference of use between Palestinian and Diaspora Jewish literature must be related to the fact that the title 'the Most High'

---

[59] *Apoc. Ab.* 19:4; *2 En.* 20–2; *Ques. Ezra* A21

[60] Ps. 8:1; 57:5, 11; 108:5; 113:4; cf. Isa. 66:1; *1 En.* 84:2; Ps-Orpheus B 33–34

[61] God as sole Ruler of all things: e.g. Dan. 4:34–35; Bel 5; Add. Esth. 13:9–11; 16:18, 21; 3 Macc. 2:2–3; 6:2; Wis. 12:13; Sir. 18:1–3; *Sib. Or.* 3:10; 19; *Sib. Or.* frg. 1:7, 15, 17, 35; *1 En.* 9:5; 84:3; *2 Bar.* 54:13; *2 En.* 33:7; 1QH[a] 18:8–10; Josephus, *A.J.* 1.155–6.

[62] See chapter 1 above.

[63] It is worth noting that Celsus, the pagan critic of Christianity, seems to know of the use of ὕψιστος by Jews (*apud* Origen, *Cels.* 1.24; 2.74). Since he also knows of the Jews' use of Adonai and Sabaoth (1.24), there may be some value in his evidence.

[64] Gen. 14:22–23: Philo, *Ebr.* 105; *Leg.* 3:24, 82; Num. 24:16: Philo, *Mut.* 202; Deut. 32:8–9: Philo, *Post.* 89; *Plant.* 59; *Congr.* 58.

(ὕψιστος with or without θεός) was in widespread use by non-Jews.[65] This made it a term for the God of Israel which Gentiles would readily understand, and a term that could, for apologetic purposes, connect with Gentile usage. This accounts for its regular use by or for Gentiles in Diaspora Jewish literature. As Dodd comments:

> the tendency to exalt and worship a supreme God above all other gods is one of the ways in which Greek religious thought approached monotheism. In the Hellenistic world it met Jewish monotheism half-way. The Jews were conscious of this.[66]

But the same currency of the term in Gentile use also made for serious ambiguity. Unlike עליון, ὕψιστος is morphologically a superlative, which might be used in an elative sense ('very high'), but can also be taken as a true superlative, meaning 'the highest' in a series.[67] The latter was its meaning in ordinary Hellenistic religious usage. The god so called was the highest of the gods. This must be why Diaspora Jewish literature, for the most part, avoided it as a properly Jewish usage.

Its absence from the voluminous works of Philo and Josephus is especially striking. Josephus uses it only once, when he is quoting the Emperor Augustus (*A.J.* 16.163). His non-use of it is conspicuous, for example, when he retells the story of Abraham's meeting with Melchizedek (*A.J.* 1.180; cf. *B.W* 6.438). In Genesis 14, the title 'the Most High God' is very prominent, and it is only to be expected that Palestinian Jewish retellings of the story retain it (*Jub.* 13:29; Ps-Eupolemus frg. 1:5). Josephus, however, does not.

Philo, as we have noted, uses the title only when addressing Gentiles or when he quotes and discusses biblical texts that use it. But one of these latter instances is very illuminating. With reference to the phrase 'priest of the Most High God' used of Melchizedek in Genesis 14:18, Philo explains:

---

[65] We have no evidence that עליון or an Aramaic equivalent was used in non-Jewish cults in the Near East at this time. Philo of Byblos (64–141 ce) writes (*ap.* Eusebius, *Praep. ev.* 1.10.14–15) that he found in the Phoenician historian Sanchunyaton (c. 1300 BCE) the divine name Elioun, which he translates as ὕψιστος. This is not evidence for the use of the name in the late Second Temple period. The Zeus Olympios, to whose worship the Jerusalem temple was dedicated (2 Macc. 6:2) by the Hellenizing faction at the beginning of the crisis under Antiochus Epiphanes, seems to have been identified with the Semitic 'Lord of heaven' (*Ba'al shamem*), but there is no evidence that he was called 'the Most High' (עליון). It would seem unlikely that the book of Daniel would have adopted the latter title so prominently if he had been. Hengel, *Judaism,* 297–9, associates too much evidence too indiscriminately.

[66] C.H. Dodd, *The Bible and the Greeks* (London: Hodder & Stoughton, 1935), 12.

[67] Dodd, *Bible,* 12.

not that there is any other [god] not Most High – for God being One 'is in heaven above and on earth beneath, and there is none besides him' [Deut 4:39] – but to conceive of God not in low earthbound ways but in lofty terms, such as transcend all other greatness and all else that is free from matter, calls up in us a picture of the Most High (*Leg.* 3.82).

Philo here deploys a classic Jewish monotheistic formula,[68] both in his own formulation ('not that there is any other') and in a peculiarly appropriate biblical version (Deut 4:39 LXX: 'the Lord your God, he is God in heaven above and in the earth beneath, and there is none besides him'), as well as an echo of the Shema' ('for God being One'). The Most High is not the highest of a pantheon of gods active throughout the heavens and the earth; he is the utterly unique One, the only one in heaven or earth. The misunderstanding of θεὸς ὕψιστος as the highest, but not the only, true God, a misunderstanding easily encountered in a Hellenistic religious context, is what Philo is careful to avert. The rarity of the term in his own writings, and in those of most other Jewish writers in the Mediterranean Diaspora, must be for this reason. As in many other instances, we find Second Temple Jewish writers deliberately dissociating their monotheism from the common pagan pattern of belief in the divine monarchy of a high God who rules as chief of the many gods.

We have confined this discussion to literature. The epigraphic evidence requires separate discussion, since there is so much uncertainty and disagreement about the extent to which Jewish usage is reflected in the inscriptions, and whether there was something like a 'cult of Theos Hypsistos' that spanned the distinctions between Jews, pagans and Christians.[69] At this point, we can only leave open the possibility that, in some popular Jewish usage in the Greek-speaking Diaspora, the title was rather more freely used than it is in the extant literature.

---

[68] Deut. 4:35, 39; 32:39; 1 Sam. 2:2; 2 Sam. 7:22; 1 Kgs. 8:60; 1 Chr. 17:20; Isa. 44:6; 45:5, 6, 14 (*bis*), 18, 21 (*bis*), 22; 46:9; Joel 2:27; cf. 2 Sam. 22:32 = Ps. 18:32; Isa. 64:4; Wis. 12:13; Jdt. 8:20; 9:14; Bel 41; Sir. 18:2; 24:24; 36:5; 1QH^a15:32; 18:9; 20:11, 31; 1Q35 1:6; 4Q377 frg. 1^r 2:8; 4Q504 [4QDibHam^a] frg. 1–2 5:9; 2 *En.* 33:8; 36:1; 47:3; *Sib. Or.* 3:629, 760; 8:377; *Apoc. Ab.* 19:3–4; Ps-Orpheus 16; Philo, *Opif.* 23, 46; *Leg.* 3.4.

[69] Stephen Mitchell, 'The Cult'; Paul R. Trebilco, *Jewish Communities in Asia Minor* (SNTSMS 69; Cambridge: CUP, 1991), 128–40; Irina Levinskaya, *The Book of Acts in Its Diaspora Setting*, vol. 5 of *The Book of Acts in Its First Century Setting* (Grand Rapids: Eerdmans/Carlisle: Paternoster, 1996), chaps. 5–6; William Horbury and D. Noy, *Jewish Inscriptions of Graeco-Roman Egypt* (Cambridge: CUP, 1992), 200–1.

， **TABLE**
God 'Most High' in early Jewish Literature (250 BCE – 150 CE)

Note: Works which can, with reasonable confidence, be identified as (non-Christian) Jewish works and dated before 150 CE are included in the main lists below and divided into works written in Palestine (or, in a few cases, perhaps the Mesopotamian Diaspora) and those written in the western Diaspora. Supplementary lists contain works which many scholars cite as evidence of early Judaism, but about which there are serious doubts as to their early date and/or their non-Christian Jewish provenance.[70]

---

[70] James R. Davila, *The Provenance of the Pseudepigrapha: Jewish, Christian, other?* (JSJSup 105; Leiden: Brill, 2005) makes an important case for greater methodological rigour and caution in judging works in the category of 'Old Testament Pseudepigrapha' to be (non-Christian) Jewish works. In particular, he shows that this cannot be assumed just because a work lacks obvious Christian features. I share his doubts about *Joseph and Aseneth* (190–5) and the *Testament of Abraham* (199–207), but I remain convinced that *Sibylline Oracles* book 3 (181–6) and the Wisdom of Solomon (219–25) are so probably non-Christian Jewish that scholars are justified in citing them as such. On the other hand, Davila is right to reject the case recently made by Rivka Nir, *The Destruction of Jerusalem and the Idea of Redemption in the Syriac Apocalypse of Baruch* (SBLEJL 20; Atlanta: SBL, 2003) for considering *2 Baruch* a Christian work. On *Joseph and Aseneth*, see also Ross Shephard Kraemer, *When Aseneth Met Joseph* (New York: OUP, 1998), and my review in *JTS* 51 (2000): 226–8. Dale C. Allison in his excellent work, *Testament of Abraham* (Commentaries on Early Jewish Literature; Berlin: de Gruyer, 2003), is clear that the texts of both recensions of this work, as we have them, have many Christian elements, but still thinks a non-Christian Jewish Ur-text underlying both 'overwhelmingly probable' (28–9). Even this judgement, however, makes the work unusable for our purposes, since there is no way of knowing whether the occurrences of 'Most High' belong to the Ur-text. David Satran, *Biblical Prophets in Byzantine Palestine: Reassessing the Lives of the Prophets* (SVTP 11; Leiden: Brill, 1995) shows that, in their present form, the *Lives of the Prophets* date from the early Byzantine period. They undoubtedly contain early Jewish material, but cannot provide reliable evidence for our present purposes. The *Testaments of the Twelve Patriarchs*, as Marinus de Jonge has long and extensively argued (most recently in *Pseudepigrapha of the Old Testament as Part of Christian Literature: The Case of the Testaments of the Twelve Patriarchs and the Greek Life of Adam and Eve* [SVTP 18; Leiden: Brill, 2003]), are similarly a Christian composition with Jewish sources that cannot be confidently delimited. (The strongest case for a substantial Jewish source is in the case of the *Testament of Levi*, owing to the existence of related Levi material in the Dead Sea Scrolls and Genizah fragments, and some of the occurrences of 'the Most High' plausibly belong to it, but the point cannot be pressed here.) The Prayer of Manasseh may well be Jewish, but a strong case has yet to be made. On the other hand, even though the *Ladder of Jacob* is one of the least studied of the Old Testament Pseudepigrapha included in recent collections, I think the case for regarding chaps. 1–6 as Jewish is strong (see James Kugel, 'The Ladder of Jacob,' *HTR* 88 [1995]: 209–27), especially now that a Hebrew version of the prayer in chap. 2 has been identified (Reimund Leicht, '*Qedushah* and Prayer to Helios: A New Hebrew Version of an Apocryphal Prayer of Jacob,' *JSQ* 6 [1999]: 140–76).

Palestine (and eastern Diaspora)	Number of Occurrences
4 Ezra[71]	68
Ben Sira[72]	47
2 Baruch[73]	24
Jubilees[74]	23
1 Enoch[75]	17
Daniel[76]	14
Genesis Apocryphon (1Qap Gen[ar])[77]	10
Prayer of Nabonidus (4Q242)[78]	4
Psalm 154 (3, 9, 10, 14; = 11Q5 18:1, 6, 7, 14)	4
Qumran War Rule[79]	4
Tobit[80]	3
Qumran Community Rule (1QS 4:22; 10:12; 11:15)	3
4QApocryphon of Joshua[a] (4Q378 26:1, 3, 4)[81]	3
Pseudo-Philo, *Biblical Antiquities* (33:14; 53:2)	2
Testament of Moses (6:1; 10:7)[82]	2
Qumran Thanksgiving Hymns (1QH[a] 12:31; 14:33)[83]	2
Cairo Geniza Testament of Levi (Bodleian b 5–6; d 16)	2

---

[71] In all cases 'the Most High' (*altissimus*). In the following notes, no attention is drawn to Hebrew texts that have only the simple עליון or Greek texts that have only the simple ὕψιστος, but, for other texts, variations (such as 'the Most High God') are noted, as are the terms used in Aramaic texts.

[72] Forty-seven is the number of occurrences in the Greek text (though in four of these cases there are variant readings without ὕψιστος). The title occurs twenty times in the (incomplete) Genizah and Masada Hebrew texts, not always corresponding to the usage in the Greek. Alexander A. Di Lella, in Patrick W. Skehan and Alexander A. Di Lella, *The Wisdom of Ben Sira* (AB 39; New York: Doubleday, 1987), 182, speaks of 'the fluidity of the divine names in the book and its translations'.

[73] 'The Lord Most High': 2 *Bar.* 6:6; 'the Most High': 2 *Bar.* 13:8; 17:1; 24:2; 25:1; 54:17; 56:1; 64:8; 67:3, 7; 69:2; 70:7; 71:2; 76:1; 77:4, 21; 80:1, 3; 81:4; 82:2, 6; 83:1; 85:8, 12.

[74] 'The Most High': *Jub.* 16:18; 'the Most High God': *Jub.* 12:19; 20:9; 22:13, 23; 25:3, 11; 32:1; 'God Most High': 13:16, 29; 16:27; 21:22, 23. 25; 22:6, 19, 27; 25:21; 27:15; 'the Lord Most High': *Jub.* 22:11; 36:16; 39:6; 'the Lord God Most High': *Jub.* 21:20.

[75] 1 *En.* 9:3; 10:1; 46:7; 60:1, 22; 62:7; 77:1; 94:8; 97:2; 98:7, 11; 99:3, 10; 100:4; 101:1, 6, 9 (all 'the Most High').

[76] 'The Most High' (עליא): Dan. 4:14(17), 21(24), 22(25), 29(32), 31(34); 7:25; 'God Most High' (אלהא עליא): Dan. 3:26, 32 (4:2); 5:18, 21; 'the Most High' (עליונין): Dan. 7:18, 22, 25, 27. For the plural form עליונין as referring to God, against other suggestions, see John J. Collins, *Daniel* (Hermeneia; Minneapolis: Fortress, 1993), 312.

[77] 'The Most High' (עליא): 1Qap Gen[ar] 2:4; 10:18; 'God Most High' (אל עליון): 1Qap Gen[ar] 12:17; 20:12, 16; 21:2, 20; 22:15, 16, 21.

[78] 'God Most High' (אלהא עליא): 4Q242 1–3 2, 3, 5, 6.

[79] 11Q14 1 2 4, 7 (= 4Q285 1 3); 4Q491 15 7; 4Q492 1 13.

[80] Tob. 1:4 (AB), 13 (AB, S); 4:11 (AB). These verses are not extant in the Qumran fragments of Tobit.

[81] 'The Most High' (עליון): 26:1, 3; 'God Most High' (אלהים עליון): 26:4.

[82] Both 'the Most High God' (*summus Deus*).

[83] Both 'God Most High' (אל עליון).

	Number of Occurrences
Ladder of Jacob (5:12; 6:8)[84]	2
4QEschatological Hymn (4Q457b 2 3 5, 6)	2
1QBook of Noah (1Q19 2 2)	1
Judith (13:18)	1
Apostrophe to Zion (11Q5 22:15)	1
Compositions of David (11Q5 27:11)[85]	1
Damascus Rule (CD 20:8)	1
4QWork Containing Prayers A (4Q291 1 3)	1
4QAramaic Apocalypse (4Q246 2 1)[86]	1
4QBeatitudes (4Q525 2 24)	1
4QParaphrase of Genesis and Exodus (4Q422 2–6 2:9)	1
4QProto-Esther[d] (4Q550c 3 1)[87]	1
4QKingdoms[a] ar (4Q552 4 2)[88]	1
4QNarrative Work and Prayer (4Q460 5 1:3)	1
4QAramaic C (4Q536 1 8)[89]	1
Pseudo-Eupolemus (frg. 1:5)[90]	1

Palestine (early date and non-Christian Jewish provenance uncertain)

Lives of the Prophets (4:3)	1

Western Diaspora

Philo[91]	13
1 Esdras (2:2[3]; 6:31; 8:19, 21; 9:46)[92]	5
Sibylline Oracles book 3 (519, 574, 580, 719)[93]	4
Sibylline Oracles book 1 (179, 200)[94]	2

---

[84] The occurrence at 7:1 belongs to the later Christian addition to the book.

[85] 'The Most High' (העליון).

[86] 'The Most High' (עליון).

[87] Aramaic עליא.

[88] 'God Most High' (אל עליון).

[89] It is a question whether עליונין should be read as a true plural ('highest ones') or as referring to God, as in Dan. 7:18, 22, 25, 27.

[90] *Apud* Eusebius, *Praep. ev.* 9.17.5. Ps-Eupolemus is widely thought to have been a Samaritan author.

[91] 'The Most High' (ὁ ὕψιστος): Philo, *Post.* 89; *Plant.* 59; *Congr.* 58; *Mut.* 202; 'the Most High God' (ὁ ὕψιστος θεός): Philo, *Leg.* 3.24, 82 [*tris*]; *Ebr.* 105; *Flacc.* 46; *Legat.* 157, 278, 317.

[92] 'The Lord Most High' (κύριος ὁ ὕψιστος): 1 Esd. 2:2(3); 'the Most High God' (ὁ θεός ὁ ὕψιστος): 1 Esd. 6:30(31); 8:19, 21; 'the Lord God Most High' (ὁ κύριος θεός ὕψιστος): 1 Esd. 9:46. It is possible that the Greek 1 Esdras originated in Palestine (see Martin Hengel, *The 'Hellenization' of Judaea in the First Century after Christ*, trans. John Bowden [London: SCM/ Philadelphia: Trinity, 1989], 25), but most scholars see it as a product of the Diaspora.

[93] 'The Most High' (ὕψιστος): *Sib. Or.* 3:519, 574, 580; 'God Most High' (ὕψιστος θεός): *Sib. Or.* 3:719.

[94] 'The Most High God' (ὕψιστος θεός): *Sib. Or.* 1:179; 'The Most High' (ὕψιστος): *Sib. Or.* 1:200.

	Number of Occurrences
3 Maccabees (6:2; 7:9)[95]	2
Wisdom of Solomon (5:15; 6:3)	2
Sibylline Oracles frg. 1 (4)	1
2 Maccabees (3:31)[96]	1
Philo the Epic Poet (frg. 3)[97]	1
Ezekiel the Tragedian (239)	1
Josephus (*A.J.* 16.163)[98]	1
Pseudo-Aeschylus[99]	1

Western Diaspora (early date and/or non-Christian Jewish provenance uncertain)

Joseph and Aseneth[100]	35
Testament of Abraham[101]	10
Greek Apocalypse of Zephaniah[102]	1

Works of doubtful provenance (geographical provenance uncertain, early date and/or non-Christian Jewish provenance uncertain)

Testaments of XII Patriarchs[103]	17
Latin Life of Adam and Eve (15:3; 28:1)[104]	2
Prayer of Manasseh (7)	1

---

[95] 'The Most High' (ὕψιστος): 3 Macc. 6:2; 'God Most High' (θεός ὕψιστος): 3 Macc. 7:9.

[96] 2 Maccabees is an epitome of a much longer work by Jason of Cyrene who, though from the Diaspora, lived in Palestine, but 2 Maccabees probably reached its present form, with the two epistles prefaced in chap. 1, in Egypt.

[97] *Apud* Eusebius, *Praep. ev.* 9.24.1. On this passage, see Carl R. Holladay, *Fragments from Hellenistic Jewish Authors*, vol. 2: *Poets* (Atlanta: Scholars, 1989), 267–8, arguing correctly that the reference is to God.

[98] 'The Most High God' (ὕψιστος θεός).

[99] *Apud* Clement of Alexandria, *Strom.* 5.14.131.3.

[100] 'The Most High': *Jos. Asen.* 8:9; 11:7, 9, 17; 14:8; 15:7 (*bis*), 8, 12 (four times); 16:14 (*bis*), 16; 18:9; 21:4, 21; 22:13; 25:6; 'God the Most High': *Jos. Asen.* 8:2; 9:1; 15:7 (*tris*); 18:9; 19:5, 8; 21:15; 22:8,13; 23:10; 'the Lord God Most High': *Jos. Asen.* 15:7; 17:6; 21:6.

[101] 'The Most High': *T. Ab.* A9:1, 2, 3, 8; 15:13; 16:1, 6; 'God the Most High': *T. Ab.* A14:9; 15:11; 16:9 (also B13:6; 14:7).

[102] This apocalypse, of which we know just one fragment, quoted by Clement of Alexandria, *Strom.* 5.11.77, is probably not the same work as the Apocalypse of Zephaniah extant in Coptic. The fragment is too short to allow any confidence as to its Jewish or Christian provenance, though its resemblance to Merkavah literature suggests the former is more likely.

[103] *T. Sim.* 2:5; 6:7; *T. Levi.* 3:10; 4:1, 2; 5:1; 16:3; 18:7; *T. Gad* 3:1; 5:4; *T. Ash.* 2:6; 5:4; *T. Jos.* 1:4, 6; 9:3; *T. Benj.* 4:5; 9:2.

[104] These passages have no parallels in the other versions of the *Life of Adam and Eve* (Greek, Armenian, Georgian, Slavonic): see Gary A. Anderson and Michael E. Stone ed., *A Synopsis of the Books of Adam and Eve* (SBLEJL 05; Atlanta: Scholars, 1994).

4

The Worship of Jesus in Early Christianity[1]

1. Introduction

The prevalence and centrality of the worship of Jesus in early Christianity from an early date has frequently been underestimated, as has its importance for understanding christological development. On the other hand, Johannes Weiss called the emergence of the worship of Jesus 'the most significant step of all in the history of the origins of Christianity'.[2] David Aune makes a similar claim, but with more historical precision: 'Perhaps the single most important historical development within the early church was the rise of the cultic worship of the exalted Jesus within the primitive Palestinian church.'[3] The decisive significance of the worship of Jesus is by no means even limited to the Christology of the New Testament, but can be seen at work right down to the definitions of Nicene and Chalcedonian orthodoxy in the fourth and fifth centuries.

Since the major types of evidence for the worship of Jesus form a continuous tradition from the New Testament onwards, this chapter will treat ante-Nicene Christianity as a whole, and will conclude with the contribution that the tradition of worshipping Jesus eventually made to the Trinitarian and christological developments of the fourth and fifth centuries.

---

[1] This is a considerably expanded and revised version of 'Jesus, Worship of,' in *ABD*, vol. 3, 812–19.

[2] Johannes Weiss, *The History of Primitive Christianity*, trans. Four Friends, ed. F.C. Grant (London: Macmillan, 1937), 1:37.

[3] David E. Aune, *The Cultic Setting of Realized Eschatology in Early Christianity* (NovTSup 28; Leiden: Brill, 1972), 5.

2. Origins

In the nature of the case, conclusive evidence of the point at which worship of Jesus began in early Christianity is unlikely to be available, but general considerations, along with the available evidence, point to the earliest Palestinian Jewish Christianity. In the earliest Christian community, Jesus was already understood to be risen and exalted to God's right hand in heaven, active in the community by his Spirit, and coming in the future as ruler and judge of the world. As God's eschatological agent, he was the source of the experience of eschatological salvation and the enthusiasm of the Spirit which characterized Christian gatherings for worship, and he was the focus of all Christian relationship, through him, to God. Psalms and hymns celebrating his exaltation by God and God's work of salvation through him were probably sung and composed from the earliest times.[4] To the living presence of a figure with this kind of religious role, thanksgiving and worship, naturally included within the worship of God, were the inevitable response.[5]

Acclamations and prayers addressed to Jesus go back to the earliest times. The Aramaic cry *Maranatha* ('Our Lord, come!': 1 Cor. 16:22; *Did.* 10:6; cf. Rev. 22:20),[6] whose preservation in Aramaic in Greek-speaking churches indicates its very early origin, implies not only the expectation of the Parousia, but present religious relationship with the one who is to come, whether or not it was associated with a eucharistic presence from the beginning. The New Testament evidence for personal prayer to Jesus as a regular feature of early Christianity has sometimes been underestimated.[7] Paul (2 Cor. 12:8; 1 Thess. 3:11–13; 2 Thess. 2:16–17; 3:5, 16; cf. Rom. 16:20b; 1 Cor. 16:23; Gal. 6:18; Phil. 4:23; 1 Thess. 5:28; 2 Thess. 3:18; Phlm. 25)[8] and Acts (1:24; 7:59–60; 13:2) take it for granted (cf. also 1 Tim. 1:12; 2 Tim. 1:16–18; 4:22).[9] The dominant practice was undoubtedly prayer to God, but since Jesus was understood as the

---

[4] Martin Hengel, 'Hymns and Christology,' in *Between Jesus and Paul,* trans. John Bowden (London: SCM, 1983), 78–96.

[5] For the very early origin of the worship of Jesus, see especially Hurtado, *One God.*

[6] On this, see Hurtado, *One God,* 106–7; idem, *Lord Jesus Christ: Devotion to Jesus in Earliest Christianity* (Grand Rapids: Eerdmans, 2003), 140–2; Martin Hengel, 'Abba, Maranatha, Hosanna und die Anfänge der Christologie,' in *Kleine Schriften IV: Studien zur Christologie* (WUNT 201; Tübingen, 2006), 496–534.

[7] E.g. by Rudolf Bultmann, *Theology of the New Testament,* trans. Kendrick Grovel (London: SCM, 1952), 1:125–8. Against Bultmann's attempt to limit prayer to Christ as personal, rather than liturgical prayer, see, rightly, Hurtado, *One God,* 105–6.

[8] Cf. Larry W. Hurtado, 'The Binitarian Shape of Early Christian Worship,' in *Jewish Roots,* ed. Newman, Davila and Lewis, 187–213, here 195.

[9] Also Ignatius, *Eph.* 20.1; *Rom.* 4:1; *Smyrn.* 4.1.

active mediator of grace from God (as in the epistolary formula, 'Grace to you and peace from God our Father and the Lord Jesus Christ': Rom 1:7 and elsewhere) and as the Lord for whose service Christians lived, prayer addressed to him was natural. John 14:14 (where the correct reading is probably 'if you ask *me*') makes prayer to Jesus a principle of regular petition.[10]

Petitionary prayer to Jesus is not, as such, *worship* of Jesus. But two phrases drawn from the language of the Old Testament cult are highly suggestive of the centrality of Jesus as object of religious devotion. First, Acts 13:2 portrays the prophets and teachers at Antioch 'worshipping [*leitourgountōn*] the Lord [Jesus]'. The verb, which in Jewish usage referred to the cultic service of God, must here, in connection with 'fasting', refer to prayer in the broadest sense with Jesus as its focus. The second phrase is more widely used and more significant. In both Acts and Paul (whose usage here certainly reflects pre-Pauline Christian usage),[11] Christians are those who 'call on the name of our Lord Jesus Christ' (1 Cor. 1:2; cf. Rom. 10:12–14; Acts 9:14, 21; 22:16; 2 Tim. 2:22; Hermas, *Sim.* 9:14:3).[12] The phrase, no doubt drawn into Christian usage especially from Joel 2:32 (Acts 2:21; Rom. 10:13), regularly in the Old Testament refers to the worship of God (e.g. Gen. 4:26; 12:8; 13:4; Ps. 105:1).[13] Its early Christian usage indicates a cultic practice of confessing Jesus as Lord that was regarded as the defining characteristic of Christians (cf. Rom. 10:9; 1 Cor. 12:3; Phil. 2:11). As Hurtado points out, this 'ritual use of Jesus' name reflects an explicit identification of Jesus as an appropriate recipient of such cultic devotion ... It represents the inclusion of Jesus with God as recipient of public, corporate cultic reverence.'[14] Hurtado also connects it with the wider use of the name of Jesus in early Christian religious practice: baptism, healings, exorcisms.[15] In all these cases, there seems

---

[10] On this topic, see E. Delay, 'A qui s'addresse la prière chrétienne?' *RTP* 37 (1949): 189–201; Alexius Klawek, *Das Gebet zu Jesus: Seine Berechtigung und Ubung nach den Schriften des Neuen Testament* (NTAbh 6/5; Münster i. W.: Aschendorff, 1921); Arthur W. Wainwright, *The Trinity in the New Testament* (London: SPCK, 1962), 97–101; Wilhelm Thüsing in Karl Rahner and Wilhelm Thüsing, *A New Christology*, trans. David Smith and Verdant Green (London: Burns & Oates, 1980), 117–21.

[11] Bultmann, *Theology*, 1:125; Werner Kramer, *Christ, Lord, Son of God*, trans. Brian Hardy (SBT 50; London; SCM, 1966), 78–9; Adalbert Hamann, *Prayer: The New Testament*, trans. Paul J. Oligny (Chicago: Franciscan Herald, 1971), 199; Hurtado, *Lord Jesus Christ*, 197–200.

[12] An important study of this phrase is Carl J. Davis, *The Name and Way of the Lord: Old Testament Themes, New Testament Christology* (JSNTSup 129; Sheffield: Sheffield Academic Press, 1996), chap. 4.

[13] Ralph P. Martin, *Worship in the Early Church* (London: Marshall, Morgan & Scott, 1964), 31.

[14] Hurtado, *Lord Jesus Christ*, 198–9.

[15] Hurtado, *Lord Jesus Christ*, 200–6.

to be an association of the Lord (*kurios*) Jesus with the divine name in the Hebrew Scriptures, often represented in Greek by *kurios* (while *Maranatha* may well attest an equivalent association already in Aramaic-speaking Jewish Christianity). As Philippians 2:11 attests, where the divine name appears, worship cannot be far behind. We must reckon with a very early inclusion of Jesus in the identity of the Lord YHWH that integrated Jesus also into the worship of YHWH. This integration was so central as to make 'those who call upon the name of the Lord' a defining characteristic of Christians from a very early date.

As the one exalted to participation in God's unique divine lordship, Jesus was the object of religious attention in Christian worship from the beginning. We should not exclude the possibility that he was deliberately included in the worship offered to God also from the very beginning. But, if there was first prayer, thanksgiving and reverence given to Jesus, and unambiguously divine worship of Jesus only somewhat later, the transition would not have been difficult. It was a natural and smooth process; there is no evidence that anyone contested or resisted it. Certainly the old view that the transition coincided with the movement of Christianity from a Jewish to a pagan Hellenistic environment[16] is mistaken. Apart from involving an over-schematized division between Jewish and Hellenistic Christianity and neglecting the continuing dominance of Jewish Christian leadership in the churches of the Gentile mission in the New Testament period, this view founders on the fact that two of the New Testament works in which the worship of Jesus is clearest – Matthew and Revelation – remain within a thoroughly Jewish framework of thought. That the worship of Jesus did not result from Gentile neglect of Jewish monotheism, but originated within, and had to be accommodated within, a Jewish monotheistic faith, which passed into Gentile Christianity along with it, is of the greatest importance for the course of later christological development.

The significance of Revelation, in which it is stressed that Jesus is worthy of explicitly divine worship, is discussed in section 6 below. As for Matthew, the issue turns on his emphasis on *proskunēsis* ('obeisance, prostration before someone as an expression of reverence or worship') paid to Jesus. Matthew uses the verb *proskunein* with Jesus as object ten times (whereas Mark uses it in this way only twice,

---

[16] Wilhelm Bousset, *Kyrios Christos: Geschichte des Christusglaube von den Anfängen des Christentums bis Irenaeus* (Gottingen: Vandenhoeck & Ruprecht, 1913), 92–125. This view is still substantially advocated by P. Maurice Casey, 'Monotheism, Worship and Christological Development in the Pauline Churches,' in *Jewish Roots*, ed. Newman, Davila and Lewis, 214–33.

Luke only in 24:52 v. 1.). On five of these ten occasions, there is no synoptic parallel (Matt. 2:2, 8, 11; 28:9, 17). On three of them, Matthew supplies the word *proskunein* where Mark has the gesture but not this word (Matt. 8:2 par. Mark 1:40; Matt. 9:18 par. Mark 5:22; Matt. 15:25 par. Mark 7:25). On the remaining two occasions, Matthew supplies the word where the Markan parallel has not even the gesture (Matt. 14:33 par. Mark 6:51; Matt. 20:20 par. Mark 10:35). There are also two occasions where Mark has the word but Matthew omits even the gesture, and one where Mark has the gesture but Matthew omits it (Mark 5:6 par. Matt. 8:29; Mark 15:19 par. Matt. 27:30; Mark 10:17 par. Matt. 19:16). However, on these three occasions, the worship (by demons, the mocking soldiers, the rich young man) would have been considered less than adequate by Matthew.

The evidence, therefore, suggests that Matthew uses *proskunein* in a semi-technical way for the obeisance that is due to Jesus, and emphasizes that it expresses the proper response to Jesus. It is true that the word *proskunein*, as well as the gesture it describes, could be used of reverence for human beings without any implication of idolatry (Matt. 18:26; Rev. 3:9; LXX Gen. 18:2; 19:1; 23:7, 12; 33:6–7; 1 Kgdms. 28:14; 3 Kgdms. 2:19; Isa. 45:14, etc.). But a large majority of Septuagintal uses of the word refer to the worship of God or false gods, and the gesture had become highly suspect to Jews in contexts where the idolatrous worship of a human being or an angel might be implied (Add. Esth. 13:12–14 [cf. Esth. 3:2]; *Apoc. Zeph.* 6:14–15; Philo, *Decal.* 64; *Legat.* 116; Matt. 4:9; Luke 4:7; Acts 10:25–26; Rev. 19:10; 22:8–9; cf. also *Mart. Pol.* 17:3). Thus, whereas in Mark and Luke the gesture of obeisance to Jesus is probably no more than a mark of respect for an honoured teacher, Matthew's consistent use of the word *proskunein*, and his emphasis on the point, show that he intends a kind of reverence which, paid to any other human being, he would have regarded as idolatrous. This is reinforced by the fact that his unparalleled uses tend to be in epiphanic contexts (Matt. 2:2, 8, 11; 14:33; 28:9, 17). Combined with his emphasis on the presence of the exalted Christ among his people (18:20; 28:20), Matthew's usage must reflect the practice of the worship of Jesus in the church.[17]

In view of the origin of the worship of Jesus in Jewish Christianity, Hurtado calls it 'a significantly new but essentially internal development within the Jewish monotheistic tradition'.[18] That it constituted a new

---

[17] On the worship of Jesus in Matthew, see Larry W. Hurtado, 'Pre-70 CE Jewish Opposition to Christ-Devotion,' *JTS* 50 (1999): 35–58, here 38–42.

[18] Hurtado, *One God*, 100.

'mutation' or 'variant' (Hurtado)[19] of Jewish monotheistic worship, rather than an abandonment of Jewish monotheism, will become evident in section 6 below. Further evidence of the worship of Jesus throughout the whole ante-Nicene period permeates the following discussion.

Two expressions of worship are of particular interest: doxologies (section 3) and hymns (section 4). Together they are strong evidence of the centrality and normality of the worship of Jesus in early Christianity, not because they are the only evidence,[20] but because they are the most pervasive types of evidence. Moreover, they have a complementary significance: the doxologies provide unambiguous evidence that the worship offered to Jesus was that appropriate to God, while the hymns help to illuminate why such properly divine worship was considered appropriately offered to Jesus.

3. Doxologies

The attribution of doxologies to Christ is particularly clear evidence of unambiguously divine worship, i.e. worship that is appropriately offered only to the one God. Moreover, an unbroken tradition of use of christological doxologies can be traced from the New Testament through the whole ante-Nicene period. We distinguish two types: the strict doxological form and the acclamatory doxology.

The strict doxological form has three or four parts: (1) the person praised, usually in the dative, often a pronoun; (2) the word of praise, usually *doxa*, quite often with the addition of other terms; (3) the indication of time, i.e. 'forever' or a fuller formula for eternity, usually followed by (4) 'Amen'. Thus the basic structure, of which many variations and expansions are possible, is: 'To whom/him/you (be/is) the glory forever. Amen.'[21] Such doxologies were typically used by

---

[19] In his later work, *Lord Jesus Christ*, Hurtado prefers the term 'variant', for reasons he explains on p. 50 n. 70.

[20] The most controversial area remains that of Pauline Christianity, where it is disputed whether Paul and his churches merely venerated Jesus in a way that did not amount to the properly divine worship that Jews accorded only to the one God (James D.G. Dunn, 'How Controversial Was Paul's Christology?' in *From Jesus to John: Essays on Jesus and New Testament Christology in Honour of Marinus de Jonge*, ed. Martinus C. De Boer [JSNTSup 84; Sheffield: Sheffield Academic Press, 1993], 148–67, here 164–5; idem, *The Theology of Paul the Apostle* [Grand Rapids: Eerdmans, 1998], 257–60; Casey, 'Monotheism'), or included Jesus in their worship in a way that can be called 'binitarian' (Hurtado, 'Pre-70 CE Jewish Opposition,' 50–7; idem, *Lord Jesus Christ*, 134–53).

[21] R. Deichgräber, *Gotteshymnus und Christushymnus in der frühen Christenheit* (SUNT 5; Göttingen: Vandenhoeck & Ruprecht, 1967), 25–7; Richard Bauckham, *Jude, 2 Peter* (WBC 50; Waco: Word, 1983), 119–20.

Jews and Christians as a conclusion to a prayer, a sermon, a letter or a part of any of these. Though they are rare in extant Jewish literature, where the benediction (a different form with an equivalent function)[22] is much more common, there is no doubt that the early Christian use of doxologies did derive from Judaism,[23] where they were an expression of monotheistic worship.[24] It is the one God of Israel to whom glory belongs eternally. There could be no more explicit way of expressing *divine* worship of Jesus than in the form of a doxology addressed to him.[25]

One common early Christian way of christianizing the doxology without addressing it to Christ was by the addition of the phrase 'through Jesus Christ' (Rom. 16:27; Jude 25; *Did.* 9:4; *1 Clem.* 58:2; 61:3; 64; 65:2; *Mart. Pol.* 14:3; 20:2; cf. 2 Cor. 1:20; 1 Pet. 4:10; Justin, *1 Apol.* 65:3; 67:2; Origen, *Or.* 33:1, 6). But doxologies addressed to Christ also came into use.[26] The commonest form was a doxology to Christ alone, of which three examples occur in the New Testament, though in relatively late New Testament documents (2 Tim. 4:18; 2 Pet. 3:18; Rev. 1:5–6). Two other New Testament doxologies (Heb. 13:21; 1 Pet. 4:11) could be, but are not very likely to be, addressed to Christ and the same can be said for two doxologies in *1 Clement* (20:12; 50:7) which, if addressed to Christ, would be roughly contemporary with the three certain New Testament examples.[27] However, the three clear New Testament examples are from different geographical areas and theological traditions and so presuppose a common Christian practice going back some time before the writing of these works.

Some examples of the strict doxological form addressed to Christ alone from the second and early third centuries are: *Acts John* 77; *Acts Paul Thecla* 42; *Acts Pet.* 20; 39; Melito, *Peri Pascha* 10, 45, 65, 105; *frg.* II 23;[28] *Mart. Perpetua* 1:6; Tertullian, *Or.* 29; Hippolytus, *Comm. Dan.* 1:33; 4:60; Origen, *Princ.* 4.1.7; 4.3.14. Two special categories of further examples should be noted. One is the doxologies that end the homilies of Origen,

---

[22] There is one New Testament benediction that may have Christ as its object: Rom. 9:5. For a later christological benediction, see *Mart. Carpus* Gk. 41.

[23] Deichgräber, *Gotteshymnus*, 35–8; Bauckham, *Jude*, 121.

[24] The doxology to 'truth' in 1 Esd. 4:59 is not really an exception.

[25] Cf. J. Jungmann, *The Place of Christ in Liturgical Prayer*, trans. A. Peeler, 2nd ed. (London/ Dublin: Chapman, 1965), 174–5.

[26] Note some examples that, while not formally doxologies, use the verb *doxazō* with Christ as the object: Ignatius, *Eph.* 2.2; *Smyrn.* 1.1.

[27] Deichgräber, *Gotteshymnus*, 32. On the New Testament doxologies to Christ, see also Wainwright, *Trinity*, 93–5. The argument of C.C. Oke, 'A Doxology not to God but to Christ,' *ExpTim* 67 (1955–6): 367–8, that 1 Tim. 1:17 is a doxology to Christ, is not convincing.

[28] Stuart G. Hall, *Melito of Sardis: On Pascha and Fragments* (Oxford: Clarendon, 1979), 94.

which are characteristically addressed to Christ alone. Of 202 such doxologies, 181 are addressed to Christ (five others may be addressed to Christ or to the Father).[29] This practice of Origen's is especially noteworthy, since it contrasts with his own theory (*Or.* 14–15; cf. 33.1) and is likely, therefore, to be evidence not only of his own devotion to Christ, but also of a normal practice of ending sermons in this way.

Secondly, the early Acts of the Christian martyrs seem always to have ended with a doxology to Christ alone (*Mart. Pol.* 21;[30] *Mart. Carp.* Lat. 7; *Mart. Pion.* 23; *Mart. Just.* Rec. B & C 6; *Mart. Perp.* 21:11; *Mart. Marc.* Rec. N 5; *Mart. Iren. Sirm.* 6; *Mart. Jul.* 4:5; *Mart. Crisp.* 4:2). In some cases, the later expansion of an original christological doxology into a later Trinitarian form can be clearly seen (*Mart. Carp.* Gk. 47; *Mart. Just.* Rec.A 6; *Mart. Das.* 12:2; *Mart. Agape* 7:2; cf. *Mart. Eupl.* Gk. 2:4). Here the Trinitarian doxology is the post-Nicene development; the purely christological doxology is the early form. In many of these cases, the christological doxology is attached to a standard form of reference to the reign of Christ (*Mart. Pol.* 21; *Mart. Carp.* Lat. 7; *Mart. Pion.* 23; *Mart. Marc.* Rec.N 5; *Mart. Iren. Sirm.* 6; *Mart. Das.* 12:2; *Mart. Agape* 7:2), so that the effect is to contrast the divine rule of Christ, to whom worship is due, with Caesar's idolatrous pretensions to divine worship. The doxology thus expresses precisely the issue of worship for which the martyrs died.

As well as the strict doxological form, acclamatory doxologies were also used with purely christological reference. Here the basic form is simply, 'Glory to ...', with the object of praise expressed in the second or third person.[31] Frequently a relative or causal clause follows, giving the reason for praise. This form is not normally a concluding formula, as the strict doxological form is (but see *Odes Sol.* 17:17), but forms an independent, or even introductory, ascription of praise.[32] Though few Jewish examples seem to be extant (cf. *2 En.* 71:11, Rec. J), a background

---

[29] These figures are calculated from those in Henri Crouzel, 'Les doxologies finales des homelies d'Origène selon le texte grec et les versions latines,' *Augustinianum* 20 (1980): 95–107. Crouzel's argument that Rufinus may be responsible for the variation of the form of the doxologies in the homilies translated by him does not affect our argument: these doxologies were certainly originally addressed to Christ.

[30] Comparison with the standard form in *Mart. Carp.* Lat. 7; *Mart. Pion.* 23, etc., shows that the doxology here is original. (Cf. also J.B. Lightfoot, *The Apostolic Fathers,* part 2, vol. 1, 2nd ed. [London: Macmillan, 1889], 626–7, for a different kind of argument to this effect.) Those manuscripts that omit it do so because, with the addition of chap. 22, which ends with its own doxology, a doxology is no longer appropriate at the end of chap. 21.

[31] Rev. 7:12 shows how closely this form is related to the fuller doxological form in three or four parts.

[32] In form and function it is, therefore, closer to the benediction than is the fuller form of doxology.

in Judaism is probable and supported by its use in the New Testament with reference to God (Luke 2:14; Rev. 19:1; cf. Luke 19:38). In early Christianity, its christological use is found especially in the apocryphal Acts (*Acts John* 43; 78; *Acts Thom.* 59; 60; 80; 153; *Acts Andr.* 29:1), though by no means exclusively there *(Odes Sol.* 17:17; *Mart. Pion.* 11:6).[33]

Besides its three purely christological doxologies, the New Testament also contains one doxology addressed to God and Christ together (Rev. 5:13; cf. 7:10). This is the nearest the New Testament comes to later *Trinitarian* doxologies in 'coordinated' form, i.e. in which glory is ascribed to all three divine persons. They are less common in the ante-Nicene period than the doxology addressed to Christ alone, but they are found. It is disputed whether this form of the doxology is original in *Martyrdom of Polycarp* 14:3,[34] but there seems to be a good case for claiming that it was regularly used by Hippolytus in the liturgy, as well as in other work,[35] as it certainly was also in the Syriac liturgies from an early date.[36] Other early doxologies to the Trinity are in *Acts John* 94; 96; *Acts Thom.* 132 (all these in the acclamatory form); Dionysius of Alexandria *(apud* Basil, *De Sp. S.* 29).[37]

4. Hymns

Hymns in praise of Christ are probably, as Martin Hengel has argued, 'as old as the [Christian] community itself',[38] and, like the doxology

---

[33] Of these, at least the *Acts of Thomas* and the *Odes of Solomon* are of Syrian origin. Later use of the form in Syria can be found in the works of Ephrem. The extended use of it in the Sermon on the Passion (Adalbert Hamman, *Early Christian Prayers*, trans. Walter Mitchell [Chicago: Henry Regnery/London: Longmans, Green, 1961], 180–1) is clearly in the same tradition as *Acts Thom.* 80.

[34] See Jungmann, *The Place*, 147 n. 4.

[35] Jungmann, *The Place*, 5–8, 151–2, 152 n. 2, 155; Jules Lebreton, *Histoire de la Trinité des Origins au Concile de Nicée*, 2 vols., 2nd ed. (Paris: Beauchesne, 1928), 2:622–5; but on the liturgy, see also J.M. Hanssens, *La Liturgie d'Hippolyte: ses documents, son titulaire, ses origins et son caractère* (Orientalia Christiana Analecta 155; Rome: Pontificium Institutum Orientalium Studiorum, 1959), 343–68.

[36] Jungmann, *The Place*, 194–200.

[37] See also Julius Africanus, *apud* Basil, *De Sp. S.* 29. The doxologies at the end of Origen, *Hom. Luc.* 3 and 37, appear to be Trinitarian, but cf. Crouzel, 'Les doxologies,' 98, for the possibility that the form is due to Jerome, who translated the Homilies. Cf. also, for praise to the Trinity, not in doxological form, *Acts Thom.* 39; Clement of Alexandria. *Paed.* 3.12; third-century hymn in Pap. Oxy. 15.1786 (Adalbert Hamman, *Early Christian Prayer*, 69, no. 98a; Lebreton, *Histoire*, 26 n. 3; Martin Hengel, 'The Song about Christ in Earliest Worship,' in *Studies in Early Christology* [Edinburgh: T&T Clark, 1995], 227–91, here 254–6). Note also Origen's interpretation (*Or.* 33:1) of the doxology *through* Christ as meaning that Christ is praised *along* with the Father (*sundoxologoumenou*).

[38] Hengel, 'Hymns,' 93.

to Christ, can be traced in a continuous tradition through the early centuries.[39] The singing of hymns 'to the Lord' [i.e. to Christ] is already attested in Ephesians 5:19, then by Pliny's report (of Christians' own testimony) that Christians habitually, in their morning worship, sang a hymn to Christ as God (*carmen Christo quasi deo*; Pliny the Younger, *Ep.* 10.96.7).[40] Ignatius' comment that, by the concord and harmony of the Ephesian Christians, the praise of Jesus Christ is being sung (*Iēsous Christos adetai*: Ignatius, *Eph.* 4:1; the following verse continues the thought in terms of singing through Christ to the Father) uses a metaphor that must reflect a practice of singing hymns in praise of Christ. A Coptic fragment of the *Acts of Paul* refers to 'psalms and praises to Christ'.[41]

Later evidence of the continuity of this tradition of christological liturgical hymns comes, interestingly, from the context of third-century christological debate. An anonymous early third-century writer, refuting the heretic Artemon who denied the deity of Christ, adduces as evidence of the antiquity of this belief the fact that 'all the psalms and hymns (*ōdai*) written by believing brothers, from the beginning, hymn Christ as the Logos of God and speak of him as God (*ton logon tou theou ton Christon humnousin theologountes)*' (*apud* Eusebius, *Hist. eccl.* 5.28.6). (In this text, as also in *Hist. eccl.* 7.30.10, note the continuity with the early Christian terminology for such hymns in 1 Cor. 14:26; Col. 3:16; Eph. 5:19.[42]) Known hymns of some antiquity (such as the *Phōs hilaron*) must be in the author's mind, since he also appeals, quite accurately, to named second-century writers who speak of Christ as God (*Hist. eccl.* 5.28.4–5). Some years later, Paul of Samosata – the first Christian reformer who attempted to abolish the worship of Christ in the interests of a low Christology – put a stop to psalms addressed to Jesus Christ, considering them to be modern compositions (*Hist. eccl.* 7.30.10). (For the practice of singing hymns in praise of Christ, see also Origen, *Cels.* 8.67; Porphyry *apud* Augustine, *Civ.* 19.23.)

---

[39] Hengel, 'Hymns,' 89, in seeming to deny this, makes no distinction between 'the composition of hymns' and 'the singing of extempore hymns'. The latter is likely to have declined, but it is wholly uncertain how far it was really characteristic of earliest Christianity in any case. A Spirit-inspired song was not necessarily composed extemporaneously.

[40] On this text, see Hengel, 'Song,' 262–4; Margaret Daly-Denton, 'Singing Hymns to Christ as to a God (Cf. Pliny, *Ep.* X, 96),' in *Jewish Roots*, ed. Newman, Davila and Lewis, 277–92 (she argues that the reference is to singing of the canonical psalms understood as being about and addressed to Jesus).

[41] Wilhelm Schneemelcher and Robin McL. Wilson ed., *New Testament Apocrypha*, (Cambridge: James Clarke/Louisville: WJK, 1992), 2:264.

[42] Cf. Hengel, 'Hymns,' 78–80.

Those fragments of early Christian hymns which are often thought to have been preserved in the New Testament[43] (and perhaps also in Ignatius)[44] are not actually *addressed* to Christ, but are forms of 'narrative praise' recounting the history of Jesus in the third person (especially Phil. 2:6–11; 1 Tim. 3:16). Like the narrative psalms of the Old Testament, such hymns are praise of God for his saving acts in the history of Jesus, but they are, at the same time, also praise of Jesus the Saviour, as Ephesians 5:19 makes plain, if it is to hymns of this type that it refers. Indeed, Philippians 2:9–11 is virtually equivalent to a doxology addressed *to* Christ and *through* him to the Father. The tradition of hymns of narrative praise must have continued, because the hymnic elements in the work of Melito of Sardis seem clearly indebted to liturgical hymnody of this type.[45] Melito makes the praise of Christ quite explicit by ending such compositions with formal christological doxologies *(Pasch.* 10, 45, 65, 105; frg. II 23). (Note also the combination of christological doxology and narrative praise in *Acts Thom.* 8 0, which may reflect a hymnic form.)

However, hymns of praise actually addressed to Christ may also have originated at a very early date. A brief acclamation of praise to Christ, drawn from the messianic Psalm 118, is found in the context of the eucharistic liturgy in *Did.* 10:6, 'Hosanna to the God of David!'[46] Revelation 5:9–10, which addresses praise to Christ in the second person, is not an actual hymn in Christian use: the seer has composed this heavenly liturgy for its context in his work. But it would be surprising if it did not reflect the use of hymns of this kind in John's churches. Moreover, Hebrew 1:8–12 understands Psalm 45:6–7 and Psalm 102:25–27 as *psalms addressed to Christ*[47] and may well reflect common Christian use of them as such,[48] while Justin later attests a

---

[43] These have often been claimed to be hymns or fragments of hymns: John 1:1–8; Eph. 2:14–16; Phil, 2:6–11; Col. 1:15–20; 1 Tim. 3:16; 1 Pet. 3:18–22; Heb. 1:3. In my view, such claims have often been made too hastily. Cf. Hengel, 'Song,' 277–91; Hurtado, *Lord Jesus Christ*, 146–9.

[44] See Ignatius, *Eph.* 7:2; 18:2; 19:2–3.

[45] Cf. also the hymn to Christ in *Sib. Or.* 6 (second or third century). But the predictive form of this means that it is not a real hymn that could have been used in worship.

[46] For the view that 'God of David' is deliberate christological heightening of the phrase 'Son of David' (Matt. 21:9), in the light of Matt. 22:41–46, see Lebreton, *Histoire*, 2:212–13; Klawek, *Das Gebet*, 102. But, for a different view, see Kurt Niederwimmer, *The Didache*, trans. Linda M. Maloney (Hermeneia; Minneapolis: Fortress, 1998), 162–3. Hengel, 'Abba,' 512–22, attributes the use of *Hosanna* in worship to the early Aramaic-speaking church and connects it closely with *Maranatha*.

[47] See chapter 7 below. Perhaps Paul in Rom. 15:9 takes Ps. 18:49 (LXX 17:50) to be addressed to Christ (Ernst Käsemann, *Commentary on Romans,* trans. Geoffrey W. Bromiley [London: SCM, 1980], 386).

[48] Cf. Wainwright, *Trinity*, 67; Raymond E. Brown, *Jesus, God and Man* (London: Chapman, 1968), 35.

Christian exegesis of some psalms as addressed to Christ (*Dial.* 37–38; 63; 73–74; 126). In line with Hengel's argument that, in the earliest Christian community, the use of Old Testament messianic psalms accompanied the composition of new songs,[49] this kind of christological exegesis of psalms could have inspired new Christian psalms addressed to Christ. So it may be to this type of hymn that Ephesians 5:19 and Pliny's report refer. Examples of such hymns which have survived from a later period are the lamp-lighting hymn *Phōs hilaron*, probably from the late second or early third century,[50] Clement of Alexandria's hymn to Christ the Saviour in *Paed.* 3.12 and, probably, the original ante-Nicene form of the *Gloria in excelsis*.[51] (It must be admitted that we have few texts of hymns composed by Christians [as distinct from the use of the canonical psalms by Christians] from the ante-Nicene period,[52] but relatively little of the Christian literature of this period, especially the second century, has survived.)

The special value of the hymns is that they help us much more than the doxologies to see how the worship of Jesus arose. As Hengel has shown in detail,[53] the earliest hymns celebrated the saving death and heavenly exaltation of Jesus as the one who now shares the divine throne and, as God's plenipotentiary, receives the homage of all creation. In offering praise to Christ, they anticipate the eschatological consummation, when all will acknowledge Christ's lordship and worship him. Thus the worship of Christ is the community's response to his eschatological history. It corresponds to the very high Christology of the earliest Christian communities, according to which Jesus exercises all the functions of God in relation to the world as Saviour, Lord and Judge, as well as to the same communities' strong sense of the living reality of Jesus as the one who reigns now and is coming. The one who functions as God shares the divine identity with God and, naturally, receives divine worship, not of course as a competitor or supplanter of God in the community's worship but as God's plenipotentiary whose praise redounds to God's glory (Phil. 2:11; Rev. 5:12–13). It is likely that the attribution of explicitly divine worship to

---

[49] Hengel, 'Hymns,' 92.

[50] Antonia Tripolitis, '*Phōs Hilaron:* Ancient Hymn and Modern Enigma,' *VC* 24 (1970): 189–96, here 196.

[51] Jules Lebreton, 'Le désaccord de la foi populaire et de théologie savante dans l'Église chrétienne du IIIᵉ siècle,' *RHE* 19 (1923): 481–506; 20 (1924): 5–37, here 29–32; Bernard Capelle, 'Le Texte du "Gloria in excelsis,"' *RHE* 44 (1949): 439–57; Maurice Wiles, *The Making of Christian Doctrine* (Cambridge: CUP, 1967), 76.

[52] Hengel, 'Song,' 246–62.

[53] Hengel, 'Hymns'; cf. also David M. Stanley, 'Carmenque Christo Quasi Deo Dicere', *CBQ* 20 (1958): 73–91.

Jesus assisted the development of more explicit statements about his divine identity.

5. Pagan Perceptions of Christianity

Interesting evidence that the worship of Jesus was the central distinguishing feature of early Christianity comes from pagan observers and critics.[54] 'To pagan observers ... Christian identity centred on the worship of Christ', writes Wilken.[55] Most second- and third-century pagan writers who discuss Christianity emphasize the worship of Jesus (Pliny, *Ep.* 10.96.7; Lucian, *Peregr.* 13; Celsus *apud* Origen, *Cels.* 8.12, 14, 15; Porphyry *apud* Augustine, *Civ.* 19:23; cf. *Mart. Pol.* 17:2). Also the third-century anti-Christian graffito from the Palatine hill depicts a man in prayer before a crucified man with the head of a donkey, and the inscription, 'Alexamenos worships [his] God' (*Alexamenos sebete theon*; cf. *Mart. Pion.* 16.4–5; Minucius Felix, *Oct.* 9.4; Tertullian, *Apol.* 16; *Nat.* 1.14).

In a sense, it was easy for pagans to see Christianity as a religious association devoted to the cult of Jesus, in the same way that other religious groups exalted particular teachers and heroes to divine or semi-divine status. But what set Christianity apart, in their eyes, was not only that Jesus was, in fact, unworthy of such a cult (as Celsus was at pains to argue), but also the *exclusivity* of Christian worship. They saw Christianity as having perverted the exclusive monotheism of the Jews, itself an objectionable superstition (Tacitus, *Hist.* 5.4–5), into the exclusive worship of Jesus as the only God. Mühlenberg persuasively interprets Pliny's report as implying this: 'The skandalon, the fanatic obstinacy, as Pliny sees it, consists in the exclusivity of the divinity of Jesus'.[56] According to Celsus, whose principal objection to Christians was their antisocial (indeed seditious) opting out of all religious

---

[54] See E. Mühlenberg, 'The Divinity of Jesus Christ in Early Christian Faith,' in *Studia Patristica XVII: Part 1*, ed. Elisabeth A. Livingstone (Oxford: Pergamon, 1982), 136–45; Robert L. Wilken, 'The Christians as the Romans (and Greeks) Saw Them,' in *Jewish and Christian Self-Definition*, vol. 1 in *The Shaping of Christianity in the Second and Third Centuries*, ed. E.P. Sanders (London: SCM, 1980), 100–25; Robert L. Wilken, *The Christians as the Romans Saw Them* (New Haven/London: Yale University Press, 1984).

[55] Wilken, 'The Christians,' 113; cf. also Mühlenberg, 'The Divinity', 144: 'From the non-Christian perspective, Christian religion appears to be the worship of the god Christ.'

[56] Mühlenberg, 'The Divinity,' 139; cf. Graham N. Stanton, 'Aspects of Early Christian and Jewish Worship: Pliny and the *Kerygma Petrou*,' in *Worship, Theology and Ministry in the Early Church: Essays in Honor of Ralph P. Martin*, ed. Michael J. Wilkins and Terence Paige (JSNTSup 87; Sheffield; Sheffield Academic Press, 1992), 84–98, here 90.

practices except their own, Christians 'want to worship only this Son of man, whom they put forward as leader under the pretence that he is a great God' (*apud* Origen, *Cels.* 8.15). Celsus cannot understand how this can be compatible with the Jewish monotheistic tradition in which Christians claim to stand: 'If these men worshipped no other God but one, perhaps they would have had a valid argument against the others. But, in fact, they worship to an extravagant degree this man who appeared recently and yet think it is not inconsistent with monotheism if they also worship his servant' (Origen, *Cels.* 8.12). In thus perceiving that Christians claimed an exclusive monotheism centred on the worship of Jesus, Celsus strikingly corroborates the accounts of the martyrs that are noted in 6.4 below.

6. Christian Adherence to Jewish Monotheism

Before the advent of Christianity, Judaism was unique among the religions of the Roman world in demanding the *exclusive* worship of its God. It is not too much to say that Jewish monotheism was defined in practice by its adherence to the first and second commandments. That the God of Israel was the one and only God meant not only that he was supreme, the Creator of heaven and earth, but also that he alone might be worshipped. By contrast, perhaps the principal religious feature of the rest of the Roman world was inter-religious tolerance: One's participation in one cult did not imply that others, or even oneself, should not participate in other cults. Where a kind of monotheism was held by the more sophisticated – deriving from the Platonic tradition, for example – it denied the legitimacy of none of the existing forms of popular religion. Worship of the supreme transcendent God (in any case known by different names to different nations) was entirely compatible with also worshipping the lesser divine beings who were more immediately involved in affairs here on earth. The difference between Jewish and pagan monotheism did not, of course, turn on the *existence* of supernatural beings inferior to the supreme God, but on whether they might be worshipped.

It was this intolerant Jewish monotheism, with its condemnation of all other cults as idolatrous, that also made Christianity an objectionable oddity in the Roman world, with the additional scandal that Christianity somehow linked this exclusive monotheism to the cult, not of an ancient hero or noble philosopher, but of a recently crucified criminal. Intelligible as the thesis might seem – a priori – that Christianity adopted the worship of Jesus to the extent that it abandoned exclusive Jewish monotheism under the influence of the pagan environment, the evidence does not bear it out. On the contrary, it indicates that, from the New Testament period onwards, Christians held to exclusive monotheism as tenaciously as they did to the worship of Jesus, because both features were already definitive of Christian worship when it emerged from its original Jewish context into the pagan world.

As Hurtado writes, 'The accommodation of Jesus as recipient of cultic worship with God is unparalleled and signals a major development in monotheistic cultic practice and belief. But this variant form of monotheism appeared among circles who insisted that they maintained faithfulness to the monotheistic stance of the Jewish tradition.'[57] In other words, Jewish monotheism and the worship of Jesus were mutually conditioning factors in the development of early Christian faith.

The remainder of this section examines some of the evidence that the worship of Jesus was practiced in close conjunction with an adherence to Jewish monotheism.

6.1. First Corinthians 8:6.

The worship of Jesus as Lord was undoubtedly practised in the churches of the Pauline mission, but in combination with the exclusive monotheism of the parent religion. In 1 Corinthians 8:4–6, Paul takes up the issue of polytheistic and monotheistic worship by christianizing the Shema'. In other words, he aligns himself and his fellow-Christians with the Jews in their rejection of the 'many gods and many lords' of paganism, and does so by referring to the classic, constantly repeated, declaration of Jewish exclusive monotheism in the Shema' (Deut. 6:4). But he so expounds the Shema' as to include the lordship of Jesus within its terms, glossing its *theos* (God) with 'Father' and its *kurios* (Lord) with 'Jesus Christ'.[58]

6.2. The book of Revelation.

Revelation portrays the worship of Christ in heaven quite explicitly as *divine* worship (5:8–12). The heavenly worship of God the Creator (4:9–11) is followed by the heavenly worship of the Lamb (5:8–12), and

---

[57] Hurtado, *Lord Jesus Christ*, 53.
[58] N. Thomas Wright, '"Constraints" and the Jesus of History,' *SJT* 39 (1986): 189–210, here 208; Douglas R. de Lacey, '"One Lord" in Pauline Christology,' in *Christ the Lord*, ed. Rowdon, 191–203, here 200–1.

then, as the climax of the vision (5:13), the circle of worship expands to include the whole of creation addressing a doxology to God and the Lamb together. This very deliberate portrayal of the worship of Christ is noteworthy, not only because it occurs in a work whose thought-world is unquestionably thoroughly Jewish, but also because John shows himself quite aware of the issue of *monotheistic* worship. The whole book is much concerned with the question of true and false worship, with differentiating the true worship of God from the idolatrous worship of the beast. Moreover, the issue of worship is reinforced in the closing chapters of the work by the incident, included twice for strategic effect, in which John prostrates himself in worship before the angel who mediates the revelation to him. The angel explains that he is only a fellow-servant of God and directs John to worship God (19:10; 22:8–9). John is here making use of a traditional motif developed in apocalyptic literature precisely in order to protect monotheistic worship against the temptation of angelolatry.[59] The point is that the angel is not the source of revelation but only the instrument for communicating it to John. The source is God, who alone may be worshipped. But, in the same passages, Jesus is distinguished as source, not instrument, of revelation (19:10b; 21:16, 20). By implication, he is not excluded, like the angel, from the strictly monotheistic worship, but included in it. It seems clear that, in Revelation, we have the deliberate treatment of Jesus as an object of worship *along with* a deliberate retention of the Jewish definition of monotheism by worship.

Because of this combination, it seems that John is concerned not to represent Jesus as an alternative object of worship alongside God, but as one who shares in the glory due to God. He is worthy of divine worship because his worship can be included in the worship of the one God. Thus, chapter five is structured so that the heavenly worship of the Lamb (5:8–12) leads to the worship of God and the Lamb together by the whole creation (5:13). It is probably the same concern which leads to a peculiar usage elsewhere in Revelation, where mention of God and Christ is followed by a singular verb (11:15) or singular pronouns (22:3–4; and 6:17, where the reading *autou* should be preferred). (Of these texts, 22:3 is particularly noteworthy as referring to worship.) Whether the singular in these passages refers to God alone or to God and Christ as a unity, John is evidently reluctant to speak of God and Christ together as a plurality.

---

[59] Bauckham, 'The Worship of Jesus,' 322–41, here 323–7; revised version in Bauckham, *Climax of Prophecy*, chap. 4, here 120–32.

6.3. Missionary Christianity in the Apocryphal Acts.

The apocryphal Acts of the late second and early third centuries are the best evidence we have of how conversion to Christianity was represented to outsiders. With the exception of one section of the *Acts of John* (94–102, 109), they should not be labelled gnostic, and their doctrinal peculiarities are not likely to have seemed unorthodox at the time. They represent conversion to Christianity, again and again, as conversion from idolatry to the worship of the only true God *Jesus* (as well as references below, see *Acts John* 42; 44; 79).[60] Admittedly, in the *Acts of John*, this treatment of Jesus as the only God is combined with a consistent elimination of all distinction between Jesus and the Father (except in 94–102, 109, a secondary addition to the work).[61] But the other Acts are not really, as has been claimed, guilty of 'naive modalism':[62] they distinguish the Father and the Son as readily as they call Jesus the only God.[63] In fact, they exhibit a relatively unreflective combination of (a) monotheistic worship, (b) worship of Jesus as God and (c) the Trinitarian distinctions – a combination probably characteristic of much popular Christianity and capable, of course, of being condemned as modalism by more sophisticated Trinitarian thinkers. (It seems, for example, much like the position of Pope Zephyrinus, quoted by Hippolytus, *Haer.* 9:6, who condemns it as 'ignorant and illiterate'.)

What is particularly interesting, however, is the evidence that traditional Jewish monotheistic formulae, designed to assert monotheistic worship against paganism, are employed for the same purpose, but with reference to the worship of Jesus. For example, there seems to have been a form of the full doxology, attested only in early Christian literature (Rom. 16:27; 1 Tim. 1:17; 6:15–16; Jude 25; *1 Clem.* 43:6; *2 Clem.* 20:5) but surely of Jewish origin, in which glory

---

[60] Passages where conversion is to the worship of the one and only God, not said to be Jesus, are *Acts Pet.* 26; *Acts Paul Thecl.* 9; *Acts Paul* (Pap. Heid. p. 42).

[61] Eric Junod and Jean-Daniel Kaestli ed., *Acta Johanni* (Corpus Christianorum Series Apocryphorum 2; Turnhout: Brepols, 1983), 2:680; Pieter J. Lalleman, *The Acts of John: A Two-Stage Initiation into Johannine Gnosticism* (Studies on the Apocryphal Acts of the Apostles 4; Leuven: Peeters, n.d. [1998?]), 167–8 (he calls this characteristic Christomonism). Hall, *Melito*, xliii, and idem, 'Melito's Paschal Homily and the *Acts of John*,' *JTS* 17 (1966): 95–8, here 97, attempts to align Melito with the *Acts of John* in this respect. But Melito does not eliminate all distinction between Father and Son, and so is better aligned with the other apocryphal Acts. Melito helps to show that, at that time, their alleged tendency to modalism was not peculiar.

[62] Lebreton, 'Le désaccord', 24–6, rightly rejects this view.

[63] Particularly revealing here is *Acts of Paul* in Pap. Heid. p. 6: 'there is no other God save Jesus Christ, the Son of the Blessed, unto whom is glory forever. Amen'! Cf. also *Acts Thom.* 25 ('Thou [Jesus] art the God of truth and no other') with 104 ('to worship and fear one God, the Lord of all, and Jesus Christ his Son').

is ascribed to the *only* God. This turns the doxology into an explicit assertion of *exclusive* monotheistic worship. In the apocryphal Acts, this kind of doxology is addressed to Jesus *(Acts Pet.* 20; 39; *Acts John* 77; *Acts Paul* [Pap. Heid. p. 6]; and acclamatory form in *Acts John* 43; and cf. the ascriptions of praise, not in strictly doxological form, in *Acts Pet.* 21; *Acts Thom.* 25; *Acts John* 85). Furthermore, in several of these cases, the words are: 'you [Jesus] are the only God and there is no other' (or similar) *(Acts Pet.* 39; *Acts John* 77; *Acts Thom.* 25; *Acts Paul* [Pap. Heid. p. 6]). This formula derives from Deutero-Isaiah's polemic against idolatry (Isa. 43:11; 45:5, 11, 22; 46:9, etc.) and had already been taken up in Jewish propagandist literature in the Roman world *(Sib. Or.* 3:629, 760; Ps.-Orphica 16; cf. *Sib. Or.* 8:377, which is most likely Christian). It makes absolutely clear that, in the apocryphal Acts, where the worship of Jesus is so prominent, it was conceived primarily in terms of Jewish monotheistic worship.

The fact that the apocryphal Acts portray Christianity predominantly in its missionary role, and are probably, to some extent at least, missionary documents, enables us to make the following observation. The combination of Jewish monotheism and the worship of Jesus that we find in them surely accounts for much of the appeal of the Christian message in the second and third centuries. Paganism (especially in its philosophically influenced forms) offered, on the one hand, the supreme God, abstract and remote from human affairs, and, on the other hand, any number of lesser divinities involved in human affairs. The aspiration to monotheism, which is evidenced in the religious philosophies of the time, could not be satisfied at the expense of the many gods, because only they met the real religious needs of ordinary people. Christianity, however, recognized the one God, Creator of heaven and earth, who was not merely the philosophical abstraction of Platonic monotheism, but had involved himself in the human world and given himself a worldly identity in Jesus. Thus, Christianity actually could dispense with the worship of the lesser divinities and advocate *exclusive* monotheistic worship. The one God of Christian faith, unlike the supreme God of paganism, could take the place of the lesser gods, because, in Jesus himself, the one God was religiously accessible. Hence the formula 'Jesus is the only God' – however theologically problematic in other respects – did summarize the missionary appeal of Christianity.

6.4. *Persecution and Martyrdom*

It was for their 'atheism' – i.e. for their exclusive monotheistic worship – that Christians were persecuted and martyred. Probably they incurred a good deal of general dislike by their refusal to participate in what, to their neighbours, was ordinary social life but, in their eyes, would implicate them in idolatrous worship. Martyrdom resulted from refusal to worship the emperor or the traditional Roman state gods who were understood to guarantee the wellbeing of the empire.

In the conflict with the empire, which Christians saw as a conflict about monotheistic worship, they again took up traditional Jewish ways of asserting this. This is the case already in Revelation (14:7; 15:4; cf. the parody of a monotheistic formula in 13:4) and is also true of the *Acts of the Martyrs* (which, whether or not their records of the words of the martyrs are accurate, are evidence of Christian views on this issue). Repeatedly, under questioning, the martyrs claim to worship the one God who made heaven and earth,[64] call down destruction on the gods who did not make heaven and earth (Jer. 10:11 LXX),[65] appeal to Old Testament commandments prohibiting the worship of any but the one God,[66] echo traditional Jewish polemic against idols,[67] and use other standard formulae of Jewish monotheistic worship ('I know of no other God besides him';[68] 'the living and true God'[69]). But, with no sense of incongruity, the martyrs also speak of Christ – the crucified man – as God and of his worship,[70] while their own prayers and worship, as they approach and suffer martyrdom, are usually to Christ.[71] We have already noticed (section 3) how the standard literary conclusion to the accounts of martyrdom sets the eternal divine kingship of *Christ* in implicit contrast to the pretended divinity of the emperor and the eternity of the empire.

It is worth pausing over the political implications of monotheistic worship, since it has been alleged that the cult of Christ is a post-Nicene development that functioned as the ideological basis for the Christian empire of Constantine and his successors: 'The entire imperial cult

---

[64] *Mart. Pion.* 8.3; 9.6; 16.3; 19.8, 11; *Mart. Fruct.* 2.4; *Mart. Mont. Luc.* 19.5; *Mart. Jul.* 2.3; *Mart. Agape* 5.2; *Mart. Crisp.* 1.7; 2.3; *Mart. Phil.* Gk. 9–10; Lat. 3.4.

[65] *Mart. Carp.* Gk. 9; Lat. 2; *Mart. Crisp.* 2.3; *Mart. Eupl.* Lat. 2.5.

[66] *Mart. Pion.* 3.3; *Mart. Mont. Luc.* 14.1; *Mart. Jul.* 2.1; *Mart. Iren. Sirm.* 2.1; *Lett. Phil.* 10 (apud Eusebius, *Hist. eccl.* 8.10.10); *Mart. Phil.* Lat. 1.1.

[67] *Mart. Carp.* Gk. 1.6–7; *Mart. Marc.* Rec. M 1.1; *Mart. Iren. of Sirm.* 4.3; *Mart. Crisp.* 3.2.

[68] *Mart. Crispina* 1.4; cf. Dionysius of Alexander *apud* Eusebius, *Hist. Eccl.* 7.11.5.

[69] *Mart. Carp.* Lat. 3.4; *Mart. Jul.* 1.4; *Mart. Crisp.* 1.6.

[70] *Mart. Carp.* Gk. 5; *Mart. Pion.* 9.8–9; 16.4–5; *Mart. Con.* 4.2; 6.4; *Mart. Max.* 2.4; *Mart. Jul.* 3.4; *Mart. Fel.* 30; *Mart. Phil.* Gk. 5–6; *Mart. Eupl.* Lat. 2:4.

[71] *Mart. Carp.* Gk. 41; Lat. 4.6; 5; 6.5; *Mart. Fruct.* 4.3; *Mart. Con.* 6:4; *Mart. Jul.* 4:4; *Mart. Fel.* 30; *Mart. Iren. Sirm.* 5.2, 4; *Mart. Eupl.* Lat. 2.6; 3.3. This point is apparently made by K. Baus, 'Das Gebet der Märtyrer,' *Trierer Theologische Zeitschrift* 62 (1953): 19–32, which I have not been able to see. Cf. also Adalbert Hamann, 'La prière chrétienne et la prière païenne, formes et differences,' in *ANRW* 2.25.2 (1980): 1190–1247, here 1239–42.

and ideology was refocused on Christ, while in return Christ crowned his earthly deputy and validated his rule' (Don Cupitt).[72] Jewish monotheism, of course, had always had strong political implications, precisely because of its definition by exclusive worship of the God of Israel. It entailed refusing to pay divine honours to any divinized ruler or to the Roman state gods who guaranteed the wellbeing of the empire. Christians continued to draw this consequence from exclusive monotheism. Precisely this is one of Celsus's charges against them. In Celsus's Platonism, worship is properly paid to the lesser divinities, including the emperor, because they are ministers of the supreme God: to honour them is to honour him (*apud* Origen, *Cels.* 7.68; 8.2; 63; 66). But the exclusive monotheistic cult of the Christians he sees as a threat to the religio-political order, a threat not mitigated but intensified by the fact – incomprehensible to Celsus – that *Jesus* is the object of this exclusive worship.[73] To pagans Christianity was the cult of a crucified man – ridiculous at best, but subversive at worst, because it entailed religious loyalty to a man who suffered the deserved fate of a slave or a rebel.[74] The martyrs repudiated the divine lordship of Caesar and asserted the divine lordship of Jesus who was crucified on Caesar's authority. Much as they protested their loyalty to the empire *under God*, the effect of monotheistic worship in relativizing all political authority was radicalized by the Christian focusing of monotheistic worship on a crucified man. Thus, in the pre-Constantinian period in which the worship of Jesus originated and flourished, it had quite the opposite effect from that alleged by Cupitt for the Constantinian period. So far from giving earthly rule divine sanction, it deprived political authority of divine sanction and aligned the rule of God with people condemned by political authority – the crucified Jesus and his worshippers, the martyrs.[75]

7. Relationship to patristic christological development

How could Jewish monotheism accommodate the worship of Jesus? It seems clear, from what we know of popular Christianity in the first

---

[72] D. Cupitt, 'The Christ of Christendom,' in *The Myth of God Incarnate*, ed. John Hick (London: SCM, 1977), 133–47, here 139.

[73] Mühlenberg, 'The Divinity,' 141–2.

[74] Martin Hengel, *Crucifixion*, trans. John Bowden (London: SCM, 1977), chap. 1.

[75] For a broader response to Cupitt's account of the relationship of Christology to Roman politics, see Colin Gunton, *Yesterday and Today: A Study of Continuities in Christology* (London: Darton, Longman & Todd, 1983), chap. 9.

three centuries, that for most Christians this was not a real problem. Worship of Jesus was worship of God. Jesus was not an alternative, competitive object of worship alongside the Father. His worship was included within the worship of the one God. In this way, popular Christianity combined the exclusive monotheism of its parent religion with the worship of Jesus that the central datum of Christian faith and experience – the divine activity of Jesus – required. However, in order to maintain and safeguard this position, it was necessary for reflective theology to reach a doctrinal understanding of the being of God and the being of Christ which could do justice to the two propositions: that only God may be worshipped, and that Jesus is such that he must be worshipped. The search for such an understanding, within the intellectual context of the time, occupied Christian thinkers for the whole of the patristic period. The worship of Jesus was a major factor determining the result. As Frans Jozef van Beeck puts it, 'The divinity of Christ was defined precisely because Christians worshipped Christ.'[76]

By means of a necessary oversimplification, we can identify two important trends in ante-Nicene Christianity's reflection on the relation of Jesus to God.[77] One trend remained close to the worshipping life of the church *and* to Jewish monotheism; it reflects very faithfully the evidence just surveyed for the worship of Jesus and for the retention, in Christian witness, of exclusive monotheistic worship against the polytheistic worship of paganism. It is easy to see how this combination might lead in the direction of modalism, in which the distinction between the Father and the Son was simply denied. As we have already remarked, in connection with the apocryphal Acts, by no means everything that, taken in isolation, sounds modalistic really is. But the danger was present. If only God may be worshipped and if Jesus may be worshipped, then the conclusion could be drawn that there can be no real distinction between God the Father and God as incarnate in Jesus.

Such a proposition was not likely to succeed in the long run. It neglected too much in the witness of the Bible and the tradition to the personal distinction between Jesus and his Father and, while doing justice to the worship of Jesus, abolished his mediatorial role, which was

---

[76] Frans Jozef van Beeck, *Christ Proclaimed: Christology as Rhetoric* (New York: Paulist, 1979), 114.

[77] For the distinction between popular faith and academic theology in this period, see Lebreton, 'Le désaccord'; H.J. Carpenter, 'Popular Christianity and the Theologians in the Early Centuries,' *JTS* 14 (1963): 294–310.

equally strong in the tradition, not least in the liturgy. But it is easy to see why it made an immediate appeal and was at first tolerated by the early third-century bishops of Rome.[78] Noetus, defending his modalistic teaching against the elders of the church of Smyrna, asked, 'What evil am I doing by giving glory *(doxazōn)* to Christ?' (Hippolytus, *Noet.* 1.6; the importance of the point is shown by the way Hippolytus takes it up in 9.2; 14.6–8; and concludes the work with his own doxology addressed to the Son along with the Father and the Holy Spirit: 18.2).

The other trend is represented by the tradition of intellectual theology, which was relatively more independent of the worship and witness of ordinary Christianity. This tradition begins in the apologists of the second century and continues in the Alexandrians and the Origenist tradition. At first sight, it may seem surprising that the danger of a paganizing of Christianity arose here rather than in popular Christianity, but there is a clear reason why this was, in fact, the case. Christianity had no difficulty in distinguishing itself from popular paganism, towards which it was consistently intolerant, but the Christian intellectuals were engaged in a critical appropriation of pagan philosophy. The result was that they tended to use Platonic monotheism as the model for understanding the relation of Jesus to God. God, the Father, is the supreme God, while Christ, the Logos, is god in a subordinate and derivative sense. And, just as the Platonist did not confine worship to the supreme God but allowed the worship of lesser divinities to appropriate degrees, so the Christian practice of the worship of Jesus could be permissible as the relative worship of the principal divine intermediary, while absolute worship is reserved for the one who is God in the fullest sense. The danger in this Christian Platonism was the loss of monotheism in the Judeo-Christian sense.

In relation to worship, we can see one possible effect in a surprising passage of Justin Martyr's first Apology, in which he defends Christians against the charge of atheism by claiming that, in fact, they worship a number of divine beings: not only God, but also 'the Son who came from him …, and the host of other good angels who follow him and are made like him, and the prophetic Spirit, we worship and adore *(sebometha kai proskunoumen)'* (1 *Apol.* 6). The inclusion of the angels represents an attempt to assimilate the Christian view of the divine world as closely as possible to the Platonic hierarchy of divinity: first God, second God, and a multitude of lesser divine beings (cf. also Athenagoras, *Leg.* 10.5; Origen, *Cels.* 8.13). This is apologetic and should

---

[78] Cf. Carpenter, 'Popular Christianity,' 304–6.

not be taken as a serious claim that Christians worship angels, but it illustrates how Platonic influence could undermine the Jewish principle of monotheistic worship.

In Origen, we see the growing gap between a platonically influenced intellectual theology and the popular faith and practice of the church precisely in relation to this principle.[79] Origen distinguishes four types of prayer and worship.[80] Three of them (supplication, intercession and thanksgiving) may quite properly be made to human beings as well as to God, but the fourth, which is prayer in the fullest sense of the word *(kuriolexia)* and is accompanied by praise, is properly offered only to the unoriginated God, not to any derived being and so *not even to Christ (Or.* 14–15; cf. *Cels.* 5.11; 8.26). Origen is conscious of how far this diverges from the practice of 'uninstructed and simple' Christians (16.1), and the extent of the tension is indicated by his own divergent practice (see section 3 above) and even, apparently, divergent theory elsewhere *(Cels.* 8.67; cf. *Or.* 33.1). His ability elsewhere to accommodate actual Christian practice of worshipping Jesus is explained by *Cels.* 5.4: all types of prayer can be offered to the Logos, *provided* 'we are capable of a clear understanding of the absolute and relative sense of prayer'.

The absolute and relative sense of prayer corresponds to Origen's hierarchical view of divinity, in which only the Father, the supreme God, is God in the absolute sense, and the Son is divine in a relative sense, deriving his divinity from the supreme God and mediating between the supreme God and the rest of reality. Hence, worship in the proper sense is due only to the supreme God, but must be offered through the mediation of the Son *(Or.* 15.1–2), who himself can be worshipped only *as an intermediary* who mediates our prayers to, and himself prays to, the Father *(Cels.* 8.13, 26). Thus Origen, constrained by, on the one hand, his platonically influenced doctrine of God and, on the other hand, the Christian practice of worshipping Jesus, halts between a rigorously monotheistic worship, which would allow only the one who is God in the fullest sense, the Father, to be addressed in worship, and a Platonic permission to worship, in appropriate degrees, all subordinate divinities (cf. *Cels.* 8.66–67).

Early Arianism was, in one sense, a reassertion of Judeo-Christian monotheism. Rejecting the notion of degrees of divinity, Arius drew an absolute distinction between the Creator and all creatures. Christ could not be a lesser divinity and so he had to be, in the last resort, a creature. The effect was that Arius enabled the christological implications of

---

[79] Lebreton, 'Le désaccord,' 13–24; Wiles, *The Making,* 72–5.
[80] The idea of the four types of prayer, and the terminology, derive from 1 Tim. 2:1.

the worship of Jesus to be clearly seen: either Christians worship a creature, or Jesus belongs to the being of the one God who alone may be worshipped. If this was not at first fully recognized by the Arians, it was by Alexander of Alexandria *(Ep. Alex.* 31) and Athanasius, who continually accused the Arians of idolatry in worshipping Jesus whom they considered a creature *(Ep. Adelph.* 3; *Depos.* 2.23; 3.16). Arianism itself seems not to have entirely abolished the worship of the Son, but severely restricted it and understood it in a strongly Origenist way – as honouring the one who mediates worship to the Father who is the only proper object of worship (Theognis of Nicaea in *Serm. Ar.* frg. 16).[81]

The development of Nicene orthodoxy, on the other hand, was the attempt to do theological justice to the church's practice of worshipping Jesus with the worship due only to God. The achievement of the Trinitarian doctrine that eventually emerged from the Arian controversies was to do this without lapsing into modalism. The triumph of Nicene orthodoxy, at the fundamental level of acceptability to the church at large, was due to the justice it did to the place of Jesus in popular Christian faith, as expressed in the worship of Jesus.

Finally, the worship of Jesus again played a part as a christological principle in the christological debate that led to the Council of Chalcedon. It was the principle continually invoked by the Alexandrians, especially Cyril, against an extreme Antiochene Christology. If Jesus Christ is a man indwelt by God, a human subject alongside a divine subject in a relationship of grace, then the worship of Jesus is the worship of a man alongside the Logos (see Cyril, *Ep. Nest.* 2; and the eighth of the Twelve Anathemas in Cyril, *Ep. Nest.* 3, later adopted, in expanded form, as the ninth anathema of the Second Council of Constantinople in 553). Only if Jesus is the divine Logos incarnate is the worship of Jesus not idolatry but the worship of God incarnate. So the Council of Ephesus (431) decided.

8. Theological Conclusion

John MacIntyre, in a rather neglected but important book, *The Shape of Christology* (1966), is one of several modern writers on Christology who make the Christian practice of the worship of Jesus a methodological principle for Christology:

---

[81] T.A. Kopecek, 'Neo-Arian Religion: The Evidence of the Apostolic Constitutions,' in *Arianism: Historical and Theological Reassessments*, ed. Robert C. Gregg (Philadelphia: Philadelphia Patristic Foundation, 1985), 153–79, here 170–2.

[W]e shall not be satisfied with any christological analysis which eliminates from its conception of who he [Jesus Christ] is all valid basis for an attitude of worship to him. It is on this very score that humanistic interpretations of the person of Jesus Christ fail, that they present to us someone who cannot sustain human *worship*; admiration, perhaps, even a sense of wonder at the courage he had in the face of danger and death, but never worship. That is given only to God.

One of the questions MacIntyre proposes we should put to any christological analysis is: 'To what degree is the analysis organically united with the worship of Christ, so that it may finally come to inform, to deepen and enrich the worship of Christ?'[82]

As we have seen, the worship of Jesus was central to the character of early Christianity throughout the early centuries, beginning in the early Palestinian Christian movement. At the same time as a worshipping response to Jesus was integral to Christian faith, the early church also clung tenaciously to the Jewish understanding of monotheism, according to which belief in the one God was defined in religious practice by the exclusive worship of the one God. In time it became clear that the practice of the worship of Jesus in the context of Jewish monotheism constituted both a christological principle – that Jesus is such that he can be worshipped – and a theological (Trinitarian) principle – that God is such that Jesus can be worshipped. These were the principles that governed the development of the Nicene and Chalcedonian dogmas, and they constitute the fundamental continuity of these dogmas with the faith of the first Christians in the God and Father of the Lord Jesus Christ.

---

[82] John McIntyre, *The Shape of Christology* (Philadelphia: Westminster, 1966), 45.

5

The Throne of God and the Worship of Jesus[1]

1. Second Temple Jewish monotheism

That YHWH, the God of Israel, is the only God and that he alone may be worshipped are at the heart of Jewish religious self-understanding in the late Second Temple period. Some recent discussion might lead one to doubt this, but the evidence is abundant. For example, there is strong evidence that, in this period, Jews who were serious about the practice of Torah recited the Shemaʿ twice daily, morning and evening, as they supposed the Torah itself required.[2] Nothing could be more conducive to the inculcation of a highly self-conscious monotheism, in the sense not simply of belief that there is one God, but also in the sense of understanding this God to require exclusive devotion: to be loved and served (Heb. ʾābad, Gk. latreuō): words that refer primarily to cultic worship) with all one's heart and soul (Deut. 6:5; 10:12; 11:13). There is evidence that, at this period, the sections of Deuteronomy recited daily also included the Decalogue,[3] at least on some occasions, but, in any case, the first and second commandments of the Decalogue were clearly also central to Jewish religious self-understanding. Despite our modern problems of understanding precisely what the Shemaʿ and the first commandment of the Decalogue originally meant, we need have no

---

[1] A shorter version of this essay was published in *The Jewish Roots of Christological Monotheism*, ed. Carey C. Newman, James R. Davila and Gladys S. Lewis (JSJSup 63; Leiden: Brill, 1999), 43–69. It was written before the publication of the major study by Timo Eskola, *Messiah and Throne: Jewish Merkabah Mysticism and Early Christian Exaltation Discourse* (WUNT 2/142; Tübingen: Mohr Siebeck, 2001), with which I agree to a significant extent, while disagreeing on some key points.

[2] Josephus, *A.J.* 4.212; Aris. Ex. 160; 1QS 10:10.

[3] This is suggested by the contents of *mezuzōt* and *tefillîn* found at Qumran; by Josephus, *A.J.* 4.212; and perhaps also by the Nash Papyrus; cf. also m. Tam. 4:3 – 5:1.

doubt of how they were understood in the late Second Temple period. Josephus' paraphrase of the first commandment, in which in effect he uses the Shema᷄ to interpret it, would have met general assent: 'The first word teaches us that God is one and he only must be worshipped (*sebesthai*)' (*A.J.* 3.91). Philo paraphrases the first commandment in very similar terms: 'to acknowledge and to honour (*nomizein te kai timan*) the one God who is above all' (*Decal.* 65), while Pseudo-Philo has Abraham, the paradigm of monotheistic faith (see below), similarly combining, in effect, the Shema᷄ and the first commandment: 'We know one Lord, and him we worship' (*L.A.B.* 6:4). This was common Judaism, uncontroversial in spite of the many other things about which Jews of this period differed. Of course, there may have been exceptions, but the evidence is such that the burden of proof lies with establishing such exceptions.

Thus, the central texts of the highly scriptural religion that Second Temple Judaism was themselves forge a necessary link between the uniqueness of the God of Israel and the exclusive worship of this God. Many other texts of Second Temple Judaism support the point. But was the Jewish monotheism of this period really as 'strict' or 'inflexible' as such statements of it suggest? Recent debate has highlighted significant texts which earlier scholars did not know or neglected but, at the same time, itself tends to neglect the bulk of the evidence.

Since I first stated, in 1981, that 'in [Jewish] religious practice it was worship which signalled the distinction between God and every creature, however exalted',[4] the importance of the link between the uniqueness of God and exclusive worship of God for the definition of Jewish monotheism in our period has been quite widely recognized. The issues of definition have become, it seems to me, the twin issues of defining God (or divinity) and of defining worship. It is tempting to cut the Gordian knot by defining each in terms of the other. Worship is the honour paid to the one God, and the one God is the one to whom worship is given. This circularity is not entirely alien to the texts, so closely are monotheism and monolatry linked, but it clearly will not suffice. The texts make clear that worship can, but should not, be given to other purported gods, other heavenly beings, other creatures. But

---

[4] Richard Bauckham, 'The Worship of Jesus,' 322–3; cf. also idem, 'Jesus, Worship of,' *ABD*, 3:816 ('Judaism was unique among the religions of the Roman world in demanding the *exclusive* worship of its God. It is not too much to say that Jewish monotheism was defined by its adherence to the first and second commandments'); idem, *Climax of Prophecy*, 118 ('In the exclusive monotheism of the Jewish religious tradition, as distinct from some other kinds of monotheism, it was worship which was the real test of monotheistic faith in religious practice'); idem, *Theology*, 58–9.

why not? Instead of going first to those intriguing, and now so much debated, texts which seem to portray other heavenly beings as in some way divine, or which suggest that some kind of veneration of beings other than God was practised, we might try, for once, attending to the way the many texts (much the largest part of our evidence) that speak so emphatically of the uniqueness of the one God and condemn worship of any but him actually understand God's uniqueness and justify the restriction of worship to the one God.

The question we are asking is about the *unique identity* of YHWH the God of Israel. I do not take this term 'identity' from the texts, but all discussions of this kind find it necessary to analyze the texts with terms they do not themselves use (divine agency, divine function, hypostasis, personification and so on). I find the term 'divine identity' more useful than many of these, and certainly more useful than the concept of divine nature, even though the latter is found in a few of the texts.[5] I mean that, for the Jewish religious tradition in general, what is primary is not what God is, or what divinity is (divine nature or essence), but *who God is, who YHWH the God of Israel is*. In the Hebrew Bible and in Second Temple Jewish literature, God is depicted as a unique personal agent, identified by his distinctive activities and personal characteristics. In Second Temple Jewish literature, some of these come to special prominence in statements of his unique identity. They are those that most easily identify him as absolutely unique by attributing to him a unique relationship to the rest of reality.

Briefly, God is the only Creator of all things (heaven and earth and sea and all that is in them), and God is the only sovereign Ruler of all things (all nature and history). It is not insignificant that the phrase 'all things' is itself commonly used in the texts in these connections,[6] as well as more elaborate ways of speaking of all of creation.[7] The point is that both of these features of the divine identity define an absolute distinction between God and all other reality. He alone is Creator; all else is created by him. He alone is supreme Ruler; all else is subject to his will. Even the most exalted of creatures is created and subject to God, while God is uncreated and subject to none. These two identifying features of the unique God, both alone and together, constantly recur in non-polemical evocations of God's absolute superiority to all

---

[5] E.g. Josephus, *A.J.* 1.15, 19; 8.107; C. *Ap.* 2.167–8.

[6] E.g. Isa. 44:24; Jer. 10:16; 51:19; Sir. 43:33; Wis. 9:6; 12:13; Add. Esth. 13:9; 2 Macc. 1:24; 3 Macc. 2:3; *1 En.* 9:5; 84:3; 2 *En.* 66:4; *Jub.* 12:19; *Apoc. Ab.* 7:10; *Jos. Asen.* 12:1; *Sib. Or.* 3:20; 8:376; *Sib. Or.* frg. 1:17; Josephus, *B.J.* 5.218; 1Qap Gen^ar 20:13; 4QD^b 18:5:9.

[7] E.g. Bel 5; Add. Esth. 13:10; *Sib. Or.* 3:20–3; *Sib. Or.* frg. 1:35; Ps-Sophocles; *T. Job* 2:4; Pr. Man. 2–3.

creatures[8] and in polemical assertions of the uniqueness of the one God, YHWH, in comparison with pagan gods or creatures pagans worship as gods.[9] The second category includes many instances which base on these unique characteristics of God the restriction of worship to God alone; it is because God alone is Creator and Ruler of all that he alone is worthy of worship.[10] It is important to notice that this conforms to the way Jewish literature regularly speaks of the worship due to God alone as different in kind, not merely in degree, from whatever kind of honour may appropriately be given by inferior to superior creatures. In these many Jewish texts, worship is understood precisely as the acknowledgement of God's qualitative uniqueness, God's unique identity as only Creator and only Sovereign. I should mention that some other characteristics unique to God are also mentioned frequently in the literature, such as that God is the only Eternal One[11] or that God alone sees all things, including the secrets of human hearts.[12] But these are all corollaries or implications of the two I have emphasized.

The understanding of God's unique identity in these terms is found throughout Second Temple Jewish literature. I cite passages from *1 Enoch*, *2 Enoch*, *2 Baruch*, the *Apocalypse of Abraham*, Ben Sira, *Jubilees*, 2 Maccabees, the Additions to Daniel and Esther, Wisdom, the *Sibylline Oracles*, *Joseph and Aseneth*, the *Testament of Job*, Pseudo-Sophocles, Philo, Josephus.[13] This is once again common Judaism. Most Jews must have been well aware of these very easily grasped and easily stated ways of specifying the uniqueness of the God they worshipped. Asked why they worshipped only this God, there were answers ready to hand.

I will give one interesting and significant illustration: the story of Abraham's conversion from idolatry to monotheism. Abraham was widely regarded as the first (for many generations) to worship the only true God, the paradigm monotheist of exemplary faith. The story of his conversion, not told in the Bible, appears in four very different Jewish

---

[8] Macc. 1:24; 3 Macc. 2:2; Sir. 43:33; *2 En.* 47:3–4; *2 Bar.* 21:4–9; *1 En.* 84:2–3; Wis. 12:13; 1Qap Gen^ar 20:12–13; 1QH^a 18:8–10.

[9] Jer. 10:6–12; Bel 5; *Sib. Or.* 3:19–25; *Sib. Or.* 8:375–377; *Sib. Or.* frg. 1:5–8, 15–18; *Sib. Or.* frg. 3; *Sib. Or.* frg. 5; *2 En.* 2:2; 66:4–5; *Jos. Asen.* 12:1–2; *Apoc. Ab.* 7:10; Philo. *Opif.* 171.

[10] Bel 4–5; *Sib. Or.* 3:19–35; *Sib. Or.* 8:375–94; *Sib. Or.* frg. 1; *Sib. Or.* frg. 3; *2 En.* 66:2–5; *Jos. Asen.* 12:1–5; *Apoc. Ab.* 7; *T. Job* 2–3; Philo, *Decal.* 52–65; *Spec.* 1.13–22; Josephus, *A.J.* 1.155–6; Ps-Sophocles.

[11] *T. Mos.* 10:7; 2 Macc. 1:25; cf. 'the only living One': *2 Bar.* 21:10; 4 Macc. 5:24.

[12] E.g. 1 Kgs. 8:39; 2 Chr. 6:30; Ps. 33:13–15; Sir. 15:18–19; 42:18–20; Jdt. 8:14; Sus. 42; *1 En.* 9:5; 84:3; *2 En.* 66:3–5; 4QTLevi^a 1:10–11; *Sib. Or.* 3:12; 8:369, 373; *Sib. Or.* frg. 1:4, 8; Aris. Ex. 132–8; Josephus, *A.J.* 4.41; *C. Ap.* 2.166–7.

[13] See notes 8 and 9 above.

writers: *Jubilees*, Philo, Josephus and the *Apocalypse of Abraham*.[14] A similar story told of Job in the *Testament of Job* (3–5) is probably modelled on it. It must have been a popular story. The four accounts, different in various respects, agree that Abraham's crucial recognition was that the only true God is the Creator of all things, himself uncreated. While in *Jubilees* this is contrasted only with the worship of idols, in the other three accounts Abraham recognizes that all creatures, even the heavenly bodies that many worship as gods, are created and subject to the Creator and, therefore, not to be worshipped. Josephus' account is especially noteworthy:

> God, the creator of the universe, is one (*hena*), and that, if any other being contributed aught to man's welfare, each did so by His command and not in virtue of its own inherent power. This he inferred from the changes to which land and sea are subject, from the course of sun and moon, and from all the celestial phenomena; for, he argued, were these bodies endowed with their own power, they would have provided for their own regularity, but, since they lacked this last, it was manifest that even those services in which they cooperate for our greater benefit they render not in virtue of their own authority, but through the might of their commanding sovereign, to whom alone it is right to render our homage (*timēn*) and thanksgiving (*eucharistian*) (*A.J.* 1.155–6, tr. Thackeray).

It is very clear here (and equally in Philo and the *Apocalypse of Abraham*) that the worship due to God alone is contrasted not only with worship of purported (pagan) gods but also with worship of creaturely servants of God. There does not seem to be any room for worshipping such servants of God as his subordinates so long as God is acknowledged as supreme. Josephus' reasoning would apply equally to angels, such as those whom Jews generally believed to control the movements of the heavenly bodies and all other inanimate parts of nature. Worship is due only to the one who alone created and commands all creatures. It is notable that the words Josephus uses for worship (*tēn timēn kai tēn eucharistian aponemein*) do not in themselves obviously specify an activity directed appropriately only to God (though in Jewish use of Greek, *eucharistia* and *eucharisteō* are very predominantly used with reference to God). It is not so much these words, but the context that defines their peculiar significance here. In effect, Josephus is defining worship as the kind of homage and thanksgiving that acknowledges the only Creator and Ruler of all as the true source

---

[14] *Jub.* 12:1–5, 19; Josephus *A.J.* 1.155–6; *Apoc. Ab.* 7:1 – 9:4; Philo, *Virt.* 212–19.

of all benefits and blessings. Such an understanding of the one God and his worship entails a radical relativizing of all relationships of inferiority and superiority among his creatures, such as Philo expresses when he designates all created beings, even the most exalted, as our brothers:

> Let us ... refrain from worshipping those who by nature are our brothers, even though they have been given a substance purer and more immortal than ours, for created things, in so far as they are created, are brothers, since they have all one Father, the Maker of the universe (*Decal.* 64).

The same relativizing of differences between creatures is present in the motif to be found in some apocalypses, when an angel rejects the worship offered him by the seer on the grounds that they are both fellow-servants of God (*Ascen. Isa.* 8:5; Rev. 19:10; 22:9; cf. also Tob. 12:18).[15]

The evidence of the literature is clear that the overwhelming tendency in Second Temple Judaism was to depict God as absolutely unique, to differentiate God as completely as possible from all other reality, and to understand the exclusive worship of God as marking, in religious practice, the absolute distinction between God and all creatures. This is not to say that there are no traces remaining in Second Temple Jewish literature of the notions that God is the most eminent example of the species 'deity' or that God is the chief of a divine hierarchy. Jewish monotheism was a historical phenomenon, whose ways of portraying God and his uniqueness were often fashioned out of older or non-Jewish materials that lacked the typically sharp Second Temple Jewish understanding of divine uniqueness. It would be surprising if nothing at all in the least open to a less strictly monotheistic interpretation remained. But such traces are, in fact, only rarely and weakly discernible, and can usually be seen to have been subordinated and neutralized by the dominant tendency. We shall miss this dynamic of Jewish monotheistic thought and misconstrue the evidence, placing the weight in the wrong places, unless we take fully seriously the ways of characterizing the unique identity of God that I have very briefly indicated in this section.

2. Intermediary figures

We have seen that Jewish literature itself defines monotheism for us. It understands the unique divine identity as distinguished from all

---

[15] Cf. Bauckham, *Climax of Prophecy*, 120–48; Stuckenbruck, *Angel Veneration*, 75–103.

other reality, especially in that God is sole Creator and sole supreme Ruler of all things. It is this unique identity that monotheistic worship acknowledges and to which it responds. It is important to grasp that it is intrinsic to the divine identity, intrinsic to who God is, that God is sole Creator and sole Ruler of all things. These are not mere functions that can be delegated to creatures. Hence the literature finds it important to deny that God had co-workers or assistants in the work of creation[16] and to make clear that those servants who carry out God's will in the governance of the universe are no more than servants who do his will.[17] In the light of this understanding of the divine uniqueness, we can now turn to the various intermediary figures who have seemed, to so many recent scholars, to blur the distinction between God and other heavenly beings. The key question to ask about such figures is: Is this figure included within the unique divine identity or not? To put the issue in this way is not to attempt to impose uniformity on the diversity of the literature, since the understanding of the unique identity of God that I have sketched can often be found in precisely the texts in which the intermediary figures appear.

In chapter 1, I have argued that answers to the question, 'Is this figure included within the unique divine identity or not?' reveal two distinct categories of figures. First, there are those which are included in the unique identity of God. These are personifications or hypostatizations of aspects of God himself, such as his Spirit, his Word or his Wisdom.

---

[16] Isa. 44:24; 2 *En.* 33:4; 4 *Ezra* 3:4; Josephus, *C. Ap.* 2.192. Even Philo's exegesis of Gen. 1:26 in *Opif.* 72–5; *Conf.* 179 is only a minor qualification of this denial: he insists that God acted alone in the creation of all things *except* humanity, and holds that the plural in Gen. 1:26 ('let *us* make humanity in *our* image and *our* likeness') involves subordinate co-workers of God so that, while good human actions may be attributed to God as their source, sins may not. On Jewish interpretations of this plural, see Menahem Kister, 'Some Early Jewish and Christian Exegetical Problems and the Dynamics of Monotheism,' *JSJ* (2006): 548–93, here 563–89.

[17] Unlike the later rabbinic discussions, there is no evidence in the texts that such monotheistic safeguards have an inner-Jewish polemic as their context. The polemic, where it exists, is against pagan idolatry and polytheism. (This explains why the polemical assertions of monotheism are more plentiful in literature written in the Diaspora than in literature written in Palestine, though anti-pagan polemic was not irrelevant in Palestine.) I am inclined to regard even the motif of an angel refusing worship, which has been studied by myself and Stuckenbruck (see n. 381 above), as directed not against a Jewish practice of venerating angels, but against the pagan worship of heavenly beings who could be seen by Jews as comparable with angels. As also in New Testament texts, ways of accentuating the distinction between God and angels functioned as ways of positively highlighting the uniqueness of God without being necessarily aimed negatively against other views of angels.

As aspects of the unique divine identity, they are included in it. They are fully compatible with the absolute uniqueness of God, as understood in the Jewish monotheism of this period, and are not seen as, in any way, qualifying or threatening it. The second category is of figures who, though they act as servants of God exercising some degree of delegated divine authority, are not included in God's unique identity and in no way qualify or threaten its uniqueness. These are principal angels and exalted patriarchs. Once we take full account of the ways in which Jewish monotheism itself characterized the unique identity of God, it becomes possible to see that one category, the personifications or hypostatizations of aspects of God, falls unproblematically within it, while the other category, the principal angels and exalted patriarchs, falls (in every case but one) unproblematically outside it.

Without being able to demonstrate these conclusions in the present context, I want to make a few important points about them before narrowing our focus to the specific interest of this chapter:

(1) The texts, in my view, are concerned for the unique identity of God, not for the unitariness of God, which became a facet of Jewish monotheism only later. In other words, there is no reason why there should not be real distinctions within the unique identity of God. To say that the Wisdom of God and the Word of God are portrayed as intrinsic to the unique identity of God does not, in itself, decide the highly debated question of the extent to which their portrayal as personal agents is merely literary personification or real hypostatization. I am inclined to think this varies in the various texts. What my conclusion does deny is either that they are divine beings subordinate to the one God or that they are non-divine creatures of God. However much real existence of their own they are envisaged to have, they belong to the one God's own unique identity, to *who he is*. Similarly, it is not because high-ranking angels are portrayed as personal agents that they should not be seen as intrinsic to the unique divine identity.

(2) Of the two key aspects of the uniqueness of God – sole Creator and sole Ruler – the first operates as a criterion of divinity very straightforwardly. None of the principal angels or exalted patriarchs is portrayed as participating in the work of creation, and it has hardly ever been suggested that they are. God's Wisdom and God's Word, on the other hand, are regularly portrayed as participants in creation.

(3) I dissent from the rather popular view among recent scholars
that Jewish writers of this period commonly envisaged a single
grand vizier or plenipotentiary of God, who, as second to God
in the government of the universe, has the whole of the divine
sovereignty delegated to him.[18] When the image of God as the
great emperor ruling the universe by means of a great hierarchy
of angelic servants is employed, as it often is, the general view is
that God governs by means of a council of angelic ministers with
differentiated areas of responsibility. Some may rank higher than
others (though the texts offer no consistent evidence of this), but
none has overall responsibility for all areas of government. I find
the idea of a single vicegerent of God in only a few cases where
special considerations can be seen to be at work: the archangel
(probably Michael) in *Joseph and Aseneth*, where his role in heaven
is modelled on Joseph's in Egypt (14:8–9; cf. Gen. 45:8);[19] the Spirit
of truth or Prince of light (also identified with Michael) in some
Qumran texts (especially 1QS 3:15 – 4:1), where the role is due to
the rather distinctive features of Qumran dualism; and the Logos
in Philo, who had his own philosophical-theological reasons for
envisaging a single mediator of all divine relationship to the
world. The other so-called intermediary figures have much more
limited roles.

(4) I do not consider visible appearance a criterion of divine identity,
and theories of divine bifurcation or binitarianism or angels
as visible manifestations of God that depend on resemblances
between visual descriptions of God and those of other heavenly
beings[20] are based on a fallacy. Descriptions of the form of God
(which are quite rare in the literature) do not employ elements
of description which are specific or unique to God, but borrow
a standard set of descriptives that could be used to describe any
heavenly being, including quite ordinary, as well as quite exalted,
heavenly beings. The basic idea behind all these descriptions is
that heaven[21] and its inhabitants are shining and bright. Hence
the descriptions especially employ a stock series of images

---

[18] E.g. Segal, *Two Powers*, 186–200; Hurtado, *One God*, 71–82; Hayman, 'Monotheism,' 11;
Barker, *Great Angel*.

[19] In addition, the date and provenance of *Joseph and Aseneth* are problematic, and so as
evidence for Second Temple Judaism it can be considered only tentatively.

[20] E.g. Rowland, *Open Heaven*, 94–111; idem, 'A Man Clothed in Linen: Daniel 10:6ff. and
Jewish Angelology,' *JSNT* 24 (1985): 99–110; Gieschen, *Angelomorphic Christology*, 32. Against
Rowland's theory of 'bifurcation', see Hurtado, *One God*, 85–90.

[21] For the unimaginable brightness of the heavenly world, see *Ascen. Isa.* 8:21–5.

of brightness, the more resplendent and dazzling the better: heavenly beings or appropriate parts of them or their dress are typically shining like the sun or the stars, gleaming like bronze or amber or precious stones, fiery bright like torches or lightning, dazzling white like snow or pure white wool. The most that can be said of such descriptions is that, as a literary convention, they are a survival of the old notion of a species identity that YHWH shared with all heavenly beings (gods). All such beings have glorious, shining bright appearances, like the heavenly bodies that can be seen in the sky. But in Second Temple Jewish literature, in which YHWH has been exalted beyond species identity to an absolutely unique identity, such descriptions no longer function to indicate a common species to which he and other heavenly beings alike belong.

3. The heavenly throne of God

In the rest of the chapter, we shall focus on the role of the divine throne in the highest heaven as symbolizing the sole sovereignty of God over all things, a role which it has already in the Hebrew Bible: 'YHWH has established his throne in the heavens, and his kingdom rules over all' (Ps. 103:19).[22] We should notice a number of important aspects of the depiction of this throne, often called 'the throne of [his] glory',[23] in Second Temple Jewish literature.

3.1. God's throne and other thrones

In most cases, the throne of God is unique, being the only throne in heaven,[24] though we should note a few exceptions and apparent exceptions to this rule. The most important (since it is the only scriptural instance) is Daniel 7:9, which speaks of 'thrones' set up, on one of which the Ancient One takes his seat. However, the scene does not describe God's permanent rule over the world, but the eschatological session of the divine court of judgement, and so could readily be understood as set

---

[22] Cf. Pss. 2:4; 9:8; 29:20; 55:20; 93:2; 102:13; 1 Kgs. 22:19.

[23] Jer. 14:21; 17:12; *1 En.* 9:4; 71:7; 4Q405 23.1.3; 11QShirShabb 3–1-9.5–6; *Lad. Jac.* 2:7; *T. Levi* 5:1; Wis. 9:10; *T. Adam* 2:9; b.Hag. 13a; Visions of Ezekiel; ARN (a) 37.

[24] E.g. 1 Kgs. 22:19; Sir. 1:8; Pr. Azar. 32–33; *1 En.* 9:4; 14:18; 71:7; *2 En.* 20:3; 25:4; *2 Bar.* 21:6; *Apoc. Ab.* 18:3; *Ques. Ezra* A21; *T. Levi* 5:1; *T. Adam* 2:9. The *Songs of the Sabbath Sacrifice* refer on occasions to several thrones or chariots in the heavenly temple, but they are all thrones of God, like the thrones in the seven heavens in the later Visions of Ezekiel.

on earth rather than in heaven (cf. 4Q530 2.16–17;[25] *1 En.* 90:20; Rev. 20:4). The plural thrones could be understood as those of the divine council of heavenly beings who sit, under God's presidency, in judgement (cf. 7:10, 26), or they could be thought to include a throne on which the humanlike figure is implicitly enthroned in verse 14.[26] Surprisingly, neither interpretation seems to be attested in the literature of Second Temple Judaism, despite the considerable influence this chapter of Daniel exercised. In the *Parables of Enoch*, it is not on a second throne but on the single divine throne that the Son of Man takes his seat for eschatological judgement, while the divine council, though mentioned in a description of the judgement otherwise closely based on Daniel 7, are explicitly said to stand (*1 En.* 47:3; cf. 60:2). A few New Testament texts speak of a plurality of thrones occupied by followers of Jesus, who exercise judgement with him in the end-time (Matt. 19:28; Luke 22:30; Rev. 20:4; cf. 3:21). In our period, there is no evidence of controversy over the interpretation of the thrones in Daniel 7:9, such as is attested later in rabbinic literature, but the silence of the texts about these plural thrones is eloquent. Not only God's throne in heaven, but also the throne on which he sits for the eschatological judgement, is usually unaccompanied by any others (*4 Ezra* 7:33; *1 En.* 90:20; Rev. 20:11).

Secondly, among exceptions to the rule that God's throne is the only throne in heaven, we should note that the old notion of a council of heavenly beings seated with, and ruling with, God apparently survives in some texts (some Christian, but in continuity with Jewish tradition), but in significantly modified forms that make it clear that those who sit on thrones are not co-rulers with God but strictly subordinates. One form is found in Revelation 4, where the twenty-four elders seated on thrones in heaven are best understood as angelic figures governing the cosmos on God's behalf. But their continual action of getting down off their thrones, prostrating themselves before the throne of God and casting down their crowns before it (4:9–10) – so that apparently they are never more than momentarily seated on their thrones – makes their subordination to God's rule emphatically obvious. Revelation does not depict a series of heavens, but a few texts that do achieve

---

[25] For this text (a fragment of the Enochic Book of Giants), see Loren T. Stuckenbruck, 'The Throne-Theophany of the Book of Giants: Some New Light on the Background of Daniel 7,' in *The Scrolls and the Scriptures*, ed. Stanley E. Porter and Craig A. Evans (JSPSup 26; Roehampton Institute London Papers 3; Sheffield: Sheffield Academic Press, 1997), 216–17. He translates: 'Behold, the ruler of the heavens descended to earth, and thrones were erected and the Great Holy One sat down.'

[26] This is the interpretation attributed to R. Aqiva in b.Hag. 14a: 'one for him [God] and one for David' (presumably presupposing that the humanlike figure in Daniel 7 is the Davidic Messiah).

the same end by placing angels on thrones in lower heavens, where they are occupied in praising God in the highest heaven (*Apoc. Zeph. ap.* Clement of Alexandria, *Strom.* 5.11.77; *Ascen. Isa.* 7:14, 19, 24, 29, 33; 8:7–10). Similarly, an order of angels known as 'thrones' are located by the Testament of Levi (3:8) in the fourth heaven, where they are occupied in praising God, and are the eighth of ten angelic ranks who stand (!) praising God on his throne far above them in 2 *Enoch* (20:1–4J).[27] The only case in which the idea of the divine council seated on thrones seems to appear without any evident trace of a relativizing modification is the enigmatic fragment 11 of 4Q491,[28] in which an unknown speaker claims to have sat on 'a mighty throne in the congregation of the gods'. The speaker appears to be a human being who has had the unique honour of sitting in the divine council in heaven. In the fragmentary state of the text, it is difficult to say more.

Thirdly, in a few texts (but mostly, if not entirely, Christian ones), the righteous after death are depicted as sitting on thrones in heaven (*T. Job* 33; *1 En.* 108:12; *Ascen. Isa.* 9:24–5; 11:40; *Apoc. El.* 1:8; 4:27, 29).

3.2. Sitting and standing in heaven

Corresponding to the fact that in most of the texts the only throne in heaven is God's is the fact that, in heaven, God alone sits, while the angels who attend him are regularly described as standing.[29] Standing is the posture of the servant (cf. 3 *En.* 16:2). The prevalence of this image shows how the Second Temple Jewish emphasis on the sole sovereignty of God has functioned to reduce all other heavenly beings to the role of subservience and service, effecting the will of the one enthroned Being.[30] In most literature of the period, the most exalted of angels, the archangels, do not participate in God's rule but function as servants, standing ready to carry out his orders.[31] Enoch also, exalted to heaven, is to 'stand in front of my face forever' (2 *En.* 22:6).[32] The rule that 'on

---

[27] For the thrones as an order of angels, see also *Apoc. El.* 1:10–11; 4:10; *Hist. Rech.* 16:1a; *T. Adam* 4:8; Col. 1:16.

[28] For a discussion, see Martin G. Abegg, 'Who Ascended to Heaven? 4Q491, 4Q427, and the Teacher of Righteousness,' in *Eschatology, Messianism, and the Dead Sea Scrolls*, ed. Craig A. Evans and Peter W. Flint (Grand Rapids: Eerdmans, 1997), 61–73.

[29] E.g. Dan. 7:10; 4Q530 2.18; *1 En.* 14:22; 39:12; 40:1; 47:3; 60:2; 2 *En.* 21:1; *Ques. Ezra* A26, 30; 2 *Bar.* 21:6; 48:10; *4 Ezra* 8:21; *T. Ab.* A7:11; 8:1; 9:7; *T. Adam* 2:9.

[30] For this emphasis, see already Ps. 103:19–22.

[31] Tob. 12:15; *T. Ab.* A7:11; 8:1–4; 9:7–8; cf. also Luke 1:19.

[32] Though Enoch is also, in the same work, invited to sit on God's left by Gabriel [24:1], this is simply a temporary posture from which Enoch can see the creation as God explains it to him.

high there is no sitting', found later in rabbinic tradition (b.Hag. 15a; Gen. Rab. 65:1; cf. *3 En.* 18:24), seems already to have been operative in the Second Temple period.

3.3. In the heights of heaven

The symbolism of the throne as indicative of God's absolute sovereignty over the whole cosmos is assisted by the prevalent image of height. Following Isaiah 6:1 (which for later Jewish readers referred to God's throne in the heavenly temple), the great height of the throne itself is sometimes stressed. In the oldest version of Enoch's vision of God, he sees the 'lofty throne' of God (*1 En.* 14:18), to which not even the most exalted of angels can come close (14:22). In *2 Enoch*, even when he is among the angelic hosts on the threshold of the seventh heaven, he can see the Lord only 'from a distance, sitting on his exceedingly high throne' (*2 En.* 20:3J). The heavens, we should remember, were imagined as vast in height, and each one much higher than the one below it.[33] The throne of God, at the summit of them all, is envisaged as unimaginably high above the earth, and even above the various ranks of angels who serve God in the lower heavens. It represents the absolute divine rule, not merely over human society, but over the whole cosmos, the world of nature, the unseen worlds of the heavens and Hades, the whole of reality which God, the sole cosmic emperor, governs by his myriads of angelic servants.

3.4. Conclusion

In Second Temple Judaism, then, the throne of God in the highest heaven became a key symbol of monotheism, representative of one of the essential characteristics definitive of the divine identity. While a few traces of other enthroned figures associated with God's rule can be found, the subordination of such figures to God's rule is almost always stressed, while the overwhelming trend of the literature is towards emptying heaven of all thrones except God's. There is no indication that this was a controverted issue, as it was later in rabbinic discussions of Daniel 7:9 and of Metatron.[34] The uniqueness of the heavenly throne of God belongs to the logic of the monotheism that dominated common Judaism in the Second Temple period.

---

[33] Cf. *3 Bar.* 2:2; 3:2; 4:2; *Ascen. Isa.* 7:18, 28; Visions of Ezekiel.
[34] b.Hag. 14a, 15a; *3 En.* 16.

4. Figures on the throne

The symbolic function of the unique divine throne is such that, if we find a figure distinguishable from God seated on God's throne itself, we should see that as one of Judaism's most potent theological means of including such a figure in the unique divine identity.[35] This is the hypothesis to be tested in consideration of the three relevant cases in Second Temple Jewish literature, and of the case of Jesus in early Christianity. The three non-Christian Jewish instances are each very different and each in its own way very instructive.

4.1. Wisdom on the throne

There are two texts in which Wisdom is represented as sharing God's throne. One is in *1 Enoch* 84:2–3, a prayer in which the reference to Wisdom occurs within a fine example of the kind of monotheistic rhetoric of the sole divine sovereignty with which we have been concerned:

> Blessed are you, O Lord, King,
> great and mighty in your majesty,
> Lord of all the creation of the heaven,
> King of kings and God of all eternity.
> Your power and your reign and your majesty abide for ever and for ever
> and ever abide for ever and ever,
> and to all generations your dominion.
> All the heavens are your throne forever,
> and all the earth is your footstool for ever and for ever and ever.
> For you have made and you rule all things,
> and nothing is too difficult for you;
> Wisdom does not escape you,
> <and it does not turn away from your throne,>[36] nor from your
>   presence.
> You know and see and hear all things
> and there is nothing that is hidden from you.[37]

---

[35] So, rightly, Gieschen, *Angelomorphic Christology*, 93–4: 'Texts in which a figure shares the divine throne with God, or is its sole occupant, make a profound theological statement in a Jewish context: divinity could be ascribed to the enthroned figure.' I would say: 'divinity must be ascribed to the enthroned figure.'

[36] Nickelsburg and VanderKam have emended the text here.

[37] Translation from George W.E. Nickelsburg and James C. VanderKam, *1 Enoch: A New Translation* (Minneapolis: Fortress, 2004), 119.

The picture is of God's Wisdom seated beside him as his adviser, constantly present to advise him in all the exercise of his rule. The picture is not in the least tension with the monotheistic emphasis on God's rule over all things or with the insistence found in other monotheistic texts that God needs no counsellor (Isa. 40:13; Sir. 42:21; *1 En.* 14:22; and cf. Wis. 9:13, 17; 1QS 11:18–19), because Wisdom is not someone other than God, whose advice God needs, but God's own Wisdom, intrinsic to his own divine identity. As *2 Enoch* 33:4 (J) puts it, without contradiction, 'there is no adviser ... My Wisdom is my adviser'.

The picture of Wisdom seated beside God on the throne of the universe is found also in the book of Wisdom, where Solomon asks God to 'give me the Wisdom who sits as your assessor on your throne (*tēn tōn sōn thronōn paredron sophian*)' (9:4) and to send her 'from the throne of your glory ... that she may labour at my side' (9:10). The picture is again of Wisdom as God's supremely knowledgeable adviser who will, therefore, be able to instruct and advise Solomon as only God's Wisdom could (9:9–12). The fact that the image occurs in two such different texts as *1 Enoch* 84 and Wisdom suggests that it should not be regarded as eccentric. It is part of the general tendency to portray the Wisdom of God as intrinsic, not extrinsic, to the unique divine identity.

4.2. Moses on the throne

Ezekiel the Tragedian's remarkable account of Moses' dream, in which he sees himself seated on the cosmic throne of God, has been widely discussed but, in my view, has been misunderstood by almost all interpreters,[38] and so I have to treat this particular text in some detail. The real interpretative crux is the relationship between the dream itself and Raguel's interpretation of the dream, between the extravagant exaltation of Moses to the throne of the universe in the dream and the much more modest account of Moses' role in the biblical story which Raguel gives as the meaning of the dream. None of the proposed

---

[38] The major discussions are listed in C.R. Holladay, *Fragments from Hellenistic Jewish Authors: Volume II: Poets* (SBLTT 30; Atlanta: Scholars, 1989), 437–8; but add Pieter W. van der Horst, 'Moses' Throne Vision in Ezekiel the Dramatist,' in *Essays on the Jewish World of Early Christianity* (NTOA 14; Göttingen: Vandenhoeck & Ruprecht, 1990), 63–71; William Horbury, 'The Gifts of God in Ezekiel the Tragedian,' in *Messianism Among Jews and Christians* (London/New York: T&T Clark, 2003), 65–82; Eskola, *Messiah*, 86–90; Jane Heath, 'Homer or Moses? A Hellenistic Perspective on Moses' Throne Vision in Ezekiel Tragicus,' *JJS* 58 (2007): 1–17.

interpretations succeed in doing justice to both: either they cannot admit that it is really the divine throne of the cosmos on which Moses is seated in his dream, or they are obliged to see Raguel's interpretation as seriously incomplete and inadequate.

What seems to have been missed is the clear evidence that Raguel takes the dream, like most symbolic dreams and visions in Jewish literature, as figurative. What the dream means is something other than what it says, and this is why it needs interpretation. Raguel cites the fact that Moses in the dream sees, as one would from God's throne, the three parts of the cosmos: the inhabited earth, the depths below it and the heavens above it. Then he interprets this to mean something else: that Moses will see things present, past and future – not the three parts of the cosmos, but the three parts of time (87–9). This clearly refers to the common Jewish understanding of Moses as an inspired prophet, who wrote in the Torah not only of things present but also of the past and of the future (cf. *Jub.* 1:4). A feature of the dream's account of Moses' *cosmic* exaltation is thus interpreted as an aspect of Moses' role in the *earthly* history of God's people. Once we recognize this, we can see that the other part of Raguel's interpretation works in the same way: 'you will raise up a great throne, and you yourself will judge and govern *mortals* (*brotōn*)' (85–6). In the dream itself, there are no mortals.[39] There it is the stars, the immortal heavenly beings, who fall on their knees before the enthroned Moses (79). Once again, a feature of the dream's account of Moses' *cosmic* exaltation – his sovereignty over the host of heaven – is interpreted as an aspect of Moses' role in *earthly* history, in this case his rule over Israel. Raguel's interpretation of the dream is, in fact, quite complete, that is, it interprets each major facet of the dream. But it takes Moses' exaltation to the throne of the universe, sovereign over and surveying the whole cosmos, to be a figurative prediction of Moses' biblical career, as understood by post-biblical Jews: Moses will rule Israel as king and exercise prophetic powers. Only in this way can the proper match between dream and interpretation be appreciated.

Why should Ezekiel have used a depiction of Moses seated on the cosmic throne of God as figurative of the much more limited role of Moses as king and prophet on earth? In answering this question, it is worth remembering the extent to which Jewish theology in this period was fundamentally exegetical, even when not explicitly so.

---

[39] Note that Ezekiel uses the same word of Moses himself in pointed contrast with God (102).

Our problems with Jewish texts can often be solved by detecting the underlying basis in exegesis of Scripture. So, in this case, we should note, first, that there was good precedent within the Torah itself for a dream of the kind Ezekiel gives Moses. The patriarch Joseph dreamed that the sun, the moon and the stars bowed down to him. In other words, he received the obeisance that only God receives from the heavenly bodies. However, the interpretation of the dream is that his parents and brothers will bow down to him (Gen. 37:9–10). Cosmic rule, equivalent to God's, functions in the dream as a figure for earthly rule. This is how Ezekiel will have read Joseph's dream. But, secondly, we can discern a particular reason why he should have fashioned a similar dream for Moses. For Jewish exegetes, one of the most remarkable, but also problematic, things said about Moses in Scripture is in Exodus 7:1: 'I have made [literally, given] you God (Heb. *ᵉlōhîm*, Gk. *theos*) to Pharaoh' (cf. 4:16).[40] Ezekiel's account of Moses' dream, and Raguel's interpretation of it, is an exegesis of these words of God to Moses: 'I will make you God.'[41] The dream simply elaborates on this image: it *depicts* Moses *as God*, replacing God in his unique sovereignty over the whole universe. Raguel's interpretation of the dream then explains what the image *signifies*, when understood, as it has to be, metaphorically. Of course, Moses is not actually to be understood as literally God, exercising the uniquely divine sovereignty from the throne of the cosmos. The *image* of Moses as God is interpreted to *signify* that Moses will be a king and a prophet. The dream and the interpretation of it together explain how the use of the word 'God' for Moses (Exod. 7:1) is a metaphor for Moses' rule over Israel and his inspired knowledge of the past, the present and the future. Moses is like God only in these respects.

Thus the dream depicts Moses quite literally as God, but the meaning of the dream is not its literal meaning. On this reading we can recognize the unparalleled, and otherwise extraordinary, fact that, in the dream, God actually *vacates* his throne and puts Moses there in his place. This is what it would literally mean for God, as Exodus says, to 'make' Moses 'God'. Moses would have to replace God in the unique divine sovereignty. The other features of the dream are also designed to depict unequivocally the uniquely divine sovereignty: Moses surveys

---

[40] The claim by Horbury, 'Jewish,' 16–44, here 33, that Jewish exegetes read this text to mean that God appointed Gentile worship of their gods, seems to me wholly unconvincing.

[41] For this divine statement taken out of its context, treated as a kind of epitome of Moses' supremely significant role and status, and therefore echoed in a prophecy, given early in Moses' life, of his future greatness; cf. Visions of Amram³ 3:1 (4Q543).

the whole cosmos, seeing all things, as only God does from his throne (e.g. Ps. 33:13–15); he counts the stars, as only their Creator can (Ps. 147:4; Isa. 40:26); he receives their obeisance, as only God does (Neh. 9:6). Everything in the dream contributes to a picture of Moses quite literally taking the place of God on his throne and exercising the unique divine sovereignty in God's stead. No wonder that, at this point, Moses wakes from his dream in terror. Ezekiel is well aware that the cosmic throne of God symbolizes the unique sovereignty that is intrinsic to the unique identity of God. He can place Moses on it only for the sake of a similitude: as God is in relation to the cosmos, so Moses will be in relation to Israel.

4.3. The Son of Man on the throne

In the *Parables of Enoch*, God places on his own throne the figure known as the Righteous One, the Elect One, the Messiah and the Son of Man, the figure to whom God delegates the eschatological judgement. The controlling text behind the portrayal of this figure is Daniel 7:13 in its context, with the human figure in heaven understood as the heavenly representative of the people of God on earth, instrumental in delivering them from their oppressors. Daniel 7:14 has been understood (cf. the LXX) to mean that God will give the Son of Man the role of judging the kingdoms which oppress the elect. In the *Parables of Enoch*, the Son of Man, hidden in heaven until the time of the eschatological judgement, has no role until that time. His role is primarily and centrally to execute the eschatological judgement in both the angelic (61:8–9) and the human spheres, though he will also dwell with the elect in blessedness thereafter (45:4; 62:14).

In one scene only, reminiscent of Daniel 7:9–10, God himself sits in judgement, along with his heavenly council (47:3). This is probably to be understood as the preliminary divine decision that the time for judgement has come.[42] The judgement itself is then given to the Son of Man, the one God has appointed as judge (42:9). Because of the centrality of the theme of sovereign judgement, the divine throne is a central symbol. It is 'the throne of glory' (45:3; 55:4; 61:8). It is the throne of God's glory on which God himself sits (47:3; 60:2; 71:7). But it is also the throne of the Elect One's or the Son of Man's glory on which he will

---

[42] Thus it is not strictly true that 'there is fluctuation within 1 Enoch 37 – 71 with respect to the executor of Final Judgement. Sometimes God is specified as this executor while, at other times, the messianic agent is so designated' (Larry J. Kreitzer, *Jesus and God in Paul's Eschatology* [JSNTSup 19; Sheffield: JSOT Press, 1987], 106).

sit to judge (62:2, 5; 69:27, 29; cf. 51:3).[43] That it is the same throne that is called both God's throne of glory and the Elect One's throne of glory is made certain by the statement that God placed the Elect One on the throne of glory (61:8). This picture of God placing another figure on his own throne is paralleled in the Jewish literature of our period only in Moses' dream in Ezekiel the Tragedian, where, as we have seen, it is not intended to be read literally. That it derives from Psalm 110:1, as some have suggested,[44] is not likely, since there are no allusions to this psalm (in particular, no reference to the distinctive image of sitting at the right hand of God, which the *Parables of Enoch* could easily have used to portray the Son of Man on the throne of glory, as the New Testament in many indisputable allusions to Ps. 110:1 does) or even to the themes of the rest of the psalm in the *Parables of Enoch*. Rather, the idea that God places the Son of Man on his own throne probably derives from observing that the terms in which the sovereignty of the Son of Man are described in Daniel 7:14 are closely similar to those used elsewhere in Daniel of God's own sovereignty (Dan. 4:3; 4:34; 6:26).[45] The author has concluded from these passages that the Son of Man participates in God's unique sovereignty, and accordingly portrays him seated on the divine throne. The Son of Man does not participate in the divine sovereignty until the time for eschatological judgement arrives; until that time he is only destined for this role. But by calling the divine throne his, the *Parables of Enoch* evidently intends this participation in divine sovereignty seriously.

That it is intended seriously can also be seen in the passages that portray the worship of the Son of Man when he is seated as Judge on the throne of glory (46:5; 48:5; 62:6, 9). In two of these cases, the wicked are said to prostrate themselves before him and to worship him (48:5; 62:9), while in another, unfortunately obscure passage, they 'bless and glorify and exalt him who rules over the all' (62:6). If this is the Son of Man, as the sequence of verse 7 makes most plausible, then the worship of the Son of Man is here described in terms used elsewhere of the worship of God (cf. 39:12; 48:5; 61:9, 11, 12; 69:24). In 48:5 and 62:9, the language could be used of submission to a ruler without necessarily connoting

---

[43] For the attempts to argue that 'his' in these passages originated in Ethiopic translation, see Matthew Black, 'The Messianism of the Parables of Enoch: Their Date and Contributions to Christological Origins,' in *The Messiah*, ed. J.H. Charlesworth (Minneapolis: Fortress, 1992), 154–5.

[44] Hengel, *Studies*, 186; Black, 'Messianism,' 153–5, both following J. Theisohn, *Der auserwählte Richter* (SUNT; Göttingen: Vandenhoeck & Ruprecht, 1975), 94–8.

[45] For the probable influence of these passages in the Parables, see the allusion to Dan. 4:35 in *1 En.* 41:9, and the allusion to Dan. 4:17 in *1 En.* 46:5.

divine worship but, as in so many cases, it is not the gesture or the terms used but the context which must determine whether the Son of Man is receiving the worship due only to God. That he is seated on the divine throne, the symbol of the unique divine sovereignty, is sufficient to establish that he does receive divine worship. It is a mistake, in such a context, to distinguish merely political submission from cultic worship. Kingship or lordship is the overwhelmingly dominant image of God's relation to the world in Second Temple Judaism. The cultic worship of God expresses precisely the submission to God's rule required of all creatures. If the Son of Man, seated on the divine throne itself, receives obeisance, he receives that recognition of the unique divine sovereignty that is divine worship. Certainly, the dominant emphasis of the Parables is on the worship of God, but the Son of Man also receives worship that does not detract from, but is in some way included in, the worship of God (cf. 48:5). If so, worship of the Son of Man is appropriate because his participation in the divine sovereignty, symbolized by his sitting on the divine throne, includes him in the unique identity of God that is recognized in worship. It is when they 'see and recognize that he sits on the throne of his glory', that the kings and the mighty ones worship him as the one 'who rules over all' (62:3, 6), i.e. as exercising the unique divine sovereignty.

Thus the Son of Man in the *Parables of Enoch* is unique among exalted human or angelic figures depicted in Second Temple Jewish literature in two respects: he sits on the divine throne and he receives worship. Because he participates in a key aspect of the unique identity of God – rule over all things – he receives the recognition which, in Second Temple Judaism, is restricted to that unique divine identity: worship. What Ezekiel the Tragedian attributes only figuratively to Moses, the *Parables of Enoch* attribute literally to the Son of Man, though only in the eschatological future. The contrast enables us to see that, in all other portrayals of exalted human and angelic figures, there is no question of participation in the unique divine identity: they fall unproblematically outside it. They execute God's will, but they do not participate in the divine sovereignty in the way which sitting on the divine throne signifies. They do not receive worship, which is often refused by them or forbidden. The Son of Man in the *Parables of Enoch* is the exception that proves the rule.

Wisdom, portrayed as sharing God's throne, and the Son of Man, according to the *Parables of Enoch*, provide the only precedents for the Christian claim that the exalted Jesus shares the heavenly throne of God. They show, to a very limited extent, how Jewish thought could move in the direction taken by early Christian Christology. I do not think they are likely to have influenced Christology,[46] any more than the later, and in some ways more impressive, Jewish parallel to christological thinking, the enthronement of Metatron in heaven,[47] did. Apart from other considerations, the decisive role which Psalm 110:1 played in Christology is missing from these Jewish precedents. Their value is in showing us that, in a Second Temple Jewish understanding of monotheism, sitting on the heavenly throne of God did signify inclusion in the unique divine identity and could be recognized in divine worship.

5. Jesus on the heavenly throne of God

When New Testament Christology is read within the context of the understanding of the Second Temple Jewish monotheism we have sketched, it can readily be seen that early Christians applied to Jesus all the well-established and well-recognized characteristics of the unique divine identity in order, quite clearly and precisely, to include Jesus in the unique identity of the one God of Israel. Primary among these characteristics was the unique divine sovereignty over all things. From the earliest post-Easter Christology that we can trace, Jesus' exaltation was understood as his sharing the divine throne in heaven and thus participating in the divine rule over the cosmos. Other uniquely divine characteristics followed logically and swiftly, notably Jesus' participation in the work of creation. Worship of Jesus, as his inclusion in the monotheistic worship due exclusively to the one God, followed as the necessary recognition of his inclusion in the divine identity, again primarily in recognition of his exercise of the unique divine sovereignty from the heavenly throne of God. In the present context, we must restrict our interest to the main features of the New Testament's understanding of Jesus' exaltation to the divine throne.

---

[46] The claim that Matt. 25:31 reflects the influence of the Parables of Enoch is far from compelling, given that the divine throne is commonly called 'the throne of glory' (see n. 23 above). At most, one could argue for common dependence on a tradition of exegesis of Dan. 7:13–14.

[47] Cf. D. Abrams, 'The Boundaries of Divine Ontology: The Inclusion and Exclusion of Metratron in the Godhead,' *HTR* 87 (1994): 291–8. I do not consider it possible to draw any direct line from the Son of Man, identified with Enoch, in the Parables of Enoch and Metratron, identified with Enoch, in 3 *Enoch*. The enthronement and role of the former are wholly eschatological; the enthronement and role of the latter wholly present with no reference to eschatology at all.

5.1. Psalm 110:1: the key text

Early Christian theology developed mainly through the exegesis of the Scriptures, which was both traditional in method, pursued with the exegetical expertise of Jewish learned exegesis, and frequently novel in its results, since it was deployed to interpret events, understood as decisive eschatological acts of the God of Israel, which did not neatly conform to any existing Jewish expectation. One remarkable datum in the exegetical development of early Christology is that verse 1 of Psalm 110 is the verse of the Hebrew Scriptures to which christological allusion is most often made in early Christian literature. Clear allusions to it occur across a very wide range of the literature from the first hundred years of the Christian movement (Synoptic Gospels, Acts, major Pauline letters, Ephesians, Colossians, Hebrews, 1 Peter, Revelation, Longer Ending of Mark, 1 Clement, Polycarp, Barnabas, Epistle of the Apostles, Apocalypse of Peter, Ascension of Isaiah, Apocryphon of James).[48] Within the New Testament itself, there are twenty such quotations or allusions.[49] Impressive is not only the widespread use of this verse, but also the fact that motifs associated with its interpretation and links made between this verse and other scriptural texts recur in various, otherwise unrelated, Christian writings, which must therefore reflect underlying traditions of interpretation of this verse. There are probably kerygmatic or confessional formulations, of a relatively though not completely fixed character, reflected in some of the texts, which can make even a late text such as Polycarp, *Phil.* 2:1 useful evidence for understanding earlier developments. It is very clear that Psalm 110:1 was not only cited, but also interpreted with care, both very early and very widely in the early Christian movement. Texts with which it was often linked in interpretation are Psalm 8:6 and Daniel 7:13–14. It is notable that it is *in conjunction with Psalm 110:1* that these other texts play their principal roles in the New Testament. They facilitated the Christian reading of the key text as referring to Jesus' participation in precisely God's cosmic rule over all things.

---

[48] See the list of quotations and allusions in Hay, *Glory*, 45–6, and add *Ep. Apos.* 3; *Ascen. Isa.* 10:14; 11:32. All the allusions can be regarded as certain, with the exception of Rev. 3:21, which is probable.

[49] The count of twenty-one in Hengel, 'Sit at My Right Hand!' 133, includes Mark 16:19, excludes Eph. 2:6; Heb. 12:2; Rev. 3:21, while counting Acts 2:33 and 2:34–35 as two instances, whereas I have counted them as one.

5.2. Novel exegesis and novel claim

The clearly foundational importance of Psalm 110:1 for early Christology is a major impediment in the way of attempts to see early Christology as the transference to Jesus of a Jewish model already well-developed and well-known in relation to various principal angels and exalted patriarchs. There is no convincing case of allusion to Psalm 110:1 (or to any other part of the psalm) in Second Temple Jewish literature,[50] apart from *Testament of Job* 33:3, where it used quite differently[51] and which may, in any case, be a Christian work influenced by the New Testament. This does not prove that Psalm 110 was not read messianically in pre-Christian Judaism. The tendency to read all the royal psalms messianically would suggest that it probably was understood messianically when it was read, but the absence of allusion shows that it was of no *importance* in Second Temple Jewish thinking and that, if interpreted at all, it was probably not read in the way that early Christians read it, as referring to the participation of a human figure in the unique cosmic sovereignty of God.[52] The fact that Second Temple Jewish theology, including early Christian theology, was primarily a tradition of exegesis, not a tradition of ideas passed on independently of exegesis, makes this a fact of prime importance for the origins of

---

[50] Psalm 110 could very appropriately have been applied to Michael-Melchizedek as he is depicted in his eschatological role in 11QMelchizedek (but Joel Marcus, *The Way of the Lord: Christological Exegesis of the Old Testament in the Gospel of Mark* [Louisville: WJK, 1992], 133, overstates the relationship when he says that Melchizedek 'has been exalted to God 's right hand': there is no reference to the right hand of God in 11QMelch). Eskola, *Messiah*, 130, claims, by hypothesizing dependence on Ps. 110, that 11QMelch 'may be regarded as one of the earliest examples of exploiting Psalm 110 in an apocalyptic Jewish writing' (which are the other examples?). But no allusion to Ps. 110 is found in the extant fragments of 11Q13 [11QMelch]. In 11QMelch 2:10, Melchizedek *stands* in the heavenly council (according to Ps. 82:1). Is it possible that Psalm 82:1 explains the enigmatic and much discussed fact that, in Acts 7:55–56, the Son of Man *stands* at the right hand of God? He stands in order to pronounce judgement on Stephen's unjust judges, as Elohim does in Psalm 82:1–2. For standing to pronounce a judicial sentence, see also Ps. 76:9; Isa. 3:13.

[51] The point of Job's enthronement at the right hand of God, as Job develops it (*T. Job* 33:2–9), is that, in place of his throne and his splendour in this world, which is passing away and all of whose splendour fades (33:4), Job has an eternal splendour reserved for him in heaven. The point is not to give him a position of authority in God's rule over the world, but to depict his heavenly reward as the eternal reality of which his kingdom in this world has been only a worthless shadow. Probably the psalm is being read in accordance with the idea that all the righteous will after death receive thrones in heaven (*1 En.* 108:12; *Ascen. Isa.* 9:24–5; 11:40; *Apoc. El.* 1:8; 4:27, 29; cf. 4Q521 [4QMessAp] 2.2.7). The allusion provides no precedent for early Christian use of the text, in which Christ's enthronement at God's right hand is not merely his individual heavenly reward, but his unique cosmic status and role.

[52] Some later rabbinic readings of the psalm take it to mean that the one appointed to be the Messiah in the future sits waiting in heaven until God installs him in his kingdom on earth (Hay, *Glory*, 54–5).

Christology. Teachers and writers of the period did not work primarily by transferring models from one heavenly or eschatological figure to another, but by asking to which figure particular texts applied or which texts applied to a particular figure, and what such texts said about the figure in question. The extent to which early Christology is novel in its Jewish context is the extent to which, in view of the unique features of Jesus' history, it applied to Jesus a particular selection and configuration of key texts, some already well used for certain heavenly or messianic figures, some not previously so used, but *as a particular selection and configuration novel.* Psalm 110:1, perhaps the most foundational text for the whole configuration, was a novel choice, evidence of the exegetical and theological (the two are inextricable) novelty of the earliest Christian movement. The explanation of its role in early Christology, contrasted with its absence from Second Temple Jewish literature, is that, for early Christians, it said about Jesus what no other Jews had wished to say about the Messiah or any other figure: that he had been exalted by God to participate now in the cosmic sovereignty unique to the divine identity.

Of the two partial precedents we have identified, the idea of Wisdom sharing God's throne could have had a formative influence on the earliest Christology only if the identification of Jesus with Wisdom preceded the application of Psalm 110:1 to him, which is unlikely. The *Parables of Enoch* are moving, to some extent, in the same direction as the earliest Christology, with dependence on some of the same key texts as also featured in early Christian use, but without allusion to Psalm 110. This suggests that they represent a parallel rather than a source. In substance, the key difference is that the Son of Man in the Parables will sit on the divine throne in the future. It was Jesus' participation in the unique divine sovereignty already in the present that obliged early Christians to take his inclusion in the divine identity much more seriously than the Son of Man's in the Parables, both in including Jesus in other uniquely divine characteristics, such as creation, and in envisaging and practising the divine worship of Jesus.

Some recent work on New Testament Christology seems to be working with the conviction that it is only possible to understand how a high Christology could have developed within a Jewish monotheistic framework, if we can show that something rather like it already existed in pre-Christian Judaism. This is a mistake.[53] In order to understand how early Christology was possible without any infringement of

---

[53] So also Eskola, *Messiah*, 383–4.

Jewish monotheism, we need only to show that the ways in which Second Temple Jewish monotheism understood the uniqueness of the one God were such that the inclusion of Jesus within them was not precluded. The concern of early Christology was not to conform Jesus to some pre-existing model of an intermediary figure subordinate to God. The concern of early Christology, from its root in the exegesis of Psalm 110:1 and related texts, was to understand the identification of Jesus with God. Early Jewish monotheism provided little precedent for such a step, but it was so defined and so structured as to be open for such a development.

5.3. *Divine sovereignty over all things*

That it is on God's own heavenly throne itself, the throne of glory, that Jesus sits beside God is explicit in some of the texts (Heb. 8:1; 12:2; Rev. 3:21; 5:6; 7:17; 22:3) and should probably be assumed for all.[54] Partly with the exegetical help of Psalm 8:6, this participation in God's cosmic rule is frequently expressed by the formulae 'all things'[55] or 'heaven and earth' (or fuller cosmic formulae)[56] or, for emphasis, both.[57] This language, constantly used of God's relationship with his creation in Second Temple Jewish texts,[58] is significant because it is the way Jewish monotheism distinguishes God from all other reality ('all things'), as Creator and Ruler of all. By including Jesus in the full cosmic scope of God's sovereignty, New Testament terminology places Jesus clearly on the divine side of the distinction between God and 'all things'. While Daniel 7:14 and Psalm 2:8 provided the basis for thinking of a universal rule on earth by the Messiah (*Sib. Or.* 5:416; *1 En.* 62:6), it is the cosmic scope of Christ's sovereignty which places it in that unique category which his enthronement on the divine throne in the highest heaven symbolizes. Of no principal angel or exalted human in Second Temple Jewish texts is it said that he has authority over all things or over heaven and earth.[59]

---

[54] Pol. *Phil.* 2:1, evidently thinks of a throne for Jesus beside God's throne, but makes it quite clear that this image implies nothing less than if Jesus shared God's own throne: that he exercises the unique divine rule over all things.

[55] Matt. 11:27; Luke 10:22; John 3:35; 13:3; 16:15; Acts 10:36; 1 Cor. 15:27–28; Eph. 1:22; Phil. 3:21; Heb. 1:2; 2:8; cf. Eph. 1:23; 4:10.

[56] Matt. 28:18; Phil. 2:10; Rev. 5:13.

[57] Pol. *Phil.* 2:1; cf. Matt. 11:25–27; Luke 10:21–22; Eph. 1:10; Col. 1:20.

[58] See nn. 6, 7 above.

[59] Fragment 2 of 4Q521 (4QMessAp) begins '[. . . the heav]ens and the earth will hear [*or* obey] his Messiah (*lmšyhw*)' (2.2.1). Since the rest of this fragment makes no reference to the Messiah, it is difficult to guess the significance of this statement. Karl-Wilhelm Niebuhr

Another way in which the fully cosmic rule of the exalted Christ is stressed is by reference to the subjection of all the heavenly powers to him. The texts portray the submission both of the rebellious angelic powers (1 Cor. 15:24–28; *Ascen. Isa.* 11:23) and of the obedient ones (Eph. 1:20–21;[60] 1 Pet. 3:22; *Ascen. Isa.* 11:24–32; cf. Rev. 5:11–14; *Ep. Apos.* 3). It is noteworthy that the specific ranks of angels are those in high authority in the heavens: 'principalities' (*archai*: 1 Cor. 15:24; Eph. 1:21), 'authorities' (*exousiai*: 1 Cor. 15:24; Eph. 1:21; 1 Pet. 3:22), 'powers' (*dunameis*: Eph. 1:21; 1 Pet. 3:22) and 'dominions' (*kuriotētes*: Eph. 1:21).[61]

5.4. In the heights of heaven

The imagery of height, which we have seen to be important in depictions of the divine throne, also reinforces the New Testament picture of Jesus' participation in the unique divine sovereignty. He ascended 'far above all the heavens' (Eph. 4:10), 'far above every principality and authority and power and dominion and every name which is named' (Eph. 1:21). He 'sat down at the right hand of the Majesty on high, having become as much superior to angels as the name he has inherited is more excellent than theirs' (Heb. 1:3–4). God 'highly exalted him and gave him the name that is above every name' (Phil. 2:9). These three passages are linked by the motif of height applied both to the divine throne which is higher than all the heavens and to the name which is higher than all other names. Probably in all three cases, it should be understood that Jesus, seated on the divine throne above every angelic authority, also receives the divine name, which is far superior to all the names by which God alone names all the host of heaven.[62] These various ways

---

(in an unpublished paper) proposes that there is in fact no reference to a single Messiah; he reads *lmšyhw* as plural (for *lmšyhyw*, 'his anointed ones') and parallel to 'the holy ones' (*qdwšym*) in line 2, so translating: 'the heavens and earth will obey his anointed ones, and all that is in them will not turn away from the commandments of the holy ones'. In that case, the reference could be to the angelic governors of the natural world, and the text would refer to the restoration of proper order in the natural world, after the period before the end of history when nature has strayed from its God-ordained regularities and orders (cf. *1 En.* 80:2–8; *4 Ezra* 5:4–9).

60 In light of Eph. 2:2; 6:12, the rebellious angelic powers are presumably included, but the very general statement of 1:21, like that of 1 Pet. 3:22, must also include the heavenly authorities subordinate and obedient to God.

61 These constitute, after 'the great archangels', the second, third, fourth and fifth of the ten ranks of highest angels listed in *2 En.* 20:1–3(J). See also *1 En.* 61:10, where 'powers' and 'dominions' are found with cherubim, seraphim and ophanim, and *T. Levi* 3:3, 8, where 'powers' are in the third heaven and 'authorities' in the fourth.

62 Cf. Isa. 40:25–26; *1 En.* 43:1; 69:21; *Jos. Asen.* 15:11–12; *Ascen. Isa.* 7:4. The phrase 'which is named' (Eph. 1:21) is a divine passive, meaning 'which God names' (cf. *1 En.* 48:3).

of stating Jesus' absolute supremacy over all the angels need not be understood as polemical in any way. They simply apply to Jesus the well-recognized ways in which God himself on his heavenly throne was understood as absolutely supreme over all his angelic creatures.

5.5. *Worshipped by angels and all creation*

A series of texts concerned with Jesus' enthronement in heaven portray the worship given him specifically by all the heavenly beings (Heb. 1:6; *Ascen. Isa.* 10:15; 11:23–32; *Ap. Jas.* 14:26–30), while others portray his worship by all creation (Phil. 2:10–11; Rev. 5:12–14; Pol., *Phil.* 2.1). That this is the worship due to God alone is clear from the context of Jesus' enthronement on God's own heavenly throne, the symbol of the uniquely divine sovereignty over all things. It should be noted that it goes much further than the very limited worship accorded the Son of Man in the *Parables of Enoch*, who is worshipped neither by angels nor by any other part of the non-human creation, but only by the wicked at the day of judgement. The Christian texts draw out the full consequences of Jesus' exaltation to the divine throne, and deliberately deploy the strongest Jewish theological means of placing Jesus emphatically on the divine side of the line between the one God of Israel and the rest of reality, his creation. It is worship by the angels that differentiates God absolutely from them; it is worship by the whole creation that differentiates God absolutely from all other reality. However we may evaluate the evidence adduced for some kind of veneration of angels in some parts of Second Temple Judaism,[63] no angel is worshipped by other angels in Second Temple Jewish literature. These texts do not place Jesus in some ambiguous semi-divine position on a spectrum.

---

[63] Stuckenbruck, *Angel Veneration*, 45–203; Clinton E. Arnold, *The Colossian Syncretism* (Grand Rapids: Baker, 1996), 32–89; Loren T. Stuckenbruck, '"Angels" and "God": Exploring the Limits of Early Jewish Monotheism,' in *Early Jewish*, ed. Stuckenbruck and North, 45–70. Both Stuckenbruck, *Angel Veneration*, 50, and Gieschen, *Anthropomorphic Christology*, 35, speak of 'various degrees' of veneration of angels. Even if 'veneration' is accepted as a suitable term for all the evidence adduced, it seems to me that it would be better to speak of 'various different kinds' of veneration: they are not easily graded on a scale. But the most important point is that Second Temple Judaism forces a distinction in kind, not merely in degree, between any attention paid to angels or humans and the worship which is exclusive to God because it is precisely recognition and adoration of the unique divine identity. Nothing in the evidence seems to me inconsistent with such a view. The principle that divine worship is recognition of the unique divine identity, characterized especially by God's sole sovereignty in creation and providence, seems to me much more useful than the attempt to distinguish cultic worship from other kinds of worship, a distinction difficult to apply consistently (e.g. Jews prayed individually in their homes or elsewhere at the times of the morning and evening burnt-offerings in the temple).

In Second Temple Judaism, there was not a continuous spectrum of reality through which a developing Christology could gradually move Jesus until eventually he shared the divine identity. There was a gulf that Christology could cross only by seeing Jesus surpassing all at once every heavenly creature and, seated on the throne of God, receiving their worship as God does. These texts place Jesus unequivocally within the unique divine identity.

5.6. Human worship as recognition of the unique divine sovereignty

The texts discussed in 5.5 do not portray directly the early Christian practice of worshipping Jesus, but they constitute vital evidence for understanding it. That early Christian worship of Jesus was understood to be the inclusion of Jesus in the monotheistic worship due only to the one who rules all things from his heavenly throne can be confirmed by two other passages which speak specifically of human worship given to Jesus.

One is Matthew 28:17–18. Matthew does not reserve worship of Jesus for the post-Easter situation. His consistent use of *proskunein* (from 2:2 onwards), differently from Mark's and Luke's,[64] shows that he reserves it for a gesture of obeisance that expresses what is properly due to Jesus. But that what is properly due to Jesus is divine worship is not clear in most instances. Matthew's usage through the Gospel anticipates the last occurrence of *proskunēsis* in his Gospel, when the full significance of the gesture finally becomes clear. This act of worship (Matt. 28:17) introduces Jesus' declaration, 'All authority in heaven and on earth has been given to me' (28:18). The scene forms a kind of antithesis to the temptation of Jesus which, in Matthew's temptation narrative, is the climactic last of the three. In this, the devil offers Jesus sovereignty over all the kingdoms of the world: 'All these things I will give you,

---

[64] He uses it ten times with Jesus as its object (whereas Mark uses it in this way only twice, and Luke only in 24:52 *v.l.*). In half of these cases, there is no synoptic parallel (Matt. 2:2, 8, 11; 28:9, 17). On three occasions, Matthew supplies the word *proskunein* where Mark has the gesture but not the word (Matt. 8:2 par. Mark 1:40; Matt. 9:18 par. Mark 5:22; Matt. 15:25 par. Mark 7:25), and on the remaining two occasions supplies the word where the Markan parallel has not even the gesture (Matt. 14:33 par. Mark 6:51; Matt. 20:20 par. Mark 10:35). There are also two occasions where Mark has the word, but Matthew omits even the gesture, and one where Mark has the gesture, but Matthew omits it (Matt. 8:29 par. Mark 5:6; Matt. 27:30 par. Mark 15:19; Matt. 19:16 par. Mark 10:17). But, on these latter three occasions, the worship (by demons, the mocking soldiers, the rich young man) would have been considered less than adequate by Matthew. On *proskuneō* in the Gospels and Matthew's distinctive usage, see Larry W. Hurtado, *How on Earth Did Jesus Become a God? Historical Questions about Earliest Devotion to Jesus* (Grand Rapids: Eerdmans, 2005), 134–51.

if you will fall down and worship (*proskunēsēs*) me' (Matt. 4:9). Jesus replies by citing a commandment from the passages recited daily with the Shema͏ͨ (Deut. 10:20; cf. 6:13), and which sums up the first two commandments of the Decalogue: 'Worship (*proskunēseis*) the Lord your God and serve him alone (*autō monō latreuseis*)' (Matt. 4:10).[65] Matthew takes his use of *proskunein* from this commandment, and shows its appropriateness to Jesus, when the unique divine sovereignty over all things – which had not been the devil's to give – is given to Jesus by his Father, thereby including him in the unique divine identity to which alone *proskunēsis* is due.

The second text is John 5:23, the Fourth Gospel's one clear reference to the worship of Jesus. The context, 5:19–23, depicts the Son's activity as the exact replication of his Father's:

> just as the Father raises the dead and gives them life, so also the Son gives life to whomever he wishes. The Father judges no one but has given all judgement to the Son, so that all may honour (*timōsi*) the Son just as they honour the Father. Anyone who does not honour the Son does not honour the Father who sent him (5:21–23).

The verb *timaō* may not seem adequate to describe the worship due exclusively to the one God, but it is so used by Philo (*Decal.* 65), while Josephus uses *timē* for the same purpose (*A.J.* 1.156). But more important is the context in John. The two divine activities cited are exercises of the uniquely divine sovereignty. Deuteronomy 32:39, the most important monotheistic text of the Torah after the Decalogue and the Shema͏ͨ, speaks of YHWH's unique sovereignty over life in terms frequently echoed and later understood to include the resurrection of the dead (cf. 1 Sam. 2:2; 2 Kgs. 5:7; Tob. 13:2; Wis. 16:12–14; 4 Macc. 18:18–19). In the same context, YHWH declares, 'Vengeance is mine' (Deut. 32:35). The uniqueness of the divine throne, of course, included the unique role of 'the Judge of all the earth' (Gen. 18:25; cf. Ps. 94:2) to pronounce ultimate judgement. In terms of God's eschatological sovereignty, which is at stake in John 5, the giving of life and the passing of final judgement are closely connected (5:24; cf. Rev. 20:12). Thus, it is because the Son exercises the uniquely divine sovereignty that he will and should be honoured just as his Father is.

---

[65] By comparison with the LXX text of both Deut. 10:20 and Deut. 6:13, Matthew's text has *proskunēseis* in place of *phobēthēsē* and adds *monō*. The latter is an interpretative addition (cf. 1 Sam. 7:3) which the NRSV also finds it necessary to add in its version of Deut. 10:20.

Examination of the New Testament texts that offer theological rationale for the worship of Jesus thus confirms our argument. Worship is given to Jesus precisely as recognition of characteristics of the divine identity that were regarded in Second Temple Judaism as distinguishing the uniqueness of the one God. The worship of Jesus serves to focus in conceptuality, as well as making most obvious in religious practice, the inclusion of Jesus in the unique identity of the one God of Jewish monotheism. It was not only the natural religious response of Jewish Christians to the status they perceived the exalted Jesus to have and to the role he played in their religious experience and life. It was also reflectively understood in the context of Jewish monotheistic understanding of God.

6

Paul's Christology of Divine Identity

1. Early Jewish monotheism and early Christology

In chapter 1, I have set out in broad outline a particular thesis about the relationship of early Jewish monotheism and early Christian Christology, which also entails a relatively fresh proposal about the character of the earliest Christology. I argued that the monotheism of Second Temple Judaism was indeed 'strict'. Most Jews in this period were highly self-consciously monotheistic, and had certain very familiar and well-defined ideas as to how the uniqueness of the one God should be understood. In other words, they drew the line of distinction clearly between the one God and all other reality, and were in the habit of distinguishing God from all other reality by means of certain clearly articulated criteria. So-called intermediary figures were not ambiguous semi-divinities straddling the boundary between God and creation. Some (such as God's Wisdom and God's Word) were understood as aspects of the one God's own unique reality. Most were regarded as unambiguously creatures, exalted servants of God whom the literature often takes pains to distinguish clearly from the truly divine reality of the one and only God. Therefore, differing from the second view, I do not think such Jewish intermediary figures are of any decisive importance for the study of early Christology. (We shall return to the issue of Jewish precedents for early Christology after our study of Paul, which will enable us to focus on the most relevant of such alleged precedents.)

In my view, high Christology was possible within a Jewish monotheistic context, not by applying to Jesus a Jewish category of semi-divine intermediary status, but by identifying Jesus directly with the one God of Israel, including Jesus in the unique identity of this one God. I use the term 'unique identity' as the best way of speaking of the uniqueness of God as generally conceived in early Judaism. The concept of identity is more appropriate, as the principal category for understanding Jewish monotheism, than is that of divine nature. In other words, for Jewish monotheistic belief, what was important was *who* the one God is, rather than what divinity is.

The one God of Second Temple Jewish belief was identifiable as unique by two kinds of identifying features. The first concerns his covenant relationship with Israel. He is the God of Israel, known from the recital of his acts in Israel's history and from the revelation of his character to Israel (Exod. 34:6). He has revealed to Israel his name YHWH, which was of great importance to Jews of the Second Temple period because it names precisely the unique identity of their God. As well as such identifications of God from his relationship with Israel, this God was also characterized as unique by his relationships to the whole of reality, especially that he is the only Creator of all things and that he is the sole sovereign Ruler of all things. Such identifications of YHWH are extremely common in Second Temple Jewish literature.[1] They were the simplest and clearest way of answering the question, What distinguishes YHWH, the only true God, from all other reality? In what does his uniqueness consist? These characteristics make a clear and absolute distinction between the true God and all other reality. God alone created all things; all other things, including beings worshipped as gods by Gentiles, are created by him. God alone rules supreme over all things; all other things, including beings worshipped as gods by Gentiles, are subject to him. These ways of distinguishing God as unique formed a very easily intelligible way of defining the uniqueness of the God they worshipped which most Jews in most synagogues in the late Second Temple period would certainly have known. However diverse Judaism may have been in many other respects, this was common: only the God of Israel is worthy of worship, because he is sole Creator of all things and sole Ruler of all things. Other beings who might otherwise be thought divine are, by these criteria, God's creatures and subjects. (Thus so-called intermediary figures either *belong to* the unique identity of God or *were created by* and remain *subject to* the one God, as his worshippers and servants, however exalted.)

---

[1] God as Creator of all things: e.g. Isa. 40:26, 28; 42:5; 44:24; 45:12, 18; 48:13; 51:16; Neh. 9:6; Hos. 13:4 LXX; 2 Macc. 1:24; Sir. 43:33; Bel 5; *Jub.* 12:3–5; *Sib. Or.* 3:20–35; 8:375–6; *Sib. Or.* frg. 1:5–6; *Sib. Or.* frg. 3; *Sib. Or.* frg. 5; 2 *En.* 47:3–4; 66:4; *Apoc. Ab.* 7:10; Ps-Sophocles; *Jos. Asen.* 12:1–2; *T. Job* 2:4. God as Ruler of all things: e.g. Dan. 4:34–35; Bel 5; Add. Esth. 13:9–11; 16:18, 21; 3 Macc. 2:2–3; 6:2; Wis. 12:13; Sir. 18:1–3; *Sib. Or.* 3:10, 19; *Sib. Or.* frg. 1:7, 15, 17, 35; 1 *En.* 9:5; 84:3; 2 *En.* 33:7; 2 *Bar.* 54:13; Josephus, *A.J.* 1:155–6.

We could characterize this early Jewish monotheism as *creational* monotheism, *eschatological* monotheism and *cultic* monotheism. That God alone – absolutely without advisors or collaborators or assistants or servants – created all other things was insisted on (even when he was understood to have created out of pre-existing chaos rather than out of nothing). That God was the sole Creator of and the sole Lord over all things required the expectation that, in the future when YHWH fulfils his promises to his people Israel, YHWH will also demonstrate his deity to the nations, establishing his universal kingdom, making his name known universally, becoming known to all as the God Israel has known. This aspect I call *eschatological* monotheism. Finally, there is *cultic* monotheism. Only the sole Creator of all things and the sole Lord over all things should be worshipped, since worship in the Jewish tradition was precisely recognition of this unique identity of the one God.

The early Christian movement, very consciously using this Jewish theological framework, created a kind of *christological* monotheism by understanding Jesus to be included in the unique identity of the one God of Israel. Probably the earliest expression of this to which we have access – and it was certainly in use very early in the first Christian community's history – was the understanding of Jesus' exaltation in terms of Psalm 110:1. Jesus, seated on the cosmic throne of God in heaven as the one who will achieve the eschatological lordship of God and in whom the unique sovereignty of the one God will be acknowledged by all, is included in the unique rule of God over all things, and is thus placed unambiguously on the divine side of the absolute distinction that separates the only Sovereign One from all creation.[2] God's rule over all things defines who God is: it cannot be delegated as a mere function to a creature. Thus the earliest Christology was already *in nuce* the highest Christology. All that remained was to work consistently through what it could mean for Jesus to belong integrally to the unique identity of the one God. Early Christian interest was primarily in soteriology and eschatology, the concerns of the gospel, and so, in the New Testament, it is primarily as sharing or implementing God's eschatological lordship that Jesus is understood to belong to the identity of God. But early Christian reflection could not consistently leave it at that. Jewish eschatological monotheism was founded in creational monotheism. If Jesus was integral to the identity of God, he must have

---

[2] For the significance of God's cosmic throne in Jewish monotheism and in the earliest Christology, see chapter 5 above. The topic is now also well developed, in a way that coheres closely with my arguments, in Eskola, *Messiah*.

been so eternally. To include Jesus also in the unique creative activity of God and in the uniquely divine eternity was a necessary corollary of his inclusion in the eschatological identity of God. This was the early Christians' Jewish way of preserving monotheism against the ditheism that any kind of adoptionist Christology was bound to involve. Not by adding Jesus to the unique identity of the God of Israel, but only by including Jesus in that unique identity, could monotheism be maintained. This applies also to the worship of Jesus, which certainly began in Palestinian Jewish Christianity.[3] This expressed the inclusion of Jesus in the unique identity of the sole Creator of all things and sole Sovereign over all things.

Early Christology was framed within the familiar Jewish framework of creational, eschatological and cultic monotheism. The first Christians developed a *christological* monotheism with all three of these aspects. From this perspective, I call the Christology of all the New Testament writers, rooted as it was in the earliest Christology of all, a Christology of divine identity, proposing this as a way beyond the standard distinction between 'functional' and 'ontic' Christology. This latter distinction does not correspond to early Jewish thinking about God and has, therefore, seriously distorted our understanding of New Testament Christology. When we think in terms of divine identity, rather than of divine essence or nature, which are not the primary categories for Jewish theology, we can see that the so-called divine functions which Jesus exercises are intrinsic to who God is. This Christology of divine identity is already a fully divine Christology, maintaining that Jesus Christ is intrinsic to the unique and eternal identity of God.

My purpose in the rest of this chapter is to examine some of the evidence for this kind of Christology of divine identity in the letters of Paul. We shall begin with the phenomenon of christological interpretation of scriptural passages about YHWH, which we shall see to be closely connected with a deliberate attempt by Paul to reformulate Jewish monotheism as christological monotheism. We shall then examine three important christological passages in Paul that combine an explicit monotheistic concern with the inclusion of Jesus in the divine identity (Rom. 10:13; Phil. 2:6–11; 1 Cor. 8:5–6). Finally, we shall return to two examples of intermediary figures in Second Temple Judaism that have often been cited as precedents for early Christology and demonstrate how little they parallel the phenomenon of divine identity Christology in Paul.

---

[3] See chapter 4 above.

2. Christological reading of scriptural YHWH texts

Paul's christological interpretation of scriptural passages about YHWH, taking the name YHWH (*kurios* in LXX) to refer to Jesus Christ, is an important phenomenon that has often been underestimated both in extent and in significance. A signal exception is Gordon Fee's *Pauline Christology*,[4] to which I had access only at the final stage of revising the present chapter. Fee both recognizes the wide extent of this phenomenon and its indispensable value for understanding Paul's Christology.

The basic data are set out here:[5]

2.1. YHWH texts with Jesus Christ as referent:[6]

(1) Five quotations including *kurios*

Rom. 10:13	Joel 2:32
1 Cor. 1:31	Jer. 9:24 (= 1 Kgdms. 2:10)
1 Cor. 2:16	Isa. 40:13
1 Cor. 10:26[7]	Ps. 23(24):1
2 Cor. 10:17	Jer. 9:24 (= 1 Kgdms. 2:10)

(2) One quotation to which Paul adds *legei kurios*

Rom. 14:11	Isa. 45:23

---

[4] Gordon D. Fee, *Pauline Christology* (Peabody: Hendrickson, 2007).

[5] In compiling these lists I am indebted especially to the work of David B. Capes, *Old Testament Yahweh Texts in Paul's Christology* (WUNT 2/47; Tübingen: Mohr [Siebeck], 1992), chap. 3, but I have significantly extended the data and I have sometimes differed from his judgements. Cf. also his later article, 'YHWH Texts and Monotheism in Paul's Christology,' in *Early Jewish*, ed. Stuckenbruck and North, 120–37. Fee, *Pauline Christology*, which reached me only at the stage of finally revising this chapter for publication, has persuaded me of several allusions I had not noticed previously. His work is unusual as a study of Pauline Christology that takes Paul's application of YHWH texts to Jesus very seriously. See also Hurtado, *Lord Jesus Christ*, 110–11. Kreitzer, *Jesus and God*, 112–28, speaks of a 'referential shift of "Lord" from God to Christ' (113), but only discusses texts relating to the future 'Day of the Lord'. The phrase 'referential shift of "Lord" from God to Christ' rather begs the question whether Paul thought he was transferring the reference of these texts from God to Christ or discerning the reference to Christ that was divinely intended in these texts. Richardson, *Paul's Language*, 283–4, evidently did not have Capes' work available to him, and grossly underestimates the extent of the phenomenon of YHWH texts applied to Christ in Paul.

[6] For the purposes of this essay I am including evidence only from the undisputed Pauline letters, 2 Thessalonians and Colossians. For instances in Ephesians and the Pastorals, see section 8 below.

[7] I am persuaded by the arguments of Capes, *Old Testament Yahweh Texts*, 140–5, and Fee, *Pauline Christology*, 133–4, that the referent of *kurios* here is Christ.

(3) One quotation not including *kurios*[8]

    Rom. 9:33   Isa. 8:14[9]

(4) Thirteen allusions including *kurios*[10]

1 Cor. 8:6	Deut. 6:4
1 Cor. 10:21	Mal. 1:7, 12
1 Cor. 10:22	Deut. 32:21 (*kurios* not in LXX)
2 Cor. 8:21	Prov. 3:4 (*kurios* in LXX, *'elōhîm* MT)
Phil. 2:10–11	Isa. 45:23
Phil. 3:8, 12	Hos. 6:3[11]
1 Thess. 3:13	Zech. 14:5[12]
1 Thess. 4:16	Ps. 47:5 (LXX 46:6)[13]
2 Thess. 1:7	Isa. 66:15
2 Thess. 1:9	Isa. 2:10, 19, 21
2 Thess. 1:12	Isa. 66:5
2 Thess. 3:5	1 Chr. 29:18[14]
2 Thess. 3:16	Num. 6:26[15]

(5) Twelve stereotyped OT phrases including *kurios*

   'to call on the name of the Lord'[16]

   1 Cor. 1:2 (cf. Rom. 10:13)   Joel 2:32; Zeph. 3:9; Zech. 13:9;
                                       Jer. 10:25; etc.

---

[8] In Rom. 8:36, Paul quotes Ps. 43(44):23, probably as addressed to Christ. In LXX, the following verses use the address *kurie* (43:24, 27), but this translates *'ªdōnî* (MT 44:24; there is no equivalent to *kurie* in MT 44:27) not *yhwh*. So I have not included this quotation.

[9] In Isa. 8:14 the stone (LXX: *lithou proskommati … petras ptōmati*; cf. Rom. 9:33: *lithon proskommatos kai petran skandalou*) is YHWH (8:13).

[10] Many scholars, including Capes and Fee, put 2 Cor. 3:16 in this category but, in my view, 3:17 means that in this case, uniquely, Paul took the *kurios* of the text (Exod. 34:34) to be the Spirit, not Christ. I am not quite persuaded that 1 Thess. 4:6 is an allusion to Ps. 94:1 (LXX 93:2), as, for example, Fee, *Pauline Christology*, 47, argues, or that 2 Thess. 2:13 alludes to Deut. 33:12, as Fee, *Pauline Christology*, 65, argues.

[11] This allusion to the opening words of Hos. 6:3 ('Let us know, let us press on [LXX *diōxomen*] to know YHWH') seems not to have been noticed, but it seems probable to me, especially since the context in Hosea is interpreted christologically in early Christian literature (Hos. 6:2: 1 Cor. 15:3; Hos. 6:3b: Jas. 5:7).

[12] There may also be an allusion to Zech. 14:5 in 2 Thess. 1:7; and cf. *Did.* 16:7; *Ascen. Isa.* 4:14.

[13] For this allusion, see Fee, *Pauline Christology*, 44–5.

[14] I agree with Fee, *Pauline Christology*, 65–6, that *kurios* in 2 Thess. 3:5 is probably Christ.

[15] I have not attempted to list allusions to YHWH texts where *kurios* does not appear in the Pauline texts. It would be much more difficult to compile a comprehensive list of these. An example is Phil. 3:4, where 'boast in Christ Jesus' may well allude to Jer. 9:23–24 (quoted in 1 Cor. 1:31).

[16] See Davis, *The Name*, 129–33, 159–60.

'the name of the Lord' (other uses)

1 Cor. 1:10; 5:4; 6:11; 2 Thess. 1:12; 3:6; Col. 3:17	Gen. 12:8; Mic. 4:5; etc.

'the day of the Lord'[17]

1 Cor. 1:8; 5:5; 2 Cor. 1:14; 1 Thess. 5:2; 2 Thess. 2:2	Joel 1:15; 2:1, 11, 31; Amos 5:18; Isa. 13:6, 9; etc.

'to serve the Lord'

Rom. 12:11; 16:18; Col. 3:24	1 Kgdms. 12:20; Pss. 2:11; 99(100):2; 101(102):22; etc.

'the word of the Lord'

1 Thess. 1:8; 4:15; 2 Thess. 3.1	Isa. 2:3; etc.

'the Lord be with you'

2 Thess. 3:16	Ruth 2:4; 1 Kgdms. 17:37; 20:13; etc.

'the fear of the Lord'

2 Cor. 5:11; cf. Col. 3:22	Isa. 2:10, 19, 21; etc.

'the Spirit of the Lord'

2 Cor. 3:17	Judg. 3:10; 6:34; etc.[18]

'the glory of the Lord'

2 Cor. 3:18; cf. 2 Thess. 2:14	Exod. 24:16, 17; 40:34, 35; etc.[19]

'the fear of the Lord'

2 Cor. 5:11	Isa. 2:10, 19, 21; Prov. 1:7; etc.

'the command of the Lord'

1 Cor. 14:37	Deut. 11:27–28; etc.

'the Lord is near'[20]

Phil. 4:5	Pss. 34:18 (LXX 33:19); 145:18 (LXX 144:18); cf. 119:151 (LXX 118:151)

---

[17] See Kreitzer, *Jesus and God,* 112–13, 161–3.

[18] See Fee. *Pauline Christology,* 179.

[19] See Fee. *Pauline Christology,* 180–2.

[20] I treat this as a stereotyped phrase because I see no decisive reason for choosing Ps. 34:18 or Ps. 145:18 as the text to which Paul alludes, though the latter may be more likely in view of its continuation ('The Lord is near to all who call upon him') that approximates to Joel 2:32 (Rom. 10:13; 1 Cor. 1:2). Commentators discuss whether *engus* ('near') in Phil. 4:5 is spatial or temporal, but it is not impossible that Paul read the phrase in the psalms as referring to the nearness of the Parousia.

2.2. YHWH texts with God as referent:

(1) Nine quotations including *kurios*

Rom. 4:7–8	Ps. 31(32):1–2
Rom. 9:27–28	Hos. 2:1 + Isa. 10:22–23[21]
Rom. 9:29	Isa. 1:9 (*kurios sabaōth*)
Rom. 10:16	Isa. 53:1 (*kurios* in LXX, no equivalent in MT)[22]
Rom. 11:3	3 Kgdms. 19:10 (*kurios* not in LXX, no equivalent in MT)[23]
Rom. 11:34	Isa. 40:13
Rom. 15:11	Ps. 116(117):1
1 Cor. 3:20	Ps. 93(94):11
2 Cor. 6:18	2 Kgdms. 7:14, 8 (*kurios pantokratōr*)

(2) Three quotations to which Paul adds *legei kurios*

Rom. 12:19[24]	Deut. 32:35
1 Cor. 14:21	Isa. 28:11–12
2 Cor. 6:17	Isa. 52:11 + Ezek. 20:34

(3) Twelve quotations in which the speaker ('I') is identified as YHWH in the OT context

Rom. 4:17	Gen. 17:5
Rom. 9:9	Gen. 18:14
Rom. 9:13	Mal. 1:2–3
Rom. 9:14	Exod. 33:19
Rom. 9:17	Exod. 9:16
Rom. 9:25	Hos. 2:25
Rom. 9:33	Isa. 28:16
Rom. 10:19	Deut. 32:21[25]
Rom. 10:20	Isa. 65:1
Rom. 10:21	Isa. 65:2
Rom. 11:26–27	Isa. 59:20–21
2 Cor. 6:2	Isa. 49:8

---

[21] Isa. 10:22–23: LXX has *ho theos*, but for the strong probability that Paul did not change *ho theos* to *kurios* but found *kurios* in his *Vorlage*, see Christopher D. Stanley, *Paul and the Language of Scripture* (SNTSMS 74; Cambridge: CUP, 1992), 118.

[22] Readers of Isa. 53:1 LXX would surely take *kurie* to stand for YHWH.

[23] I include this case because Paul's addition of *kurie* to the text presumably imitates Elijah's address to God in other places, where LXX has *kurie* for MT's YHWH (3 Kgdms. 17:20, 21; 18:36, 37; 19:4).

[24] It is possible that the referent here is Christ; cf. 1 Thess. 4:6; 2 Thess. 1:8.

[25] In the allusion to the first half of this verse in 1 Cor. 10:22, Paul takes the divine 'I' to be Jesus, and so it is possible that he reads the second half of Deut. 32:21 in the same way when he quotes it in Rom. 10:19.

(4) One quotation in which the addressee ('you') is identified as YHWH
     in the OT context

Rom. 15:9   Ps. 18:49 (LXX 17:50) = 2 Sam. (LXX
                                       2 Kgdms. 22:50)[26]

How are these phenomena of Paul's usage to be understood? We may
quickly discount two possible interpretations: (1) It is not plausible
that, where Paul takes the *kurios* of the Septuagint to refer to Jesus, he
is not aware that *kurios* is functioning as a reverential substitute[27] for
the divine name. Paul certainly knew the Hebrew text as well as the
Greek, but, in fact, even a Greek-speaking Jewish Christian who knew
the Jewish Scriptures only in Greek could not have been unaware of
the function of *kurios* as representing the Tetragrammaton. In many
manuscripts of the Septuagint, what appeared in the written text was
not *kurios*, but the Hebrew letters of the Tetragrammaton or a Greek
equivalent (ΠΙΠΙ) or a Greek transliteration (ΙΑΩ). Readers substituted
kurios in reading (whether to themselves, since ancient readers usually
pronounced the words when reading alone, or in public reading). When
kurios was written in manuscripts as the substitute for YHWH,[28] it was
usually differentiated from other uses of *kurios* by its lack of the article,
indicating that it was being used as a proper name. In a phrase such as
'the name of the Lord', this is particularly clear, since its Greek form in
the Septuagint (*to onoma kuriou*) breaks the normal rule that in such a
construction either both nouns should have the article or both nouns
should lack it.[29]

---

[26] This is a somewhat puzzling instance, because the OT explicitly includes YHWH (LXX
kurie) as the addressee, but Paul's text omits this. It is possible that Paul understands the
addressee to be Christ (cf. Käsemann, *Romans*, 386), but the correspondence between
exomologeō in this citation and the same verb in Rom. 14:11 (= Isa. 43:25), where God is
the object, together with the context in Rom. 15:8, strongly suggest that Paul understands
the addressee to be God and probably Christ to be the speaker (cf. Heb. 2:12). Perhaps
Christ (here identified with YHWH) is also the speaker in 15:10 (Deut. 32:43 LXX), but is
certainly not in 15:11. If Paul takes the addressee in Ps. 18:49 (Rom. 15:9) to be God, then
the omission of *kurie* may well be a deliberate means of excluding the possible identification
of the addressee as Christ. The same step is not taken in 15:11 (Ps. 116:1), but the words *ton
kurion* there are more integral to the text.

[27] NT scholars often speak of *kurios* as a 'translation' of the divine name. This is inaccurate. It
was not normally understood as a translation, but as a conventional *substitute* for the divine
name.

[28] Whether this occurred in pre-Christian manuscripts of the LXX has been disputed, but for
the most recent case for regarding it as the original practice of the Greek translators, see
Martin Rösel, 'The Reading and Translation of the Divine Name in the Masoretic Tradition
and the Greek Pentateuch,' *JSOT* 31 (2007): 411–28.

[29] Cf. Davis, *The Name*, 90–2, 135.

We can also discount (2) the notion that Paul read the Jewish Scriptures in a 'ditheistic' way, distinguishing between the high God (Heb. *'ēl 'elōhîm*, Gk. *ho theos*) and YHWH as a 'second god'.[30] It is clear from our summary of the evidence that, more often than not, Paul took the referent of YHWH to be God and, less frequently, took it to be Christ. It is indeed noteworthy that Paul seems only very rarely, if at all, to take 'God' (Heb. *'ēl 'elōhîm*, Gk. *ho theos*) in the text to refer to Christ,[31] and we shall return to this point. But it is equally significant that he clearly does not simply equate YHWH with Christ, but can take the divine name to designate either God or Christ, occasionally even in the same text cited on different occasions (Rom. 11:34; 1 Cor. 2:16: Isa. 40:13).

The texts about YHWH that Paul applies to Jesus rather than to God are quite diverse and cannot all be explained by one principle. But what has rarely been noticed is that many of these texts are (or would have been read by Paul as) expressions of eschatological monotheism. We can certainly claim that a major factor in Paul's application of texts about YHWH to Jesus is his christological reading of the eschatological monotheism of the Jewish Scriptures.

3. Eschatological monotheism in the christological YHWH texts

When we consider the scriptural texts about YHWH that Paul applies to Jesus within their scriptural context, it is remarkable how many of them either function as monotheistic assertions in themselves or relate to a monotheistic assertion in the fairly immediate context:[32]

Joel 2:32 [Rom. 10:13; cf. 1 Cor. 1:2]: A standard monotheistic formula occurs in 2:27, 'You shall know ... that I the Lord (YHWH) am your God, and that there is no other besides me.'

---

[30] Barker, *Great Angel*, chap. 11. In idem, *The Risen Lord: the Jesus of History as the Christ of Faith* (Edinburgh: T&T Clark, 1996), chap. 4, she argues that Jesus himself took this view and identified himself with the second god YHWH.

[31] Zech. 14:5 is a partial exception, since LXX reads *kurios ho theos mou*. Also exceptions would be the allusions to Pss. 89:7 (LXX 88:8) and 68:35 (LXX 67:36) in 2 Thess. 1:10, if these are to be accepted as real allusions (see Fee, *Pauline Christology*, 60–1, with n. 518). It is not clear to me why Kreitzer, *Jesus and God*, 124, speaks of a 'Referential Shift of Pronouns from God to Christ' in connection with the mixed quotation of Isa. 28:16 and Isa. 8:14 in Rom. 9:33. In Isa. 8:13–14, the stone represents YHWH.

[32] The translations that follow are from LXX.

Isaiah 40:13 [1 Cor. 2:15; cf. Rom. 11:34]: This verse is a monotheistic denial that, in the creation of the world, YHWH needed or received any advice from any other being. It was the source of a standard Jewish way of claiming that God created the world alone and denying any polytheistic notion of creation as a collaborative project of several gods (Isa 40:13 is echoed in this sense in Sir. 42:21; *2 En.* 33:4aJ; Philo, *Opif.* 23; cf. also *4 Ezra* 6:6; Josephus, *C. Ap.* 2.192). In its own context in Isaiah 40, verse 13 belongs to that chapter's lengthy exposition of the incomparability of YHWH, which, in turn, relates to the eschatological monotheism of the following chapters: the expectation that, since YHWH is the one and only Creator and Lord, YHWH will come to be acknowledged by all the nations as the incomparable One.

Jeremiah 9:24 [1 Cor. 1:31; 2 Cor. 10:17]: This verse is implicitly monotheistic in the sense that it makes YHWH the only proper subject of boasting, and counters the self-deification of the arrogant who boast of their own wisdom, power or wealth (9:23; cf. Isa 2, discussed below). In Jeremiah 9:23–24, there is no indication of an eschatological context, but this passage also occurs, inserted into the song of Hannah, in 1 Kingdoms 2:10 in connection with words that would certainly have been read as messianic in early Judaism ('he will judge the ends of the earth . . . and will exalt the horn of his Messiah').

Isaiah 45:23 [Rom. 14:11; Phil. 2:10–11]: The accumulation of monotheistic assertions in Isaiah 45:18–25 ('I am the Lord and there is none besides'; 'I am God and there is no other besides me'; 'there is none but me'; 'I am God and there is no other') make it the most insistently monotheistic passage in Isaiah 40 – 55. Moreover, verses 22–3 are the most explicit assertion of eschatological monotheism in these chapters. The accumulation of monotheistic rhetoric climaxes in YHWH's oath that all will in the end acknowledge him as the only righteous and saving God.

Deuteronomy 32:21a [1 Cor. 10:22]: This half-verse is itself a mono-theistic assertion that the idols are 'no gods' (appropriately to the context in which Paul alludes to it; cf. 1 Cor. 8:4), but it also belongs to a passage that leads up to the solemn divine self-declaration: 'Behold, behold, I am he, and there is no god besides me' (32:39). The whole Song of Moses (Deut. 32) was read, in early Judaism, as an eschatological prophecy of God's coming deliverance of his people from pagan oppression. Paul's several quotations and allusions (Rom. 10:19 [Deut. 32:21b]; Rom. 12:19 [Deut. 32:35]; Rom. 15:10 [Deut. 32:43]; 1 Cor. 10:19 [Deut. 32:21a]) show that he also read it holistically and understood it as eschatological prophecy.[33]

---

[33] Richard B. Hays, *Echoes of Scripture in the Letters of Paul* (New Haven/London: Yale University Press, 1989), 163–4; Bell, *Provoked,* chap. 7.

Zechariah 14:5b [1 Thess. 3:13; cf. 2 Thess. 1:7]: The coming of YHWH, of which this verse speaks, leads to the following result: 'And the Lord (YHWH) will become king over all the earth; and in that day the Lord (YHWH) will be one, and his name one' (14:9). This puts the Shema' into eschatological form: YHWH will be one – the only God in the eyes not just of Israel, but of all – when his rule is acknowledged by all.

Isaiah 2:10, 19, 21 [2 Thess. 1:9]: Alongside this repeated refrain ('from the presence of the terror of the Lord [YHWH] and from the glory of his might'), referring to the fate of the arrogant when the Lord comes in judgement in the last days, there is another repeated refrain: 'and the Lord (YHWH) alone will be exalted in that day' (2:11, 17).

Isaiah 66:5, 15 [2 Thess. 1:7, 12]: These references to eschatological judgement by YHWH on his enemies occur in a prophetic sequence that climaxes in the recognition and worship of YHWH by all (66:18, 23).

By contrast, only a relatively small proportion of the scriptural texts in which Paul takes YHWH to be God can arguably be related to eschatological monotheism (Isa. 10:22–23; Isa. 40:13; Deut. 32:35; Isa. 52:11; Deut. 32:21b; Isa. 59:20–21), and few of these have a clear monotheistic assertion in their context (Isa. 40:13; Deut. 32:35; Deut. 32:21b), whereas almost all of the texts just discussed, in which YHWH is taken to be Jesus, do have such a monotheistic assertion in their context.

Eschatological monotheism is not explicit in all of the contexts in which Paul places his quotations of and allusions to these passages, but it is prominent in some of those contexts and it may be assumed to lie behind Paul's christological reading of most or all of these passages. This means that it is very often in scriptural texts that refer to the final and universal manifestation of the unique identity of the one God that Paul understands Jesus to be YHWH. Jesus himself is the eschatological manifestation of YHWH's unique identity to the whole world, so that those who call on *Jesus'* name and confess *Jesus* as Lord are acknowledging YHWH the God of Israel to be the one and only true God. It becomes clear that Paul's purpose is to include Jesus in the unique identity of the one God, not to add Jesus to the one God as a non-divine agent of God, for Jesus can manifest the unique identity of the one God and receive the universal acknowledgement of that God's sole lordship only if he himself belongs to the unique identity of God. (We should also note, without having space to develop the point here, that many of the scriptural texts we have discussed in this section refer not only to the eschatological manifestation of YHWH's sole lordship but also to eschatological salvation by YHWH. Not only as the one who manifests YHWH's lordship but also as the one who enacts YHWH's role as Saviour, Jesus belongs to the unique identity of God.)

4. Creational monotheism in the christological YHWH texts

In early Jewish theology, eschatological monotheism was closely connected with creational monotheism. That YHWH alone created all things is the basis for his sole lordship over all things, which must finally be fulfilled in the universal acknowledgement of him as only Creator and Lord. Among the biblical sources of early Jewish monotheism, this is especially clear in Isaiah 40 – 55 and appears in the context of the two passages from these chapters that were discussed in the last section. Isaiah 40:13 is most immediately a statement of creational monotheism, declaring YHWH to be unique in that he created the world without any collaborators or assistants. This incomparability as the sole Creator of all things is closely related, in the rest of Isaiah 40 – 55, to the eschatological monotheism that expects him to make his unique deity known to all the nations. The passage of divine speech to which Isaiah 45:23 belongs (45:18–25) is probably the best example of this close relationship between creational and eschatological monotheism. While verse 23 is a strong assertion of eschatological monotheism, the passage begins with a statement of creational monotheism ('Thus says the Lord [YHWH] who made the heaven, this God who set forth the earth and made it . . . I am the Lord and there is none besides') on which all the monotheistic rhetoric of the following verses is based. Thus, it was no great step, exegetically at least, from the inclusion of Jesus in the identity of God as sole eschatological Ruler to the inclusion of Jesus in the identity of God as sole Creator. These two aspects of the unique divine identity were inseparable.

In view of the creation context of both these Isaianic texts in which Paul clearly takes YHWH to be Jesus, there is no difficulty in supposing that he also takes YHWH in Psalm 23(24):1 (1 Cor. 10:26: 'the earth and its fullness are the Lord's') to be Jesus. Paul here returns to the creational monotheism with which he began his discussion of meat offered to idols (1 Cor. 8:5–6). By virtue of his role in God's creation of all things, not only do 'the cup of the Lord' and 'the table of the Lord' (10:20) belong to the Lord Jesus, but also the whole realm of created things.

We shall now proceed by looking more closely at several Pauline passages in which a monotheistic concern is especially evident, and in which Paul also interprets Jewish monotheism christologically: Rom. 10:13; Phil. 2:6–11 (with reference also to Rom. 14:10–12);

1 Cor. 8:5–6. These texts will be much better understood if we treat them not merely individually, but in the context of the broader christological phenomenon of Paul's identification of Jesus with YHWH in scriptural texts, especially in relation to creational and eschatological monotheism.

5. Romans 10:13

C. Kavin Rowe has recently published a fine study of Romans 10:13 in its context which coheres closely with the argument of this chapter.[34] He argues that 10:13 is the climax of Paul's argument in Romans 10:1–13, and that the use of Joel 2:32 there,

> if taken at all as instructive for the way in which Paul conceives of God's relation to Christ, eliminates the possibility of thinking of the God of Israel, YHWH, as apart from the human being Jesus. This unitive relationship is dialectical and hinges in fact on unreserved identification of one with the other as well on clear differentiation.[35]

I cannot here repeat all of his important observations. For our present purposes, the relationship between Paul's application of this YHWH text to Christ and eschatological monotheism is especially significant. The relationship is clear in the context in Romans, where verse 12 is an emphatically monotheistic assertion: 'For there is no distinction between Jew and Greek; the same Lord is Lord of all and is generous to all who call on him.' The 'Lord' here must be Jesus. This is clear from the relationship of the last clause ('all who call on him') to the quotation from Joel that follows in the next verse ('Everyone who calls on the name of the Lord shall be saved'), as well as from the wider context of reference to confession of Jesus as Lord (v. 9), belief in Jesus (v. 11), and calling on the one in whom they have believed (v. 14).

It is instructive to compare the monotheistic statement of 10:12 with that of Romans 3:29–30. In both cases, Paul bases the salvation of Jew and Gentile alike on the Jewish belief that there is only one God. In 3:29–30, an explicit allusion to the Shema‛ ('God is one') grounds Paul's claim that the same *God* is *God* of both Jews and Gentiles and, therefore, will justify both Jews and Gentiles alike through faith. In 10:12, the claim that the same *Lord* is *Lord* of all entails that 'there is

---

[34] C. Kavin Rowe, 'Romans 10:13: What is the Name of the Lord?' *HBT* 22 (2000): 135–73. I do not think that his disagreement with me (166–9) is a point of real difference between us.

[35] Rowe, 'Romans 10:13,' 136–7.

no distinction' between Jews and Gentiles and that all who call on his name will be saved. The argument is the same in each case, except that in one case there is only one God of both Jews and Gentiles, while in the other case the one Lord of both Jews and Gentiles is Jesus. The relationship between these two parallel arguments is similar to the way, as we shall see, Paul divides up the Shema' in 1 Corinthians 8:6, finding in it both one God, the Father, and one Lord, Jesus. In Romans 10:9–13, Paul propounds a christological version of Jewish eschatological monotheism, such that confessing Jesus as Lord or calling on the name of the Lord Jesus is tantamount to acknowledging YHWH as the one and only God. In this context, there is nothing incidental or unconsidered about Paul's identification of 'the name of YHWH' in Joel 2:32 as the name of Jesus. It is the climax of a clear statement of christological monotheism, which makes a very serious *identification* of Jesus with YHWH. The identifying name YHWH names Jesus as well as God his Father, and in such a way that they are certainly not two gods. As Rowe puts it well, 'Paul's God and the God of Israel are the same God only if YHWH is so identified with Jesus and Jesus with YHWH that the first two commandments are not violated.'[36]

It is typical of the early Jewish mode in which early Christians, including Paul, developed their theology that this remarkable conclusion is reached *exegetically*. We have already noticed that Joel 2:32 itself occurs in a context of formulaic monotheistic reference: 'You shall know that I am in the midst of Israel, and that I the Lord (YHWH) am your God and that there is no other besides me' (2:27). Paul was aware of this monotheistic context in Joel (understanding it as a context of eschatological monotheism) and his awareness of it is reflected in the way in which he uses Joel 2:32 as the climax of his argument. We can be sure of this because of the other scriptural quotation that he makes in this immediate context: 'No one who believes in him will be put to shame (*kataischunthēsetai*)' (Isa. 28:16, quoted in Rom. 10:11). This is linked to the quotation from Joel by the Jewish exegetical principle of *gezera shawa*, according to which passages including identical words or phrases may be used to interpret each other. The connection here is with the repeated promise in Joel: 'my people shall never again be put to shame' (2:26, 27: *kataischunthē, kataischunthōsin*), the two occurrences of which frame the monotheistic formula: 'You shall know that ... I the Lord (YHWH) am your God and that there

---

[36] Rowe, 'Romans 10:13,' 171.

is no other besides me' (2:27). It follows that Paul knew, and attended to, the monotheistic context of his quotation from Joel.

6. Philippians 2:6–11

Obviously, it is quite impossible to do justice here to this extraordinarily rich and also very much debated passage.[37] We shall focus on aspects that bear on the relation of Christology to Jewish monotheistic faith in the one God of Israel and the world. Of particular significance in this respect is the fact that the passage depicts the worship of Jesus by the whole creation (2:10–11) and is, therefore, the most unequivocal reference in Paul's writings to the worship of Jesus in connection with the monolatry or cultic monotheism that is one of the defining characteristics of Second Temple Jewish monotheism. Furthermore, since the worship of Jesus is depicted as the eschatological goal of God's purpose in Christ, we have in this passage a convergence of eschatological and cultic monotheism.

About the worship of Jesus in this passage, we can make three observations. In the first place, worship of Jesus by the whole creation is here associated with his exaltation to the position of divine sovereignty over the whole creation. This, as we have argued throughout these essays, was the essential catalyst for the early Christians' inclusion of Jesus in the unique divine identity. For Jewish monotheism, sovereignty over all things was definitive of *who God is*. It could not be seen as delegated to a being other than God. The corollary of recognizing Jesus' participation in God's universal sovereignty was the worship of Jesus, since worship is recognition of and response to the unique identity of the God who uniquely rules all creation.

---

[37] A few of the more important recent contributions are: Martin and Dodd ed., *Where Christology Began*; James D.G. Dunn, *The Theology of Paul the Apostle* (Grand Rapids: Eerdmans, 1998), 245–52, 281–93; Markus Bockmuehl, *The Epistle to the Philippians* (Black's NT Commentary; London: A. & C. Black, 1998), 114–48; Adela Yarbro Collins, 'The Worship of Jesus and the Imperial Cult,' in *Jewish Roots*, ed. Newman, Davila and Lewis, 234–7; Denny Burk, 'On the Articular Infinitive in Philippians 2:6: A Grammatical Note with Christological Implications,' *TynBul* 55 (2004): 253–4; Hurtado, *How on Earth*, chap. 4; Fee, *Pauline Christology*, 373–401; Joseph H. Hellerman, *Reconstructing Honor in Roman Philippi: Carmen Christi as Cursus Pudorum* (SNTSMS 132; Cambridge: CUP, 2005). Some of these contributions, notably those of Bockmuehl, Collins and Hellerman, rightly situate the passage in the political and social context of the Roman colony of Philippi, where the religio-political implications of Jesus' lordship over all things, implicitly but unavoidably contrasted with those of Caesar, would be important. In my view, Paul's christological monotheism must have had anti-imperial force and this is a key passage for recognizing that. Cf. chapter 4, section 6 above.

There are three passages about the exaltation of Jesus in early Christian literature that both allude to Psalm 110:1 (the master text for the earliest Christology of divine identity) and also refer to the worship of Jesus by all the angelic powers of the heavens (Heb. 1:3–6; *Ascen. Isa.* 10:14–15; 11:23–32; *Ap. Jas.* 14:26–30). These quite independent passages attest a common theme which singles out the angels in order to make clear precisely Jesus' exaltation to the divine throne, high above all the angelic powers, from which, unlike any mere angelic minister of God, he exercises the divine rule over all things, even the angels. Three other passages (Pol., *Phil.* 2:1; Rev. 5; Phil. 2:9–11) include the angels in a depiction of the worship of Jesus by all creatures, heavenly and earthly. Only one of these alludes to Psalm 110:1:

> believing in the One who raised our Lord Jesus Christ from the dead
> and gave him glory and a throne at his right hand;
> to whom are subject all things heavenly and earthly;
> whom all that breathes worships;
> who is coming as the judge of the living and the dead
>
> (Polycarp, *Phil.* 2:1).

This is clearly a traditional creedal formula, quite independent of Philippians 2:9–11, with which it shares no terminology or biblical allusions. Philippians 2:9–11 itself refers to the exaltation of Jesus, not with allusion to Psalm 110:1, but with allusion to Isaiah 52:13, a text elsewhere associated with Psalm 110:1 in reference to the exaltation of Jesus (Acts 2:23; 5:31).

The correspondence between Philippians 2:9–11 and Revelation 5 is particularly noteworthy. In both cases, it is explicitly the crucified Christ (depicted symbolically as the slaughtered Lamb in Revelation) who is exalted and worshipped. In Philippians 2:9–11 and Revelation 5:13, there are strikingly similar accounts of the worship of Christ by all creation. Philippians 2:10–11 echoes Isaiah 45:23 ('To me every knee shall bow, every tongue shall swear'), but expands the 'every knee ... every tongue' of Isaiah, emphasizing the universality of the worship given to Christ with a formula encompassing the whole creation: 'every knee shall bow, in heaven and on earth and under the earth' (Phil. 2:10). Revelation 5, having portrayed the exalted Christ as the Lamb in the midst of the divine throne in heaven (5:6; cf. 7:17), includes the Lamb in the worship of God on his throne in heaven, and then expands the circle of worship to include the whole creation:

every creature in heaven and on earth and under the earth and in the sea, and all that is in them, singing, 'To the one who is seated on the throne and to the Lamb be blessing and honor and glory and might forever and ever!' (Rev. 5:13).

It may not be accidental that these formulae for the whole cosmos have one of their closest parallels in the second commandment of the Decalogue (Exod. 20:4; Deut. 5:8–9; cf. also Neh. 9:6, Ps. 146:6; Rev. 10:6, which lack 'under the earth'): all those creatures whom it is forbidden to worship are depicted as themselves giving the worship due to God alone to Christ who shares his throne. In any case, the emphasis on universality makes it clear that it is the uniquely divine sovereignty over all creation that the exalted Jesus exercises and which is therefore acknowledged in worship by the whole creation.

It is unlikely that Revelation 5 is dependent on Philippians. Together with the other passages, they attest a widespread – and therefore early – christological schema, in which the exaltation of Jesus meant his participation in the unique divine sovereignty over all things, and therefore also its Jewish monotheistic corollary: the worship of Jesus by the whole creation in recognition of this divine sovereignty.

The second aspect of Philippians 2:9–11 which we shall consider is that worship of Jesus by the whole creation is associated with the giving of the divine name to Jesus at his exaltation. There can be no doubt that 'the name that is above every name' (v. 9) is YHWH: it is inconceivable that any Jewish writer could use this phrase for a name other than God's own unique name.[38] Contrary to much comment on this passage, the name itself is not 'Lord' (*kurios*: v. 11), which is not the divine name nor even a Greek translation of the name, but a conventional Greek reverential *substitute* for the name.[39] However, the fact that it was a

---

[38] The phrase 'the name of Jesus' (Phil. 2:10) has led some to suppose that 'Jesus' must be 'the name that is above every name' (v. 9). But the phrase 'the name that is above every name' itself, together with the allusion to Isa. 45:23 in vv. 10–11 (see below), require that it is at the divine name YHWH that every knee shall bow. So it would seem that 'the name of Jesus' is not the name Jesus, but the name YHWH that the exalted Jesus bears. But there is also a possibility that seems not to have been noticed. The name Jesus, like many Jewish names, contains the divine name. It means, 'YHWH is salvation' (the full form of the name *Yehôšua'* = YHWH *yēša'*). The name is peculiarly appropriate to the context of the allusion to Isa. 45:23 in Phil. 2:10–11 (Isa. 45:21–22: 'a righteous God and a Saviour ... Turn to me and be saved'). It could be that the name Jesus is regarded as a new kind of substitute for or even form of the divine name, such that Phil. 2:10–11 means, 'at the name YHWH-is-Salvation every knee should bend, ... and every tongue should confess that Jesus Christ is LORD (i.e. YHWH).'

[39] J.A. Fitzmyer, 'The Semitic Background of the New Testament Kyrios-Title,' in *A Wandering Aramean* (SBLMS 15; Missoula: Scholars, 1979), 115–42; A. Pietersma, 'Kyrios or Tetragram: A Renewed Quest for the original Septuagint,' in *De Septuaginta* (Mississauga, Ontario: Benben Publications, 1984), 85–102.

substitute for the Tetragrammaton is certainly relevant to the meaning of the passage. It connects the unique identity of God (YHWH) closely with his sovereignty (*kurios*) as a key identifying characteristic of his uniqueness. Jesus is given the divine name because he participates in the divine sovereignty. Thus, confession 'that Jesus Christ is Lord' (v. 11) is both a surrogate for calling on him by his name, YHWH, and also a confession of his lordship.

In associating Jesus' exaltation to participation in the unique divine sovereignty with the bestowal of the unique name of God on Jesus, our passage again resembles another depiction of the exaltation of Jesus. According to Hebrews 1:3–4, Jesus 'sat down at the right hand of the Majesty on high, having become as much superior to angels as the name he has inherited is more excellent than theirs.' Both passages associate the imagery of height – Jesus exalted to the divine throne in the height of heaven – with the unique superiority of the name he acquires. Only a divine name, superior to all other names (Phil. 2:9), can be superior to the names of angels (Heb. 1:4). This parallel itself makes it extremely likely that Hebrews, like Philippians, refers to the name YHWH. Most commentators think that the name in Hebrews must be 'the Son', since it is this term which distinguishes the Son's status from that of angels in verses 5–7. But this makes little sense of the expression 'the name he has inherited'. A son does not inherit the title 'son'; rather his being a son is the basis for his inheriting other things from his father. The meaning is that since Jesus, as the Son, inherited his Father's sovereignty over all things (v. 2), he also inherited his Father's name which names the unique divine identity as sovereign over all things.[40] The association of the unique divine name with the unique divine sovereignty is common to the depiction of the exaltation of Jesus in both Philippians and Hebrews, and probably therefore dates from very early christological reflection.

In Jewish monotheism, the unique name of God, YHWH, names his unique identity. It is exclusive to the one God in a way that the sometimes ambiguous word 'god' is not. Hence, the bearing of this divine name by the exalted Jesus signifies unequivocally his inclusion in the unique divine identity, recognition of which is precisely what worship in the Jewish monotheistic tradition expresses.

The third and final aspect of the worship of Jesus in Philippians 2:9–11 that we must consider is that worship of Jesus by the whole creation expresses the *eschatological* monotheism of the Jewish tradition. This was

---

[40] See chapter 7 below.

most powerfully expressed in the prophecies of Deutero-Isaiah, whose great monotheistic assertions were formative of Second Temple Jewish monotheism and constantly re-echoed in its literature. YHWH's great act of eschatological salvation, the new exodus, will be accomplished in the sight of all the nations (Isa. 52:10), will manifest his glory to all flesh (40:5), and bring all the nations to acknowledge him as the only God. This is especially the theme of Isaiah 45 (see especially vv. 5–6, 14), culminating in YHWH's invitation and solemn oath:

> There is no other god besides me,
>   a righteous God and a Savior;
>   there is no one besides me,
> Turn to me and be saved,
>   all the ends of the earth!
> For I am God and there is no other.
> By myself I have sworn,
>   from my mouth has gone forth in righteousness
>   a word that shall not return:
> 'To me every knee shall bow,
>   every tongue shall swear' (Isa. 45:21b–23).

The repetition of the standard monotheistic formula[41] in the first, third and fifth lines should be noted: the theme of the passage is emphatically the acknowledgement of the one and only God as the only God and the only Saviour. The universal obeisance, prophesied with God's most solemn guarantee (v. 23), is therefore unequivocally a matter of monotheistic worship. As a result of his eschatological act of salvation, YHWH's sole deity is universally acknowledged.

It is Isaiah 45:23 to which Philippians 2:10–11 plainly alludes. This is agreed by almost all scholars, but its full significance is not always appreciated. It shows the concern of the Philippians passage to be a typically Jewish monotheistic one and the worship of Jesus it depicts to be precisely a matter of the exclusive monotheistic worship of the Jewish religious tradition. The claim of Philippians 2:9–11 is that it is in the exaltation of Jesus, his identification with and as YHWH in YHWH's universal sovereignty, that the unique deity of the God of Israel comes to be acknowledged as such by all creation. YHWH's sole sovereignty and unique deity are recognized when the exalted

---

[41] For this formula, see Deut. 4:35, 39; 32:39; 1 Sam. 2:2; 2 Sam. 7:22; Isa. 43:11; 44:6; 45:5, 6, 14, 18, 21, 22; 46:9; Hos. 13:4; Joel 2:27; Wis. 12:13; Jdt. 8:20; 9:14; Bel 41; Sir. 24:24; 36:5; 4Q504 [4QDibHam^a] 5:9; 1Q35 1:6; Bar. 3:36; *2 En.* 33:8; 47:3; *Sib. Or.* 3:629, 760; 8:377; Orphica 16; Philo, *Leg.* 3.4, 82.

Jesus exercises that sovereignty and bears the name YHWH. The eschatological monotheistic expectation of Deutero-Isaiah and Second Temple Judaism is fulfilled through the revelation of Jesus' inclusion in the unique divine identity. Eschatological monotheism proves to be christological monotheism.

Philippians 2:9–11 is, therefore, a christological version of Deutero-Isaianic eschatological monotheism. We may expand on this conclusion by way of four additional observations.

First, we may note that, in this as in the other respects already noticed, the parallel with Revelation 5 is striking. There too worship is a matter of the eschatological acknowledgement of the divine sovereignty by all creation. The worship of the Lamb is the inclusion in the worship of God (5:13) of the one who has 'conquered' (5:5), i.e. has achieved the decisive victory in the establishment of God's eschatological kingdom, in which he will reign with God on the divine throne (11:15; 22:3). Worship of God and the Lamb on the throne in Revelation 5 anticipates the worship in the New Jerusalem (22:3). Thus, Revelation 5 also provides a christological version of eschatological monotheism.[42]

Secondly, it is noteworthy that both Philippians 2 and Revelation 5 take care to include Jesus in the worship of God, not to present him as an object of worship alternative to God his Father.[43] This is essential if the worship of Jesus is to be an expression of eschatological monotheism. In Philippians 2:9–11, kneeling at the name of Jesus and confessing him to be Lord are 'to the glory of God the Father'. In Revelation 5, the angelic worshippers who continually worship God (4:8–11) now worship the Lamb, along with myriads of angels (5:11–12), while the climax of the scene is the worship by every creature in the whole cosmos of both God and the Lamb (5:13). These are two ways of including Jesus in the cultic acknowledgement of the unique divine identity. The first does so no less than the second. It cannot mean that merely *honouring* Jesus is a way of *worshipping* God,[44] since this was precisely the way sophisticated pagans related polytheistic worship to recognition of a single supreme God. Jewish monotheists always rejected it (e.g. Philo, *Spec.* 1.31). Jesus is not here honoured as a servant of God. He is worshipped, because

---

[42] Revelation 5 does not have an explicit allusion to Deutero-Isaiah, comparable with that in Philippians 2:10–11, but elsewhere Revelation takes up the eschatological monotheism of Deutero-Isaiah explicitly, when it applies the monotheistic formula 'the First and the Last' (Isa. 44:6; 48:12), with the variations 'the Alpha and the Omega' and 'the Beginning and the End', to Christ (Rev. 1:17; 2:8; 22:13) as well as to God (Rev. 1:8; 21:6).

[43] On Revelation, see Bauckham, *Theology,* 59–61; idem, *Climax of Prophecy,* 133–40.

[44] Cf. James D.G. Dunn, *The Partings of the Ways* (London: SCM, 1991), 194.

he participates in the unique divine sovereignty and bears the name that names the unique divine identity. Since he does so as the Son of his Father, sharing, not rivalling or usurping, his Father's sovereignty, worship of Jesus is also worship of his Father, but it is nonetheless really worship of Jesus.

Thirdly, Philippians 2:9–11 cannot be understood as an expression of an Adam Christology. Jesus is not here exalted to the human dominion over other earthly creatures given to humans at creation (Gen. 1:28), but to the uniquely divine sovereignty that is acknowledged by all creation when God's sole deity as the one and only God is universally confessed.

James Dunn, who attempts to read the whole of the christological passage in Philippians 2 in terms of an Adam Christology,[45] has cited as a parallel to Philippians 2:9–11 a passage from the *Life of Adam and Eve* in which God requires the angels to worship Adam.[46] In this passage (13 – 15), Satan refuses to worship Adam when the angels are commanded to do so. Adam is introduced to the angels by God as 'our image and likeness' (13:3), and Michael commands the angels, 'Worship the image of the Lord God, as the Lord God has instructed' (14:1). The devil refuses to worship, because he 'will not worship one inferior and subsequent to me' (14:3). It is clear that worship here is intended to indicate the angels' recognition of Adam's superiority to them, in that he is the image of God. It should be said that the scene is exceptional in the literature of Second Temple Judaism[47] and, in view of the very uncertain history of the Adam literature, this passage (which does not appear in the Greek or Slavonic, but only in the Latin, Armenian and Georgian versions of the Adam cycle, which represent later developments[48]) cannot be

---

[45] Dunn, *Christology*, 114–21.

[46] Dunn, *Partings*, 194–5; others who take this passage as evidence that Jews could imagine – or even practice – the worship of Adam are: A. Chester, 'Jewish Messianic Expectations and Mediatorial Figures and Pauline Christology,' in *Paulus und antike Judentum*, ed. Martin Hengel and U. Heckel (WUNT 58; Tübingen: Mohr [Siebeck], 1991), 17–89, here 64; D. Steenburg, 'The Worship of Adam and Christ as the Image of God,' *JSNT* 39 (1990): 77–93; Crispin H. T. Fletcher-Louis, 'The Worship of Divine Humanity as God's Image and the Worship of Jesus,' in *Jewish Roots*, ed. Newman, Davila and Lewis, 112–28, here 127–8.

[47] It appears in later Christian texts about Adam: Jarl E. Fossum, *The Name of God and the Angel of the Lord* (WUNT 36; Tübingen: Mohr [Siebeck], 1985), 171–2. The rabbinic traditions about complaints by the angels against God's creation of Adam, summarized by Gary A. Anderson, *The Genesis of Perfection: Adam and Eve in Jewish and Christian Imagination* (Louisville: WJK, 2001), 30–5, significantly say nothing about obeisance to or worship of Adam.

[48] Marinus de Jonge and Johannes Tromp, *The Life of Adam and Eve and Related Literature* (Guides to Apocrypha and Pseudepigrapha; Sheffield: Sheffield Academic Press, 1997), chap. 2.

presumed to be a Jewish text of our period.[49] But, in any case, the 'worship' of Adam here can be distinguished from properly divine worship. The Latin uses *adorare*, but since the Armenian and Georgian versions both use words which mean 'to bow down, to prostrate oneself',[50] we can be fairly sure that the Greek original used *proskunein*. The word describes a gesture that, in itself, was not exclusive to divine worship (and, indeed, not employed in most Jewish worship).[51] It could be an acceptable way of acknowledging a human superior (e.g. Gen. 18:2; 19:1; 23:7, 12; 33:2; 1 Sam. 28:14; 1 Kgs. 2:19; 2 Kgs. 2:15) or even an angelic superior (*L.A.B.* 18:9: *adoravit eum in terra*). In Isaiah 45, where the universal acknowledgement of YHWH's lordship is expressed by the bowing of every knee (45:23), the Gentile captives who 'bow down' to Israel are clearly not worshipping, since they say 'God is with you alone, and there is no other; there is no god besides him' (45:14; cf. Rev. 3:9). The context in each case gives the gesture a different significance. The gesture of prostration became unacceptable to Jews in contexts which gave it idolatrous overtones, such as reverence for monarchs who claimed divinity (cf. Add. Esth. 13:12–14; Philo, *Legat.* 116; cf. Acts 10:25–26). But the context determined its meaning. It was worship of God where the context indicated that God's unique sovereignty was being acknowledged. In the context in the *Life of Adam and Eve*, it is clear that the gesture is required of the angels because Adam is the image of God, which suggests both his superiority to them and his inferiority to God. Adam does not occupy the divine throne.

This example does show that not the gesture of prostration but what is being recognized or acknowledged about the object of worship is the real issue. In Revelation, the gesture of prostration before the Lamb (5:8, 14) is worship because it takes place in the divine throne-room where all prostration must be to the unique divine sovereignty, and because it accompanies doxologies (a form reserved, in Jewish usage,

---

[49] We cannot in fact be sure that there is a (non-Christian) Jewish text behind the Adam cycle at all: de Jonge and Tromp, *Life*, chap. 4.

[50] Anderson and Stone ed., *Synopsis*, 11–12.

[51] J. Lionel North, 'Jesus and Worship, God and Sacrifice,' in *Early Jewish*, ed. Stuckenbruck and North, 186–202, here 187–93, rightly argues that the semantic spectrum of *proskuneō* is broad, but he does not take sufficient account of the way the context (such as reference to enthronement or the divine name) helps to determine the meaning in the New Testament examples. He goes on to argue that *proskunēsis* as worship of a deity is 'only complete when it includes or is followed by sacrifice to the deity' (198), so that sacrifice, rather than mere *proskunēsis* is what distinguishes properly divine worship. But he fails to provide *Jewish* evidence that 'it was sacrifice that was the acid test and criterion of deity' (198) in a sense that *proskunēsis* was not. After all, the second commandment of the Decalogue makes no reference to sacrifice.

to the worship of the one God) addressed to the Lamb, and to God and the Lamb together (5:12, 13). Similarly Christ's enthronement at God's right hand and the subjection of all things heavenly and earthly to him make the worship of Christ by the whole creation in Polycarp's confessional formula (*Phil.* 2:1) clearly a matter of acknowledging the exalted Christ's participation in the unique divine sovereignty. It is arbitrary to distinguish these close parallels from the scene in Philippians 2:9–11 and to treat the latter as expressive of no more than an Adam Christology. When one who bears the name YHWH receives the universal acknowledgement of his lordship portrayed in Isaiah 45:23 as the eschatological achievement of YHWH's unique rule, it is strictly worship that is portrayed. It is not a matter of restoring human dominion over other creatures, but of establishing YHWH's own unique rule over all of creation.[52] This is made certain by the clear allusion to Isaiah 45:23, by contrast with the absence of any convincing reference to Adam in these verses.[53]

Fourthly, although this point cannot be fully developed here,[54] it is worth pointing out that the whole of the christological passage in Philippians 2:6–11 can be understood as a christological reading of Deutero-Isaianic prophecy. The allusion to Isaiah 45:23 in verses 10–11 is all but universally agreed, though its full significance is by no means always appreciated. More debatable are allusions to Isaiah 52 – 53 in verses 7–9,[55] but a good case can be made especially for allusions to Isaiah 52:13 and 53:12, the summarizing verses at the beginning and the end of the Suffering Servant passage, in these verses of the Philippians passage ('poured himself out ... to death.... Therefore also God exalted him to the highest place'). The basic conceptual structure of verses 6–9 of Philippians 2 is that *because* Christ humiliated himself to the point of death, *therefore* God has highly exalted him. This structure is given by Isaiah 52:13, according to which it is because the Servant poured himself out to death that God will allot him a portion with the great, i.e. will highly exalt him (cf. 52:13). But since the terminology describing the

---

[52] This formula is not used for Adam's dominion, which is usually limited to the earth (e.g. *Jub.* 2:14; 2 *En.* 31:3), though 4 *Ezra* 6:46, 54 includes the heavenly bodies (cf. 2 *Bar.* 14:18ff.), and Wis. 10:2 makes Adam ruler of 'all things' (following Ps. 8:6).

[53] N.T. Wright, *Climax of the Covenant*, 93–4, unsuccessfully attempts to have his cake and eat it, i.e. an Adam Christology *and* a full recognition of the monotheistic significance of the allusion to Isa. 45:23. The two are incompatible. Against Adam Christology in Phil 2:6–11, see, recently, Hurtado, *How on Earth*, 88–101; Fee, *Pauline Christology*, 390–3.

[54] See also chapter 1 above.

[55] Martin, *Carmen Christi*, rev. ed. (Grand Rapids: Eerdmans, 1983), 167–8, 182–90, 211–13, 240, 313–15; N.T. Wright, *Climax of the Covenant*, 60–2.

Servant's exaltation in Isaiah 52:13 also describes the exalted position of God on his throne in Isaiah 6:1 and 57:15, Isaiah 52:13 can easily be read (by means of the Jewish exegetical principle of *gezera shawa*) to mean that the Suffering Servant is exalted to share the divine throne in heaven.

What has rarely been noticed, even by those who agree that Philippians 2:7–9 has Servant of Isaiah 52 – 53 in view, is the way the allusions to Isaiah 52 – 53 and to Isaiah 45 cohere. Early Christians, for whom Isaiah 40 – 66 was *the* scriptural account of the meaning of the events of Jesus Christ and his future, the influence of which can traced throughout the New Testament, did not read the so-called Servant passages in isolation from the overall themes of eschatological salvation and eschatological monotheism which dominate these chapters. The Servant of the Lord is the one through whom God accomplishes the new exodus, the eschatological act of salvation, in the sight of the nations, thereby manifesting his glory and demonstrating his unique deity to the nations. Thus Paul, in Philippians 2:6–11, reads Deutero-Isaiah to mean that the career of the Servant of the Lord, his suffering, humiliation, death and exaltation, is the way in which the sovereignty of the one true God comes to be acknowledged by all. God's unique rule receives universal acclaim when it is exercised by the one who humiliated himself in obedience to God to the point of death and was, therefore, exalted to the divine throne.

In Philippians 2:9–11, therefore, Paul sets out a christological version of eschatological and cultic monotheism. We now proceed to detailed comments on two specific expressions used in verses 6–11 that have strong monotheistic resonances: *to einai isa theō* ('being equal with God', 'equality with God') (2:6) and *ho theos auton huperupsōsen* ('God has highly exalted him', 'God has raised him to the position of highest honour') (2:9). Understanding these phrases is essential for demonstrating that the passage does not mean that Christ only begins to belong to the divine identity at his exaltation. Rather only one who already belonged to the divine identity could occupy this position of eschatological supremacy. It is part of the function of the opening words of the passage (2:6), which I understand, with the large majority of scholars,[56] as depicting the pre-existence of Christ, to make clear his identity with the one God from the beginning.

First, the phrase *to einai isa theō* ('being equal with God', 'equality with God') (Phil. 2:6). In my view, the best linguistic argument suggests that

---

[56] Dunn's strong advocacy of the view that pre-existence is not in view seems to have made very few converts.

the debated clause within which this phrase occurs is best understood: 'he did not think equality with God something to be used for his own advantage'.[57] There is no question here either of gaining or of losing equality with God. The pre-existent Christ has equality with God; the issue is his attitude to it. He elects to express it, not by continuing to enjoy the 'form of God' (*morphē theou*), which is the visible splendour of divine status in heaven,[58] but by exchanging this glorious form for the humble status of the human form (*morphēn doulou*) on earth (2:7). What has been given surprisingly inadequate attention in the complex discussion of this opening section of the passage is the phrase *to einai isa theō* itself. Scholars have been distracted by its alleged contribution to an Adam Christology. But, even if there were an Adam Christology at work here, it would not be enough to refer to Genesis 3:5 to explain the phrase *to einai isa theō* since, while this could give it the sense of the blasphemous ambition which Adam attempted to snatch, it does not explain the phrase in its positive application to Christ. Whatever reading of the verse is offered, 'equality with God' has to be something Christ had, has or will have,[59] but which it is not blasphemous to ascribe to him.

The phrase does not mean simply 'like God' in a sense that would be unexceptionable when applied human beings created 'in the image of God'. There is no good evidence that the adverb *isa* used with *einai* has a weaker force than the adjective *isos*.[60] It does not denote mere similarity (in Dunn's curious phrase, 'the degree of equality with God which [Adam] already enjoyed'[61]), but equivalence, being on a level with.[62] Even if *isa* itself could be used on occasion somewhat loosely, a loose use of *to einai isa theō* in a Jewish monotheistic context is intrinsically very unlikely. We can appreciate this when we notice that the phrase has a close parallel in the New Testament itself: in John 5:18 ('making himself equal with God': *ison heautou poiōn tō theō*), where

---

[57] N.T. Wright, *Climax of the Covenant*, 62–90.

[58] Charles A. Wanamaker, 'Philippians 2:6–11: Son of God or Adam Christology?' *NTS* 33 (1987): 183–7.

[59] It would hardly do justice to the passage to see 'equality with God' as something Christ never had and was never to have, but only something he refused to attempt to have.

[60] L.D. Hurst, 'Christ, Adam and Preexistence,' in *Where Christology Began*, ed. Martin and Dodd, 91–2 n. 17. For the usage, see BDF §434 (1).

[61] Dunn, *Christology*, 116. The examples Dunn quotes from LXX (*Theology*, 285 n. 89), where Hebrew כ is translated *isa*, are all in similes (e.g. Job 5:14: 'let them grope in the noon-day just as [*isa*] in the night') (there are ten such instances of use in similes in LXX Job). This is a kind of usage that cannot be compared directly with *to einai isa theō*. The phrase *ton ison autou* [i.e. God] (Job 41:4) is an attempt at literal translation of *'erᵉkô*.

[62] See the abundant evidence in LSJ and Lampe.

it constitutes an accusation of blasphemy against Jesus. Equality with God was something which pagan kings claimed[63] – blasphemously in Jewish eyes. In Philippians 2:6–12, with its strong evocation of Deutero-Isaianic monotheism, *to einai isa theō* cannot fail to have strongly monotheistic resonances. In the light of the God who asks, 'To whom do you compare me?' (Isa. 40:25; cf. 18 LXX), declares, 'I will not give my glory to another' (Isa. 42:8; 48:11 LXX) and insists, 'I am God and there is no other besides me' (Isa. 45:21 LXX), 'equality with God' is conceivable only for one who is not 'another' besides God, but actually belongs to the identity of this unique God.

Secondly, the words *ho theos auton huperupsōsen* ('God has highly exalted him', 'God has raised him to the position of highest honour') (Phil. 2:9). The verb does not indicate that God has exalted Jesus to a higher status than he had previously occupied (whether in pre-existence or in mortal life), but that God has exalted him to a higher status than that of anyone or anything else, i.e. to the pre-eminent position in the whole cosmos. This sense coheres so well with the following phrase ('and bestowed on him the name that is above [*huper*] every name') that this coherence is surely sufficient to establish the meaning of *huperupsōsen*. God gives him the name that is 'higher' than any other, his own uniquely divine name, because he exalts him to the status that is higher than any other, his own uniquely divine status. In my view, this statement echoes Isaiah 52:13, 'Behold, my servant shall understand and shall be exalted (*hupsōthēsetai*) and shall be glorified greatly' (LXX). This verse, connected by *gezera shawa* with passages which speak of God himself as exalted on his heavenly throne (Isa. 6:1 [LXX: *hupsēlou*]; 57:15 [LXX: *hupsistos, en hupsēlois*]), has been understood to mean that the Servant is exalted to God's own position of pre-eminence on his heavenly throne.[64]

Although I consider Isaiah 52:13 the principal scriptural background to Philippians 2:9, it is also instructive to observe the Septuagint's use of the verb *huperupsoō*. It is used once of the arrogant wicked person who exalts himself in competition with God (Ps. 36[37]:35; similarly also Dan. 12:11 *v.l.*) and once in the Psalms of YHWH:

> For you are the Lord [*kurios* for YHWH] the Most High [*hupsistos*]
>   over all the earth;
> you are greatly exalted [*sphodra huperupsōthēs*] above all the gods
>   (Ps. 96[97]:9).

---

[63] Examples (*isa theou, isotheos*, etc.) in BDAG 431.
[64] See chapter 1 above.

Elsewhere it occurs only in the Song of the Three (in the Greek additions to Daniel), where it occurs thirty-five times in the refrains: 'to be praised and highly exalted forever'; and 'sing praise to him and highly exalt him forever' (*humneite kai hyperupsoute auton eis tous aiōnas*). It is worth noticing that this latter refrain is used to call on all created beings to praise God and to acknowledge him as Lord – which is what occurs with reference to Jesus in Philippians 2:11–12.

As a final comment on Philippians 2:6–11, it is worth noting the possibility that the exegesis of Isaiah 45:23 that lies behind it distinguished two divine subjects in that verse. In the Septuagint (MT is different), it reads: 'By myself I swear, righteousness shall go out from my mouth, my words will not be frustrated: that to me every knee shall bow and every tongue shall confess to God (*exomologēsetai ... tō theō; v. l. omeitai ... ton theon*).' The speaker is YHWH (v 18) but in this verse he speaks not only of himself ('to me every knee shall bow') but also in the third person of 'God' ('every tongue shall confess to God'). When Paul quotes this verse in Romans 14:11, he seems to take advantage of this possibility of distinguishing two divine subjects, identifying 'the Lord' (YHWH) as Jesus and 'God' as the Father. He makes this clear by inserting 'says the Lord' into the first part of his quotation:

> As I live, says the Lord, every knee shall bow to me,
> and every tongue shall confess to God (*exomologēsetai tō theō*).

The same interpretation could lie behind Philippians 2:10–11, where the first part of this quotation is interpreted as 'at the name of Jesus every knee should bow', while the interpretation of the second part also refers to Jesus but goes on to make clear that the confession of Jesus as Lord redounds to the praise of God the Father: 'every tongue should confess that Jesus Christ is Lord, to the glory of God the Father'.

Such a reading of Isaiah 45:23 could have been encouraged also by the fact that verse 25 (LXX) has two parallel statements, one about the Lord (*kurios* for YHWH), the other about God (*tō theō*). But we must also note that, in this passage, it is unambiguously YHWH (*kurios*) who makes the emphatic series of monotheistic claims: 'I am the Lord and there is none besides'; 'I am God and there is no other besides me'; 'there is none but me'; 'I am God and there is no other' (vv. 18–22, LXX). If the Christian exegesis has distinguished two divine subjects and identified YHWH as Jesus, then the implication is clearly that Jesus is not added alongside the one God of Israel but included in the unique identity of that God. Maurice Casey, who suggests that an exegesis that found two figures in Isaiah 45:23–25 lies behind Philippians 2:10–11, entirely misses this implication, asserting that, for the author of this passage, 'Jesus was not fully divine'.[65]

7. First Corinthians 8:5–6

The context of this passage in Paul's discussion of the issue of eating meat offered to idols and participation in temple banquets supplies its clear monotheistic concern. The issue is the highly traditional Jewish monotheistic one of loyalty to the only true God in a context of pagan polytheistic worship. What Paul does is to maintain the Jewish monotheistic concern in a Christian interpretation for which loyalty to the only true God entails loyalty to the Lord Jesus Christ.

In the first place, we should note the statement which Paul takes up in verse 4 in order to explain it in the following verses: 'we know that there is no idol in the world and that there is no God except one (*oudeis theos ei mē heis*)'. No doubt the statement comes from the Corinthians' letter, but they may be citing back to Paul what he himself had taught them, and, in any case, the statement is a typically Jewish monotheistic one. The designation of other gods as 'idols' can, of course, only be Jewish.[66] The statement is reminiscent of the very common Jewish monotheistic formula which claims that there is no other God besides YHWH,[67] especially those versions of this formula which give it an explicitly cosmic context, like the *en kosmō* ('in the world') of 1 Corinthians 8:4, which Paul echoes in the *eite en ouranō eite epi gēs* ('in heaven or on earth') of the following verse, and especially also those versions of the formula which link it with an allusion to the Shema''s assertion of the uniqueness of God. For example:

> YHWH is God; there is no other besides him … YHWH is God in heaven above and on the earth beneath; there is no other (Deut. 4:35, 39).

> For there is no other besides the Lord, neither in heaven, nor on the earth, nor in the deepest places, nor in the one foundation (2 *En.* 47:3J).

---

[65] Casey, *Jewish Prophet*, 114.

[66] *En kosmō* shows that *eidōlon* here does not mean the physical object as such (which, of course, undeniably exists), but the pagan god Jews frequently regarded *as* the idol.

[67] Deut. 4:35, 39; 32:39; 1 Sam. 2:2; 2 Sam. 7:22; 1 Kgs. 8:60; 1 Chr. 17:20; Isa. 44:6; 45:5, 6, 14 (*bis*), 18, 21 (*bis*), 22; 46:9; Joel 2:27; Wis. 12:13; Jdt. 8:20; 9:14; Bel 41; Sir. 18:2; 24:24; 36:5; 1QHᵃ 15:32; 18:9; 20:11, 31; 1Q35 1:6; 4Q377 frg. 1ʳ 2:8; 4Q504 [4QDibHamᵃ] frg. 1–2 5:9; 2 *En.* 33:8; 36:1; 47:3; *Sib. Or.* 3:629, 760; 8:377; *Apoc. Ab.* 19:3–4; *T. Ab.* A8:7; Orphica 16; Philo, *Opif.* 23, 46; *Leg.* 3.4, 82; cf. also Dan. 3:29; Add. Esth. 13:14.

There is an ancient saying about him: 'He is one ... And there is no other' (Ps-Orphica, lines 9–10, 17).

He is one, and besides him there is no other (Mark 12:32).[68]

This sets the context of strict Jewish monotheistic belief within which Paul works in his discussion with the Corinthians that follows. He fully accepts the statement in verse 4 (though not, as becomes clear, the implications for behaviour which the Corinthians draw from it). But he goes on to give, in verse 6, a fuller monotheistic formulation, which is remarkable in that, while it follows the structure of Jewish monotheistic assertions, it also incorporates Jesus Christ into the unique divine identity. This is probably Paul's most explicit formulation of what we have called christological monotheism. That Paul has here produced a Christian version of the Shemaʿ has now rightly been recognized quite widely,[69] but the fully decisive way in which he has here included Jesus in the Jewish definition of the unique identity of the one God can be appreciated only in the light of the account of Jewish monotheism that we offered in the first section of this chapter.

In verse 5, Paul acknowledges the context of pagan polytheism to which the Jewish monotheism he continues to maintain is polemically opposed. His point is not to affirm the existence of many gods and many lords, and certainly not to affirm their existence *as* gods and lords, but to introduce the contrast between the *allegiance* of pagans to the many whom they call gods and lords and the exclusive, monotheistic loyalty of Christians, which is specified in verse 6 ('but for us'). He is, in fact, shifting the emphasis from the mere existence or otherwise of gods (which the Corinthians' use of the statement quoted in verse 4 stressed) to the question of allegiance, devotion and worship. There is nothing alien to Jewish monotheism in this shift. The monotheism expressed in the Shemaʿ is precisely a matter not merely of believing that only one God exists, but of according this God ('YHWH our God') the exclusive and whole-hearted devotion that his uniqueness requires. Hence, it is entirely appropriate that it should be by means of a version

---

[68] This is given as the scribe's interpretation of Jesus' literal quotation of the Shemaʿ in v. 29.

[69] E.g. Frederick F. Bruce, *1 and 2 Corinthians* (NCB; London: Oliphants, 1971), 80; Douglas R. de Lacey, '"One Lord" in Pauline Christology,' in *Christ the Lord*, ed. Rowdon, 191–203 (a significant and pioneering study which has gone surprisingly unnoticed or unacknowledged by the other authors); Dunn, *Christology*, 180; Hurtado, *One God*, 97; Wright, *Climax of the Covenant*, 128–9; Donald A. Hagner, 'Paul's Christology and Jewish Monotheism,' in M. Shuster and R. Muller ed., *Perspectives on Christology* (Grand Rapids: Zondervan, 1991), 28–9; Richardson, *Paul's Language*, 300; Ben Witherington III, *Jesus the Sage* (Edinburgh: T&T Clark, 1994), 316; Anthony C. Thiselton, *The First Epistle to the Corinthians* (NIGTC; Grand Rapids: Eerdmans/Carlisle: Paternoster, 2000), 636–7.

of the Shemaʿ that Paul, in verse 6, formulates Christian monotheism. However, verse 5 prepares for this version of the Shemaʿ also in another way. When Paul moves in this verse from calling the pagan deities 'gods' to calling them not only 'gods' but also 'lords' (*kurioi*), he introduces a term which was, in fact, used in many pagan cults, but he introduces it in order to provide a more complete contrast to the version of the Shemaʿ which is to come in verse 6. Whereas pagans profess allegiance to many gods and many lords, Christians owe exclusive allegiance to one God *and* one Lord.

The carefully structured formulation of verse 6 reads:

> *allʾ hēmin heis theos ho patēr*
>   *ex hou ta panta kai hēmeis eis auton,*
> *kai heis kurios Iēsous Christos*
>   *diʾ hou ta panta kai hēmeis diʾ autou.*

> but for us [there is] one God, the Father,
>   from whom [are] all things and we for him,
> and one Lord, Jesus Christ,
>   through whom [are] all things and we through him.

In stating that there is one God and one Lord, Paul is unmistakably echoing the monotheistic statement of the Shemaʿ ('YHWH our God, YHWH, is one'),[70] whose Greek version in the Septuagint reads: *kurios ho theos hēmōn kurios heis estin*. He has, in fact, taken over all of the words of this statement,[71] but rearranged them in such a way as to produce an affirmation of both one God, the Father, and one Lord, Jesus Christ. If he were understood as *adding* the one Lord to the one God of whom the Shemaʿ speaks, then, from the perspective of Jewish monotheism, he would certainly be producing, not christological monotheism, but outright ditheism. Jewish understanding of the Shemaʿ in this period certainly saw it as a profession of the absolute uniqueness of YHWH, besides whom there is no other. Over against the many gods and many lords (v. 5) whom pagans worshipped, the Shemaʿ demands exclusive allegiance to the unique God alone. Even if 'Lord' in verse 6 means no more than 'lords' in verse 5 – and it must mean at least this – there can be no doubt that the *addition* of a unique Lord to the unique God of the Shemaʿ would flatly *contradict*

---

[70] The many allusions to the Shemaʿ in Second Temple Jewish literature which have the form 'God is one' suggest that this is the way the Shemaʿ was normally understood (rather than 'YHWH our God is one YHWH' or 'YHWH is our God, YHWH alone').

[71] The *hēmōn* appears as the *hēmin* and repeated *hēmeis* of Paul's formulation.

the uniqueness of the latter. Paul would be, not reasserting Jewish monotheism in a Christian way nor modifying or expanding[72] the Shema͑, but repudiating Judaism and radically subverting the Shema͑. The only possible way to understand Paul as maintaining monotheism is to understand him to be including Jesus in the unique identity of the one God affirmed in the Shema͑. But this is, in any case, clear from the fact that the term 'Lord', applied here to Jesus as the 'one Lord', is taken from the Shema͑ itself. Paul is not adding to the one God of the Shema͑ a 'Lord' the Shema͑ does not mention. He is identifying Jesus as the 'Lord' (YHWH) whom the Shema͑ affirms to be one. Thus, in Paul's quite unprecedented reformulation of the Shema͑, the unique identity of the one God *consists of* the one God, the Father, *and* the one Lord, his Messiah (who is implicitly regarded as the Son of the Father). Contrary to what many exegetes who have not sufficiently understood the way in which the unique identity of God was understood in Second Temple Judaism seem to suppose, by including Jesus in this unique identity Paul is precisely *not* repudiating Jewish monotheism, whereas were he merely associating Jesus with the unique God he certainly *would* be repudiating monotheism.

Paul rewrites the Shema͑ to include both God and Jesus in the unique divine identity. But the point might not have been sufficiently clear had he not combined with the Shema͑ itself another way of characterizing the unique identity of YHWH. Of the Jewish ways of characterizing the divine uniqueness, the most unequivocal was by reference to creation. In the uniquely divine role of creating all things, it was for Jewish monotheism unthinkable that any being other than God could even assist God (Isa. 44:24; Sir. 42:21; *4 Ezra* 3:4; 6:6; Josephus, *C. Ap.* 2.192; Philo. *Opif.* 23).[73] But to Paul's unparalleled inclusion of Jesus in the Shema͑, he adds the equally unparalleled inclusion of Jesus in the creative activity of God. No more unequivocal way of including Jesus in the unique divine identity is conceivable within the framework of Second Temple Jewish monotheism.

It has not been sufficiently clearly recognized that, as well as dividing the wording of the Shema͑ between God and Jesus, Paul divides a description of God as the Creator of all things between God and Jesus. The description in its undivided, unmodified form is used elsewhere by Paul – in Romans 11:36a: 'from him and through him and to him [are] all things' (*ex autou kai di᾿ autou kai eis auton ta panta*).

---

[72] Richardson, *Paul's Language*, 300.
[73] Even Philo's exegesis of Gen. 1:26 in *Opif.* 72–5 is only a minor qualification of this conviction: he insists that God acted alone in the creation of all things *except* humanity.

It is true that there are some non-Jewish Hellenistic parallels to the formulation which relates 'all things' (*ta panta*) to God by a variety of prepositions. The best examples are in Pseudo-Aristotle, *Mund.* 6 (*ek theou panta kai dia theou sunestēke*); Marcus Aurelius, *Medit.* 4.3 (*ek sou panta, en soi panta, eis se panta*); and Asclepius 34 (*omnia enim ab eo et in ipso et per ipsum*).[74] The point of such formulae is that they describe God as the cause of all things, indicating the various types of causation (as standardly recognized in ancient philosophy) which are appropriate to God's relation to the world by means of the various prepositions: i.e. efficient causation (*ek*), instrumental causation (*dia* or *en*), and final causation (*eis*).[75] But such formulae would clearly be very congenial to Jewish usage, since Jews were, in any case, very much in the habit of describing God as the Creator of 'all things'.[76] Josephus (*B.J.* 5.218), without the use of the prepositions, says much the same as the non-Jewish Hellenistic formulations: 'all things are from God and for God (*tou theou panta kai tō theō*)'. Philo explicitly takes up the standard philosophical set of types of causation, and applies to God's relation to the world the three which can be so applied: God himself is the efficient cause ('by whom [*huph' hou*] it was made'), his Word is the instrumental cause ('by means of which [*di' hou*] it was made'), and the final cause ('on account of which [*di' ho*]') is 'the display of the goodness of the Creator' (*Cher.* 127).[77] In Hebrews 2:10, God is final and instrumental cause of his creation: the one 'on account of whom (*di' hon*) are all things and through whom (*di' hou*) are all things'.[78]

We can, therefore, be confident that Paul's formulation – 'from him and through him and to him [are] all things' – is neither original to

---

[74] The quotation from Seneca, *Ep.* 65.8, given by Dunn, *Christology*, 329; idem, *Romans 9–16* (WBC 38; Dallas, Word, 1988), 701, is relevant only in the sense that it shows that the four or five types of causation could be indicated by difference prepositions, while the reference to Philo, *Spec.* 1.208 is scarcely relevant at all.

[75] Material and formal causation could not appropriately describe the relationship between God and the universe. Eph. 4:6 uses a different kind of formula, which also relates God to all things by means of three different prepositions, but has the prepositions governing *panta*, 'one God and Father of all, who is above (*epi*) all and through (*dia*) all and in (*en*) all'.

[76] E.g. Isa. 44:24; Jer. 10:16; 51:19; Jdt. 16:14; 2 Macc. 1:24; 7:23; 3 Macc. 2:3, 21; 4 Macc. 11:5; Sir. 18:1; 24:8; 43:33; 51:12 iv; Wis. 1:14; 9:1; 1QS 11:18; 1QH^a 8:16; *Jub.* 2:31; 11:17; 12:4, 19; 17:3, 26; 22:4; 23:27; *Sib. Or.* 3:20; 8:376; *1 En.* 9:5; 84:3; *2 En.* 33:8; 66:4; *Apoc. Ab.* 7:10; Aris. Ex. 16; *Jos. Asen.* 12:1; *Pr. Jac.* 1–2; Aristob. frg. 4 13:4; Aristob. frg. 5 12:12; Josephus, *A.J.* 8.280; *B.J.* 5:218; *C. Ap.* 2.190; Philo, *Opif.* 28, 88, 135; *Decal.* 64; *Spec.* 1. 20, 30, 62.

[77] The citation of *Cher.* 125, by Dunn, *Christology*, 329; idem, *Romans 9–16*, 701, to illustrate the use of the prepositions in Rom. 11:36; 1 Cor. 8:6 is somewhat misleading, since Philo here uses *ek* for material, not efficient, causation: with reference to creation, it refers to the four elements of which the world was composed (*Cher.* 127).

[78] It is very surprising that this parallel to Rom 11:36 is missing from those displayed in Dunn, *Romans 9–16*, 701.

Paul nor borrowed directly from non-Jewish sources, but was known to him as a Jewish description precisely of God's unique relationship to all other reality. That God is the instrumental cause (*dia*) as well as the agent or efficient cause (*ek*) of all things well expresses the Jewish monotheistic insistence that God used no one else to carry out his creative work, but accomplished it solely by means of his own Word and/or Wisdom.

When Paul uses this formulation in Romans 11:36, there is no christological reference, but when he incorporates it into his christianized version of the Shema' in 1 Corinthians 8:6, he divides it between God and Christ, just as he divides the wording of the Shema' between God and Christ. The relationship to God expressed by the first and the last of the three prepositions (*ek* and *eis*) is attributed to the one God, the Father ('from whom [are] all things and we for him'), while the relationship expressed by the second of the three prepositions (*dia*) is attributed to the one Lord, Jesus Christ ('through whom [are] all things and we through him'). The fact that, in Romans 11:36, all three prepositions apply to God whereas, in 1 Corinthians 8:6, one of them applies to Christ does not mean[79] that they no longer all describe the Creator's relationship to the whole of creation. On the contrary, it means precisely that Christ is included in this relationship as the instrumental cause of creation.[80]

The variation between 'all things' and 'we' in 1 Corinthians 8:6 results from Paul's desire to situate himself and his readers within the 'all things' who are thus related to their Creator. In this way, Paul is continuing the emphasis of the *hēmin* ('for us') with which he began his adaptation of the Shema', and reflecting the Shema''s own reference to 'the Lord *our* God'. He wishes it to be clear that the God whose unique identity is characterized by being the Creator of all things has that identity not only for all things in general, but specifically *for us*, who, therefore, owe exclusive allegiance to this God. The fact that Paul associates 'all things' with one preposition ('from whom all things'), 'we' with another ('we for him'), and both 'all things' and 'we' with the last preposition ('through whom all things and we through him') is a rhetorical variation adapted to the needs of verbal symmetry. Paul does not mean that 'we' are not also 'from God' or that 'all things' are not also 'for God'. The whole is a condensed form

---

[79] Contra Richardson, *Paul's Language*, 297.

[80] Col. 1:16 goes further and sees Christ as both the instrumental and the final cause of creation.

of what would otherwise have been the more cumbersome and less symmetrical formulation:

> one God, the Father,
> from whom [are] all things and we from him,
> for whom [are] all things and we for him,
> and one Lord, Jesus Christ,
> through whom [are] all things and we through him.

The rather extensive scholarly discussion as to whether all or part of the formulation in 1 Corinthians 8:6 refers to the work of salvation rather than to the work of creation is redundant. All three prepositions, as in Romans 11:36, describe the unique divine relationship to the whole of created reality. Since they designate God as the final cause or goal of creation (*eis*) as well as its origin (*ek*) and instrumental cause (*dia*), the whole formulation encompasses not only God's bringing of all things into being, but also his bringing of all things to final fulfilment in himself, in new creation. In this sense, salvation as well as creation is envisaged, but in no less cosmic a sense and scope than in the case of creation. This point is missed when, in support of a soteriological rather than a creational reference in 1 Corinthians 8:6, it is claimed that Paul uses the phrase *ta de panta ek tou theou* either with reference to God's creative work (1 Cor. 11:12) *or* with reference to God's salvific work (2 Cor. 5:18).[81] In fact, 2 Corinthians 5:18 refers to God's work of salvation precisely as *new creation* (cf. 5:17). There is no evidence that, when Paul says *ta panta*, he means anything less than Jewish writers normally meant by this phrase: the whole of reality created by God, all things other than God their Creator.

The purpose of what is said about Jesus Christ in 1 Corinthians 8:6 is not primarily to designate him the 'mediator' (a not strictly appropriate term in this context, but frequently used) of God's creative work or of God's salvific work, but rather to include Jesus in the unique identity of the one God. Jesus is included in God's absolutely unique relationship to all things as their Creator. The purpose of the whole verse, in its context, is strictly monotheistic. Its point is to distinguish the God to whom Christians owe exclusive allegiance from the many gods and many lords served by pagans. Just as in all Second Temple Jewish monotheistic assertions of this kind, what is said about God is said as a means of *identifying God as unique*. What is said about Jesus Christ

---

[81] Richardson, *Paul's Language*, 297–8.

only serves this purpose if it *includes Jesus in the unique identity of God*. Paul apportions the words of the Shema' between Jesus and God in order to include Jesus in the unique identity of the one God YHWH confessed in the Shema'. Similarly, he apportions between Jesus and God the threefold description of God's unique identifying relationship as Creator to all things, in order to include Jesus in the unique identity of the one Creator.

That of the three prepositions that characterize the Creator's unique relationship to all things Paul chooses 'through' (*dia*) for Jesus Christ's relationship to all things is a secondary issue, but the choice is certainly not arbitrary. Paul knew that Jewish language about creation did customarily distinguish between God as the agent of creation and that through which or by which God created – the instrumental cause of creation. This instrumental cause – God's Word and/or God's Wisdom – was not other than God, but was included in God's unique identity, as his own Word or his own Wisdom. For example:

The Lord made the earth by (*en*) his power,
prepared the world by (*en*) his wisdom,
and by (*en*) his understanding stretched out the heaven (Jer. 28:15 LXX
   [= 51:19 Heb.]).

who have made all things by (*en*) your word,
And by your wisdom have formed humankind (Wis. 9:1–2).

You have made all things by (*en*) wisdom (Ps. 103:24 LXX
   [= 104:24 Heb.]).

you devised and spoke by means of your word (*2 Bar.* 14:17).

There are also other texts, some undoubtedly known to Paul, which develop this language by means of a personification of God's Word or God's Wisdom portrayed as acting as a personal subject. Whether Paul, in formulating 1 Corinthians 8:6, had in mind the Word of God or the Wisdom of God or both it is hardly possible to say. Nor, in the last resort, is it of decisive importance whether the texts he knew employed the personification of either or both concepts as a mere literary device or as indicating some degree of real hypostatization of these aspects of God. Paul's thinking did not *start* from a distinction in God with which Jewish accounts of creation provided him. His purpose was to include Jesus Christ in the Jewish characterization of the unique identity of God, which entailed including him as participant in God's creative activity. He came to the texts with this theological-christological purpose. What he certainly found in the Jewish descriptions of creation was a distinction within the divine *relationship* to creation. He found a distinction between, on the one hand, God as the agent of creation, and, on the other hand, God's own Wisdom devising the creation or God's own Word accomplishing the work of creation. It was this distinction that facilitated his apportionment of the language of creation between God the Father and the Lord Jesus Christ, without introducing an associate other than God into the uniquely divine work of creation. The Jewish language and conceptuality of creation, we may say, left room for Paul to include Jesus Christ as the instrumental cause of creation within the unique divine identity as it was characterized by the relationship of Creator to creation.

Neil Richardson uses the apt term 'theological *inclusio*' for a chiastic pattern which he finds widely in Paul's writings and which comes to a particular grammatical expression in the use of the prepositions in 1 Corinthians 8:6. The pattern is: God > Christ > Christ > God. This 'corresponds with the observation made by many commentators that God is the source and goal, Christ the mediator and instrument'.[82] But it also forms a literary pattern in which Paul's 'thinking begins and ends with God. Yet between the "movement" from God and back to God there is Christ. Thus Paul's language about God has been opened up, amplified, explicated, justified by language about Christ'.[83] Richardson's observation of and observations about this pattern are illuminating and important. He does not, however, quite see its full significance, which is that Paul is not just including language about Christ *between* his language about God, but including Christ *in* the identity of God. The literary *inclusio* reflects Paul's theological *inclusion* of Jesus Christ in the unique identity of the one God of Jewish monotheism. This is the theological basis for what Richardson calls the 'interplay between Paul's language about God and his language about Christ', which means not only that Paul 'uses God-language in order to interpret and "define" Christ', but also 'that language about Christ in turn redefines the identity of God'.[84] In our terms, if Jesus Christ is included in the identity of God, that inclusion must itself affect the way the identity of God is understood. This last point is of very considerable significance, but our task in the present essay stops short of developing it.

---

[82] Richardson, *Paul's Language,* 301
[83] Richardson, *Paul's Language,* 304.
[84] Richardson, *Paul's Language,* 307.

8. Christological reading of scriptural YHWH texts outside Paul

The christological reading of scriptural passages about YHWH was practised not only by Paul, but also by many other early Christian teachers and writers. The evidence presented in this section is doubtless not complete, but will serve the purpose simply of demonstrating that the practice is not likely to have been invented by Paul and was widely practised in early Christianity. The phenomenon of christological reading of scriptural YHWH texts outside Paul has received even less scholarly attention than the phenomenon within Paul's writings. Individual instances have been discussed,[85] but there have not even been any attempts to assemble lists of such cases. The following list classifies the texts in the same way as the Pauline instances were classified in section 2. The material deserves close examination that cannot be given here.

8.1. YHWH texts with Jesus as referent

(1) Quotations including *kurios*

Matt. 3:3	Isa. 40:3
Mark 1:3	Isa. 40:3
Luke 3:4	Isa. 40:3
John 1:23	Isa. 40:3
Acts 2:21	Joel 2:32
2 Tim. 2:19	Num. 16:5[86]
Heb. 1:10–12	Ps. 102:25–27 (LXX 101:26–28)
	(*kurie* only in LXX)
1 Pet. 2:3	Ps. 34:8 (LXX 33:9)
1 Pet. 3:10–12	Ps. 34:12–16 (LXX 33:13–17)

---

[85] The passages in 1 Peter receive particularly helpful discussion in William L. Schutter, *Hermeneutic and Composition in 1 Peter* (WUNT 2/30; Tübingen: Mohr Siebeck, 1989). The quotations of Isa. 40:3 in the Gospels are discussed in Davis, *The Name*, chap. 3, and that in Mark 1:3 in Joel Marcus, *Way of the Lord*, chap. 2; Rikki E. Watts, *Isaiah's New Exodus in Mark* 2nd ed. (Grand Rapids: Baker, 200), chap. 3. On Rev. 1:17; 22:13, see Bauckham, *Theology*, 25–8, 54–8. On Jude 14 in relation to comparable use of OT YHWH texts in the NT, see Richard Bauckham, *Jude and the Relatives of Jesus in the Early Church* (Edinburgh: T&T Clark, 1990), 288–95.

[86] Num. 16:5 MT has YHWH, but LXX has *ho theos*.

(2) Quotations to which the authors add *kurios*

1 Pet. 1:24–25	Isa. 40:6–8
Jude 14	*1 En.* 1:9[87]

(3) Quotations not including *kurios*

Eph. 4:8	Ps. 68:18 (LXX 67:19)[88]
1 Pet. 2:8	Isa. 8:14[89]
Rev. 1:17; 22:13	Isa. 44:6; 48:12

(4) Allusions including *kurios*

Luke 1:76	Mal. 3:1
Eph. 6:19	Ps. 27:6 (LXX 26:6)[90]
2 Tim. 4:14	Ps. 62:12 (LXX 61:13); Prov. 24:12[91]
2 Tim. 4:17	Exod. 34:5[92]
Jas. 5:7	Hos. 2:3

(5) Allusions not including *kurios*

John 12:41	Isa. 6:1 (LXX)
2 Tim. 4:17–18	Ps. 22:20–21 (LXX 21:21–22)[93]
1 Pet. 3:14–15	Isa. 8:12–13
Rev. 2:23	Jer. 17:10
Rev. 22:12	Isa. 40:10[94]

(6) Stereotyped OT phrases including *kurios*

'to name the name of the Lord'

Acts 19:13; 1 Tim. 2:19[95]	Isa. 26:13; Lev. 24:16; Amos 6:11; etc.

'to call on the name of the Lord'

Acts 9:14;[96] 22:16; 2 Tim. 2:22	Joel 2:32; Zeph. 3:9; Zech. 13:9; Jer. 10:25; etc.

---

[87] The book of Enoch is here treated comparably with the Hebrew Scriptures.

[88] It is possible that in the author's reading of this verse, he did not identify the subject (third person singular in LXX) as YHWH, but for the view that he did, see, for example, Timothy Gombis, 'Cosmic Lordship and Divine Gift-Giving: Psalm 68 in Ephesians 4:8,' *NovT* 47 (2005) 367–79; Fee, *Pauline Christology*, 356–9.

[89] In Isa. 8:14, the stone is YHWH (8:13).

[90] For this allusion, see Margaret Daly-Denton, 'Singing Hymns to Christ as to a God (Cf. Pliny, *Ep.* X, 96),' in Newman, Davila and Lewis ed., *Jewish Roots*, 277–92, here 280–1.

[91] See Fee, *Pauline Christology*, 459–60.

[92] See Fee, *Pauline Christology*, 461.

[93] See Fee, *Pauline Christology*, 461–4.

[94] For christological reading of this text, see also *1 Clem.* 34:3; *Barn.* 21:3.

[95] The phrase is here used in an unknown (probably conflated) scriptural quotation, perhaps based on Num. 16:26–27 and Isa. 26:13. For the reference to Christ as *kurios*, see Fee, *Pauline Christology*, 455–8.

[96] Cf. also 9:21.

'the name [of the Lord] invoked over' people

Jas. 2:7; cf. Hermas, *Sim.* 8.6.4   Amos 9:12 (quoted Acts 15:17);
2 Chr. 7:14; Jer. 14:9; etc.

'the name of the Lord' (other uses)

Acts 9:29; 10:48; 19:17; 21:13;   Gen. 12:8; Mic. 4:5; etc.
Eph. 5:20; Jas. 5:14

'the day of the Lord'

2 Pet. 3:10   Joel 1:15; 2:1, 11, 31; Amos 5:18;
Isa. 13:6, 9; etc.

'the way of the Lord'

Acts 18:25; cf. the absolute use   Isa. 40:3
of 'the Way' (Acts 9:2; 18:25–26;
19:9, 23; 22:4; 24:14, 22)

'the word of the Lord'

Acts 8:25; 13:44, 48, 49; 15:35, 36;   Isa. 2:3; etc.
16:32; 19:10

'to serve the Lord'

Acts 21:19   1 Kgdms. 12:20; Pss. 2:11;
99(100):2; 101(102):22; etc.

'the servant of the Lord'

2 Tim. 2:24   Josh. 7:14; 24:29; Judg. 2:8 etc.[97]

'the fear of the Lord'

Acts 9:31   Isa. 2:10, 19, 21; Prov. 1:7; etc.

9. Jewish precedents for Paul's Christology of divine identity?

Two of the so-called intermediary figures most often cited as resembling some of the Pauline christological material we have discussed are: Melchizedek in 11QMelchizedek and the angel Yahoel in the *Apocalypse of Abraham*. For example, Carl Davis suggests that 11QMelchizedek 'gives a parallel to the New Testament applications of texts about God to Jesus', though he rather strongly qualifies this: 'the nature of the second figure here [i.e. Melchizedek] is so unclear that one may not with any confidence use it as an explanation of the New Testament application of

---

[97] See Fee, *Pauline Christology*, 459.

passages about God to Jesus'.[98] Maurice Casey is one of many scholars who have referred to the angel Yahoel, who has the name of God in him, in connection with Philippians 2:10–11: 'this ... parallel shows quite how exalted a being could be perceived to be without being thought of as a deity'.[99] A third possibility we shall discuss is that certain portrayals of the Messiah in Second Temple Jewish literature are antecedents of Paul's application of YHWH texts to Jesus.

(1) **Melchizedek**: In 11QMelchizedek, Melchizedek is the name of a principal angel, probably to be regarded as another name for Michael, who is the angelic patron of Israel elsewhere in the Qumran texts. The text proceeds by quoting and interpreting a series of scriptural texts, which are understood to refer to the coming eschatological events in which Melchizedek will act on God's behalf in salvation and judgement. He is the agent of the eschatological salvation of God's elect by delivering them, with the help of the other good angels (called *'ēlîm* in 2:14, as frequently in the Qumran literature), from the power of Belial and his evil angels. In this way, he fulfils the prophecy of Isaiah 61:1–2, delivering the captives and executing God's vengeance. For our purposes, the interest is in the application to Melchizedek of biblical texts in which the *'ᵉlōhîm* of the text is taken to refer to Melchizedek.

The first of these is Psalm 82:1:

> *'ᵉlōhîm* will stand up in the assembly of *'ēl*,
> in the midst of the *'ᵉlōhîm* he judges (quoted in 11QMelch 2:10).

The exegete who composed our text saw that *'ᵉlōhîm* could not have the same meaning in both of its occurrences, since, in the first, it is treated as singular and, in the second, as plural. He, therefore, took the second occurrence to refer to the angels who compose the assembly. But he also, quite understandably, supposed that, in the first statement (' *'ᵉlōhîm* will stand up in the assembly of *'ēl*'), *'ᵉlōhîm* must be a different person from *'ēl*. Since the assembly – the heavenly council of judgement – is said to be that of *'ēl*, he naturally supposed that *'ēl* is YHWH, while *'ᵉlōhîm* is the angel Melchizedek, who stands up in the divine council to condemn Belial and his evil angels (Ps. 82:2, as interpreted in 11QMelch 2:11–12). The reason, therefore, for the unusual exegesis of a singular use of *'ᵉlōhîm* as referring to an angelic being is a strictly exegetical one. Since the word here cannot,

---

[98] Davis, *The Name*, 47.
[99] Casey, *Jewish Prophet*, 113.

for exegetical reasons, refer to YHWH, it must refer to a principal angel.

The next text quoted, as a reference also to Melchizedek, is Psalm 7:8b–9a:

> Above it [the assembly] on high return;
> 'ēl will judge the peoples (quoted in 11QMelch 2:10–11).

This text is quoted because it too refers to the heavenly council[100] in a context of judgement, and also because it too is understood as distinguishing between YHWH and a figure who takes an exalted position in the assembly. 'ēl is here the scribal substitute for the Tetragrammaton, a standard practice in Qumran texts, and (especially in view of the fact that our exegete has taken 'ēl in Psalm 82:1 to be YHWH) it must be understood to refer here not to Melchizedek but to YHWH. However, since the first line quoted (Ps. 7:8b) is an imperative, whereas the second line (Ps. 8:9a) speaks of YHWH in the third person, our exegete has supposed that the person addressed in the first line must be someone other than YHWH, and takes him to be Melchizedek. Thus, the quotation and implied interpretation of this biblical text make very clear that there is no confusion between Melchizedek and YHWH. Melchizedek is found by our exegete in these two texts only because he reads both texts as referring not only to YHWH but also to a member of his council, distinguished from YHWH, who plays an important role in the process of judgement. In both texts, Melchizedek is understood to be this prominent angelic member of YHWH's council. In the second text, it is clear that it is YHWH who actually judges, though Melchizedek executes his judgement.

Finally, Isaiah 52:7 (concluding '... saying to Zion, "Your god reigns"') is quoted (11QMelch 2:15–16, 23) and, although the text is fragmentary and the name has to be restored, it seems likely that 'your God' in the text is interpreted as another reference to Melchizedek. This exegesis is presumably possible because it has already been established, from Psalm 82:1, that Melchizedek can be called 'ᵉlōhîm and also because his name ('king of righteousness'), indicating that he rules, makes this particular text appropriate to him. Once again, the point is not that Melchizedek is in some way identified with YHWH or included in his identity, but that in this particular text the term 'your god' does not refer to YHWH, but to Melchizedek, the angelic king of Israel.

---

[100] The use of (*ēdāh* in both Ps. 82:1 and Ps. 7:8a provides an exegetical link (the principle of *gezera shawa*) between the two texts.

These interpretations of scriptural occurrences of *'elōhîm* as referring to Melchizedek highlight the significance of the fact (which we observed) that Paul does *not* provide christological applications of scriptural texts about 'God' (Heb. *'ēl*, *'elōhîm*, Gk. *ho theos*) but only of texts about YHWH.[101] Although the use of 'divine' terms (gods, sons of the gods, sons of God) for heavenly beings other than the one God YHWH almost disappeared in Second Temple Jewish literature other than the Qumran writings and (for different reasons) Philo, exegetes were well aware that the words *'elîm* and *'elōhîm* were sometimes used in Scripture to refer to beings other than the one God (some clear cases were Exod. 7:1; 15:11; Pss. 82:1, 6; 86:8; 97:9). They did not think this terminology made such angelic beings semi-divine beings who straddled the otherwise clear distinction between the one God and all other reality, but simply that these words could be used for heavenly beings created by and subject to the unique Creator and Lord YHWH. This is also true of the Qumran community where much more use of this scriptural terminology was made with reference to angels. For late Second Temple Judaism, it is not that occasional use of the word 'god' for angels qualifies monotheism, but simply that the decisive issue in defining monotheism is not the use of the *word* 'god', but the understanding of the absolute uniqueness of YHWH.

If Paul had applied scriptural statements about 'god' to Jesus, we could have understood him to be doing what 11QMelchizedek does with reference to Jesus,[102] that is, interpreting the 'god' to whom the scriptural texts refer in these particular instances to be not YHWH, the unique Creator and Lord of all things, but an angelic being created and ruled by YHWH. Such an exegetical practice would not constitute what we have called a Christology of divine identity. Identifying Jesus with the YHWH of some scriptural texts is another matter altogether.[103] YHWH is the identifying name of the unique Creator and Lord of all things. But may not the case of Yahoel – who bears the divine name – provide some kind of a precedent for the identification of Jesus with YHWH?

(2) **Yahoel**: The depiction of this angel in the *Apocalypse of Abraham* is clearly intended to represent him as the angel of Exodus 23:31, where

---

[101] I leave aside here the difficult question whether *ho ōn epi pantōn theos* in Rom. 9:5 is Jesus, but, even if it is, this is not a case of applying a scriptural text about God to Jesus.

[102] When Barker, *Risen Lord*, 86–93, supposes that 11QMelch provides background for the identification of Jesus with the divine figure of Melchizedek, she seems to forget her ditheistic distinction between Elohim and YHWH and her claim that Jesus identified himself and was identified as the latter. In 11QMelch, Melchizedek is *distinguished from* YHWH and identified instead with the El and Elohim of Ps. 82.

[103] Capes, *Old Testament Yahweh Texts*, 167, correctly stresses this difference.

God says, of the angel who will lead and protect the Israelites in their entry into the promised land, that 'my name is in him' (cf. *Apoc. Ab.* 10:8). His special characteristic is, therefore, that the power of the divine name is operative through him (10:3, 8). His special functions, in addition to those indicated in Exodus 23 (cf. *Apoc. Ab.* 10: 13–14, 16), seem to be those for which the special power of the divine name is required (10:9–12; 18:9–11), though there are also indications that he leads or supervises the worship of God in heaven (12:4; 17:2–6; 18:11). The description of his appearance (11:2–3) is best understood if he is the heavenly high priest. He wears a turban, an article of dress nowhere else attributed to a heavenly being. The Greek word (*kidaris*), which is here preserved in the Slavonic translation, occurs thirteen times in the Septuagint, on eleven of these occasions describing the headdress of the Aaronide priests (see also *Aris. Ex.* 98; Philo, *Mos.* 2.116, 131). The high priest in the Jerusalem temple wore on his headdress the letters of the divine name (cf. Sir. 45:12; *Aris. Ex.* 98; Wis. 18:24) and was the only person who, at this period, was permitted to pronounce the divine name in blessing (Sir. 50:20), just as Yahoel is sent 'to bless you [Abraham] in the name of God' (*Apoc. Ab.* 10:6). It seems likely that the author of the *Apocalypse of Abraham* has connected the angel in whom is God's name (Exod. 23:21) with the fact that the high priest wears and, alone among human beings, uses the divine name, and so has concluded that the angel in question is the heavenly high priest.

Later traditions make Michael the high priest of the heavenly temple, but, in the *Apocalypse of Abraham*, Michael appears alongside Yahoel (10:17). Perhaps the author thinks of Michael as the commander of the heavenly armies (cf. Dan. 8:11 LXX, Theod.; *Jos. Asen.* 14:8; *2 En.* 22:6; 33:10; 71:28; 72:5; *3 Bar.* 11:6; *T. Ab.* 1:4; 2:1) who protect Israel and Yahoel as the heavenly high priest who employs the divine name in protective blessing of Israel. So whereas Michael is depicted with a crown and a royal sceptre (*Jos. Asen.* 14:9), Yahoel has a turban and a golden sceptre (*Apoc. Ab.* 11:3), which, in this case, would represent not royal but high-priestly authority. There is no indication that Michael is subordinate or subject to Yahoel.

The name Yahoel (*Yahō'ēl* – a combination of *yhw[h]* and *'ēl*) is a form of the divine name, applied to God himself not only in the *Apocalypse of Abraham* itself (17:13),[104] but also elsewhere (*Lad. Jac.* 2:18; *Apoc. Mos.* 29:4; 33:5). However, it is no accident that precisely this name (rather than

---

[104] Capes, *Old Testament Yahweh Texts*, 171, makes the extraordinary suggestion that this reference to Yahoel among the names and attributes of God actually refers to the angel Yahoel (even though Yahoel is said to be singing this hymn of praise to God: 17:7).

yhwh itself or some other form of the divine name) is given also to the angel in whom is the divine name. It conforms to the standard pattern of angelic names, which usually end in -el. Moreover, as the name of an angel, it could readily be understood as the statement 'YHWH is God',[105] like the human name Elijah (*'ēlîyâh* or *'ēlîyāhû*), which also means 'YHWH is God'. The name Yahoel consists of the same two elements as the name Elijah in reverse order, and Jews would readily recognize them as versions of the same name.[106] In a Jewish tradition already attested in the first century CE (*L.A.B.* 48:1), Elijah was identified with the high priest Phinehas (grandson of Aaron) and expected to return as the eschatological high priest of Israel.[107] So it is probably quite deliberate that the angelic high priest, Yahoel, bears another version of the same name as the ideal human high priest, Elijah.[108] This name for the heavenly high priest is thus a suitable parallel to the name of the chief angel who commands God's heavenly armies, Michael, which means 'Who is like God?' (cf. Exod. 15:11).

The polyvalent character of the name Yahoel is precisely what makes it so appropriate for the angel the *Apocalypse of Abraham* describes. Whereas many human names contain the divine name, Yahoel seems to be the only angelic name attested in this period[109] that contains the divine name YHWH. This makes it appropriately the name of the angel in whom is God's name. It is identical to a form of the divine name as used of God, but used as an angel's name it need not be understood as actually naming the angel by God's name. Rather it can be taken as

---

[105] That it could be understood in this way is surely shown by its occurrence in Sefer ha-Razim, where it is the name of the first of the fourteen angels who stand on the third step in the second firmament (cf. also the name Yehoel among those of the angels on the tenth step of the second firmament). This is a rather unimportant position among the hundreds of angels named in Sefer ha-Razim, and would surely not have been given to an angel understood to bear the same name as God. See also the angel Yehoel, correlated with Gabriel, in a magic bowl text (J. Naveh and S. Shaked, *Amulets and Magic Bowls* [Jerusalem: Magnes Press/Leiden: Brill, 1985], 161).

[106] Other pairs of equivalent names (the two elements of the name in alternative orders) are even used for the same person: King Jehoiachin (e.g. 2 Kgs. 24:8) is also called Jeconiah (e.g. Jer. 24:1); Jehoahaz (2 Chr. 21:17) is also called Ahaziah (2 Chr. 22:1); Eliam (2 Sam. 11:3) is also called Ammiel (1 Chr. 3:5).

[107] See Martin Hengel, *The Zealots*, trans. David Smith (Edinburgh: T&T Clark, 1989), 162–8. Elijah as the eschatological high priest is found also in Justin, *Dial.* 8:4; 49:1; Tg. Ps.-J. Exod. 6:18; 40:10; Deut. 30:4; cf. Exod. 4:13; Num. 25:12. The idea was probably based, not only on identifying Elijah with Phinehas, but also on reading Mal. 2:7; 3:1; 4:5 together.

[108] Although one rabbinic tradition speaks of Elijah officiating as high priest in the heavenly temple, the *Apocalypse of Abraham*, which has Yahoel active already in the time of Abraham, cannot intend Yahoel actually to be the exalted Phinehas-Elijah.

[109] Even among the several hundred angelic names in Sefer ha-Razim, only eleven, including Yahoel, seem to contain the divine name.

an affirmation that 'YHWH is God'. It does not identify Yahoel with God (any more than the equivalent name Elijah identifies that prophet with God), but it designates him the angelic high priest who bears the divine name and employs its authority in priestly blessing.

Careful investigation of this figure, therefore, makes wholly redundant scholarly speculations that Yahoel is some kind of embodiment of the divine glory or participant in divine nature or even a personification of the divine name.[110] Yahoel is wholly intelligible as a principal angel (one of at least two), who exercises a delegated authority on God's behalf as the angelic high priest, the heavenly and cosmic equivalent of the Aaronide high priest in the Jerusalem temple. He is neither included in the unique identity of YHWH, as understood by Jews of this period, nor any sort of qualification of or threat to it. Throughout the work he is, as a matter of course, distinguished from God and never confused with God. He worships God (17:3), but there is no suggestion at all that he himself might be worshipped. To God himself are attributed the usual characteristics of the unique divine identity: he is the Creator of all things (7:1 – 9:3), the Eternal One who preceded all things (9:3; 12:4, 9; 14:2, 13; 17:8, etc.), the Mighty One who is sovereign over all the events of history (9:3; 14:13; 17:8; 20–32), the one apart from whom 'there is no other' (19:3–4). Yahoel shares none of these characteristics. Against those scholars who would see him as the divine name personified or hypostatized, it is very noteworthy that he is not associated with the creative work of God, despite the fact that Jewish literature of this period sometimes sees the name of God as the instrument by which God created the world (*Jub.* 36:7; *1 En.* 69:13–26; Pr. Man. 3; cf. *3 En.* 13:3).[111] Moreover, once God embarks on his revelation of creation, history and eschatology to Abraham, Yahoel drops out of the book and is wholly absent for the rest of it (19–32). In God's account of how he will exercise his sovereignty over creation and history, Yahoel plays no part. The *Apocalypse of Abraham* portrays him as one, rather special, angelic servant of God, no more.

The passage of the *Apocalypse of Abraham* in which Yahoel appears (10–17) is an elaboration of the vision of Abraham in Genesis 15. Comparison with the text of Genesis 15 shows that, so far from attributing to Yahoel the role of YHWH in the biblical text, the author has carefully avoided any overlap between what YHWH does in Genesis 15 and what Yahoel does in his account. The words of YHWH to Abraham in Genesis 15:8

---

[110] Rowland, *Open Heaven*, 101–3; Fossum, *The Name*, 318–21. Against these arguments, see also Hurtado, *One God*, 87–9.
[111] Cf. Fossum, *The Name*, 245–56.

are reproduced as words of YHWH himself in *Apocalypse of Abraham* 9:5. It is only when Abraham passes out as a result of this direct audition of the divine voice that YHWH sends Yahoel to strengthen Abraham by the power of the divine name and bring him up to the seventh heaven (*Apoc. Ab.* 10). He gives Abraham further instructions as to how to make his sacrifice (*Apoc. Ab.* 12:8), which correspond to what Abraham is said to do in Genesis 15:10. But these are precisely further instructions introduced by the author to explain how Abraham, according to Genesis 15:10, knew what to do in addition to what YHWH had expressly commanded him. YHWH's revelation of the future to Abraham, as developed at length by the *Apocalypse of Abraham* from the text of Genesis 15:13–21, is once again given directly by God to Abraham (*Apoc. Ab.* 19–32), after Yahoel has dropped entirely out of the narrative. All this shows how far the author of this apocalypse is from applying scriptural texts about YHWH to Yahoel in the way that Paul does to Christ.

It has to be admitted that the alleged precedents of Melchizedek and Yahoel offer no help at all in understanding how Paul acquired and developed his Christology of divine identity.

(3) William Horbury has argued that the background to 'divine' Christology, including the worship of Jesus, lies in Jewish messianism, which, in certain cases at least, portrays 'a messiah endued with divine traits'. Such traits are not necessarily exclusive to YHWH but were attributed also to other 'gods', i.e. angels. But Horbury does also find evidence 'that some biblical theophanies could be understood to speak of an angelic messiah acting on behalf of God himself'.[112] To be precise, he points to three passages in Second Temple Jewish literature in which 'biblical theophany passages' are 'strikingly applied to a messianic figure'. These are *1 Enoch* 52:6, *4 Ezra* 13:3–4 and *Psalms of Solomon* 17:31.[113] These passages, he suggests, 'may form an antecedent for the familiar New Testament phenomenon of the application to Christ of biblical texts which in their own context refer to God'.[114]

The passage from the Psalms of Solomon is not a convincing example.[115] The other two passages are as follows (I have added *1 En.*

---

[112] William Horbury, *Jewish Messianism and the Cult of Christ* (London: SCM, 1998), 103–4.

[113] Horbury, *Jewish Messianism*, 103.

[114] Horbury, *Jewish Messianism,* 104.

[115] Horbury, *Jewish Messianism*, 103, thinks that both the phrase 'to see his [the Messiah's] glory' and the phrase 'to see the glory of the Lord' allude to 'they shall see my [YHWH's] glory' in Isa. 66:18. But (1) the correct reading in the first line may be 'her [Jerusalem's] glory' (*tēn doxan autēs* rather than *tēn doxan autou*), alluding to Isa. 60:1–3. In the context of vv. 31b–32, a

53:7 which, accepting a probable emendation of the text, is close to *1 En.* 52:6):

> These *mountains* your eyes saw – the mountains of iron,
> And the mountains of copper, and the mountains of silver,
> And the mountains of gold, and the mountains of soft metal,
> And the mountains of lead –
> All these will be *before* the Chosen One *like wax* before the fire,
> And *like water that comes down from above upon these mountains*,
> And they shall be weak before his feet (*1 En.* 52:6).[116]

> And these *mountains* will be in the presence of his [the Chosen One's] righteousness *as <wax>*[117]
> And the hills will be like a fountain of *water*,
> And the righteous will rest from the oppression of sinners (*1 En.* 53:7).[118]

> [3]And I looked, and behold, this wind made something like the figure of a man come up out of the heart of the sea. And I looked, and behold, that man flew with the clouds of heaven; and wherever he turned his face to look, everything under his gaze *trembled*, [4]and wherever the voice of his mouth issued forth, all who heard his voice melted *as wax melts* when it feels *the fire* (*4 Ezra* 13:3–4).[119]

The passages in the Hebrew Bible to which there are probable allusions in these two texts are:

> [3]For lo, the LORD is coming out of his place,
> and will come down and tread upon the high places of the earth.
> [4]Then the *mountains* will melt under him,
> and the valleys will burst open,
> *like wax* near the fire,
> *like waters poured down a steep place* (Mic. 1:3–4 NRSV).

> [4]His [the LORD's] lightnings light up the world;
> the earth sees and *trembles*.
> [5]The *mountains will melt like wax before* the LORD,
> before the Lord of all the earth (Ps. 97:4–5 NRSV).

---

reference to Jerusalem's glory here seems more appropriate, though it does make v. 31 rather tautologous. (2) If the reference is to the messianic king's glory, there is no reason to think this phrase echoes Isa. 66:18, as the second phrase 'to see the glory of the Lord' certainly does.

[116] Translation from Nickelsburg and VanderKam, *1 Enoch*, 66.
[117] 'wax' is an emendation (MSS have 'earth').
[118] Translation from Nickelsburg and VanderKam, *1 Enoch*, 67.
[119] Translation from Stone, *4 Ezra*, 381.

> As smoke is driven away, so drive them [God's enemies] away;
> *as wax melts before the fire,*
> let the wicked perish before God (Ps. 68:2 NRSV).

> [The LORD] looks on the earth and it *trembles,*
> who touches the mountains and they smoke (Ps. 104:32 NRSV).

The first three of these passages from the Hebrew Bible are the only ones that contain the simile of melting wax, but it is worth noticing that two other Second Temple Jewish texts pick up the image of mountains melting like wax in the face of a theophany (Jdt. 16:15;[120] 1 *En.* 1:6[121]). It was evidently a vivid image that caught the attention of Jewish writers.

I have italicized the words that link the later Jewish texts with those from the Hebrew Bible. Curiously, although both 1 *Enoch* and 4 *Ezra* pick up the image of wax melting, they seem each to have drawn it from a different biblical passage. 1 *Enoch* 53:7 is dependent on Micah 1:3–4, which supplies the image of water as well as that of wax. The other biblical texts using the image of wax (Ps. 68:2; 97:5) contribute nothing that the author of 1 *Enoch* 53:7 could not have found in Micah 1:3–4. In 4 *Ezra* 13:4, on the other hand, the image of wax melting is applied to people rather than mountains, and so is closer to Psalm 68:2. The notion that it is the Messiah's voice that has this effect is not found in any of these biblical passages, but may well derive from Isaiah 11:4b (a passage about the Davidic Messiah), to which this vision of Ezra certainly alludes later (4 *Ezra* 13:10–11). The statement that everything trembles under the Messiah's gaze (13:3) may allude to Psalm 97:4 or to Psalm 105:32 (the latter has the advantage of referring to YHWH's look, but the former that of close proximity to the image of melting wax).[122]

A similar kind of allusion is found in 1 *Enoch* 46:4, which borrows another vivid image of judgement from the Psalms:

> He [the Son of man] will loosen the reins of the strong,[123]
> And he will crush the teeth of the sinners (1 *En.* 46:4b).[124]

---

[120] 'For the mountains shall be shaken to their foundations with the waters; Before your glance the rocks shall melt like wax' (Jdt. 16:15a NRSV).

[121] 'The high mountains will be shaken and fall and break apart, And the high hills will be made low and melt like wax before the fire' (1 *En.* 1:6; translation from Nickelsburg and VanderKam, 1 *Enoch*, 20). This passage belongs to the first part of 1 *Enoch* (chaps. 1–36) which was originally quite distinct from the *Parables* (chaps 37–71).

[122] Trembling may be a response to a theophany, but could be no more than the natural response to the brightly shining face of any heavenly figure: Stone, 4 *Ezra*, 385.

[123] Cf. perhaps Isa. 45:1.

[124] Translation from Nickelsburg and VanderKam, 1 *Enoch*, 60.

For you [God] strike all my enemies on the cheek,
You break the teeth of the wicked (Ps. 3:7B NRSV).

O God, break the teeth in their mouths (Ps. 58:6a NRSV).

How are we to understand these allusions? They plausibly relate to
what Larry Kreitzer, referring to *1 Enoch* and *4 Ezra*, calls a 'functional
overlap between messianic agent and God'.[125] In both cases, the Messiah
is acting as agent of God's judgement.[126] We should note that, in both the
Parables of Enoch and *4 Ezra* 13, the Messiah of Isaiah 11:1–5 is identified
with the 'one like a son of man' of Daniel 7, who was often understood
to be the agent who carries out God's judgement on the final kingdom
of evil on earth. Of the Messiah of Isaiah 11:1–5, it is said that 'he shall
strike the earth with the rod of his mouth, and with the breath of his
lips he shall kill the wicked' (11:4; echoed in *1 En.* 62:2; *4 Ezra* 13:10–11).
It is easy to see how the Messiah's judgement of the wicked could be
seen as the judgement of God[127] and, accordingly, the *Parables of Enoch*,
uniquely in early Jewish literature, depicts God seating the Messiah on
the throne of glory, God's own throne of judgement.[128] Kreitzer judges
that this 'functional overlap' between the Messiah and God 'tends to
slide into an identification between God and his agent in which the
boundaries separating them are breached'.[129]

That these texts do tend in that direction is clear, but it is also
clear that they stop far short of the kind of identification of God and
Jesus Christ that we find in Paul and other early Christian literature.
The functional overlap is limited to the execution of judgement on
the wicked on earth, whereas in Paul we find a very much broader
attribution of divine prerogatives to Jesus,[130] the participation of Jesus
in God's creative work, his cosmic rule, his salvation of the world and
his judgement of the world. Within the two Jewish texts themselves,
the *Parables of Enoch* and *4 Ezra*, there is no theological logic that could
press their tendency towards identification of God and the Messiah
further than it actually goes. It is not surprising that the phenomenon
of transferring biblical language about YHWH to the Messiah is limited
in these texts to a very few instances, whereas in Paul it is pervasive.

The difference in practice is particularly clear when we consider the
way in which biblical YHWH texts are applied to the Messiah in these

---

[125] Kreitzer, *Jesus and God,* 90; cf. 156 for comparison with Paul.
[126] See also the discussion of 11QMelch in section 9 (1) above.
[127] See also Stone, *4 Ezra,* 386–7.
[128] See chapter 5, section 4.3 above.
[129] Kreitzer, *Jesus and God,* 90.
[130] These are noted and catalogued in Fee, *Pauline Christology, passim.*

works in comparison with the practice of Paul and other early Christian writers that we have examined in this chapter. In the *Parables of Enoch* and *4 Ezra*, the allusions do not include the title 'the Lord' (or other substitute for the name YHWH), whereas what is so remarkable about many of the Pauline quotations and allusions to biblical YHWH texts is that they explicitly take the *kurios* of the texts (YHWH) to be Jesus. In the two Jewish texts, there is a functional overlap; in the Pauline literature there is a personal identification.

Thus, we must conclude that Jewish precedents for Paul's Christology of divine identity are minimal. The latter (shared with the early Christian movement in general) was highly innovatory. While some continuity of exegetical practice explains some of the ways in which this Christology was developed through exegesis of biblical texts, the identification of the YHWH of many biblical texts as Jesus cannot be explained merely as continuing a Jewish practice of messianic exegesis. Nor do such intermediary figures as we find in Second Temple Jewish literature come anywhere near to the terms in which Paul includes Jesus in the unique divine identity. The Christology of divine identity that Paul shares with many other early Christian writers must have been a response to the unique events that brought the early Christian movement into existence. But how that happened is a question that requires further investigation and reflection.

7

The Divinity of Jesus in the Letter of the Hebrews[1]

1. A Christology of divine identity

In other chapters in this volume, I have argued that New Testament Christology is best characterized as a Christology of divine identity. This is a christological model that is common to all or most of the documents of the New Testament, underlying the variety that is to be found in the more specific features of Christology in these texts. The Letter to the Hebrews is no exception, and I hope to show in this chapter how Hebrews performs an original variation on the common model.

Essentially a Christology of divine identity includes Jesus in the unique identity of God as understood in Second Temple Judaism. It takes up the defining characteristics of Jewish monotheism – the ways in which the God of Israel was understood to be unique – and applies them also to Jesus. We need to begin with those divine characteristics.

We are concerned with the ways in which Jews identified their God as unique, the ways in which they distinguished him from all other reality. For this purpose, I believe that the category of unique identity does more justice to the material than that of divine nature (though the latter can, as we shall see, take a subordinate place within the overarching notion of identity). For Jewish monotheistic faith what was most important was who God is, rather than what divinity is.

The key features of the unique identity of God are these:

God is the sole Creator of all things
(all others are created by God)

---

[1] This chapter originated as a paper given at the St Andrews Conference on the Epistle to the Hebrews and Christian Theology in 2006, and will be published in Richard Bauckham and Nathan MacDonald ed., *The Epistle to the Hebrews and Christian Theology* (Grand Rapids: Eerdmans, forthcoming).

God is the sole sovereign Ruler over all things
   (all others are subject to God's rule)

God is known through his narrative identity
   (i.e. who God is in the story of his dealings with creation, all the
   nations, and Israel)

God will achieve his eschatological rule
   (when all creatures acknowledge YHWH's sole deity)

The name YHWH names God in his unique identity

God alone may and must be worshipped
   (since worship *is* acknowledgement of God's sole deity)

God alone is fully eternal
   (self-existent from past to future eternity)

Only with the last of these features do we encounter what could be
called an attribute of divine nature. It is the metaphysical attribute
of God most often encountered in Jewish literature. It distinguishes
God as the only truly Eternal One. God alone is inherently eternal,
existing from eternity to eternity. Already in the classic monotheistic assertions of Deutero-Isaiah, God is the First and the Last.[2]
This particular attribute of divine nature is virtually entailed by
the claims that God is the sole Creator and sole Ruler of all things.
Everything else comes into existence by his will and perdures only
by his will.

The uniquely divine attribute of full eternity was also the point at
which the Jewish understanding of the divine identity coincided most
obviously and conveniently with Hellenistic God-talk. Jewish writers
were, therefore, not afraid to use Hellenistic philosophical language
about divine eternity, a point which we shall see is important for
Hebrews.

Early Christianity, very consciously using this Jewish theological
framework, created a kind of christological monotheism by understanding Jesus to be included in the unique identity of the one God
of Israel. Probably the earliest expression of this to which we have
access – and it was certainly in use very early in the first Christian
community's history – was the understanding of Jesus' exaltation in
terms of Psalm 110:1. Jesus, seated on the divine throne in heaven as
the one who will achieve the eschatological lordship of God and in

---

[2] For God as 'the only eternal One' in early Jewish literature, see *T. Mos.* 10:7; 2 Macc. 1:25; *Sib. Or.* frg. 1:16.

whom the unique sovereignty of the one God will be acknowledged by all, is included in the unique rule of God over all things, and thus placed unambiguously on the divine side of the absolute distinction that separates the only Sovereign One from all creation. God's rule over all things defines who God is: it cannot be delegated as a mere function to a creature. Thus, the earliest Christology was already *in nuce* the highest Christology. All that remained was to work through consistently what it could mean for Jesus to belong integrally to the unique identity of the one God. Early Christian interest was primarily in soteriology and eschatology, the concerns of the gospel, and so, in the New Testament, it is primarily as sharing or implementing God's eschatological lordship that Jesus is understood to belong to the identity of God. But early Christian reflection could not consistently leave it at that. If Jesus was integral to the identity of God, he must have been so eternally; and so the great passages of protological Christology, such as the Johannine Prologue, Colossians 1 and Hebrews 1, include Jesus also in the unique creative activity of God and in the uniquely divine eternity. This was the early Christians' Jewish way of preserving monotheism against the ditheism that any kind of adoptionist Christology was bound to involve.

A Christology of divine identity thus offers a way beyond the misleading alternatives of functional Christology or ontological Christology. Certain divine 'functions', if we have to use that word, are not mere functions, but integral to who God is. If Jesus performs such functions and if monotheism is to be retained, as it was in early Christianity, then he must belong to the identity of the one God. Jesus cannot function as God without being God. The point becomes even clearer once we recognize that a clearly ontological condition attaches to the divine functions of creation and sovereign rule. Only the one who alone is eternal in the full sense can be the Creator of all things and sovereign Ruler of all things. When this uniquely divine eternity is attributed also to Jesus, it is clear that the early Christians knew precisely what they were doing in Jewish theological terms, when they understood Jesus to participate in the creative work and the eschatological rule of the one God.

One more preliminary point is worth making: that, for the early Jewish Christians, the primary medium of theological development was exegesis, meticulous and disciplined exegesis of scriptural texts deployed with the sophisticated exegetical techniques of contemporary Jewish scholarship. Thus, from the beginning, a few biblical texts were of central importance for understanding the status of the exalted Jesus, some of these closely linked by catchword or other connections. Psalm 110, as already mentioned, along with Psalms 2 and 8,[3] was prominent, and Hebrews situates itself within this christological focus especially on psalms, making the more traditional christological reading of certain psalms the basis for its more creative developments in interpreting these same psalms and others. Famously, Hebrews exploits the full implications for a Christology of divine identity already familiar in Christian reading of the first verse of Psalm 110 and extends the exegesis to verse 4. The extent to which the argument of Hebrews is structured as exegesis of Psalm 110, with other texts cited to aid this exegesis, is such that more than one scholar has called Hebrews itself a commentary on Psalm 110.[4]

2. The structure of Jesus' identity in Hebrews

The main contention of this chapter is that Hebrews attributes to Jesus Christ three main categories of identity – Son, Lord, High Priest – and that each of these categories requires Jesus both to share the unique identity of God and to share human identity with his fellow-humans. In each category, Hebrews portrays Jesus as both truly God and truly human, like his Father in every respect and like humans in every respect.

The most fundamental category is that of the Son of God who shares eternally the unique identity of his Father, the unique identity of the God of Israel and the God of all reality. But sonship to God also characterizes Jesus' human solidarity with his fellow-humans. His mission in incarnation was to bring many human sons and daughters of God to glory (2:10–12). Thus sonship in Hebrews is both a divinely exclusive category (Jesus' unique relationship with the Father) and a humanly inclusive category (a form of relationship to the Father that Jesus shares with those he redeems).

As the eternally pre-existent Son of God, Jesus Christ is destined and qualified for the two main roles in God's eschatological activity of salvation. Because he is the unique Son of the Father, appointed heir of all things (1:2), he can exercise God's eschatological rule over all things

---

[3] For the frequent use of Ps. 110:1 and Ps. 8:7 in connection with each other, see Hengel, *Studies*, 163–72.

[4] E.g. George Wesley Buchanan, *To the Hebrews* (AB 36; New York: Doubleday, 1972), 23; Eskola, *Messiah*, 202. But against this claim, see Harold W. Attridge, *The Epistle to the Hebrews* (Hermeneia; Philadelphia: Fortress, 1989), 23 and n. 188.

as Lord, and he can make full atonement for sins as the heavenly high priest.[5] But, in both cases, he must also be fully human.

In Hebrews, as elsewhere in the New Testament, the traditional expectation of the Davidic Messiah ruling Israel and the nations on earth is subsumed into the cosmic role of the exalted Lord who, seated on God's heavenly throne, brings the whole of creation to the acknowledgement of God's lordship. As such, he bears the divine name, the Tetragrammaton, and he exercises the sovereignty proper only to God. Hebrews makes little of the humanity of Jesus in this role of lordship, being more interested in developing the need for the high priest to be fully human, but does acknowledge it: the cosmic Lord is also the royal Messiah born into the tribe of Judah (7:14).

The most distinctive contribution of Hebrews to Christology is its understanding of Jesus as Melchizedekian high priest. Here it is probably the need for Jesus to be fully human, acting in solidarity with his fellow-humans on their behalf, that is most obvious in Hebrews, but, as we shall see, Hebrews also regards it as essential that Jesus, as heavenly high priest, participates in the unique identity of the one God, seated on the cosmic throne.

3. The narrative identity of the Son (1:2b–4)

Hebrews begins with an overwhelming emphasis on the full and eternal deity of the Son, carefully presented in the forms, first, of a sketch of the Son's narrative identity in seven compact descriptions (1:2b–4), and, secondly, a catena of seven scriptural texts designed to establish and expound the Son's full deity (1:5–14). The two sections are connected by the key text, Psalm 110:1: the narrative sketch concludes with an allusion to it ('sat down at the right hand of the Majesty on high') and an indication of the kind of superiority to the angels this entails. The catena itself ends with a citation of Psalm 110:1 (1:13), forming an *inclusio* and showing that its purpose is to bring the other texts to assist the theological exegesis of Psalm 110:1. The catena too is concerned with the exaltation of Jesus above the angels.

---

[5] 5:5 means that 'it is his divine sonship that qualifies Christ to be the high priest referred to in Ps. 110:4' (Donald A. Hagner, 'The Son of God as Unique High Priest: The Christology of the Epistle to the Hebrews,' in *Contours of Christology in the New Testament*, ed. Richard N. Longenecker [Grand Rapids: Eerdmans, 2005], 247–67, here 257).

The structure of the exordium (1:2b–4) is:

a Son,

whom he appointed heir of **all things,**	(1) Eschatological rule over all things (Ps. 2:8; 8:6)
through whom he also created **the worlds.**	(2) Agent of creation of all things
Being the reflection of God's glory and the exact imprint of God's very being,	(3) Eternal divine being (cf. Wis. 7:26)
sustaining **all things** by his powerful word,	(4) Providential sovereignty over all things
having made purification for sins,	(5) High priestly atonement
he **sat down** at the right hand of the Majesty **on high,**	(6) Exaltation to God's throne in heaven (Ps. 110:1)
having become as much **superior to angels** as the name he has inherited is more excellent than theirs	(7) Identification (name) as YHWH

The content of the exordium is largely traditional, with close parallels in other extended New Testament accounts of protological and cosmic Christology, including Philippians 2:6–11, Colossians 1:15–20, Ephesians 1:20–23, and the Prologue to John's Gospel. Only the fifth statement is quite unparalleled and points up, at this early stage, the aspect of Christology which this epistle is later to develop creatively: the high priestly atonement. With the only possible exception of that fifth statement, the statements are designed precisely to include the Son in the unique divine identity of Jewish monotheistic belief. The characteristic phrase 'all things' (points 1 and 4), varied with 'the worlds' (point 2), is monotheistic language designed to distinguish God from the whole of the rest of reality,[6] which he created and rules, and functioning here to put the divine Son, Jesus, on the divine side of that distinction. In this sevenfold narrative, the humanity of Jesus is no more than implicit, but, while the whole is predicated of the divine Son, it does also introduce the roles of lord and high priest that the

---

[6] E.g. Isa. 44:24; Jer. 10:16; 51:19; Sir. 43:33; Wis. 9:6; 12:13; Add. Esth. 13:9; 2 Macc. 1:24; 3 Macc. 2:3; *1 En.* 9:5; 84:3; *2 En.* 66:4; *Jub.* 12:19; *Apoc. Ab.* 7:10; *Sib. Or.* 3:20; 8:376; *Sib. Or.* frg. 1:17; Josephus, *B.J.* 5.218; 1Qap Gen^ar 20:13; 4QD^b 18:5:19; Matt. 11:27; Luke 10:22; John 3:35; 13:3; 16:15; Acts 10:36; 1 Cor. 15:27–28; Eph. 1:22; Phil. 3:21.

Son undertakes in the last days. The Son is destined for eschatological lordship ('appointed heir of all things') and is exalted to the right hand of God in order to exercise it. The Son is also the one who makes high priestly atonement.

The lack of explicit treatment of the humanity of the Son here in the exordium is supplied in chapter 2, where the human inclusivity of the sonship of the incarnate Son is expounded. However, there is one other point of importance about the divinely exclusive sonship of the Son in Hebrews. Many scholars regard Jesus' sonship in Hebrews as a status to which he is appointed at some stage of his narrative, whether at incarnation, resurrection or exaltation, and the alleged inconsistency of Hebrews on this point has been widely discussed.[7] In my view, the divine Son in Hebrews is Son of God from all eternity as well as to all eternity: sonship is the eternal truth of his very being, not simply a role or status given him by God at some point. The reasons this has not been sufficiently recognized are two. The first reason is the quotation of Psalm 2:7, 'You are my Son; today I have begotten you', cited twice in Hebrews (1:5; 5:5). We shall return to the way Hebrews understands this text at a later point in this chapter. The other reason for putting a temporal limit on Jesus' sonship is the seventh and last of the statements in the exordium, 'having become as much superior to angels as the name he has inherited is more excellent than theirs' (1:4). In view of what follows in the catena, most commentators have taken the name here to be 'Son'. But this is a confusion. The name that is so much more excellent than those of angels must be the Hebrew divine name, the Tetragrammaton,[8] which is also said to be conferred on Jesus at his exaltation in Philippians 2:9 ('the name that is above every name').[9] In our passage of Hebrews, the Son is the one who inherits the name from his Father, not what he inherits. What he inherits must be something that belongs to his Father, whereas 'Son' is uniquely the Son's title. Rather it is because he is Son, as the angels are not, that he inherits his Father's name, as the angels cannot.

---

[7] E.g. Attridge, *Hebrews*, 25–6, 54–5; Kenneth Schenck, 'Keeping His Appointment: Creation and Enthronement in Hebrews,' *JSNT* 66 (1997): 91–117.

[8] So also Rowland, *Open Heaven*, 113; Gieschen, *Angelomorphic Christology*, 197; Margaret Barker, 'The High Priest and the Worship of Jesus,' in *Jewish Roots*, ed. Newman, Davila and Lewis, 93–111, here 99.

[9] For Heb. 1:4–15 as a 'large-scale development' of Phil. 2:6–11, see Martin Hengel, *The Son of God: The Origin of Christology and the History of Jewish-Hellenistic Religion*, trans. John Bowden (London: SCM, 1976), 87–8.

4. The significance of the angels in chapters 1–2

The prominence of the angels in this part of Hebrews (a prominence significantly limited to this part of Hebrews[10]) has often been associated with a so-called angel Christology or an angelomorphic Christology, whether as the object of the author's polemic[11] or as the basis for his own Christology.[12] I think there is a much better way of understanding the function of the angels in this key christological context.[13] Psalm 110:1, along with other texts, is first expounded to show the exalted Christ to be far superior to the angels. The author then turns to another text, Psalm 8:5–7, to show that, prior to his exaltation, Christ was for a time lower than the angels. The lowliness of incarnation was necessary on the way to the exaltation described in Psalm 110. In a thoroughly Jewish cosmological way, the author is working with the imagery of height as indicative of status and identity. Traditionally the cosmic throne of God was placed above the heavens (cf. 7:26), at the summit of the

---

[10] Elsewhere they appear only in 12:22 and 13:2, references not obviously connected with the role of the angels in chaps. 1–2. The lack of reference to angels after 2:16 seems to me to tell against the argument of Kenneth L. Schenck, 'A Celebration of the Enthroned Son: The Catena of Hebrews 1,' *JBL* 120 (2001): 469–85, to the effect that the angels appear in chaps. 1–2 as the mediators of the old covenant, compared with Christ as the mediator of the new covenant. This argument has support from 2:2, where the subordination of the angels to the Son is certainly pressed into service to reinforce the author's exhortation, but, in order to present it as the sole point of 1:5–14, Schenck is obliged to minimize the ontological elements of the contrast between the Son and the angels. For example, his treatment of 1:10–12 (on pp. 475–6) is very unsatisfactory. His comment that 'one cannot assume that all the salient points of a quotation are meant to be extracted from another author's use of it' (476) misses the precise character of the kind of Jewish exegesis Hebrews employs and the meticulous composition of this catena in particular. If the author's quotation from Ps. 102 was not meant to present Christ as the personal agent of creation, he chose his text very badly, and modified its opening words incomprehensibly.

[11] For references to scholars who have taken this view, see William L. Lane, *Hebrews 1–8* (WBC 47A; Dallas: Word, 1991), 8; Attridge, *Hebrews*, 52 n. 33; Stuckenbruck, *Angel Veneration*, 124–5 n. 98. L.K.K. Dey, *Patterns of Perfection in Philo and Hebrews* (SBLDS 25; Missoula: Scholars, 1975), chap. 4, sees the polemic directed against the assimilation of Christ to intermediaries such as Philo's Logos, whom Philo can call an angel. Darrell D. Hannah, *Michael and Christ: Michael Traditions and Angel Christology in Early Christianity* (WUNT 2/109; Tübingen: Mohr [Siebeck], 1999), 137–9, acknowledges the force of arguments against the view that Hebrews 1 opposes an angel Christology, and so argues that, while angel Christology 'was not an error that appealed to his readers,... it *was* in the air', and so the author is establishing his credentials with his readers by stressing his agreement with them in opposing any confusion of Christ with angels. Others think the polemic is against the veneration of angels: for references to scholars who have taken this view, see Lane, *Hebrews 1–8*, 8; Stuckenbruck, *Angel Veneration*, 124 n. 197. Randall C. Gleason, 'Angels and the Eschatology of Heb 1–2,' *NTS* 49 (2003): 90–107, thinks that Hebrews opposes the Jewish practice of invoking angels for help, especially in relation to a coming deliverance from Roman rule.

[12] Rowland, *Open Heaven*, 113; Gieschen, *Angelomorphic Christology*, 295–303, 314.

[13] Cf. Attridge, *Hebrews*, 52–3.

cosmos, and far above all the ranks of angels within the heavens.[14] This spatial superiority of God's throne above the angels indicates God's unique transcendence over all of created reality, even those glorious beings of the heavens that might be mistaken for gods but, in reality, are created beings subject to the one and only God's rule. When the exalted Christ shares his Father's throne on high, he acquires precisely God's superiority to the angels, indicated also by his acquisition of the unique divine name. But, when the Son became incarnate as human, he undertook the humble and mortal condition of earthly creatures below the angels. The imagery of height, descent and exaltation, is used similarly to the way it is in Philippians 2, but the angels in Hebrews add precision to the picture. They mark out the cosmic territory. They function, so to speak, as measures of ontological status. To be above the angels is to be God, to be below the angels is to be human. Above the angels, Jesus transcends all creation, sharing the divine identity as Creator and Ruler even of the angels. Below the angels, Jesus shares the common identity of earthly humans in birth, suffering and death.

5. The full divinity of the Lord (1:5–14)

The catena of seven scriptural texts in 1:5–14 is a fine example of the way in which sophisticated theological exegesis could be done merely by selecting and juxtaposing texts and providing the briefest of introductory comments. It has the following basic structure:

For to which of the angels did God
ever say,

> 'You are my Son   (1) superior as Son
> today I have begotten you'?
>   (Ps. 2:7)

Or again,

> 'I will be his Father,   (2) superior as Son
> and he will be my Son'?
>   (2 Sam. 7:14)

And again, when he brings the
firstborn into the world, he says,

> 'Let all God's angels worship   (3) worshipped by angels
> him.'
>   (Deut. 32:43)

---

[14] See chapter 5 above.

Of the angels he says,

'He makes his angels (*angelous* – messengers) winds, and his ministers (*leitourgous*) flames of fire.' (Ps. 104:4)	(4) he himself created the angels to be his servants and to conduct his cult in heaven

But of the Son he says,

'Your throne, O God, is forever and ever, and the righteous sceptre is the sceptre of your kingdom. You have loved righteousness and hated wickedness; therefore God, your God, has anointed you with the oil of gladness beyond your companions.' (Ps. 45:6–7)	(5) he reigns as God forever on the cosmic throne of God (unique divine rule over all things)

And,

'In the beginning, Lord, you founded the earth, and the heavens are the work of your hands; they will perish, but you remain; they will all wear out like clothing; like a cloak you will roll them up, and like clothing they will be changed. But you are the same, and your years will never end.' (Ps. 102:25–27)	(6) he is fully eternal, the same from eternity to eternity, whereas all creation (including the angels) is created and transient

But to which of the angels has he ever said,

'Sit at my right hand until I make your enemies a footstool for your feet'? (Ps. 110:1)	(7) exalted to share God's cosmic throne and eschatological rule

There is far more subtlety in this passage than we have space here to examine. Here I can only highlight the most important points for our present purposes.[15]

---

[15] For a more detailed study of this passage, see Richard Bauckham, 'Monotheism and Christology in the Hebrews 1,' in *Early Jewish and Christian Monotheism*, ed. Loren T. Stuckenbruck and Wendy E.S. North (JSNTSup 263; London/New York: T&T Clark [Continuum], 2004), 167–85.

First, all the texts are related to the messianic rule of Jesus,[16] understood as an exercise of the properly divine sovereignty, though in some cases this is obvious only in the contexts from which the quotations have been taken.[17] Traditional texts of Davidic messianism are linked with texts describing the cosmic rule of God over all things and with references to God's sovereignty in the work of creation as well as rule. The image of the cosmic throne of God is evoked not only implicitly in the citation of Psalm 110 but also explicitly in the fifth quotation (from Ps. 45). The catena makes entirely clear that the exalted Lord Jesus is the one who shares the divine identity in the two crucial respects of creation of all things and sovereignty over all things.

Secondly, the Lord's superiority to angels is not only grounded in his sonship, by which he participates in God's own transcendence of all creatures, but is also supported by the claims that he himself created the angels (text 4), that they are his servants (text 4) and that they worship him (text 3). Thus, in three key respects – creation, sovereignty and worship – the Son is related to the angels precisely as God is. The angels themselves acknowledge his unique divinity in worshipping him.

Thirdly, for its importance for what I shall say later, I draw attention especially to the sixth quotation. The author has changed the order of the first three words from the Septuagint text,[18] so that the quotation begins, literally, 'you, in the beginning, Lord' (*su kat' archas kurie*), thus placing the person addressed (Jesus Christ) at the same beginning with which Genesis begins, the primordial eternity before the creation of the heavens and the earth, for which the pre-existent Christ is also here made responsible. This carefully selected text becomes, in its new context, a christological reading of the first verse of Genesis comparable with the christological reading of that verse at the beginning of the Johannine Prologue. But, unlike the latter, Hebrews is concerned not only with the Son's pre-existence in past eternity but also with his unchangeable identity for all future eternity. The scriptural words are used to attribute to the Son precisely what distinguishes the one God from all creation: the full eternity that God alone possesses, by contrast with the createdness, mutability and transience of all created things. Left to themselves all things perish, but God alone, here including

---

[16] Cf. Kiwoong Son, *Zion Symbolism in Hebrews: Hebrews 12:18–24 as a Hermeneutical Key to the Epistle* (Paternoster Biblical Monographs; Milton Keynes: Paternoster, 2005), 111–24.

[17] In the case of the third quotation (1:6), which is from Deut. 32:43, the theme of messianic rule is implicit in the allusion to Ps. 89[88]:27 to which the words introducing the quotation allude.

[18] Ps. 101:26 LXX: *kat' archas su, kurie*.

Christ, has in himself the indestructible life that makes it possible for the psalmist to say, 'you are the same', i.e. eternally.

6. The full humanity of the high priest (2:5–18)

My subject in this chapter is the divinity of Christ, not his humanity, and so here I merely mention the way Hebrews portrays Jesus as the high priest who can fulfil his ministry only by sharing fully the human condition, becoming like his brothers and sisters in every respect, tested in every respect through suffering and death, so that he understands human weakness and now, from his heavenly throne, exercises mercy and grace to sinners. What is perhaps less well recognized is the connection between lordship (the subject of chapter 1) and high priesthood (the subject that chapter 2 begins to treat) that the author achieves by his use of Psalm 8. The latter is used to show that it is only through incarnation, humiliation, and everything it means to be mortal humanity, that the Son could attain to his eschatological lordship over all things. This is because his lordship is exercised for the sake of his human brothers and sisters. It is no longer simply the sovereignty he shared with his Father from eternity, but now a sovereignty exercised in human solidarity with humans. The cosmic throne is now also, therefore, the throne of grace that sinners can approach with boldness (4:16). So the high priestly work of atonement is the way in which he comes to exercise his sovereignty in the way that he does – salvifically.

7. The full divinity of the high priest (7:3, 16)

The Christology of Hebrews would have been simpler if the author had merely correlated Christ's lordship with his divinity, and his high priesthood with his humanity, but this is not what he does. As we have just seen, the fellow-humanity of the high priest is an indispensable and prominent element in Hebrews' understanding of this office and, for the most part, its functions are those of representing humanity to God: the high priest makes atonement for the people, offering sacrifice on their behalf (5:1), he enters the presence of God on their behalf (6:20; 9:24), and he intercedes for them (8:25).[19] Furthermore, unlike cosmic lordship, high priesthood does not belong to the unique identity of

---

[19] Note, however, that in the activity of blessing people (7:1, 6–7) the high priest represents God to the people.

God.[20] Whereas to rule all things from the throne of God is to be God, to be high priest on earth or in heaven by no means carries such an implication. What need was there for the great high priest, the finally adequate high priest, to be divine? We shall see.

Here, as elsewhere, the theological method of Hebrews is exegetical. The starting-point is verse 4 of Psalm 110, where the same one who in verse 1 is exalted to the right hand of God on his heavenly throne is addressed, 'You are a priest forever after the order of Melchizedek.' Just as in chapter 1 of Hebrews, the implications of Psalm 110:1 are expounded with the help of other, related scriptural texts, so, in chapter 7 of Hebrews, the meaning of the obscure verse 4 of Psalm 110 is expounded through recourse to another biblical passage, which contains the only other occurrence of the name Melchizedek in the Hebrew Bible: Genesis 14:17–20. The two texts have, at least, this connection: in both cases Melchizedek is both king and priest. In that respect, he well serves the christological purpose of Hebrews, which is to develop the high priestly profile of Jesus alongside, and in connection with, his messianic lordship.[21]

Although there is not space to discuss this here, in my view the figure of Melchizedek in Hebrews has very little in common with the figure in the Melchizedek scroll from Qumran.[22] We do not really need to suppose that any pre-existing traditions about Melchizedek[23] lie behind the text of Hebrews,[24] though the author may well have shared with

---

[20] But note that Philo casts the Logos in the role of cosmic high priest (Barker, *Great Angel*, 121–2).

[21] Cf. Deborah W. Rooke, 'Jesus as Royal Priest: Reflections on the Interpretation of the Melchizedek Tradition in Heb 7,' *Bib.* 81 (2000): 81–94.

[22] See Eskola, *Messiah*, 263; James W. Thompson, *The Beginnings of Christian Philosophy: The Epistle to the Hebrews* (CBQMS 13; Washington, D.C.: Catholic Biblical Association of America, 1982), 119–20. Anders Aschim, 'Melchizedek and Jesus: 11Q Melchizedek and the Epistle to the Hebrews,' in *Jewish Roots*, ed. Newman, Davila and Lewis, 129–47, makes a case for more resemblance than is usually accepted, but his argument relies heavily on the view that the portrayal of Melchizedek in Hebrews depends on a tradition in which he was seen as a heavenly (angelic) warrior-priest. I do not think this is the case.

[23] In my view, the story of the birth of Melchizedek in 2 *Enoch* 71–2 (part of a late addition to the book, attested in only a few manuscripts) is not such a tradition, but rather a later Christian attempt to explain how it could be that Melchizedek was 'without father, without mother, without genealogy' (Heb. 7:3) and yet a priest. The story must be dependent on Hebrews. I disagree with Andrei Orlov, 'The Heir of Righteousness and the King of Righteousness: The Priestly Noachic Polemics in 2 Enoch and the Epistle to the Hebrews,' *JTS* 85 (2007): 45–65. He thinks the Melchizedek story integral to 2 *Enoch*, which he dates in the late Second Temple period, and thinks both 2 *Enoch* and Hebrews use the figure of Melchizedek to polemicize against Noah traditions.

[24] Cf. Hay, *Glory*, 153: 'With the most astonishing thrift, or resolute reserve, [the author] determined to know nothing of [Melchizedek] that could not be inferred from Gen. 14:18–20 and Ps. 110:4 (chiefly the latter).'

other exegetes an interest in this figure provoked by his mysterious and anomalous appearance in Genesis as the first priest in Scripture, a non-Levitical priest with apparently no line of descent to qualify him for what Israel knew only as an hereditary office. But our author's real interest in Melchizedek arises from the fact of his appearance in Psalm 110, the most important christological psalm for the first Christians. Indeed, the author is not really interested in Melchizedek himself, for his own sake, but turns to Genesis purely in order to understand what it would mean for the Messiah of Psalm 110 to be a priest after the order of Melchizedek.[25] Not Melchizedek himself, but Melchizedekian priesthood is the point. So what is said about Melchizedek himself in Hebrews 7 need not be taken too seriously as a statement about the historical figure in Genesis. Its point is its application to Jesus.

We need to bear this in mind especially when consider the remarkable verse 3 of Hebrews 7, which says of Melchizedek:

> Without mother,
> without father,
> without genealogy,
> having neither beginning of days nor end of life,
> but resembling the Son of God,
> he remains a priest forever.

We should notice that this is both derived from the Genesis text and used to explicate the words from Psalm 110: 'you are a priest forever'.

In an article of 1991,[26] Jerome Neyrey showed, I think conclusively, that this is Hellenistic true-god-language. In other words, it is the kind of language philosophically inclined writers used to define what it is to be a true deity, as distinct from, for example, a deified hero. True deity is, in the fullest sense, eternal, having neither origin in the past nor end of life in the future. A true deity is unbegotten or ungenerated (*agennētos*) – having no parents – and unoriginated (*agenētos*) – having no other kind of origin – as well as being imperishable forever. The three terms in Hebrews beginning with the alpha privative (*apatōr, amētōr, agenealogētos*) are typical of the negative descriptions used in Hellenistic god-language.[27]

---

[25] Thompson, *Beginnings*, 117–8.

[26] Jerome H. Neyrey, '"Without Beginning of Days or End of Life" (Heb. 7:3): Topos for a True Deity,' *CBQ* 53 (1991): 439–55; see also idem, *Render to God: New Testament Understandings of the Divine* (Minneapolis: Fortress, 2004), chap. 8.

[27] Neyrey, 'Without Beginning,' 440–1.

What is particularly important is that such language was, in Hellenistic use, meant precisely to distinguish true deity from semi-divine figures.[28] This is surely why Hebrews here lays such stress on the un-originatedness of Melchizedek: without father, without mother, without genealogy, having no beginning of days. This dimension of eternity past seems gratuitous as an explanation of the words of Psalm 110:4, in which it is only the king-priest's future that is without limit. But Hebrews understands that imperishability in the future as grounded in the kind of divine existence that neither begins nor ends, the fully eternal being of true deity.

What needs to be added to Neyrey's case is a more explicit stress on the Jewishness of this author's use of Hellenistic philosophical language. First, it is used in close conjunction with typically Jewish exegesis of the text of Genesis. Because Melchizedek simply appears in the text of Genesis at this point and almost immediately disappears, never to appear again in the biblical narrative, an argument from silence can be used to deduce that Melchizedek's life had no beginning or end. Scripture would have told us if it did.[29] What makes the argument a little less artificial is the fact that a priest might be expected to be provided with a genealogy to qualify him for his priesthood.[30] This is what accounts for the specific term 'without genealogy' that the author seems to have coined by analogy with the usual sort of god-language but to meet the precise case of his text. Nevertheless, the argument is highly artificial, and really amounts to saying that Melchizedek as portrayed in the text resembles what the Son of God really is. It is the textual, not the historical Melchizedek that explains what the Melchizedekian priesthood of the Psalm is.

Secondly, the author of Hebrews is by no means the only Jewish writer to use such language to characterize true deity. We find it not only in Philo,[31] whose usage can never be safely presumed to be representative, but also in Josephus (e.g. *C. Ap.* 2.167, 190), the Jewish

---

[28] Neyrey, 'Without Beginning,' 441–6, 449–50. For example, Neyrey cites Diodorus of Sicily 6.1.2: 'As regards the gods, men of ancient times have handed down to later generations two different conceptions: Certain of the gods, they say, are eternal and imperishable ... for each of these genesis and duration are from everlasting to everlasting. But the other gods, we are told, were terrestrial beings who attained to immortal honors and fame because of their benefactions to mankind.'

[29] For the exegetical device, see, for example, Thompson, *Beginnings*, 118. As Ben Witherington aptly puts it, the silences of Scripture 'are assumed to be pregnant' (Ben Witherington III, *The Many Faces of the Christ* [New York: Crossroad, 1998], 219).

[30] Joseph A. Fitzmyer, 'Melchizedek in the MT, LXX, and the NT,' *Bib.* 81 (2000): 63–9, here 66.

[31] For examples in Philo, see Neyrey, 'Without Beginning,' 442–4, 446.

Sibylline Oracles (3:11–12; frg. 1:7–17) and the Jewish Pseudo-Orpheus verses (short version: 10–11). More remarkably, if the Slavonic text can be trusted, we find a close parallel to Hebrews in a hymn sung to God by the angels in the _Apocalypse of Abraham_:

> Eternal One, Mighty One, Holy El, God autocrat,
> self-originate, incorruptible, immaculate,
> unbegotten, spotless, immortal,
> self-perfected, self-devised,
> without mother, without father, ungenerated (17:8–10).[32]

In such a context, one would not expect Hellenistic philosophical language. The explanation is that the Jewish tradition in any case understood God to be fully eternal, so that there was a real convergence here of Jewish and Hellenistic definitions of deity. Such Hellenistic god-language could easily be appropriated in the interests of a Jewish understanding of God without involving the kind of sophisticated assimilation of Jewish theology to Platonic philosophy that we find in Philo.[33]

Thirdly, when adopted into the context of the Jewish understanding of God, such Hellenistic god-language undergoes an important re-functioning. It becomes monotheistic language.[34] Terms which for non-Jewish writers defined _a_ true deity, for Jewish writers define _the one and only_ true deity. This is easily verified from the examples just given of Jewish works that use these terms: Josephus (_C. Ap._ 2.167), the Jewish _Sibylline Oracles_ (3.11–12), Pseudo-Orpheus (10–16) and the _Apocalypse of Abraham_ (17:8–15; cf. 19:3). In the contexts, there is usually a strong affirmation of monotheism. It is the one God that is the only fully eternal one. Re-functioned to serve monotheism, these Hellenistic

---

[32] Translation from R. Rubinkiewicz, 'Apocalypse of Abraham,' in _The Old Testament Pseudepigrapha_, vol. 1, ed. James H. Charlesworth (London: Darton, Longman & Todd, 1983), 697. The last line provides a remarkably close parallel to Heb. 7:3, 'without mother, without father, ungenerated'. Rubinkiewicz, 'Apocalypse of Abraham,' 697, notes that Slavonic _bezrodine_ probably represents Greek _agenētos_ or _agenealogētos_. In the latter case, we might suppose that these three words are a reminiscence of Heb. 7:3 introduced by a Christian scribe. But this need not be the case. Note that the terms 'without mother, without father' in _Apoc. Ab._ 17:10 are in the reverse order from that in Heb. 7:3, and that a passage drawn from Heb. 7:3 would not be a very obvious one for a scribe to think applicable to God.

[33] On the disputed relationship between Hebrews and Philo, see Kenneth L. Schenck, 'Philo and the Epistle to the Hebrews: Ronald Williamson's Study after Thirty Years,' _Studia Philonica Annual_ 14 (2002): 112–35.

[34] Cf. Michael Mach, 'Concepts of Jewish Monotheism during the Hellenistic Period,' in _Jewish Roots_, ed. Newman, Davila and Lewis, 21–42, here 27–32.

terms are really little more than a cultural translation of God's claim, in Deutero-Isaiah, to be the First and the Last (Isa. 41:4; 44:6; 48:12).

We can now see that what the author of Hebrews says of Melchizedek in 7:3 is precisely what he said of Christ in applying the words of Psalm 102 to him in chapter 1. In both cases, this is the full eternity of the only true God. Just as the God of Psalm 102 remains, whereas all his creation perishes, so the Melchizedekian high priest remains a priest, whereas Levitical priests, being merely mortal, come and go. Also important here is 7:16: Jesus 'has become a priest, not through a legal requirement concerning physical descent, but through the power of an indestructible life' (another alpha privative adjective: *akatalutos*). Jesus qualifies for his never-ending priesthood because he shares the fully eternal being, the indestructible life, of God.[35] His eternity in the future – the 'forever' of Psalm 110:4 – is not merely contingently never-ending, but due to his inherently indestructible life. Such life by definition exists from eternity to eternity. It has not only no end of life, but no beginning of days either.

Now we can easily confirm that, for Hebrews, Jesus' high priesthood entailed both true divinity and true humanity. As divine, this high priest had no father or mother or genealogy, but, as human, he shares the same kind of origin as his fellow-humans (2:11) and partakes of the same flesh-and-blood mortal nature as they (2:14). These are straight contradictions that cannot be understood other than by a notion of two natures at least embryonically related to that of later patristic Christology.

8. The high priest on the throne

The cosmic throne of God was a central symbol for the Jewish understanding of the one God and his relation to all reality.[36] It also became a central symbol for early Christology, since it was the exalted Christ's unprecedented sitting beside God on the cosmic throne, evoked in Psalm 110:1, that required his inclusion in the unique identity of the one God. Christ's sitting on the throne meant his participation in the unique sovereignty of God over all things.[37] In Hebrews, however, through its christological reading not only of verse 1 of Psalm 110, but also of verse 4, it is not only as king but also as high priest that Jesus

---

[35] Note that, in Hebrews, God is characteristically 'the living God' (3:12; 9:14; 10:31; 12:22).

[36] Chapter 4 above; Eskola, *Messiah*, Part II.

[37] Chapter 4 above; Eskola, *Messiah*, Part III.

sits down on the divine throne.[38] Just as early Christology subsumed the Davidic monarchy of the Messiah on earth into the cosmic lordship of the exalted Christ in heaven, so Hebrews subsumes the idea of an eschatological high priest into the cosmic high priesthood of the exalted Christ in heaven.

But what does it mean for Jesus *as high priest* to take his seat at God's right hand on the cosmic throne? It is certainly worth remembering that the symbolism of the throne of God combines political and cultic connotations. Just as the ark in the holy of holies on earth is the earthly throne of God, so also the throne room of God in heaven, whence he governs the universe, is also the heavenly sanctuary where he is worshipped.[39] Therefore, it is easily intelligible that, in Hebrews, the atoning work of Christ follows broadly the pattern of the Levitical high priest's activity. Jesus offers himself as the atoning sacrifice, then, taking his own sacrificial blood, he enters the heavenly presence of God and comes before God's throne, just as the high priest entered the inner sanctuary on earth on the Day of Atonement and sprinkled the blood of the sacrifice before the ark of the covenant.[40] Where the two part company, however, is when Jesus sits down on the throne. Not only did the Levitical high priest not do this; it would, of course, have been unthinkable for him to have done so.

Hebrews clearly sees this difference in terms of the finality and permanence of Christ's atoning sacrifice. He has no need, like the Levitical high priests, to return to the people and repeat the ceremony year by year. Thus, according to 10:12, when he 'had offered for all time a single sacrifice for sins, he sat down at the right hand of God'. But the point cannot be simply that, having made the once-and-for-all, finally adequate sacrifice for all sins, he stays in the heavenly sanctuary, nor even that he stays in order continually to intercede for his people on the basis of his sacrifice (7:25). For these purposes, it would be sufficient for him to stand in the presence of God, as all the angels do. The potent imagery of sitting on the cosmic throne has only one attested significance: it indicates his participation in the unique sovereignty of

---

[38] Especially in the light of 1:8, the references in Hebrews to Christ's sitting at the right hand of God are not to be understood as though he occupied a second throne beside God's but that he sits beside God on the right hand part of the one heavenly throne; cf. Hengel, *Studies*, 148–9.

[39] Eskola, *Messiah*, 251–8.

[40] For Hebrews' rather free conflation of a number of rituals from the Torah, see Daniel Stökl Ben Ezra, *The Impact of Yom Kippur on Early Christianity* (WUNT 163; Tübingen: Mohr Siebeck, 2003), 187–90.

God over the world. That Jesus sits on the throne, not only as king but also as high priest (which Hebrews clearly indicates), indicates surely that his completed work of atonement is now permanently part of the divine rule over the world. In this way, *this* high priesthood, unlike the Levitical, does belong to the unique identity of God. This high priest is the perfect mediator; he not only represents his people to God, in sacrifice and intercession, but also embodies the grace and mercy of God to which his sacrifice now gives permanent expression. Therefore, for the people of God, the heavenly throne is *the throne of grace* (4:16), where they find the mercy of God.

9. The Son begotten by the Father (1:5; 5:5 = Ps. 2:7)

The major argument of this chapter is now complete, but we need to return to the question whether the two citations of Psalm 2:7 in Hebrews indicate a temporal beginning of the Son's divine sonship. I postponed this question until we had recognized the Hellenistic god-language used in 7:3, and I want to suggest that that language may be the clue to the author's reading of Psalm 2:7. In Hellenistic philosophical parlance, true deity was unoriginated (*agennētos*) and ungenerated (unbegotten) (*agenētos*). (The two terms in Greek differ only in having a single or a double letter nu, and so are frequently confused in the manuscripts.) But true deity can also be said to be self-originated and self-begotten. This latter terminology might suggest that deity does have a temporal origin, not given it by another but spontaneously self-generated. However, this latter idea is incoherent and it is not what the terminology was used to mean. In fact, the terms 'unoriginated' and 'self-originated' are used together and not regarded as contradictory, and so are the terms 'unbegotten' and 'self-begotten'. To be self-originating is to be eternal. So, in Jewish examples, we find the third *Sibylline Oracle* describing the one eternal God as 'self-produced' (*autophuēs*: 3:12), while one of the Sibylline fragments says of the one eternal God that 'he is alone, from age to age, self-originated (*autogenēs*), unbegotten (*agenētos*)' (frg. 1:16–17; cf. 7). The passage we noted in the *Apocalypse of Abraham* includes in its list of attributes of the one eternal God that he is 'self-originated', 'unbegotten' and 'unoriginated'. Familiarity with such god-language would make it easy for the author of Hebrews to read Psalm 2:7 not as declaring a temporal origin for Christ's sonship to the Father, but as, so to speak, a binitarian variation on the idea of eternal deity as self-generating.

The 'today' of 'Today I have begotten you' would be the eternal today of the divine eternity.[41]

10. Jesus Christ the same yesterday, today and forever (13:8)

In this final section we shall see that this description of Jesus constitutes a much more emphatic assertion of the full divine eternity of Jesus Christ than has usually been supposed.[42] In the first place, we should notice how closely it corresponds to the citation from Psalm 102, understood as addressed to Christ, in the first chapter of Hebrews. That quotation affirms the full eternity – eternity past and eternity future – of the divine Christ, and, very strikingly, it uses the same phrase (*ho autos*) as Hebrews 13:8 to affirm that he is 'the same', that is, he retains his own identity throughout eternity.

Secondly, a threefold formula referring to divine eternity as past, present and future is found quite widely in ancient Hellenistic, Jewish and Christian literature.[43] Like the expressions used in 7:3, it is a means of expressing the uniquely divine eternity, part of the definition of true deity. An ancient Greek hymn reads, 'Zeus was, Zeus is, and Zeus will be',[44] while Josephus explains that the Jewish God is 'the beginning, the middle and the end of all things' (*C. Ap.* 2.190).

The following description of the god *Aiōn* on an inscription from Eleusis is especially noteworthy for our present purposes:

> *Aiōn*, who by his divine nature remains always the same (*ho autos*)
> and who altogether is the unique cosmos,
> of such a nature that he is and was and will be,
> not having beginning, middle or end,
> who does not partake of change,
> who produces the absolutely eternal divine nature.[45]

This description is remarkable, because it not only affirms the full eternity of the god *Aiōn* by means of two threefold formulae ('he is and was and will be, not having beginning, middle or end'), but it also coincides with Hebrews 13:8 in its use of 'the same' (*ho autos*) ('*Aiōn*,

---

[41] This would be different from the human 'today' of 3:7, 13, the period of human opportunity up to the judgement (3:14–15).

[42] But cf. Neyrey, *Render*, 239–41.

[43] See McDonough, *YHWH*, 41–57, 187–92.

[44] Pausanias, *Desc. Graec.* 10.12.10, quoted in Neyrey, 'Without Beginning,' 453.

[45] Translation from McDonough, *YHWH*, 51–2.

who by his divine nature remains always the same'). Hebrews 1:12 also uses this expression ('you are the same') and, in doing so, is merely reproducing the Greek text of Psalm 102:28, itself a faithful translation of the Hebrew. So this is a striking example of how, particularly on the matter of the divine eternity, Jewish tradition converged with Hellenistic god-language.

Thirdly, the threefold formula, used in a Jewish monotheistic context, not only refers to the one and only God, but also can be understood as an interpretation of the Hebrew name of God. It is certainly so in the Targumim (e.g. Tg. Ps.-J. Deut. 32:29)[46] and in the book of Revelation (1:4, 8; 4:8; cf. 11:17; 16:5),[47] which demonstrates that the targumic usage is ancient, and probably also in the Jewish *Sibylline Oracles* 3:16 ('But he himself, eternal, revealed himself as existing now, and formerly, and again in the future').[48] Is this also the case in Hebrews 13:8? This would seem to be reasonably probable in view of the fact that, according to Hebrews 1:4, the divine name was indeed conferred on Jesus at his exaltation.

Commentators often make the point that Hebrews 13:8 does not refer to metaphysical immutability but to constancy of purpose, reliability, faithfulness to promises.[49] In the context, a reference to divine faithfulness certainly makes good sense,[50] and elsewhere Hebrews, with its special interest in divine oaths, has a notable emphasis on the divine faithfulness (see especially 6:17–18). But we need not make such a sharp distinction between immutability and faithfulness, given also the emphasis Hebrews puts on the full eternity that is unique to God. Jesus, in his participation in the unique divine identity, remains eternally 'the same', that is, his identity is unchanged. He remains himself eternally and can, therefore, be trusted in the present and the future just as he was in the past.

---

[46] McDonough, *YHWH*, 183–5.

[47] McDonough, *YHWH*, chap. 4.

[48] McDonough, *YHWH*, 156–7.

[49] E.g. Floyd V. Filson, *'Yesterday': A Study of Hebrews in the Light of Chapter 13* (SBT 2/4; London: SCM, 1967), 31–2; Philip E. Hughes, *A Commentary on the Epistle to the Hebrews* (Grand Rapids: Eerdmans, 1977), 570; William L. Lane, *Hebrews 9–13* (WBC 47B; Dallas: Word, 1991), 528.

[50] But commentators differ on whether the leaders of 13:7 are compared or contrasted with Jesus in 13:8. For the former view, see, for example, Filson, *Yesterday*, 31; for the latter, Robert P. Gordon, *Hebrews* (Readings: A New Biblical Commentary; Sheffield: Sheffield Academic Press, 2000), 166–7.

8

God's Self-Identification with the Godforsaken: Exegesis and Theology[1]

This chapter is an exegetical and theological study of Jesus' cry from the cross, 'My God, my God, why have you forsaken me?' (Mark 15:39; Matt. 27:46). In the second half of the twentieth century, a number of theologians, most famously Jürgen Moltmann,[2] sought to take the theological significance of the cry with radical seriousness.[3] They did not, however, give much attention to exegesis of these words, whether within their immediate context in Mark or within their larger context in Mark's Gospel narrative, or in relation to their Old Testament intertexts. On the other hand, the interpretation of the cry of desolation by exegetes has, on the whole, been theologically shallow and has failed to recognize its climactic significance in Mark's narrative. An exception to both these observations is Gérard Rossé's fine study,[4] which combines serious exegesis with theological reflection. But even Rossé's work does not give sufficient attention either to the place of the cry within Mark's Gospel or to the intertextual web of Old Testament allusions within which Mark has placed these words of Jesus. Exploring more fully both of these aspects will yield exegetical results of theological significance.[5]

---

[1] This chapter will also be published in a volume of the papers given at the Leuven Encounters in Systematic Theology V.

[2] Moltmann, *Crucified God*, chaps. 4–6. See also Richard Bauckham, *The Theology of Jürgen Moltmann* (Edinburgh: T&T Clark, 1995), chap. 4.

[3] For Hans Urs von Balthasar's treatment of the cry, see Gérard Rossé, *The Cry of Jesus on the Cross*, trans. S.W. Arndt (New York/Mahwah: Paulist, 1987), 91–5.

[4] Rossé, *Cry of Jesus*.

[5] Space does not permit comment on the place of the cry within Matthew's narrative, or on the relationship between the accounts of Jesus' dying words in the four Gospels.

1. The cry of desolation (Mark 15:34) in biblical contexts

1.1. *Mark 15:34 in the context of the psalms of lament*

As the words of Jesus' loud cry, Mark gives the opening words of Psalm 22:1,[6] first in Jesus' own Aramaic, and then in a literal Greek translation (not LXX): 'My God, my God, why have you forsaken me?'

1.1.1. *The psalms of lament in Mark's Passion Narrative*[7]
The significance of the quotation can be fully appreciated only if it is seen not in isolation but in the context of a web of allusions both to Psalm 22 and to other psalms of lament in Mark's Passion Narrative:[8]

Mark	*Psalm*
14:18	41:10
14:34	42:5, 11; 43:5
14:55	37:32?
14:57	27:12; 35:11; 69:4
15:24	22:18
15:29	22:7
15:30–31	22:8?
15:32	22:6; 69:9
15:34	22:1
15:36	69:21
15:40	38:11

This pattern of allusions has two important implications with regard to our reading of the cry of desolation. First, with regard to Psalm 22 itself, we are justified in reading Jesus' words in the context of the whole psalm, since Mark's narrative itself alludes to other parts of the psalm. However, this does not justify the claim that has sometimes been made that we should understand Jesus' words as standing for the whole psalm, as though the words Jesus quotes matter only because they are the introductory words of the whole psalm.[9] This view is ruled out by the fact that Mark gives these words of Jesus in Aramaic (as one

---

[6] Heb. 22:2; LXX 21:1. For convenience I shall give the numbering of psalms and verses only as in English versions.

[7] On this topic, see Loren R. Fisher, 'Betrayed by Friends: An Expository Study of Psalm 22,' *Int.* 18 (1964): 20–38; John Reumann, 'Psalm 22 at the Cross,' *Int.* 28 (1974): 39–58; Marcus, *Way of the Lord,* 174–86.

[8] For some other possible allusions, see Marcus, *Way of the Lord,* 174–5.

[9] Against this view, see Rossé, *Cry of Jesus,* 103–5.

of only four occasions when he does so: cf. 6:41; 7:34; 14:36), not in the original Hebrew of the psalm (in which we should expect him to recite the whole psalm if he did).[10] Mark gives us to understand that Jesus was not merely quoting, but personally appropriating, these specific words of the psalm. We must take fully seriously the fact that it is specifically these words of the psalm Jesus cries when dying, while also following Mark's indications that the whole psalm is a relevant context for understanding his words.

Secondly, through allusions to other psalms of lament Mark places Jesus' dying words in the context not only of Psalm 22 as a whole but also of the psalms of lament in general, of which there are about forty in the Psalter.[11] It is not merely that Psalm 22 was read by Mark and other early Christians as a messianic psalm that prophesied the sufferings and subsequent vindication of the Messiah, though this doubtless was the case. It is also that, in relating the passion and death of Jesus to the psalms of lament in general, Mark relates the passion and death of Jesus to the situation of all who wrote and used those psalms, those who cried out to God from the desperate situations those psalms describe. Since these psalms were in constant use, Mark could not have regarded them as *exclusively* messianic, i.e. as referring to experience unique to the Messiah. On the contrary, a messianic reading of them would have to be *inclusively* messianic, i.e. referring to the way in which the experience of the Messiah gathers up into itself the experiences of all whose sufferings find expression in those psalms.

1.1.2. 'Forsaken' (Heb. *'āzab*, Gk. *enkataleipō)*

With God as subject and the psalmist as object, the psalms of lament use this verb not only quite frequently itself, but also in parallel and more or less synonymously with other verbs and expressions, meaning: 'to cast off', 'to reject', 'to be far [from]', 'to hide [God's] face [from]', 'to turn in anger [from]', 'to forget'.[12] These expressions and their contexts reinforce

---

[10] On the implication of Jesus' use of Aramaic in citing Scripture in prayer, see P. Maurice Casey, *Aramaic Sources of Mark's Gospel* (SNTSMS 102; Cambridge: CUP, 1998), 84, 88.

[11] Lam. 5 is also a psalm of lament.

[12] Used in parallel with *'āzab* are two verbs with the meaning 'to cast off' (*nāṭaš*: Pss. 27:9; 94:14; *šālak*: Ps. 71:9), a verb meaning 'to be far [from]' (*rāḥaq*: Pss. 22:1b; 38:21), and expressions meaning 'to turn in anger [from]' (*nāṭāh bě'ap*: Ps. 27:9) and 'to hide [God's] face [from]' (*sātar pānîm*: Ps. 27:9). Other verbs used in similar ways in the Psalter include 'to cast off' (*zānaḥ*: Pss. 88:15; 89:39), 'to reject' (*mā'as*: Ps. 89:38) and 'to forget' (*šākaḥ*: Ps. 42:9; cf. Lam. 5:20). On these expressions, see Samuel E. Balentine, *The Hidden God: The Hiding of the Face of God in the Old Testament* (Oxford: Oxford University Monographs, 1983), 136–57.

the stark meaning of being forsaken by God. It is to be abandoned and rejected by God, who withholds his gracious intervention and leaves the psalmist to suffer and to die. It is important to note that these theological statements about God's relation to the psalmist correspond to quite concrete situations of distress. The psalmists are oppressed and mocked by their enemies, in extreme peril or pain, and close to death.[13] To be forsaken by God means that he has allowed this to happen and does nothing to help. So it is somewhat misleading to say – of the psalmist or of Jesus echoing his words – that he *feels* forsaken by God as though this were an understandable mistake. What Jesus experiences is the concrete fact that he has been left to suffer and die. God has, in this sense, abandoned him, not merely in psychological experience but in the form of the concrete situation that Jesus experiences.

Most often when the psalmists speak of being forsaken by God (using this or related expressions), they plead with God not to forsake them[14] or receive assurances that God has not forsaken or will not forsake them.[15] Much more rarely do they speak of having been already abandoned by God.[16] Jesus' words, therefore, echo the most extreme of the situations in the psalms of lament: those in which the psalmist not merely fears abandonment by God, but experiences it as realized fact.

1.1.3. 'Why?'

Jesus' words do not merely state the fact of his abandonment; they ask why. Such questions are found a number of times in the psalms of lament.[17] They express the psalmist's anguished inability to see God at work in his present circumstances. They find God's absence incomprehensible. They voice real questions that only God could answer.[18] In the psalms of lament there are only rare references to sin

---

[13] E.H. Gerstenberger, '"Where is God?" The Cry of the Psalmists,' in *Where is God? A Cry of Human Distress*, ed. Christian Duquoc and C. Floristan, (*Concilium* 1992/4 (London: SCM, 1992), 13–16. On the types of violence suffered by the psalmists, see also David G. Firth, *Surrendering Retribution in the Psalms: Responses to Violence in Individual Complaints* (Paternoster Biblical Monographs; Carlisle: Paternoster, 2005).

[14] Using the verb *'āzab*, Pss. 27:9; 38:21; 71:9, 18; 119:8.

[15] Using the verb *'āzab*, Pss. 9:10; 37:28, 33; 94:14.

[16] Using the verb *'āzab*, only Pss. 71:11 (said by the psalmist's enemies); 88:5; Lam. 5:20.

[17] Pss. 10:1; 42:10; 43:2; 44:23–24; 74:1, 11; 88:14. Lam. 5:20 is the only parallel that uses the verb *'āzab*. Such why questions are also found in Job (7:20–21; 13:24). Another form of question found often in the psalms of lament is 'how long?' On such questions, see Balentine, *Hidden God*, 116–35.

[18] Balentine, *Hidden God*, 121–4, rightly argues against the view that the questions are merely preliminary to the expressions of praise and thanksgiving and are more or less cancelled by the latter.

that could be understood as the cause of God's inaction.[19] Most protest against apparently undeserved suffering.[20] They are not only psalms of lament but also psalms of complaint and protest.[21]

1.1.4. 'My God, my God'

The psalmists put even their complaints and protests into address to God. Addresses like 'my God'[22] express the psalmist's sense of a relationship with God that God appears to be breaching. Psalm 22 is notable for its emphasis on the way God had hitherto proved trustworthy in relation both to the national ancestors (22:4) and to the psalmist himself (22:9–10; cf. 71:6). It is against this background of trust and reliability that the psalmist's present situation is so bewildering. This particular emphasis in Psalm 22 coheres with its unique opening address to God: the reduplicated 'My God'. The doubled expression is found nowhere else,[23] and serves, along with its prominent position as the first words of the psalm, to emphasize the psalmist's personal relationship with God and his persistence in addressing God as 'my God' even when abandoned by God. He would not do so unless he continued, in the face of the evidence, to trust the God who has always protected him. The address to 'my God' ensures that the cry is not one of despair but of faith, even though the faith is under severe assault. Even the anguished question 'why have you forsaken me?' is an (almost desperate) appeal to the faithfulness of God. It hangs on to the possibility that, even at this extreme point, God will prove trustworthy and deliver the psalmist.

It would be a mistake to contrast Jesus' habitual address to God as 'Father' with his use of 'my God' in the cry of desolation, as though at this point he can no longer regard God as his Abba.[24] The words are used because they are the words of the psalm, but they are a very suitable substitute for Abba, indicating Jesus' continued sense of intimate and mutually responsible relationship with God. Even in abandonment and protest, Jesus does not cease to trust God.[25]

---

[19] Pss. 38:4; 39:8, 11; 69:5; 79:8; cf. Lam. 5:7. Ps. 22:1 in the LXX (21:1), differently from the Hebrew, refers to the psalmist's transgressions. In this respect, it may be significant that Mark does not cite the LXX version but gives an independent rendering of the Hebrew.

[20] Balentine, *Hidden God*, 175.

[21] For the element of protest, see Balentine, *Hidden God*, 144–5.

[22] Pss. 22:1–2, 10; 31:14; 38:21; 59:1, 10; 63:1; 71:12.

[23] For the closest cases, see Pss. 35:23; 63:1.

[24] For this view see, for example, Raymond E. Brown, *The Death of the Messiah* (New York: Doubleday, 1994), 1046.

[25] Against the view that the cry of Jesus expresses despair, see Rossé, *Cry of Jesus*, 101–2, 108.

1.1.5. Darkness

In Mark 15:33–34, the cry of desolation comes at the end of the three hours of darkness that symbolize the absence of God. It is not that with the cry Jesus emerges from the darkness; rather the cry is the awful culmination of his experience of the darkness. By then he knows that God really has left him to die and will not intervene. Mark's reference to the darkness very likely alludes to Amos 8:9,[26] but we should also notice that darkness in the Old Testament is characteristic of the state of the dead (Job 10:21–22; Ps. 23:4) and, in this sense, the psalmists, complaining that God has left them to die, can say that they are in darkness like the dead (Pss. 88:6, 12, 18; 143:3; Lam. 3:2, 6; cf. Ps. 44:19; Lam. 3:2).[27] This makes it easily intelligible that, in Mark 15:33–34, it is the three hours of darkness that finally bring Jesus to speak of his abandonment by God. In both darkness and forsakenness (cf. Ps. 88:5), he is already at the gates of death.

1.1.6. Deliverance after abandonment

In all the psalms of lament, with the exception of the relentlessly dark Psalm 88,[28] there is assurance or experience of deliverance by God, beyond the situation of suffering from which the psalmist cries to God. The psalmist's trust in God, even while complaining and protesting, is vindicated in the end. Nowhere is this aspect of these psalms more emphatically and extensively represented than in Psalm 22. It is not surprising that early Christians read this second part of the psalm christologically,[29] with reference to the resurrection and exaltation of Jesus (cf. Heb. 2:12, citing Ps. 22:22), especially in the light of the psalm's references to the coming universal kingdom of God (22:27–28) and, apparently, general resurrection (22:29). In this part of the psalm, the complaint of forsakenness is superseded thus:

> For he did not despise or abhor
> the affliction of the afflicted;
> he did not hide his face from him,
> but heard when he cried to him (Ps. 22:24, NRSV altered).

---

[26] 'I will make the darkness go down at noon, and darken the earth [or, the land] in broad daylight.' The reference to noon, as in Mark, makes this a closer parallel to Mark 15:33 than other texts that refer to darkness as a form or symbol of God's judgement (Exod. 10:22; Isa. 8:22; 13:10; 60:2; Ezek. 32:7–8; Joel 2:10; Amos 5:20).

[27] Since this darkness of death is the darkness of God's absence, there is also a contrast with the psalmists' experience of God as their light (Pss. 27:1; 43:3; 44:3).

[28] Cf. also the almost despairing conclusion to the book of Lamentations (5:20–22).

[29] Reumann, 'Psalm 22,' 41–2.

This does not mean that the psalmist was mistaken in thinking himself forsaken by God, but that God heard and answered his cry out of his forsakenness. Beyond the forsakenness, God intervened to deliver.

Though Mark does not allude to the second part of the psalm, the several allusions to the first part of the psalm certainly invite competent readers to recall the whole psalm. In Jesus' case, his cry of abandonment is answered by God beyond his death – in resurrection. But this does not make the abandonment unreal or *merely* how Jesus felt. God did leave him to die. His dying cry expresses the abandonment by God that death is. Therefore, unlike the psalmists themselves, whose deliverance saves them *from* death, God's intervention to vindicate Jesus is a creative act of intervention *in* death that overturns death.[30]

1.1.7. Individual and communal

In most of the psalms of lament, it is an individual who laments his suffering,[31] but there are some in which the whole community of Israel laments the nation's fate, rejected or abandoned by God (Pss. 40; 60; 74; 79; 80; 83; Lam. 5). The same kinds of expressions of suffering and complaint are found in both the individual and the corporate laments. Thus Jesus' dying cry aligns him not only with individuals who made the words of these psalms their own but also with his people as a whole. As well as the individual in Psalm 22:1, Israel also cries to God: 'why have you forsaken us?' (Lam. 5:20). Psalm 22, with its extraordinary expression of the significance of the psalmist's vindication for Israel and for the whole world (22:22–28), could even be seen as a kind of mediation of the two – the forsaken individual and the forsaken people. In a messianically inclusive reading of Psalm 22, the speaker, like the Isaianic Servant, could be seen as bearing the forsakenness of his people.

Such a link with the Isaianic Servant is the more attractive in that these later chapters of Isaiah themselves portray Israel, in the persistence of exile, lamenting her abandonment by God in terms that are close to the psalms of lament (including Lamentations 5). Israel says, 'YHWH has forsaken me, my Lord has forgotten me' (Isa. 49:14; cf. 40:27), and God responds that he can never forsake or forget (49:15–18; cf. 41:17; 42:16), that 'for a brief moment I abandoned you, but with great compassion I will gather you' (54:7). Israel's salvation

---

[30] Cf. Rossé, *Cry of Jesus*, 109.

[31] I am not considering here the claim that the 'I' is a corporate self representing Israel, though Marcus, *Way of the Lord*, 184–6, wishes to connect this with a messianically inclusive understanding of Mark's allusions to the psalms of lament.

here corresponds to the pattern of the psalms of lament, especially those that cry to God out of realized experience of abandonment. The moment of abandonment is real but transitory. It does not negate God's continued faithfulness to his people. Into this pattern, Isaiah 52 – 53 inserts the figure of the Suffering Servant who bears, along with the sins of his people, the abandonment to death that they entail. In this perspective, the allusions in Mark's passion narrative to the psalms of lament, especially 22, converge with those to the Isaianic Servant (Mark 14:24 [Isa. 53:11–12]; 14:61 [Isa. 53:7]; 14:65 [Isa. 50:6]; 15:27 [Isa. 53:12]).[32]

1.1.8. Jesus' self-identification with all the godforsaken

Some commentators argue that the citation of Psalm 22:1 in Jesus' cry of desolation belongs to a Markan presentation of Jesus as the exemplary suffering righteous person, the innocent sufferer who maintains faith in God even in the extremity of suffering. We have already suggested that the significance of the cry of desolation is greater than this. It is a messianically inclusive cry with which Jesus identifies himself with forsaken Israel and with all who can take the words of the psalm as their own. Two features of Mark 15:33–34 support this reading.

First, the darkness lay over the whole earth (15:33).[33] It is the universal darkness of death,[34] the abandonment experienced by all who are left by God to suffer and die, that Jesus enters on the cross.

Secondly, if we take the cry of desolation seriously as a why question put to God, it does not seem that Mark's Jesus can credibly ask it on his own account. Mark's Jesus not only knows that it is God's will that he die (8:31; 9:31; 10:34, 38), but also why this must be (Mark 10:45; 14:24). He knows the Father's will is that he die for others. Of course, it might be psychologically plausible for Jesus to question this knowledge, even to lose it, in the extremity of his dying. But it is doubtful that a psychological explanation can account for Mark's very theological text. On the level of a theological understanding of the cry, it must be that

---

[32] For these and some other allusions, see Marcus, *Way of the Lord*, 186–90.

[33] The Greek is ambiguous: *holēn tēn gēn* could be the whole land or the whole earth. Commentators often prefer the former because it seems easier to treat as historical. For the kind of reading we suggest, 'land' might express Jesus' identification with the whole people of Israel, were it not for the fact that most of Israel lived outside the land. Gospel of Peter 5:15 says that the darkness was over 'all Judaea', but reads it as a sign of God's judgement on the Jews who crucify Jesus.

[34] Cf. the image of death as the shroud that covers all the nations in Isa. 25:7.

Jesus asks the question, not on his own behalf, but as the question asked by those with whom his use of the words identifies him. It is their protest that he voices on their behalf. This is fullest meaning of the fact that the words of Jesus' cry are borrowed from the psalms of lament.

1.1.9. *New and old in Jesus' quotation of the psalm*

It can be argued that the words of the cry of desolation gain their meaning, not from their Old Testament context within the psalms, but from their context at the end of the life of Jesus.[35] In other words, does Jesus' use of the words give them new meaning? The best answer to this is that there is a new meaning that nevertheless presupposes and cannot supersede the old. The fact that Jesus the Messiah, the one uniquely identified with God, prays these words not exclusively but inclusively, identifying himself with all other godforsaken people, gives them a new meaning of self-identification with others in their godforsakenness. But the new meaning is possible only because the words already express the godforsakenness of these others with whom Jesus identifies.[36]

1.2. Mark 15:34–39 in the narrative structure of the Gospel

The Gospel of Mark is both a narrative account of the divine identity of Jesus and, at the same time, a narrative account of his inauguration of the kingdom of God. He is the beloved Son of God who participates in his Father's own divine identity, and he is the messianic king who brings about God's rule. Who he is and what he does are, in this Gospel, inseparable. What he does reveals who he is, and who he is entails what he does.

In order to appreciate fully how the cry of desolation forms the narrative climax of Mark's narrative, the two most important structuring elements of the whole narrative need to be noted.

1.2.1. *Authority and passion*

The Gospel's account of who Jesus is and his way to the kingdom falls into two parts. Peter's confession (8:29) is usually identified as the point of transition between the two, but it is probably better to see the two parts as overlapping, with the first ending at 9:29 and

---

[35] Cf. Rossé, *Cry of Jesus*, 61–2, following Moltmann.

[36] Michael Jinkins and Stephen Breck Reid, 'God's Forsakenness: The Cry of Dereliction as an Utterance within the Trinity,' *HTB* 19 (1997): 37, speak of a two-way hermeneutical process, which rereads the psalm through the passion narrative, and then returns through an appreciation of the psalms of lament to the passion narrative.

the second beginning at 8:30. The two parts are distinguished by the predominating themes in each.

In the first part, Jesus is shown speaking and acting with divine authority. Almost all of Jesus' healings and exorcisms occur in this first half of the Gospel (the only exception is 10:46–52), as well as the stilling of the storm and the walking on the water. These narratives of Jesus' authoritative teaching and exercising of miraculous power are the basis for Peter's recognition that he is the Messiah (8:29).

However, Peter's confession immediately proves inadequate when he opposes Jesus' first prediction of his passion and death (8:31–33). From this point on, the need for Jesus to suffer and to die becomes a major theme of the Gospel and leads to the passion narrative itself. The way to the kingdom lies not only through Jesus' exercise of divine authority but also through his betrayal, rejection, ignominy and death.

Significant for our purposes is the fact that this twofold structure of the Gospel is evoked by the taunts of the chief priests and scribes as Jesus hangs on the cross: 'He saved others; he cannot save himself' (15:31). For readers of Mark, the words are ironic, since it is precisely by not saving himself that Jesus is saving others. But the words also highlight the fact that, in the first part of the Gospel, Jesus saved others by acts of evident divine power, whereas his path to death follows a different course.

The placing of the transfiguration in the overlap between the two parts is also significant, as we shall see in the next section.

1.2.2. Three revelatory events

The two parts of the Gospel narrative are framed by three key events of revelation, one at the outset of the first part, one at the transition between the two, and one at the conclusion of the second part and the climax of the whole narrative. The parallelism between the accounts of these three events is striking:[37]

Mark 1:9–11	**Mark 9:2–8**	**Mark 15:34–39**
baptism	transfiguration	cry of desolation
by John (= Elijah)	with Moses and Elijah	Elijah does not come
		Jesus dies
		(*exepneusen*)

---

[37] This parallelism is set out, with some differences from my analysis, by Chad Myers, *Binding the Strong Man: A Political Reading of Mark's Story of Jesus* (Maryknoll, New York: Orbis, 1988), 390–1.

Mark 1:9–11	Mark 9:2–8	Mark 15:34–39
heavens rent (*schizomenous*)	overshadowing cloud	temple veil rent (*eschisthē*)
Spirit (*pneuma*) descends on Jesus		
voice from heaven: 'You are my Son, the Beloved; with you I am well pleased.'	voice from cloud: 'This is my Son, the Beloved; listen to him!'	centurion: 'Truly this man is the Son of God.'

The transfiguration, following Jesus' saying about seeing the kingdom come with power (9:1), is a revelation of Jesus in the divine glory of his messianic rule. It could form a natural culmination of the first part of the Gospel narrative, and this is how Peter initially takes it. But Jesus has already begun to teach the disciples that the way to the kingdom lies through his rejection and death. The transfiguration is not the actual arrival of the kingdom in power, but only a preview of what cannot happen until after his passion and death. The heavenly voice provides for the disciples both a confirmation of who Jesus' mighty works in the first part of the Gospel narrative have shown him to be, but also indicates that they also still have much to learn ('listen to him!').

The verbal parallels between the first and third of the three events are closer than those that link each with the second, but there is also the remarkable difference that, whereas at the baptism and the transfiguration it is a heavenly voice, conveying the words of the Father, that declares the significance of what has been revealed, in the case of the cross it is the centurion. Nevertheless, these three designations of Jesus as the Son of God clearly belong in some kind of sequence.

One aspect of the correspondences of the events can be appreciated only when we see that the revelatory event in the third case – the cry of desolation – is an act of identification of Jesus with the godforsaken. Retrospectively, we can recognize that so also was the baptism. In submitting to the act that symbolized repentance and forgiveness of sins, Jesus identified with his people in their need of such. The transfiguration, on the other hand, reveals Jesus in the glory of his divine identity.

1.3. The revelation of Jesus' divine identity in Mark

A purely functional account of Jesus' divinity in this Gospel is not adequate; rather Mark shares with early Christian writers in general what I have elsewhere called a Christology of divine identity.[38] This is already clear in the carefully crafted conflated quotation from the prophets that forms the prologue to Mark's narrative (1:2–3). The parallelism of 'your [i.e. Jesus'] way' and 'the way of the Lord' (where 'Lord' represents the divine name YHWH in the text of Isa. 40:3) is an instance of the common early Christian practice of applying to Jesus Old Testament texts that use the divine name.[39] God's name refers, not to divine functions, but to the unique divine identity. Jesus, according to Mark, participates in this unique identity of the God of Israel. Mark is often credited with a messianic secret, but his narrative, in fact, contains a more profound secret: that of Jesus' divine identity.

Throughout the narrative, Mark provides indications for his readers that Jesus does not merely act on God's behalf, as the messianic king might be expected to do, but actually belongs to the divine identity.[40] It is doubtful whether anyone within the narrative, other than the demons, really perceives this, and so, after the prologue, Mark does not state it outright but implies it for readers as the true implication of what Jesus or others say.[41] The culmination of these indications comes in Jesus' words to the high priest (14:62), where Jesus' claim to be seated beside God on the cosmic throne from which God rules all things can only be, from a Jewish theological perspective, a claim to share in the unique divine identity of the God who alone rules over all things.

The title 'Son of God' is rare in Mark and by no means merely synonymous with 'Messiah', though he knows that others could use it in that sense (14:61).[42] For Mark, the title indicates Jesus' unique relationship to God as one who participates in the divine identity. It features in the words of the heavenly voice at the baptism and the transfiguration, and the demons recognize Jesus' divine sonship (3:11; 5:7), but, apart

---

[38] See especially chapter 1 above.

[39] See chapter 5 above.

[40] Especially 2:7; 4:41; 6:50; 10:18; 11:27–33; 12:37; 14:62.

[41] There is the fact that in his teaching, exorcisms and healings, Jesus never appeals to any authority beyond himself (cf. 1:27; 2:10, 28). There are the almost rhetorical questions: 'Who can forgive sins but God alone?' (2:7); and 'Who then is this, that even the wind and sea obey him?' (4:41). There is the theophany scene in which Jesus tramples the sea and uses the self-identification, 'It is I' (*egō eimi*), apparently innocuous words that in fact correspond to a formula of divine self-identification in the Old Testament (6:50; cf. 14:62). There are Jesus' words, 'Why do you call me good? No one is good but God alone', which seem actually to disclaim divine identity, but for competent readers mean precisely the opposite (10:18). There is Jesus' cleverly evasive refusal to disclose the source of his authority (11:27–33), and his exegetical question about the Messiah: 'David himself calls him [the Messiah] Lord. So how can he be David's son?' (12:37).

[42] Even here Mark doubtless intends readers to see more in the title than the high priest intends, as probably also in 15:39.

from the high priest, no human uses the term until the centurion at the cross, perceiving how Jesus dies, declares: 'Truly this man was a/the son of God.' The Greek is ambiguous, and the centurion, as a pagan, may appropriately be thought to recognize Jesus not as the unique Son of God, but merely a son. But Mark has not placed this christological confession at the climax of his narrative in order to highlight no more than this weak pagan sense of divinity. Whatever the centurion might credibly have meant in a merely historical reading, in the light of the rest of the Gospel his words tell the readers far more.

The significance of 'Son of God', together with the parallelism of the three key revelatory events, means that Jesus' divine identity is revealed not only in his deeds of divine authority, nor merely in his coming participation in God's cosmic rule, but also in his godforsaken death. Like the narrative as a whole, this last event reveals – indeed, actually is – Jesus' way to the kingdom and at the same time, inseparably, who Jesus is. This point of his radical identification with those who suffer and die in God's absence is actually the climax of the revelation of his divine identity. Mark's Jesus is no less divine in his identification with the godforsaken than he is in his exercise of divine authority or the coming theophany of his divine glory. Moreover, it is his self-identification with the godforsaken in his death that finally brings a human being to recognize his divine identity.

1.4. Mark's narrative of Jesus' death

Mark's presentation of the death of Jesus is remarkable for the exclusiveness with which it focuses on Jesus' godforsakenness. In the whole passion narrative, from the Last Supper onwards, there is a crescendo of forsakenness[43] that prepares for this presentation of Jesus' death. In the wake of his abandonment by friends and disciples, Jewish and Roman authorities, the theological heart of this abandonment emerges in its own right with Jesus' crucifixion. The mockery that fills the first three hours in Mark's account (15:29–32) throws Jesus' godforsakenness in his face. There follow the three hours of darkness (15:33), in which the bystanders are silent and Jesus is alone with the absence of God. In the end, Jesus summons all his remaining strength to voice the great cry of desolation (15:34, 37).[44] Its loudness perhaps matches the universality of the darkness: Jesus himself acknowledges

---

[43] Cf. Rossé, *Cry of Jesus*, 64–5.
[44] I take it, with some commentators, that the loud cry of v. 37 is not a second cry but a resumptive reference to the cry of desolation itself.

his godforsakenness for all to hear, while, at the same time, he prays to God out of it. The incident that follows, when someone thinks he is calling for Elijah (15:35–36), serves to underline Jesus' abandonment. God does not answer. He does not send Elijah to rescue Jesus from death just in the nick of time.

The rending of the veil of the temple, if we read it in parallel with the rending of the heavens in Mark's account of Jesus' baptism (1:10), signifies revelation. It signifies that this godforsaken death is the climactic event of revelation in the Gospel narrative. More than that, it transfers the place of God's presence from its hiddenness in the holy of holies to the openly godforsaken cross of the dead Jesus.[45] The centurion does not, of course, respond to the torn veil, which he could not see, but to what it represents: that the presence of God can now be recognized in how Jesus died (15:39), godforsaken and yet faithful to his God. The centurion represents all the godforsaken who find the presence of God in Jesus' self-identification with them, the godforsaken.

2. Brief Theological Reflections

(1) In the light of Jesus' divine sonship, the cross is God's act of self-identification with all people in that extremity of the human condition and that heart of all suffering that is the absence of God. It is the furthest point to which God's self-giving love in incarnation goes. We must be careful not to weaken the force of this statement by seeing the cross as merely an illustration of God's self-identification with the godforsaken or even an instance of it. In its unique particularity as the godforsaken death of this man Jesus on the cross, it is God's unique act of self-identification with the godforsaken. It does not simply reveal God's passionate love for the godforsaken; it reveals what it itself is: God's unique and particular act of self-giving love for the godforsaken.[46]

(2) For the cross to be the act of God's love for the godforsaken, it is essential to recognize both that the godforsakenness of Jesus is quite

---

[45] Christian Duquoc, '"Who is God?" becomes "Where is God?" The shift in a Question,' in *Where is God?*, ed. Duquoc and Floristan, 8, points out an implication of this 'relocation' of God: 'The New Testament moved the location of God by shifting his abode from the temple to the body of Jesus. But he is the very one who dies on the cross, outcast. The outcast is from henceforth a pointer to the presence of God. This does not mean that the outcast is a perfect witness; but he is an indication that the world is not the kingdom of God ... [God] is where a concrete being points to the kingdom of God which has not come; he is where a concrete being vitiates the claims of our society to fulfil all desires.'

[46] See Richard Bauckham, 'Jesus the Revelation of God,' in *Divine Revelation*, ed. Paul Avis (London: Darton, Longman & Todd/Grand Rapids: Eerdmans, 1997), 174–200

concretely real and also that both Jesus and the Father remain faithful to each other. In crying out to God from his abandonment, Jesus, desperately we must suppose but really, trusts God to be still his God, the 'my God, my God' of the cry.[47] The Father's faithfulness to Jesus is, indeed, contradicted by Jesus' death, but reaffirmed in his raising Jesus from the dead. For God to identify with the godforsaken, to share their suffering in the absence of God, this contradiction is necessary. It constitutes the radical nature of God's self-giving love. But only because Jesus and the Father remain faithful to each other can Jesus' forsakenness be *God's* self-identification with the godforsaken.

(3) God redeems and renews humanity in this way, by entering the situation of humanity at the deepest level of the human plight: the absence of God. In the light of the psalms of lament, we may see humanity as godforsaken, not only because, as sinners, humans suffer their own forsaking of God, but also because those who suffer, for whatever reason, are left by God to suffer. Soteriology should encompass both these aspects of human godforsakenness.

(4) I spoke of the secret of Jesus' divine identity in Mark's narrative; we might also speak of the hiddenness of God in this story. As the story nears its provisional end, the death of Jesus, so God becomes less and less evident in it, and yet paradoxically the godforsaken death of Jesus is the climactic event of revelation in this Gospel's story.[48] This paradox is entailed by the fact that God, in self-giving love for humanity, has chosen to be most truly Godself in self-identification with the godforsaken.

(5) Although the centurion already recognizes God's salvific presence in Jesus' godforsaken death, we could scarcely do so were it not for the resurrection. This puts the cross in the context of an eschatological story that is not finished until the coming of the kingdom in power.

---

[47] Rossé, *Cry of Jesus*, 67, speaks of 'the loss of God for the love of God'.
[48] Thus the chief priests can see Jesus' abandonment as disproving his claim while the centurion sees it as vindicating Jesus' claim.

Index

Index of Scripture, Apocrypha and Old Testament Pseudepigrapha